49 -

Trust and Legitimacy in Criminal Justice

Gorazd Meško • Justice Tankebe
Editors

Trust and Legitimacy in Criminal Justice

European Perspectives

Springer

Editors
Gorazd Meško
Faculty of Criminal Justice and Security
University of Maribor
Maribor, Ljubljana
Slovenia

Justice Tankebe
Institute of Criminology
University of Cambridge
Cambridge
United Kingdom

ISBN 978-3-319-09812-8   ISBN 978-3-319-09813-5 (eBook)
DOI 10.1007/978-3-319-09813-5
Springer Cham Heidelberg New York Dordrecht London

Library of Congress Control Number: 2014954232

Printed on acid-free paper

Springer is part of Springer Science+Business Media (www.springer.com)

Preface

Criminal Justice in Europe: A Study of Aspects of Trust and Legitimacy

Legitimacy and trust are not new concepts to criminology. For example, in *Causes of Delinquency*, Hirschi (1969: 127) hypothesized and tested the influence of legitimacy on delinquency: "If a person feels no emotional attachment to a person or institution, the rules of that person or institution tend to be denied legitimacy." However, it was Tyler's work that has sparked the explosion in research on trust and legitimacy over the last two decades. Tyler's *Why People Obey the Law* (Tyler, 2006) offered an analysis and interpretation of results of a telephone survey of residents in Chicago. A major strength of the book was the methodological and theoretical insights that would guide future empirical analysis of these concepts, in particular legitimacy. What emerges from Tyler's analysis is the centrality of *procedural justice* in people's judgments about the legitimacy of criminal justice institutions.

Trust and legitimacy have featured prominently in the various studies that have followed the initial work by Tyler. Although closely related, legitimacy and trust are conceptually distinct. The former describes "power that is *acknowledged as rightful* by relevant agents, who include power holders and their staff, those subject to the power and third parties whose support or recognition may help confirm it" (Beetham, 2013: 19). In addition to its emphasis on the normative character of legitimacy, Beetham's (ibid.) definition has the additional merit of drawing our attention to a need to conceptualize and investigate legitimacy from the perspectives of all relevant parties in a power relationship. Also implicit in this definition is legitimacy's focus on judgements about the present; in other words, it is concerned with recognition of claims to exercise power here and now, rather than in the future (Bottoms & Tankebe, 2012). Trust, on the other hand, is future oriented: it is a "positive feeling of expectation regarding another's future actions" (Barbalet, 2009: 375).

There is now a large body of evidence to show that legitimacy is a key mechanism fostering social order in different settings. Specifically, legal compliance and support for criminal justice institutions have been linked to the levels of trust and legitimacy these institutions command among their various audiences. Over the two decades of legitimacy research, various extensions and innovations have occurred. Some studies have sought to examine the extent to which the legitimacy-compliance and legitimacy-cooperation relationships are replicable in sociopolitical contexts beyond North America. Others have focused on improving methodological and theoretical issues within the field (e.g., Bottoms & Tankebe, 2012; Jackson, Bradford, Stanko, & Hohl, 2012; Reisig, Bratton, & Gertz, 2007). The papers collected in this book represent an attempt to extent further our knowledge in what is still a relatively nascent field. The papers present in this volume address in varying combinations the meaning of trust and legitimacy across different contexts, across time, among different demographic groups. It is not solely from the standpoint of power audiences but also power holders.

The book is organized into two major parts. In the opening chapter, *Susanne Karstedt* focuses on legitimacy in transitional democracies in order to address various important questions: first it explores how the processes of transition shape the legitimacy of criminal justice institutions. Second, it discusses why institutions lose moral recognition and the processes involved in repairing or recovering from illegitimacy. Finally, Karstedt investigates the kinds of institutional changes within the broader society that mostly impinge on the legitimacy of criminal justice.

In Chap. 2, *Julian Roberts* and *Mojca M. Plesničar* explore the relationship between the nature of a sentencing regime and public perceptions of penal legitimacy, or what we refer to as "empirical legitimacy," in terms of public attitudes to sentencing and the reasons why the public in many countries may perceive their sentencing systems as *lacking* legitimacy, on the one hand, and ways of enhancing public perceptions of sentencing legitimacy, on the other, outlining a "high-legitimacy" sentencing regime's features.

The chapter by *Jan van Dijk* focuses on victims and their perceptions of legitimacy, and how these perceptions predict the willingness of former victims to subsequently report their victimization, revising the results of older rounds of the International Crime Victims Surveys (ICVS) from a procedural justice perspective to finally arrive at the conclusion that procedural justice for victims should be at the center of programs aimed at strengthening legitimacy of police forces in the European Union.

Witold Klaus, *Konrad Buczkowski*, and *Paulina Wiktorska* discuss victim empowerment from a victimological perspective and on three levels: legislative issues (selected Polish statutes aimed at giving greater protection to victims of crime); verifications of how these legislative assumptions actually work in practice (i.e., to what extent the justice system actually supports and protects the interests of victims of crime, preventing their secondary victimization); and a relevant discourse analysis. These and other issues raised allow for an evaluation of whether or not the rights of victims have been incorporated into the real aims of the Polish justice system, or whether or not they remain no more than a pipe dream.

Paul Ponsaers in a chapter discusses the issue of whether or not the police themselves can manage the problem of legitimacy, for in need of public trust and confidence, they cannot but increase their effectiveness. Contrary to this position, Ponsaers argues that the police are not active agents in building their legitimacy, drawing on the classic Weberian sociological meaning of legitimacy by invoking the distinction between normative and empirical legitimacy. Trust seems to be tied to variations in social mechanisms beyond the reach of the police, and a vicious circle is established: while police legitimacy is not police property, it is political decision makers who influence public confidence, institutional trust, and, ultimately, police legitimacy.

Benjamin Flander and *Aleš Bučar Ručman* focus on legitimacy of criminal-justice systems in Central and Eastern Europe (CEE) in transition. Legitimacy issues are addressed through critical assessment of crime trends, crime policy, criminal law reforms, imprisonment, and trust in legal and criminal justice institutions. With vast political, economic, and social changes starting with the 1980s and resulting in disturbing changes in social and value systems inducing growing public fear of crime and criminal justice policies yielding to the populist neoliberal and neoconservative law-and-order solutions implementing ever-harsher penalties, lower standards of substantive/procedural rights, and wider powers of the formal social control agencies, criminal-justice systems of CEE countries seem to have experienced a transformation from illegitimate communist criminal-justice systems into democratic models of criminal justice pestered by the crisis of legitimacy.

Part II begins with a chapter by *Jonathan Jackson*, *Mike Hough*, *Ben Bradford*, and *Jouni Kuha*. They examine the proposition that legitimacy judgments involve two interconnected beliefs: one related to the concepts of consent and authorization (Do people believe that an entity of authority has the right to dictate appropriate behavior?), and the other to moral validity (Do people believe that this authority exercises its powers in the ways consistent with the prevailing norms of appropriate conduct?). Marshaling data from Round 5 of the European Social Survey, they first assess the scaling properties of measures of police legitimacy using the data from the UK and then examine usefulness of three different ways of representing legitimacy within a larger model of public cooperation with the police.

In this contribution, *Jerneja Šifrer*, *Gorazd Meško*, and *Matevž Bren* summarize the findings of previous legitimacy studies and claim that legitimacy is a strong predictor of compliance with the law and public trust in fairness of justice officials, substantiating their claims on four surveys conducted in Slovenia using structural equation modeling (SEM): trust in the justice module of the European Social Survey (Round 5); test of Tyler's model on "why people obey the law" in Slovenia; adult high school student survey—Slovenia; and the study on law students about legitimacy in Slovenia. Despite different formulations of legitimacy and a different focus of its prediction in different studies, their message is one and the same: relationships between dimensions of public trust and fairness of justice officials and dimensions of legitimacy are clear and strong, but trust in (fairness of) the police is paramount.

Branko Lobnikar, *Andrej Sotlar*, and *Maja Modic* in a chapter on trust in plural policing begin their reflection with the statement that there exist many studies of public confidence in authorities in Western Europe and the USA, but not in the countries of Central and Eastern Europe, as these governments and police forces lack awareness of the level of their performance being based not only on their effective investigation of criminal offenses and maintenance of public order, but also on the adoption, support, and trust that citizens show the police and the plural police community. They analyze the existing research findings on public confidence in policing bodies from the countries of Central and Eastern Europe and draw attention to the gaps existing in this field of study.

Nathalie Guzy and *Helmut Hirtenlehner* believe that according to Tom Tyler's procedural justice theory, public trust in or perceived legitimacy of the police plays a central role in enhancing citizens' cooperation with this institution. As reporting a crime to the police marks an important form of public cooperation, the authors examine the interrelationships between personal experiences with the police, various dimensions of trust in the police, and victims' reporting behaviors through means of a large-scale victimization survey carried out in Germany. The results support, in part, the hypothesized relationships and reveal dangerous pitfalls in approaching this issue with the data collected in standard victimization surveys.

Gorazd Meško and *Katja Eman* present findings from a cross-national survey of law students relating to legitimacy of policing and criminal justice in seven Central and Eastern European countries, implying a certain degree of significance of legitimacy and trust in police and criminal justice, and of similar findings on the effect of procedural justice, police effectiveness, and authority on legitimacy. The results imply that legitimacy and trust in the police are related to particular levels of democratization. Nevertheless, they also show differences among the studied countries and a negative attitude towards the police. Improvements in this segment are needed, as these respondents are future legal professionals.

The standard empirical focus of legitimacy is on what Bottoms and Tankebe (2012) call *audience legitimacy*. That is to say the recognition of the rightness of power from the standpoint of those who are subject to power (e.g., suspects, offenders, and victims). What still remains largely unexplored is power-holder legitimacy or self-legitimacy. This refers to power holders' own belief in their entitlement to power. This latter dimension of legitimacy is the subject of *Justice Tankebe* and *Gorazd Meško's* chapter. Using survey data from a sample of police officers in Slovenia, the authors examine the correlates of power-holder legitimacy, and explore the influence of power-holder legitimacy on police decision choices, including the decision to use force and self-reported pro-organizational behavior.

As this volume is a result of a fruitful scientific cooperation of the leading European criminologists studying different aspects of legitimacy of criminal justice in contemporary Europe, we believe that it will deserve attention by social scientists, especially criminologists, policy makers, criminal justice practitioners, and students of criminology, criminal justice, and police studies.

Ljubljana, Slovenia — Gorazd Meško
Cambridge, UK — Justice Tankebe

References

Barbalet, J. (2009). A characterization of trust, and its consequences. *Theory and Society*, *38*(4), 367–382.

Beetham, D. (2013). Revisiting Legitimacy, Twenty Years On. In J. Tankebe & A. Liebling (eds.), *Legitimacy and Criminal Justice: An International Exploration*. Oxford: Oxford University Press.

Bottoms, E. A., & Tankebe, J. (2012). Beyond procedural justice: A dialogic approach to legitimacy in criminal justice. *Journal of Criminal Law and Criminology*, *102*(1), 119–170.

Hirschi, T. (1969). *Causes of delinquency*. Berkeley: University of California Press.

Jackson, J., Bradford, B., Stanko, E. A., & Hohl, K. (2012). *Just authority? Trust in the police in England and Wales*. Oxford: Routledge.

Reisig, M. D., Bratton, J., & Gertz, M. G. (2007). The construct validity and refinement of process-based policing measures. *Criminal Justice and Behaviour*, *34*(8), 1005–1028.

Tyler, T. R. (2006). *Why people obey the law*. Princeton: Princeton University Press.

Acknowledgements

This book would not have been possible without the financial support of the Slovenian Research Agency and its funding of the research project on legitimacy of policing, criminal justice, and execution of penal sanctions in Slovenia and other Eastern European countries. In September 2013, some of the authors had met at the Faculty of Criminal Justice, University of Maribor, to discuss early drafts of the chapters of this volume.

We are grateful to the authors for their original contributions and persistence during the editing process and deeply thankful to numerous colleagues for their comments on early drafts of the papers and later in the peer review process. We would like to thank Barbara Błońska, Ben Bradford, Avi Brisman, Elke Devroe, Jan van Dijk, Chuck Fields, Benjamin Flander, Christian Grafl, Helmut Hirtenlehner, Mike Hough, Katrin Hohl, David Jenks, Michael Levy, Ian Loader, Kristina Murphy, Mahesh Nalla, Mike Reisig, Judah Schept, Wesley Skogan, Tal Jonathan-Zamir, and Aleš Završnik, the peer reviewers, for harnessing their expertise, creativity, and constructive criticism to improve the quality of the chapters and the entire volume on exploring legitimacy of criminal justice in Europe, as their contributions are huge. Without their help this volume would fail to be such an academic achievement.

We are indebted to Maja Modic, Nataša Knap, Barbara Čuvan, Jerneja Šifrer, and Branko Ažman, from the Faculty of Criminal Justice and Security, University of Maribor, for their administrative support, correspondence with the authors, and technical editing of the manuscript. Special thanks go to Ms. Katherine Chabalko for encouraging us to publish this volume and her support in the process of editing. Last but not least, we hugely appreciate and are thankful for the support given by Springer's copyediting service.

Ljubljana and Cambridge, 2014

Gorazd Meško
Justice Tankebe

Contents

List of Contributors

Ben Bradford Centre for Criminology, University of Oxford, Oxford, UK

Matevž Bren Faculty of Criminal Justice and Security, University of Maribor, Ljubljana, Slovenia

Institute of Mathematics, Physics and Mechanics, Ljubljana, Slovenia

Konrad Buczkowski Institute of Legal Studies, Polish Academy of Sciences, Warsaw, Poland

Jan van Dijk INTERVICT, University of Tilburg, Tilburg, The Netherlands

Katja Eman Faculty of Criminal Justice and Security, University of Maribor

Benjamin Flander Faculty of Criminal Justice and Security, University of Maribor, Ljubljana, Slovenia

Nathalie Guzy Department of Police Crime Statistics, Criminology and Criminal Investigation Analysis, Federal Criminal Police Office, Wiesbaden, Germany

Helmut Hirtenlehner Centre for Criminology, Johannes Kepler University Linz, Linz, Austria

Mike Hough Institute for Criminal Policy Research, Birkbeck, University of London, London, UK

Jonathan Jackson Department of Methodology, London School of Economics, London, UK

Susanne Karstedt Centre for Criminal Justice Studies, School of Law, University of Leeds, Leeds, UK

Witold Klaus Institute of Legal Studies, Polish Academy of Sciences, Warsaw, Poland

Jouni Kuha Department of Methodology, London School of Economics, London, UK

Branko Lobnikar Faculty of Criminal Justice and Security, University of Maribor, Ljubljana, Slovenia

Gorazd Meško Faculty of Criminal Justice and Security, University of Maribor, Ljubljana, Slovenia

Maja Modic Faculty of Criminal Justice and Security, University of Maribor, Ljubljana, Slovenia

Mojca M. Plesničar Institute of Criminology at the Faculty of Law Ljubljana, Ljubljana, Slovenia

Paul Ponsaers Research Unit Social Analysis of Security, Department of Penal Law & Criminology, Faculty of Law, Ghent University, Ghent, Belgium

Julian V. Roberts Centre of Criminology, Oxford University, Oxford, UK

Aleš Bučar Ručman Faculty of Criminal Justice and Security, University of Maribor, Ljubljana, Slovenia

Jerneja Šifrer Faculty of Criminal Justice and Security, University of Maribor, Ljubljana, Slovenia

Andrej Sotlar Faculty of Criminal Justice and Security, University of Maribor, Ljubljana, Slovenia

Justice Tankebe Institute of Criminology, University of Cambridge, Cambridge, UK

Paulina Wiktorska Institute of Legal Studies, Polish Academy of Sciences, Warsaw, Poland

Part I
Legitimacy and Criminal Justice

Trust in Transition: Legitimacy of Criminal Justice in Transitional Societies

Susanne Karstedt

1 Police and Justice in Transition

Over the past decades, the institutions of criminal justice have emerged as a key—if not the key—to successful transitions to stable post-conflict and democratic societies. This has been registered in a dramatic expansion in the number and scope of international and multinational police operations and in supranational and regional efforts to establish the rule of law and to improve the efficiency and functioning of the justice system. This includes the establishment of the European Commission for the Efficiency of Justice in 2002, which aimed particularly at the postcommunist and transitional societies of Central and Eastern Europe. Post-conflict countries like Bosnia & Herzegovina and Kosovo (see EULEX, 2010; Wilson, 2006) were provided with ample assistance to rebuild their criminal justice system and to firmly embed the rule of law into its institutional framework. Worldwide operations include countries as diverse as Haiti and East Timor (Oakley, Dziedzik, & Goldberg, 2002), African (Albrecht & Buur, 2009; Baker, 2009a, 2009b; Kyed, 2009) and Asian countries (Broadhurst & Bouhours, 2009; Dinnen & Braithwaite, 2009). One significant characteristic of these international and multinational operations is the claim that the legitimacy of criminal justice institutions—the police and the courts—is vital in securing legitimacy for the transition to democracy, for democratic government, and thus these institutions contribute to the political stability in the transitional environment (Loader, 2006; Roberts, 2008). Police and courts are tasked to promote the rule of law, a culture of human rights and generally "democratic political development," as Bayley (2001: 13) terms it; these tasks are saddled upon the more mundane ones of preventing crime and disorder and assisting in the prosecution of criminals and crimes. As Loader astutely remarks, in more secure

S. Karstedt (✉)
Centre for Criminal Justice Studies, School of Law, University of Leeds, The Liberty Building, Moorland Road, Leeds LS2 9JT, UK
e-mail: s.karstedt@leeds.ac.uk

G. Meško, J. Tankebe (eds.), *Trust and Legitimacy in Criminal Justice*,
DOI 10.1007/978-3-319-09813-5_1

settings of liberal democracies police officers or judges are not explicitly thought of contributing to "democratic political development" and do not "see protecting the rule of law and respect for human rights listed as one of police's core functions" (Loader, 2006: 203). Notwithstanding widespread agreement that trust and confidence in these institutions, and thus their legitimacy is decisive for their functioning in democratic societies (e.g., Bradford, Murphy, & Jackson, 2014; Jackson & Bradford, 2009), their impact on the legitimacy of government institutions and political stability is not seen as a priority objective in firmly established democracies.

Further claims have been made about the role of international and transitional justice procedures in establishing the rule of law and fostering human rights regimes in countries that emerge from authoritarian rule or conflict (e.g., Stromseth, 2009). Intuitively such a role seems to be obvious, both in terms of addressing past violations of the law and ending impunity, and providing models for the rule of law to be installed in the future. As Goldsmith (2005) points out impunity for illegal action of law enforcers has a negative impact on trust in police and courts. In terms of indicators of police performance that impact on trust and legitimacy, pre-transitional police forces are tainted by excessive use of force, intimidation, petty, and large-scale corruption (Goldsmith, 2005: 455–456). Karstedt (2013a) found for all regime types that trust in and legitimacy of police forces which have been highly implicated in all types of human rights abuses, crimes against humanity and mass atrocities, is consistently lower. However, in which ways and if at all prosecution of police officers and judges, or general lustration procedures in the criminal justice system through transitional or international justice procedures can rebuild a trustworthy criminal justice system has hardly been assessed. One exception is Horne's (2012) study of trust in government institutions including the judiciary, police, army, parliament, and political parties. She found that lustration procedures alone rather than the type and diversity of procedures increase trust in all these institutions combined. In addition the trust effects are dependent on time, with trust increasing immediately after lustration until reaching a tipping point, from where it declines.

Transitional justice procedures—domestic or international—have been claimed to be missionaries of the rule of law, and essential in establishing the rule of law. The rule of law emerges here as the overarching framework and institutional design, and implanting or restoring the rule of law in transitional and post-conflict societies as a foremost task of transitional governments and the international community in order to establish legitimate and stable democratic governance (see Burlyuk, 2014; Cheesman, 2014). Policing and police reform are a lynchpin in these packages of transformation, with the ultimate aim of establishing a trustworthy and therefore legitimate police force.

More recently, these claims have been increasingly questioned as to their conceptual validity, practicality, and ultimately achievements. Perhaps the most critical blow to these claims was the EULEX (2010: 5) report, which assessed the European Rule of Law Mission in Kosovo. It admitted to "some positive, gradual, realistic and sustainable progress" that had been achieved, but continued "that the problems that are being tackled are substantial and there are no quick fixes". The extraordinary level of money spent on the program and the lack of visible achievements were damning (Capussela, 2011); already in 2006 Wilson, who had been involved in delivering the program had warned that little was achieved in particular among the judiciary, and only slightly more among the police. Similarly, the World Bank states that "the numerous rule of law assistance programs in post-conflict societies or fragile countries so far resulted in few lasting consequences" (Samuels, 2006: 15). Two strands of criticism, which are interrelated, stand out. The first of these questions the legitimacy of international intervention and transitional administration (Stahn, 2005) and the capacity and achievements of such interventions (Baker, 2009a; Call & Cousens, 2007). Rather than decreeing and trying to implement sweeping changes to applicable law with a sense of urgency, building up governmental institutions, and state capacity is seen as more promising. Such a perspective is ultimately based on effective performance of governments and institutions, which generates trust and establishes trustworthy institutions (Mishler & Rose, 1997, 1998, 2001). Hutchison and Johnson (2011) found that in 16 African countries, with one third being post-conflict or even conflict countries, higher institutional capacity is associated with increased levels of individual political trust, which includes trust in police and the courts in a combined measurement. Criminal justice institutions become less important for engendering societal trust than, e.g., the delivery of welfare and health to the population in post-conflict societies (Roberts, 2008).

The second and stronger strand comprises critics who generally reject the transfer of the Western model of democratic policing, and its implementation in mostly rural societies, and in hybrid political orders with a mixture of strong local and weak central government. Dinnen and Braithwaite (2009: 161) argue against the "excessive transplantation of urban policing models" from the North into rural societies in the Global South. Importantly, the state-centered models of policing and police reform, as well as of legitimacy have turned out to be inadequate for these societies. Instead, non-state actors need to be accepted and included in building institutions of security and justice in transitional societies, in particular in those that emerge from conflicts. In-depth studies of policing in these societies find parallel state and non-state forms of governance and order, and they all stress the necessity to accept and strengthen what is in place rather than trying to establish what had not existed before, including societal legitimacy of these local institutions (e.g., Sierra Leone: Albrecht & Buur, 2009; Liberia and Southern Sudan: Baker, 2009b; Melanesia: Dinnen & McLeod, 2009; Mozambique: Kyed, 2009).

However, the experiences with establishing democratic policing and the rule of law in transitional societies had repercussions on perspectives of legitimacy and trust in criminal justice for established liberal democracies. Starting with Loader in 2006 there is now agreement on the "expressive nature" of trust in policing, and its production through shared values, and local cohesion (Jackson & Bradford, 2009; Jackson & Sunshine, 2006). Trust and legitimacy are communicated to individuals and groups in terms of their membership in a political community, thus denying or affirming identity (Loader, 2006: 204). Democratic policing and the building of trust relationships with ethnic minorities has become a major occupation of policing in western democracies, as democratic governments aim at "inclusionary legitimacy" (Karstedt, 2013a) and eliciting support from minority and migrant groups (Bradford et al., 2014; Sargeant, Murphy, & Cherney, 2014). The problems involved in relationships between police and ethnic minorities have been the driving force in assigning a more prominent role to the police in producing and maintaining democratic legitimacy in established democracies. Though performance and the perceived competence of governments and the criminal justice system are not neglected, trust and legitimacy are seen as engendered by the quality of interaction, by recognition of citizens in fair procedures and their generally fair treatment at the hands of the authorities. Even in the extreme situation of high levels of security threats, procedural justice is and remains the primary antecedent of police legitimacy, as Jonathan-Zamir and Weisburd (2013) found for two cities in Israel. Trust and legitimacy link citizens to institutions that are intended to represent them, and both are voluntarily granted. Bottoms and Tankebe (2012) therefore stress the "dialogic" and "interactive" nature of legitimacy and trust, where the dialogue provides the link between civil society and the institutions of state and government, including the police and the courts.

Trust however is at extremely low levels in societies in transition (for postcommunist countries see Mishler & Rose, 1997, 2001). As part of the transition is the withdrawal of legitimacy from the previous regime and its untrustworthy institutions, transitional societies are burdened with a legacy of distrust in governments and their institutions, while the new institutional framework has not yet elicited confidence and legitimacy in the majority of the population. Trust and legitimacy are especially critical for new regimes, but also in short supply. In a comparative study on legitimacy of police and justice in democratic and nondemocratic regimes, the "nearly democratic" countries, which included mostly transitional societies, had notoriously low levels of general government legitimacy as well as of confidence in police, justice and the civil service, levels that were significantly lower than in democracies and in stable autocratic regimes (Karstedt, 2013a). Mishler and Rose (1997) found for postcommunist countries in Europe that in 1994 skepticism rather than outright distrust prevailed and was the majority opinion. A decade later, the four postcommunist and post-conflict countries Estonia, Slovenia, Poland, and Czech Republic still had the lowest levels of trust in the police in a sample of sixteen European countries (Kääriäinen, 2007). In a sample of African countries of similar size, prior transitions had a negative impact on trust in political institutions, including a number of countries with ongoing conflicts (e.g., Uganda: Hutchison & Johnson, 2011). It seems that transitions are periods when citizens loose trust and confidence, and withdraw legitimacy from institutions, and consequently periods of fragility and instability. As Esty and his colleagues showed in 1998, democracies in transition are particularly at risk of deteriorating into state failure and conflict (Esty et al., 1998).

Even if in the period following the transition trust and legitimacy are at low levels, they should improve over time as institutions have been rebuilt and acted with a certain degree of consistency and reliability. By delivering public services, reforming corrupt practices, protecting freedoms of citizens and being accountable to civil society, government institutions generally and criminal justice in particular should accrue legitimacy and trust. Roussey and Deffains (2012) have shown for 47 European countries, including stable and transitional societies, that support for democracy as well as resources poured into the justice system increase trust in the justice system. Similarly, general institutional capacity of the state, measured as the relationship between realized and potential tax revenue, is a strong predictor of trust in government institutions generally, including the police and the courts (Hutchison & Johnson, 2011).

Given the level of domestic and international financial and technical support trust in police and justice should increase over time, though this might not be a linear relationship (Horne, 2012). Several factors that impede the increase of trust in police and justice in transitional societies have to be taken into account. High levels of violence in transitional societies are signals of a lack of performance of criminal justice, and therefore might have a negative impact on confidence in police and criminal justice. Karstedt (2013a) found for a global sample that violent crime reduces trust in police and justice, however, significantly only in fully democratic societies. In six Central American countries, including transitional and post-conflict societies like Guatemala, Honduras, Nicaragua and El Salvador besides Costa Rica and Panama, crime control performance significantly impacted on trust in the justice system as well as in its key institutions; in countries with weak and underperforming criminal justice systems (Guatemala, El Salvador and Honduras) the police was in particular affected by the erosion of trust if citizens had been victimized (Malone, 2010). The reform of corrupt institutions and overall control of corruption is of utmost importance for improving levels of trust and legitimacy in all regime types, whether democracies, nearly democratic, mixed, or autocratic (Karstedt, 2013a).

There is little evidence for the claim that criminal justice institutions are the lynchpin for legitimacy and ultimately political stability in transitional societies. Further to this, we know very little about the post-transition trajectories of legitimacy of these institutions, and the actual improvements of legitimacy and how these are achieved in societies that are in transition towards democracy. Goldsmith (2005) provides an impressive list of trust-building measures of police reform, however, little is known about their actual impact. How important are the establishment of the rule of law, the control of corruption or general institutional and governmental stability for achieving long-term increase of trust from rather low levels? Or is performance of the police and criminal justice the decisive signal for citizens to trust these institutions more than they had done before, as Mishler and Rose (1998) argue? Is the end of impunity a necessary condition, and do procedures of transitional justice, whether domestic or international, provide models of institutions that can be trusted and thus have a role in establishing the dialogue that engenders legitimacy? We can also assume that a transition that coincides with a post-conflict situation presents particular challenges for developing legitimate and trustworthy criminal justice institutions (Hutchison & Johnson, 2011).

These questions and issues will be addressed based on a global sample of transitional societies, which spans transitions from 1974 to 2010. We thus can establish post-transition trajectories of legitimacy of police and criminal justice for more than two decades for some of the early transition countries. As each country trajectory begins with the transition, the post-transition period ranges from a few years up to more than 30 years. This time-related perspective is complemented by a comparative perspective in order to explore whether levels of legitimacy in transitional societies caught up with those in established and mature democracies, or were in some ways affected by the general decline of trust in government and criminal justice from which mature democracies suffer since the 1990s. This group of countries comprises two regional samples from Europe and the Americas, and a smaller time frame is used during which transitions took place. Finally, we analyzed those conditions that have been claimed to improve trust in criminal justice institutions in transitional societies, including transitional justice procedures. To this purpose we use a "cohort" of societies that experienced a transition between 1988 and 1998, with trajectories between 1995 and 2010 (for the samples see Tables 1A and 2A in the Appendix).

2 Defining Transitions and Contextualizing Trust and Legitimacy

Transitions do not have an unambiguous direction, and they can go both ways, towards democracy or towards a more nondemocratic regime. As Esty et al. (1998) have shown, it is neither a one-way street; societies may oscillate between transitions towards democracy and back again, with Argentina a prominent example during the decades up to the 1980s, and more recently the countries of the Arab Spring. Among the 85 authoritarian countries that Geddes (1999) records as having collapsed during the third wave of democratization since the 1970s, 34 reverted to more authoritarian regimes and 21 remained unstable. Even though democracies are not by default better in generating legitimacy for criminal justice institutions than nondemocratic regimes, in fully established democracies levels of trust in police and justice are generally higher than in nearly democratic or mixed regimes, a group in which most of the transitional countries are included (Karstedt, 2013a: 145). Therefore only transitions towards a more democratic regime, civil liberties and the rule of law are considered, and those countries are excluded in which a democratic transition was rescinded and the process of democratization reversed. If a country went through more than one transition between 1974 and 2010, only the last transition that ultimately paved the way toward democracy is used as the starting point of the transition respectively the post-transition trajectory. A number of countries, e.g., the post-soviet countries that were founded when the USSR dissolved, are included as transitional countries as their political systems and institutions were nondemocratic, even if they did not exist as sovereign states before.

All measurements of regime change and regime type are based on the Polity Index. The Polity Index (Epstein, Bates, Goldstone, Kristensen, & O'Halloran, 2006; Marshall & Jaggers, 2010) uses a range of different indicators of institutional and structural characteristics of democracies (for an overview see Karstedt, 2006). The Index rates countries on a continuous scale rather than providing discrete and mutually exclusive forms of governance. It comprises two "institutional indicators" of democracy and autocracy, respectively. Both are based on key qualities of democracies: the competitiveness of political participation, to which the regulation of participation is added for autocracies; the openness and competitiveness of executive recruitment; and constraints on the chief executive. Each is measured on an additive 11-point scale; combining the two scales results in a continuous scale which ranges from −10 indicating autocracies, to +10, indicating full democracies.

Some transitions are more incremental; they start peacefully and develop step-by-step across a longer period. Others originate in more sudden and disrupting events and start with the precipitous demise of the previous regime, like for example in the Central and East European countries in 1989/1990, from where societies embark on the road towards democracy. Transitions are measured according to the Regime Transition Index of the Polity Index (Marshall, Gurr, & Jaggers, 2013: 36–37; Epstein et al., 2006). According to the Regime Transition Index, countries with democratic transitions have an increase of at least three points towards a higher democracy level within three consecutive years. Using these criteria, 78 countries were defined as going through a regime transition towards democracy across the whole period from 1974 to 2010.[1] In each case the start of the transition toward democracy is the first year of the transition period. The total post-transition period is subdivided into four periods, during which legitimacy and trust are measured: the first five years after the transition, between 6 and up to 10 years, between 11 and 15 years, and finally more than 15 years after the transition. Measurements of trust in police and justice that fall within this period for the respective country are used. As several indicators on corruption, rule of law and institutional development were only available from the 1990s onward, a subsample of transitional countries was used that included only countries that experienced a democratic transition between 1988 and 1998. Comparisons between countries that had established transitional justice procedures or did without, and between post-conflict countries and where the transition was done peacefully, were also based on this cohort of transitional societies.

In order to compare trust in police and justice in established and transitional democracies, "full" or "mature" democracies were defined as those countries that ranked between +8 and +10 on the Polity Score. Accordingly, 24 countries were defined as mature democracies (Epstein et al., 2006), most of which were in Europe and the Americas (see Tables 1A and 2A in the Appendix). However, for such a comparison countries had to be selected that were either mature democracies or

[1] Germany was excluded, as only East Germany experienced a transition, while West Germany ranked as a mature democracy throughout the period.

transitional countries during the same time period; accordingly a much more restricted time frame during which transitions took place had to be used. Further to this, account had to be taken of the fact that in some global regions trust in criminal justice is generally low, even in democracies. Therefore, two cohorts of transitional countries were used for the comparison between transitional and mature democracies. The European cohort included countries with transitions between 1988 and 1993 (excluded: Greece, Portugal, Spain, and Croatia, where transitions were either earlier or later), which resulted in 11 mature democracies and 17 transitional countries. The American cohort comprised of 20 countries, with 15 transitional countries between 1978 and 1990, and only 5 that were classified as mature democracies during this and the follow-up time period (Table 2A in the Appendix).

Measuring legitimacy on the aggregate level of countries or regimes is particularly difficult. Research on legitimacy and procedural justice has generated a wealth of conceptualizations, and tried to distinguish between legitimacy, trust and confidence, and satisfaction with authorities, as well as between process and outcome on the individual level, which need to be translated into aggregate measurements (see Smith, 2007). In this analysis, aggregate attitudinal indicators will be used. The most common measurements of legitimacy of criminal justice in domestic as well as in international and comparative research are the proportion of citizens of the country who have "confidence in the police" and "confidence in the justice system." This measure throws a wide net over the different dimensions of trust, satisfaction, and legitimacy that have been identified at the individual level, and is deemed approximately to capture essential characteristics of legitimacy. These are expectations as to the future performance of authorities, of what they are obliged to do, what is justifiable, what they should do, and what can be rightly expected from them. These data were retrieved for the whole period between 1980 and 2010 from the World Value Surveys, the European Value Surveys, the Arab Barometer, Afrobarometer, and Latinobarometro, and measured as the proportion of citizens, who either had "a great deal" or "quite a lot" (or equivalent response categories) of confidence in the police and the justice system.[2]

Next, indicators of democratic development were used that are claimed to be related to trust in police and justice in the transition period. The Bertelsmann Transformation Index [BTI] (Bertelsmann Stiftung, 2012) comprises a number of indicators of successful transitions to democracy. These include the rule of law, stability of state and government, and the establishment of a state with adequate power structures; the stability of democratic institutions, and their acceptance and

---

[2] Sources for "confidence in police," "confidence in justice," "generalized trust," and "satisfaction with democracy": World Values Survey http://www.worldvaluessurvey.org/; European Values Survey http://www.europeanvaluesstudy.eu/; Arab Barometer http://www.arabbarometer.org/; African Barometer http://www.afrobarometer.org/; Latinobarometro http://www.latinobarometro.org/lat.jsp; if more than one wave was available during the respective period, the mean was calculated.

legitimacy among the citizenry; and finally political and social integration, indicated by a stable pattern of representation and mediation between state and society.[3] These indicators were used for the subsample of countries with transitions between 1988 and 1998. Two development indicators were retrieved from the CIRI Human Rights Data Project (Cingranelli, Richards, & Chad Clay, 2012). In order to capture the strength and impact of civil society, as Goldsmith (2005) suggests, the Empowerment Rights Index was included; it comprises indicators of freedom of movement, assembly, religion, and others. The second indicator measures the independence of the judiciary from other government institutions.[4] Finally, control of corruption has been identified as decisive for the transition to fairness and even-handedness in government decision making. This applies in particular to decision making by police forces and the courts, and police corruption should severely affect levels of trust in the criminal justice system. The level of control of corruption was used as a proxy for perceived fairness of decision making, and measured by the Control of Corruption Index of the World Governance Indicators.[5]

Trust in criminal justice is part of an overarching belief system, and needs to be contextualized. During transition periods public perceptions of institutional patterns and government performance necessarily will change and might be particularly volatile. Transitional countries are low-trust countries (Mishler & Rose, 1997, 2001; Sztompka, 1993, 1996) for two reasons. First, transitions have been preceded by a deterioration of trust and legitimacy of the previous regimes, and second, authoritarian societies often breed distrust among citizens. In order to contextualize trust in criminal justice, two indicators were used. Generalized trust among the population was retrieved from the same data sources as confidence in police and justice (see above).[6] Satisfaction with democratic development and with democracy

[3] The Bertelsmann Transformation Index analyzes and evaluates democracy, market economy and political management for 128 developing and transition countries bi-annually since 2003. It is based on 17 individual criteria which are combined for each of the three dimensions, and rank the countries on each of the criteria from 1 (low) to 10 (high). The mean value for the countries for the period from 2006 to 2010 was used (Bertelsmann Stiftung, 2012).

[4] The Empowerment Index is constructed from the Foreign Movement, Domestic Movement, Freedom of Speech, Freedom of Assembly & Association, Workers' Rights, Electoral Self-Determination, and Freedom of Religion indicators. It ranges from 0 (no government respect for these seven rights) to 14 (full government respect for these seven rights). The Independence of the Judiciary index ranges from 0 (not independent) to 2 (generally independent) Cingranelli et al. (2012): The CIRI Human Rights Dataset. http://www.humanrightsdata.org; version 2013.04.02.

[5] The Control of Corruption Indicator is included in the World Bank's Worldwide Governance Indicators (Daniel Kaufmann, Aart Kraay and Massimo Mastruzzi). It reflects perceptions of the extent to which public power is exercised for private gain, including both petty and grand forms of corruption, as well as "capture" of the state by elites and private interests, and efforts to curb corruption. Percentile ranks among all countries from 0 (lowest) to 100 (highest). Version 11 was used http://info.worldbank.org/governance/wgi/index.asp.

[6] Generalized trust in others is included in all surveys that measure trust in institutions. The slightly different response categories were adapted; the category of high trust was used, either percentages of categories 7–10 from a scale from 0 (no trust) to 10 (high trust), or the equivalent categories.

as a regime was measured as percentage of the population who were highly satisfied.[7]

Legitimacy of criminal justice and government institutions more generally are based on public perceptions of their efficiency; they are also evaluated in terms of their use of repressive measures and respect for the human rights of citizens, given the often highly repressive nature of the previous authoritarian regime. Efficiency of the criminal justice system is perceived largely in terms of combating crime, in particular violent crime. In order to control for these conditions, the homicide rate[8] was used as a proxy for perceived efficiency. Past as well as ongoing violence by police and within the justice system might cast a long shadow, and should contribute to further erosion of trust and low trust levels during the transition period (Karstedt, 2013a, 2013b). Illegal violence was measured by the Political Terror Scale which combines information from the US State Department Country Reports and reports from Amnesty International. It comprises state-sanctioned/unlawful killings, disappearances, torture, and political imprisonment, and thus mainly targets the criminal justice system and its repressive use of violence. The two rankings were combined resulting in a scale from 1 indicating "no state violence" to 9 indicating "pervasive state violence."[9]

Finally, two particular characteristics of transitions were taken into account. First, the impact of transitional justice procedures was measured by identifying countries, in which at least one of the following had been initiated: criminal prosecution and trials (domestic, hybrid, or international), Truth Commissions and Reparations.[10] Second, severe armed conflict preceding the transition or even ongoing (Hutchison & Johnson, 2011) presents a particularly difficult situation for any transition. We classified a country as post-conflict, if the conflict had ceased at

Mean values for the respective time periods were used if there were more than one measurement point during the period; for sources see note 2 .

[7] Both questions ("satisfied with the way democracy is developing in this country" and "democracy a very good . . . or very bad way of governing this country") were included in the surveys that were used for all attitudinal data (see note 2). The categories for high satisfaction and "very good" or their equivalents were used to indicate support for democracy.

[8] Source: "WHO Mortality Database": Homicide rates 1974–2010 (http://www.who.int/whosis/mort/download/en/index.html). In addition, we complemented these with data from the Comparative Homicide Time Series collected at the NRILP in Finland by Lappi-Seppälä and his colleagues (Lehti, 2013).

[9] Political Terror Scale (PTS) by Mark Gibney, Linda Cornett and Reed Wood, version 2010, available at www.politicalterrorscale.org/ (Gibney, Cornett, & Wood, 2012). The PTS is combined from two sources, the US State Department and Amnesty International country reports; both are ranked from 1 (no state violence) to 5 (has expanded to the whole population) and provided separately. Here a sum scale was constructed that ranked from 1 to 9; see also Landmann & Carvalho, 2010.

[10] Data were collected from three sources: Payne, Olsen, and Reiter (2013). Transitional Justice Database Project (http://www.tjdbproject.com/); Stan and Nedelsky (2013) Encyclopedia of Transitional Justice. Cambridge: Cambridge University Press; and United States Institute of Peace (2013). Truth Commission Digital Collection (http://www.usip.org/publications/truth-commission-digital-collection).

the respective period of transition; countries with on-going conflicts were excluded. A country was classified as a non-conflict country if no armed conflict had taken place or it had ceased at least 10 years before the actual transition.[11] Results are based on regression analyses, ANOVA, and comparisons of mean (t-tests), however given the partially small numbers in our samples, cohorts and categories, significance levels should be used with caution, and more as indicative of patterns.

3 Transitions and the Production of Trust in Police and Justice

3.1 The longue Dureé of Trajectories of Trust

The trajectories of trust are followed up to more than 15 years, depending on the start time of the transition. The total post-transitional period is divided into four periods, during which legitimacy and trust are measured: the first 5 years after the transition, between 6 and up to 10, between 11 and 15 years, and finally more than 15 years after the transition. Generally, the transition countries remain low trust countries even across a rather long post-transition period, as Table 1 shows. Nearly half of the population trust the police in the immediate 5 years after the transition, which decreases slightly during the following two 5-year periods, and reaches the initial level again after 15 and more years. Trust in the justice system is at similarly high levels during the first years, but goes into continuous decline over the whole period (from 51 to 41 % after 15 and more years). Other indicators that impact on trust in criminal justice show either a decline like general trust, which decreases from barely 30 to 24 %, or show no change at all. This in particular applies to indicators of performance like homicide rates and state violence that remain at very high levels throughout the post-transition period. The exception is control of corruption, which increases by nearly 50 % (from 34 in the first 5-year period to 48 more than 15 years after the transition). Given this context, trust in criminal justice can hardly flourish in transitional countries.

Post-transitional trust trajectories differ across the global regions, as Table 1 demonstrates. Trust in both police and justice increase in African transition countries, as violence is considerably reduced and control of corruption increases. In European transitional societies trust in police increases slightly, while trust in justice decreases. As in Africa, homicide levels declined and control of corruption improved albeit insignificantly. State violence is more constrained in Africa and the Americas, while there are no changes in the comparably low levels in Europe and high levels in Asian countries.

[11] Data on conflicts were collected from the Uppsala Conflict Data Programme's Conflict Termination Dataset (Kreutz, 2010) http://www.pcr.uu.se/research/ucdp/datasets/ucdp_conflict_termination_dataset/.

Table 1 Trajectories of trust in police and justice (Transitional countries $N = 78$)

	Trust in police (%)	Trust in justice system (%)	Homicide	State violence	Control of corruption
5 years post transition					
Africa	51.62	55.61	31.8	4.8	28.6
Americas	39.01	48.40	10.95	4.59	39.15
Asia and Oceania	56.47	54.53	3.45	4.72	33.13
Europe	42.94	45.19	7.4	2.85	51.8
10 years post transition					
Africa	44.82	51.65	16.89	4.35	31.91
Americas	38.15	38.84	10.82	4.65	47.27
Asia and Oceania	43.26	50.19	3.31	4.69	33.6
Europe	43.42	41.22	7.19	2.88	47.06
15 years post transition					
Africa	52.57	57.61	16.3	4.23	37.32
Americas	35.04	36.37	12.99	4.45	46.33
Asia and Oceania	53.14	58.03	4.47	4.62	37.16
Europe	46.62	40.44	5.63	2.9	50.6
>15 years post transition					
Africa	56.27	60.23	13.47	4.03	45.65
Americas	34.46	30.31	17.86	4.01	42.18
Asia and Oceania	58.70	47.81	3.55	4.8	39.46
Europe	51.42	39.39	3.75	2.99	55.82

When comparing countries with homicide rates above and below the median for each period, the role of performance in combating violent crime is corroborated, however only for trust in police. As Figure 1 shows, there is no impact of violent crime in the immediate aftermath of the transition, but after 6 years, as homicide rates level down, the difference between countries with high and low homicide rates is more distinct ($p < .05$). No difference for trust in police was found for transition countries with high and low levels of state violence across the whole period. Efficiency rather than civilized and rule of law compliant procedures seem to impact on citizens' trust in the police. The fact that courts are capable of keeping higher levels of trust even where state violence is high mirrors findings for trust in criminal justice in nondemocratic regimes (Karstedt, 2013a). In contemporary nondemocratic regimes courts are increasingly seen by citizens as a last and also successful resort against repressive violence from other agencies of the state; these experiences might be transferred to the transitional period, resulting in partially significantly higher levels of trust in justice even under conditions of high levels of state repression.

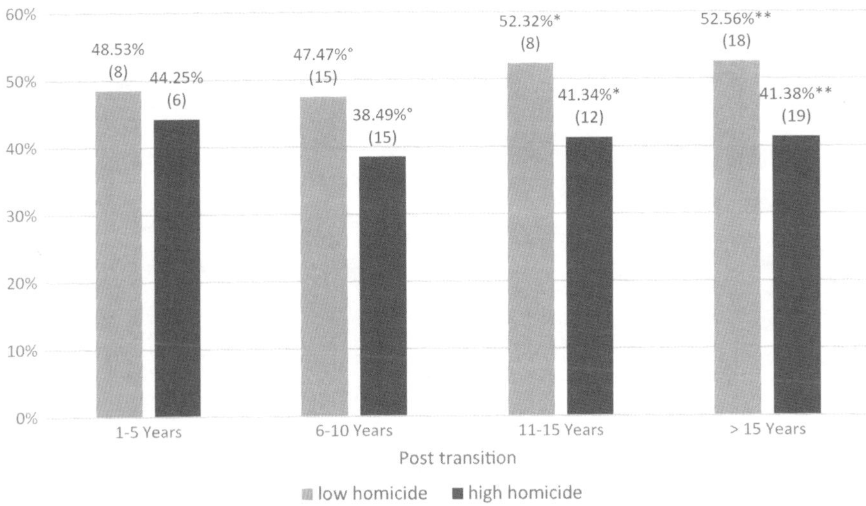

Fig. 1 Trust in police and homicide across post transition periods. Level of significance: $^{o}p < .1$; $^{*}p < .05$; $^{**}p < .01$; $^{***}p < .001$. All other: not significant

3.2 *Catching Up with Democracies: Europe and the Americas*

As the trajectories of trust in criminal justice have shown, transitional countries do not provide an environment in which such trust can flourish. When countries move toward becoming full democracies, police and the courts take center stage in sweeping reform efforts, and are seen as cornerstones for legitimacy of government and state institutions. Given the only incremental changes in trust in police and justice, which in addition are not consistently to the better, the question arises if transitional countries are capable of catching up with those countries that have been established and mature democracies since a long time. Democracies suffered from considerable losses in overall confidence in government and state institutions, and disillusion and discontent with democracy might have spread and affected transitional countries, resulting in convergence rather than divergence between transitional countries and mature democracies. In order to answer these questions we need to follow a "cohort" comprising both transitional countries, which experienced the transition within a restricted time frame, and contemporary mature democracies across the past decades. Two different cohorts of transitional countries were identified, a European cohort, which experienced the transitions between 1988 and 1993, and a cohort in the Americas (South, Central, and North), with transitions taking place within a slightly longer time frame between 1978 and 1990. Both cohorts were juxtaposed with mature democracies from their region, and trajectories of trust in police and confidence were identified between 1995 and 2010.

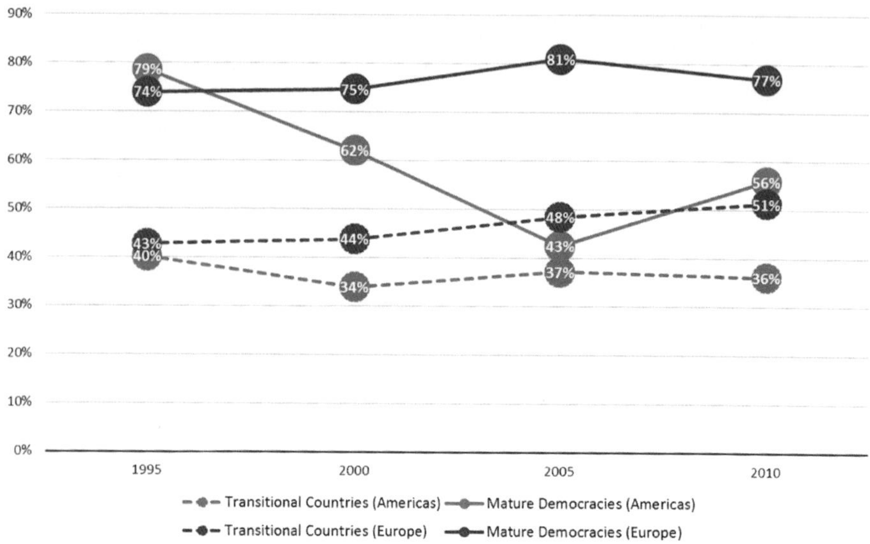

Fig. 2 Transitional societies and mature democracies: Trust in police 1995–2010 (Europe and Americas) $N(1995) = 22$; $N(2000) = 46$; $N(2005) = 25$; $N(2010) = 46$

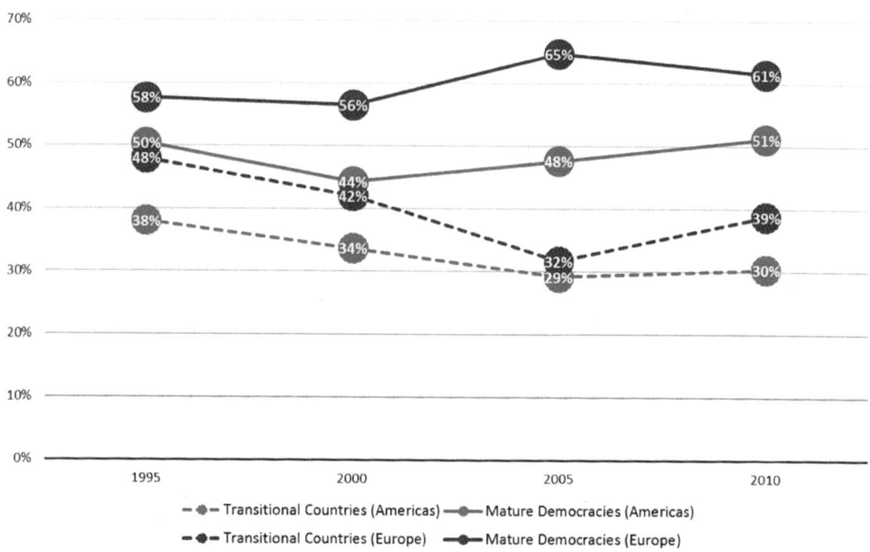

Fig. 3 Transitional societies and mature democracies: Trust in justice 1995–2010 (Europe and Americas) $N(1995) = 22$; $N(2000) = 44$; $N(2005) = 21$; $N(2010) = 46$

As both Figs.2 and 3 show, trajectories in both global regions differ considerably for transitional as well as for full democracies. However, in both regions the transitional countries do not gain on mature democracies. In Europe, the difference remains significant for trust in police across the whole period ($p < .01$) notwithstanding gains in trust for transitional countries. The gap in trust in justice between transitional countries and mature democracies increases rather than closes, and is significant from 2000 onwards. This is mainly caused by a substantive decrease of trust in justice in the transitional countries rather than by small gains of trust in mature democracies. In the Americas, trust in the police in transitional countries remains at low levels, however, in mature democracies these change quite dramatically, with a loss of trust of more than 30 % between 1995 and 2005. Differences in trust in justice increase across the period, mainly due to losses in trust in transitional countries (mostly not significant). Patterns as well as trajectories are mostly similar in both regions, and transitional countries do neither catch up with mature democracies nor do they move visibly towards this level.

Across this period, transitional countries neither made decisive gains in developing the conditions for trust in the police and justice to flourish. In Europe, civil society remains weak in transitional countries. General trust in others is at significantly lower levels ($p < .01$), as is satisfaction with democracy. Civil society empowerment is consistently at significantly lower levels ($p < .001$). While mature democracies have long established the independence of the judiciary, it is at low points in transitional countries throughout the period from 1995 to 2010. In the Americas, differences vanish as general trust deteriorates in mature democracies from 2000 onwards, and the gap in satisfaction with democracy is closed as citizens in transitional countries increasingly opt for democracy. Like in Europe, civil society empowerment remains at significantly lower levels in transitional countries ($p < .05$), and differences in the independence of the judiciary are as stark as they are in Europe ($p < .01$). Even if the Latin American countries had a longer period of transition than the European countries starting at the end of the 1980s, they do not close the gap with mature democracies in their region. Notwithstanding considerable losses of trust in police in mature democracies in the Americas, the difference is sustained throughout the period, though it is more distinct for the European countries. Transitional countries do neither provide the institutional reforms nor the environment for the empowerment of civil society that are deemed essential for creating trustworthy police and justice (e.g., Goldsmith, 2005: 463).

3.3 *Changing Institutions: Does It Matter?*

Even if transitional countries in general lag behind mature democracies in terms of legitimacy of police and justice, some transition countries might be more successful than others in creating the environment that is conducive to trust in police and justice. Reforms of police and the justice system might be more thorough, civil society might gain strength more quickly in order to fulfil its role as a "source of monitoring and resistance to government policies and practices" (Goldsmith, 2005: 463), and overall stability of democratic institutions is achieved at higher levels. Transitional countries embark on a route towards sweeping reforms of state and government institutions, which prominently include the establishment of the rule of law, as well as adequate power structures and balances of institutional power (see Karstedt, 2013b). Such reforms should give stability to flagging democratic institutions, and thus enhance their acceptance and legitimacy among the citizenry. Civil society and the state need to find a new balance between themselves, through political and social integration, and stable patterns of representation and mediation between state and society. Control of corruption is seen as pivotal among these reforms, as it increases trust and legitimacy of police and justice independent of regime type (Karstedt, 2013a).

Most of these indicators are only available since 2000; they are included in the Bertelsmann Transformation Index (BTI; see above). We therefore needed a "cohort" of transitional countries sufficiently close to the period of measurement between 2006 and 2010, and sufficiently close together in terms of their transitions. We used the cohort of transitions between 1988 and 1998, which resulted in a global sample of 43 countries with the majority from Europe (19) and Africa (12) in addition to six Asian and six Latin American countries. Performance in institutional reforms was measured as mean values between 2006 and 2010. Trust in police and justice was measured for the same period, and if there was more than one survey during this period, the mean value was used. Bivariate regression analyses were conducted.

The results reveal a pattern that corroborates the downward trajectories of trust in justice as shown in Table 1. Though none of the indicators of stability of state and democratic institutions, and in particular of civil society engagement and political and social integration is significantly related to trust in justice, this relationship mostly takes a negative direction, i.e., as more democratic institutions are established and accepted, citizens become increasingly distrustful of their criminal justice systems. Quite surprisingly, this also applies to control of corruption and the establishment of the rule of law, which is consistent with the failure of the EULEX program in Kosovo (EULEX, 2010). Figure 4 demonstrates the typical downward slope for trust in justice as rule of law credentials improve. There are two reasons behind this development. First, the justice system remains mainly intact and judges stay in their positions during the transition and beyond. Exemplary in this respect are post-war Germany (Frei, van Laak, & Stolleis, 2000; Perels, 1999), and South Africa (Dyzenhaus, 1998/2003). Second, democratic institutions give rise to critical voices and critical assessment by citizens, and thus also nourish distrust. Legitimacy of police and justice should therefore show more "elasticity" as citizens become more sensitive and well informed about practices and court cases, and are capable of voicing their distrust, which might then easily spread among the population (Karstedt, 2013a). This is corroborated by the fact that when political participation increases, trust in justice deteriorates more markedly ($p < .10$).

In the same vein, trust in police is little affected by any of the institutional reforms with one exception; Fig. 5 shows that control of corruption has a significant ($p < .01$) and quite marked positive impact on trust in police. Where control of corruption increases, citizens have more trust in police forces. Transitional countries thus do neither differ from full democracies nor from nondemocratic regimes, where control of corruption is equally essential for citizens in granting legitimacy to police (Karstedt, 2013a). However, the direction of the relationships between

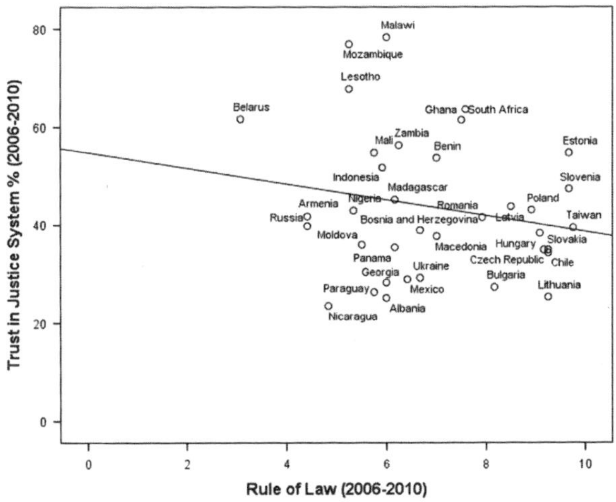

Fig. 4 Rule of law and trust in justice system 2006–2010 (% trust). $F=1.37$; $p<0.25$; $N=36$

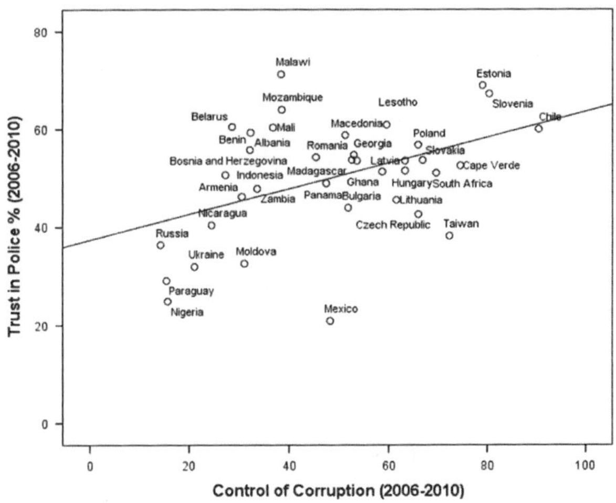

Fig. 5 Control of corruption and trust in police (% trust). $F=11.51$; $p=0.002$; $N=37$

institutional reforms and trust in police is consistently positive, in contrast to trust in justice. Given the fact that these coefficients are all nonsignificant, this should be treated with caution. Nonetheless these findings indicate that trust in police and trust in justice not only follow different trajectories across the period of transition but also institutional reforms are not unambiguous in their impact on legitimacy and trust in different institutions of government.[12] However, their overall impact is surprisingly low, and in stark contrast to the claims made about their importance in enhancing trust in police and justice.

[12] It might therefore be advisable to analyze these separately rather than in combined measures of trust in government that include a number of institutions (see e.g. Horne, 2012; Hutchison & Johnson, 2011).

3.4 Conflict and Transitional Justice: Does It Make a Difference?

Among the many hopes that are invested in transitional justice procedures the restoration of the rule of law (e.g., McAdams, 1997), delivery of justice for victims and perpetrators, and thus ultimately increasing trust in criminal justice are most often and most strongly voiced (e.g., Elster, 2006; Teitel, 2002). Impunity for perpetrators of human rights abuses among the police both in the past and in the present has been identified by Goldsmith (2005: 453) as a major obstacle to public confidence in police. As transitional justice procedures address violence and human rights abuses by police and the justice apparatus, they simultaneously delegitimize the past and (re-)legitimize the future of these institutions. In the first instance, transitional justice procedures will therefore have a detrimental impact on the legitimacy of these institutions, from which they will need to recover and regain legitimacy. Given this ambiguous nature of transitional justice procedures, a positive "net impact" might show only over the years.

The legacy of civil wars, state repression, and terror weighs heavily on transitional societies creating "societies of fear" (Koonings & Kruijt, 1999), in which trust in government and also within civil society is in short supply. Given the participation of police forces in violent repression, citizens will in particular withdraw legitimacy and trust from this institution. Ongoing and recent internal violence and massive repression, in which police are routinely implicated, have been found to have a strong and negative impact on general trust in government institutions in a sample of African countries, including police and justice (Hutchison & Johnson, 2011).

Using the cohort of 43 transitional countries from 1988 to 1998, we contrasted countries that had a conflict ("post-conflict") with countries where the transition took place without conflict or where the conflict had ceased at least 10 years before the actual transition (countries with ongoing conflicts were excluded, see above). In the next step, countries with transitional justice procedures were compared to countries that had had none. Trust in police and justice, as well as the contextual factors were measured twice: first for the 1990s, during the period of transition, and then for the decade of 2000–2010. Rule of law is an exception with only one measurement in the 2000s, as the BTI indicator was available mostly after 2006, and a mean value for 2006–2010 was calculated, which covered most of the countries.

As Figs. 6 and 7 demonstrate, in societies that leave a conflict behind, citizens are more willing to invest confidence in police and justice than in countries where the transition was not related to a conflict. It seems that ending the conflict per se gives new hope for the future, and a boost to trust both in police and in justice. The difference becomes more substantial in the 2000s, even as the conflict is left further

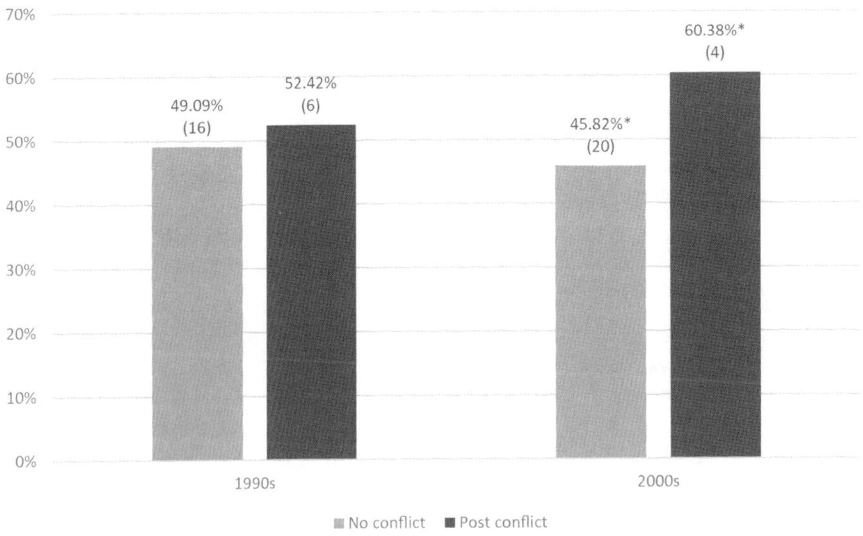

Fig. 6 Trust in police in countries with and without conflict (% trust): 1990s and 2000s . Level of significance: $^{o}p < .1$; $*p < .05$; $**p < .01$; $***p < .001$; All other: not significant

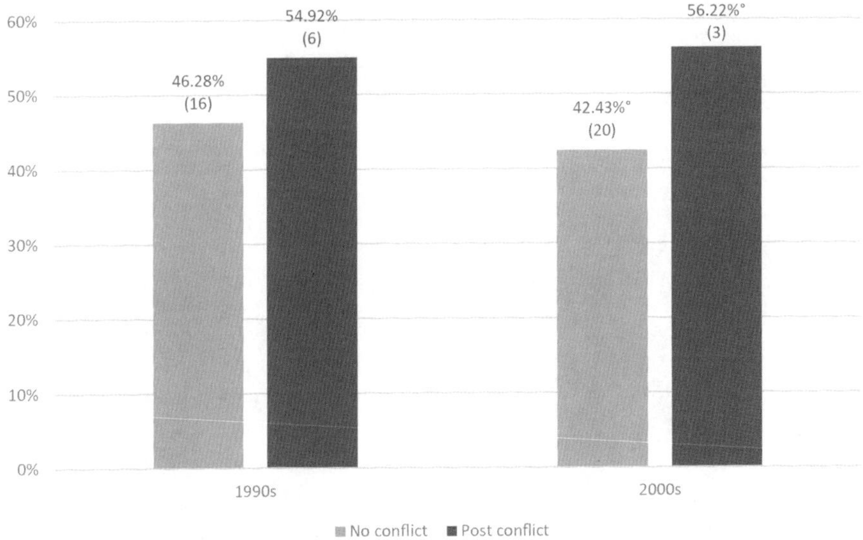

Fig. 7 Trust in justice in countries with and without conflict (% trust): 1990s and 2000s. Level of significance: $^{o}p < .1$; $*p < .05$; $**p < .01$; $***p < .001$; All other: not significant

behind. The higher levels of trust in police and justice are mirrored by higher levels of satisfaction with democracy and its development in post-conflict countries outperforming countries without conflict.

In contrast to such more optimistic attitudes among citizens, post-conflict countries lag behind in terms of structural reforms of the judiciary, implementation of the rule of law (see Fig. 10) and compliance with human rights that guarantee political participation for civil society, and ensure its capacity for "mobilizing distrust" and resistance to government policies and practices where necessary. The discrepancy between high hopes as demonstrated in the attitudes of citizens, and a deficient institutional environment in which confidence does not have a foundation and might be easily withdrawn, seems to be a breeding ground for the failure of democratic transitions that were observed by Esty et al. (1998).

Transitional justice procedures send ambiguous messages in terms of confidence in police and justice. Consequently, as Figs. 8 and 9 show, there is nearly no difference between countries with and without transitional justice procedures, and trust in justice even increases in the 2000s where no transitional justice had been implemented. Addressing past and present state violence does not automatically translate into trust among citizens. This corresponds to our findings that levels of state violence do not have an impact on confidence in police and justice across the transition period. Transitional justice seems to promote democracy as slightly more satisfaction with democratic government among the citizenry shows. It also encourages judicial reforms regarding the independence of the judiciary in the first instance (1990s), and the implementation of rights that empower citizens in the long run (2000s), however, none of these differences is marked and substantial.

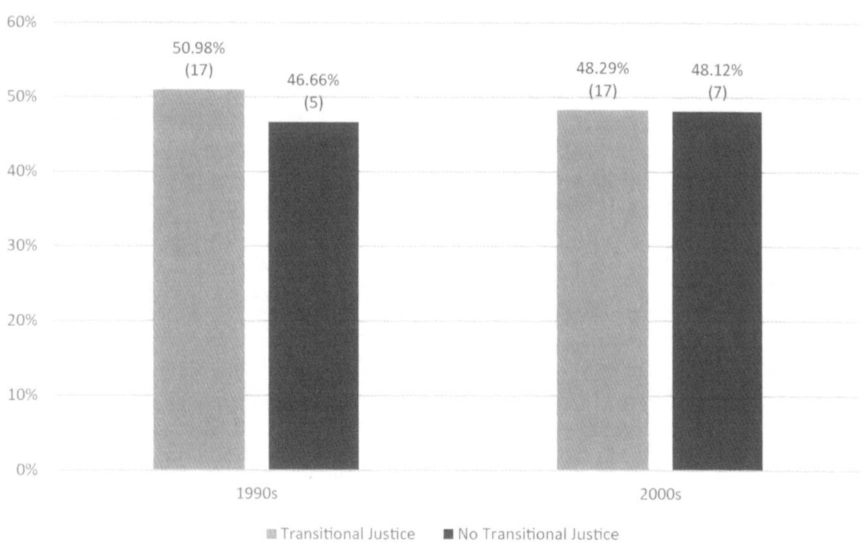

Fig. 8 Trust in police in countries with and without transitional justice (% trust) 1990s and 2000s. Level of significance: not significant

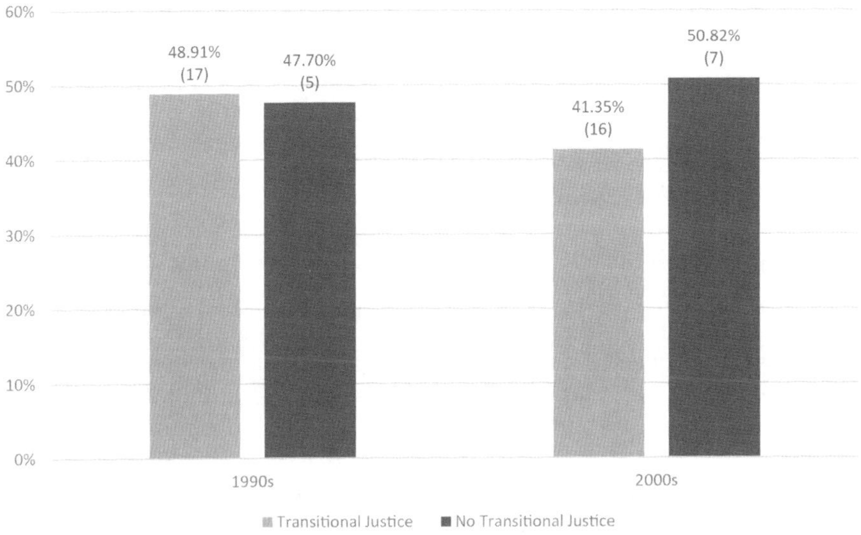

Fig. 9 Trust in justice in countries with and without transitional justice (% trust): 1990s and 2000s. Level of significance: not significant

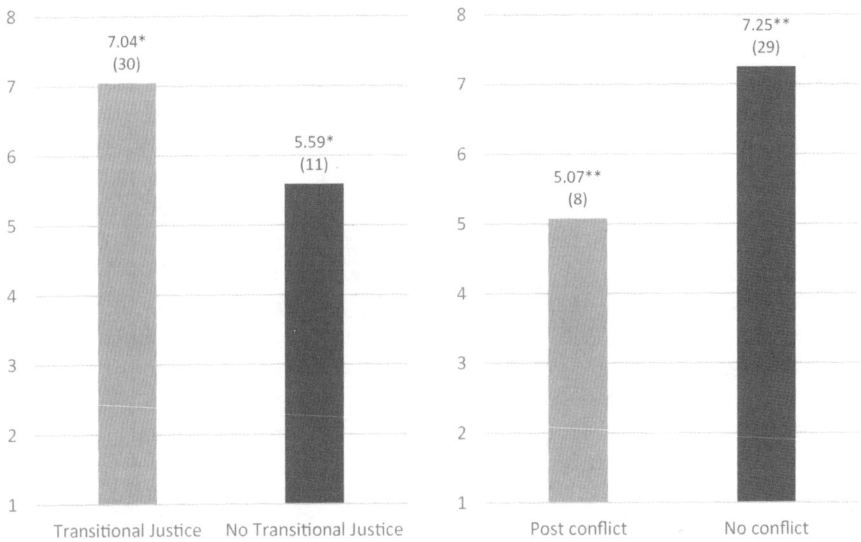

Fig. 10 Rule of Law (2006–2010): Transitional justice process and post-conflict. Level of significance: $^{o}p < .1$; $^{*}p < .05$; $^{**}p < .01$; $^{***}p < .001$

Both conflict and transitional justice impact on the implementation of rule of law reforms. As Fig. 10 demonstrates, previous violent conflict markedly impedes rule of law reforms and keeps them at low levels. In contrast, transitional justice in fact supports and promotes such reforms, and is presumably part of the establishment of the rule of law. However, as has been shown above this does not translate into trust and confidence in police and justice.

4 Building Trust in Transition

As Goldsmith (2005: 464) notes, "establishing trustworthy police forces is a key challenge for police reformers in low-trust settings", and this applies equally to trust in the justice system, courts and judges. Transitions are deeply destabilizing events that resonate throughout society with long-term effect on individual attitudes of confidence in police and justice, as well as on widely held distrust in government and state institutions (Hutchison & Johnson, 2011). Over a long time transitional societies struggle to achieve the institutional capacity and stability that gives a lasting and solid foundation for citizens to have trust and confidence in police and justice, and grant legitimacy to these institutions and their office holders. Police and justice have been identified as cornerstones for legitimacy of state and governments, and confidence in these institutions as pivotal in the process of transitions to democracy.

This comparative analysis of transitions toward democracy across the globe from 1974 to 2010 shows that building trust in transitional environments is not only challenging, but that the instruments and building blocks achieve less than is often assumed. Following transitions across more than 15 years we find only little improvement of trust in police and rather losses than gains for trust in justice. Between 1995 and 2010, transition countries in Europe and the Americas never reached the level of mature democracies in their region (with one exception for the Americas due to a drop in mature democracies). These transitional societies did neither succeed in creating the institutional context that is conducive to confidence in and legitimacy of institutions that mature democracies had at the same time. With the exception of control of corruption, none of the transformations that should achieve higher levels of legitimacy and trust had a discernable impact; the fact that improvements in the rule of law had no impact on trust in justice is perhaps less surprising in the light of recent findings of the impact of rule of law programs in Europe (EULEX, 2010). It seems to be violent crime, remaining at comparably high levels throughout the transition period that has a discernable impact on trust in police, but not in justice. Transitional justice procedures are not the panacea for enhancing trust and legitimacy among citizens, due to the ambiguous messages that they send. In countries emerging from a conflict situation, citizens indeed put more trust in police and justice, and grant more legitimacy to them. However, there is more confidence in a better future than capacity building that can retain and increase such higher levels in the long run, creating imbalances and a seedbed for political failure. As transition countries continue to struggle to build institutional capacity and create an environment conducive to legitimacy, distrust in government institutions and in particular police and justice is hardly to blame for political failure. It is questionable whether legitimacy of police and justice is the powerful glue that holds transitional societies together.

What can be done in the light of these quite sobering results? Given the global sample spanning more than three decades of transitions to democracy, only analyses of more or less trust could be conducted at the macro-level of countries, which definitely constitute limitations to these findings. Nonetheless, they pose critical questions to widely held assumptions about the positive impact of rule of law and general capacity building on police and justice legitimacy in transitional and post-conflict societies. The results point toward two routes of improving police legitimacy. First, efficacy in terms of combating crime, i.e., being competent in their everyday tasks, seems to be decisive for establishing a trustworthy police (see Mishler & Rose, 1998). Citizens in transitional and post-conflict societies might actually value law and order more than the complex system of criminal justice that the rule of law presents (Cheesman, 2014; see also Karstedt, 2013a). The fact that post-conflict societies have higher levels of trust in police and justice than non-conflict societies corroborates such an assumption. Second, control of corruption, i.e., improving fairness and equality in decision making seems to be another core requirement. For citizens in transitional countries procedural justice is as important as elsewhere. The results thus suggest a focus on police and justice reform and on the mundane delivery of security and justice in the everyday lives of citizens rather than implementing a plethora of programs of institutional capacity building across the board.

In order to overcome the limitations of this research, we need to heed Goldsmith's (2005) advice and address reasons for trust and capacity building at the local and micro-level where policing takes place and justice is done. Programs of police and justice reform that were implemented during the time, often imported models from the global North to the South, and of urban policing in western democracies to rural areas that were just recovering from conflict (Dinnen & Braithwaite, 2009). However, failures have led to a redirection of efforts towards local and non-state actors, and local initiatives of providing security and justice (e.g., Albrecht & Buur, 2009; Baker, 2009b). These probe into the local reasons for distrust and withdrawal of legitimacy. However, on all levels—from local and micro-level to country and macro-level—building of trust takes time, and mostly more than is expected and even can be afforded.

Acknowledgements I thank Gorazd Meško for giving me the opportunity to develop the research for a conference in Ljubljana in September 2013. As always I am deeply grateful to Michael Koch, University of Bielefeld, for his invaluable contributions and data collection, analyses and graphics.

Appendix

Table 1A Democracies and transitional countries, global regions

	Democracies	Transitional countries	Total
Africa	1	24	25
Americas	5	17	22
AsiaOcean	6	16	22
Europe	12	21	33
Total	24	78	102

Table 2A Countries

Country	Classification	Country	Classification
Albania (E*)	Transitional country	Guyana (*)	Transitional country
Algeria	Transitional country	Honduras (A)	Transitional country
Argentina (A)	Transitional country	Hungary (E*)	Transitional country
Armenia (*)	Transitional country	India	Mature democracy
Australia	Mature democracy	Indonesia (*)	Transitional country
Austria (E)	Mature democracy	Iraq	Transitional country
Bangladesh (*)	Transitional country	Ireland (E)	Mature democracy
Belarus (E*)	Transitional country	Israel	Mature democracy
Belgium (E)	Mature democracy	Italy (E)	Mature democracy
Benin (*)	Transitional country	Ivory Coast	Transitional country
Bhutan	Transitional country	Jamaica (A)	Mature democracy
Bolivia (A)	Transitional country	Japan	Mature democracy
Bosnia and Herzegovina (E*)	Transitional country	Kenya	Transitional country
Brazil (A)	Transitional country	Korea, South	Transitional country
Bulgaria (E*)	Transitional country	Kyrgyz Republic	Transitional country
Burundi	Transitional country	Latvia (E*)	Transitional country

(continued)

Table 2A (continued)

Country	Classification	Country	Classification
Cambodia (*)	Transitional country	Lebanon	Transitional country
Canada (A)	Mature democracy	Lesotho (*)	Transitional country
Cape Verde (*)	Transitional country	Liberia	Transitional country
Chile (A*)	Transitional country	Lithuania (E*)	Transitional country
Comoros	Transitional country	Macedonia (E*)	Transitional country
Congo, DR	Transitional country	Madagascar (*)	Transitional country
Costa Rica (A)	Mature democracy	Malawi (*)	Transitional country
Croatia (E)	Transitional country	Mali (*)	Transitional country
Cyprus	Mature democracy	Mauritius	Mature democracy
Czech Republic (E*)	Transitional country	Mexico (*)	Transitional country
Denmark (E)	Mature democracy	Moldova (E*)	Transitional country
Djibouti	Transitional country	Mongolia (*)	Transitional country
Dominican Republic (A)	Transitional country	Mozambique (*)	Transitional country
Ecuador (A)	Transitional country	Nepal (*)	Transitional country
El Salvador (A)	Transitional country	Netherlands (E)	Mature democracy
Estonia (E*)	Transitional country	New Zealand	Mature democracy
Finland (E)	Mature democracy	Nicaragua (A*)	Transitional country
France (E)	Mature democracy	Nigeria (*)	Transitional country
Gabon	Transitional country	Norway (E)	Mature democracy
Georgia (E*)	Transitional country	Panama (A*)	Transitional country
Ghana (*)	Transitional country	Paraguay (A*)	Transitional country
Greece (E)	Transitional country	Peru (A)	Transitional country
Guatemala (A)	Transitional country	Philippines	Transitional country
Guinea	Transitional country	Poland (E*)	Transitional country

(continued)

Table 2A (continued)

Country	Classification	Country	Classification
Portugal (E)	Transitional country	Switzerland (E)	Mature democracy
Romania (E*)	Transitional country	Taiwan (*)	Transitional country
Russia (E*)	Transitional country	Timor-Leste	Transitional country
Senegal	Transitional country	Trinidad and Tobago (A)	Mature democracy
Sierra Leone (*)	Transitional country	Turkey	Transitional country
Slovakia (E*)	Transitional country	Ukraine (E*)	Transitional country
Slovenia (E*)	Transitional country	United Kingdom (E)	Mature democracy
South Africa (*)	Transitional country	United States (A)	Mature democracy
Spain (E)	Transitional country	Uruguay (A)	Transitional country
Suriname (A*)	Transitional country	Zambia (*)	Transitional country
Sweden (E)	Mature democracy	Zimbabwe	Transitional country

E = European sample, *A* = American sample, *asterisk* = Transitions between 1988 and 1998

References

Albrecht, P., & Buur, L. (2009). An uneasy marriage: Non-state actors and police reform. *Policing and Society, 19*(4), 390–405.

Baker, B. (2009a). Introduction: Policing post-conflict societies: Helping out the state. *Policing and Society, 19*(4), 329–332.

Baker, B. (2009b). *Security in post-conflict Africa: The role of non-state policing*. Boca Raton: CRC Press.

Bayley, D. (2001). *Democratizing the police abroad: What to do and how to do it*. Washington: National Institute of Justice.

Bertelsmann Stiftung (2012). *Transformation index: Codebook for country assessments*. Gütersloh: Bertelsmann Stiftung.

Bottoms, A., & Tankebe, J. (2012). Beyond procedural justice: A dialogic approach to legitimacy in criminal justice. *The Journal of Criminal Law and Criminology, 102*(1), 119–170.

Bradford, B., Murphy, K., & Jackson, J. (2014). Policing, procedural justice and the (re)production of social identity. *British Journal of Criminology, 54*(4), 527–550.

Broadhurst, R., & Bouhours, T. (2009). Policing in Cambodia: Legitimacy in the making? *Policing and Society, 19*(2), 174–190.

Burlyuk, O. (2014). An ambitious failure: Conceptualising the EU approach to rule of law (in Ukraine). *Hague Journal on the Rule of Law, 6*(1), 26–46.

Call, C., & Cousens, E. (2007). *Ending wars and building peace: Coping with crisis*. New York, NY: International Peace Academy.

Capussela, A. (2011). Eulex in Kosovo: A shining symbol of incompetence. *The Guardian*. Retrieved from http://www.theguardian.com/commentisfree/2011/apr/09/eulex-kosovo-eu-mission.

Cheesman, N. (2014). Law and order as asymmetrical opposite to the rule of law. *Hague Journal on the Rule of Law, 6*(1), 96–114.

Cingranelli, D. L., Richards, D. L., & Chad Clay, K. (2012). *The CIRI human rights dataset*. Retrieved from http://www.humanrightsdata.org.

Dinnen, S., & Braithwaite, J. (2009). Reinventing policing through the prism of colonial kiap. *Policing and Society, 19*(2), 161–173.

Dinnen, S., & McLeod, A. (2009). Policing Melanesia: International expectations and local realities. *Policing and Society, 19*(4), 333–353.

Dyzenhaus, D. (1998/2003). *Judging the judges, judging ourselves: Truth, reconciliation and the apartheid legal order*. Oxford: Hart.

Elster, J. (Ed.). (2006). *Retribution and reparation in the transition to democracy*. Cambridge, UK: Cambridge University Press.

Epstein, D., Bates, R., Goldstone, J. A., Kristensen, I., & O'Halloran, S. (2006). Democratic transitions. *American Journal of Political Science, 50*(3), 551–69.

Esty, D. C., Goldstone, J. A., Gurr, T. R., Harff, B., Levy, M., Dabelko, G. D., et al. (1998). *State failure task force report: Phase II findings*. Working papers, 31 July 1998. University of Maryland.

EULEX. (2010). *EULEX programme report: Building sustainable change together*. Brussels: European Union Rule of Law Mission in Kosovo.

Frei, N., van Laak, D., & Stolleis, M. (Eds.). (2000). *Geschichte vor Gericht: Historiker, Richter und die Suche nach Gerechtigkeit*. München: Beck.

Geddes, B. (1999). What do we know about democratization after twenty years? *Annual Review of Political Science, 2*, 115–144.

Gibney, M., Cornett, L., & Wood, R. (2012). *Political terror scale 1976–2010*. Retrieved from http://www.politicalterrorscale.org/.

Goldsmith, A. (2005). Police reform and the problem of trust. *Theoretical Criminology, 9*(4), 443–470.

Horne, C. (2012). Assessing the impact of lustration on trust in public institutions and national government in Central and Eastern Europe. *Comparative Political Studies, 45*(4), 412–446.

Hutchison, M., & Johnson, K. (2011). Capacity to trust? Institutional capacity, conflict and political trust in Africa, 2000–2005. *Journal of Peace Research, 48*(6), 737–752.

Jackson, J., & Bradford, B. (2009). Crime, policing and social order: On the expressive nature of public confidence in policing. *British Journal of Sociology, 60*(3), 493–521.

Jackson, J., & Sunshine, J. (2006). Public confidence in policing: A neo-Durkheimian perspective. *British Journal of Criminology, 47*(2), 527–550.

Jonathan-Zamir, T., & Weisburd, D. (2013). The effects of security threats on antecedents of police legitimacy: Findings from a quasi-experiment in Israel. *Journal of Research in Crime and Delinquency, 50*(1), 3–32.

Kääriäinen, J. T. (2007). Trust in police in 16 European countries: A multilevel analysis. *European Journal of Criminology, 4*(4), 409–435.

Karstedt, S. (2006). Democracy, values and violence: Paradoxes, tensions, and comparative advantages of liberal inclusion. *Annals of the American Academy of Political and Social Science, 605*, 50–81.

Karstedt, S. (2013a). Trusting authorities: Legitimacy, trust and collaboration in non-democratic regimes. In J. Tankebe & A. Liebling (Eds.), *Legitimacy and criminal justice: An international exploration* (pp. 127–156). Oxford: Oxford University Press.

Karstedt, S. (2013b). State crime: The European experience. In S. Body-Gendrot, M. Hough, K. Kerezsi, & R. Lévy (Eds.), *Routledge companion to European criminology* (pp. 125–152). Oxford, UK: Routledge.

Koonings, K., & Kruijt, D. (Eds.). (1999). *Societies of fear: The legacy of civil war, violence and terror in Latin America*. London, UK: Zed Books.
Kreutz, J. (2010). How and when armed conflicts end: Introducing the UCDP conflict termination dataset. *Journal of Peace Research, 47*(2), 243–250.
Kyed, H. M. (2009). Community policing in post-war Mozambique. *Policing and Society, 19*(4), 354–371.
Landmann, T., & Carvalho, E. (2010). *Measuring human rights*. London, UK: Routledge.
Lehti, M. (2013). *NRILP comparative homicide time series (NRILP-CHTS)*. Research Brief, (32), 1–12.
Loader, I. (2006). Policing, recognition and belonging. *Annals of the American Academy of Political and Social Science, 605*, 202–221.
Malone, M. F. (2010). The verdict is in: The impact of crime on public trust in Central America. *Journal of Politics in Latin America, 2*(3), 99–128.
Marshall, M. G., Gurr, T. R., & Jaggers, K. (2013). *Polity IV project: Political regime characteristics and transitions 1800–2012: Dataset users' manual*. Vienna: Center for Systemic Peace.
Marshall, M., & Jaggers, K. (2010). *Polity IV project: Political regime characteristics and transitions 1800–2010: Polity level 2004–2008*. Retrieved from http://www.systemicpeace.org/polity/polity4.htm.
McAdams, A. J. (Ed.). (1997). *Transitional justice and the rule of law in new democracies*. Notre Dame: Notre Dame University Press.
Mishler, W., & Rose, R. (1997). Trust, distrust and skepticism: Popular evaluations of civil and political institutions in post-communist societies. *The Journal of Politics, 59*(2), 418–451.
Mishler, W., & Rose, R. (1998). *Trust in untrustworthy institutions: Culture and institutional performance in post-communist societies*. Glasgow: Centre for the Study of Public Policy.
Mishler, W., & Rose, R. (2001). What are the origins of political trust? Testing institutional and cultural theories in post-communist societies. *Comparative Political Studies, 34*(1), 30–62.
Oakley, R., Dziedzik, M., & Goldberg, E. (Eds.). (2002). *Policing the new world disorder: Peace operations and public security*. Honolulu, HI: University Press of the Pacific.
Payne, L. A., Olsen, T. D., & Reiter, A. G. (2013). *Transitional justice database project*. Retrieved from http://www.tjdbproject.com/.
Perels, J. (1999). *Das juristische Erbe des Dritten Reiches*. Frankfurt: Campus.
Roberts, D. (2008). Post-conflict state building and state legitimacy: From negative to positive peace? *Development and Change, 39*(4), 537–555.
Roussey, L., & Deffains, B. (2012). Trust in judicial institutions: An empirical approach. *Journal of Institutional Economics, 8*(3), 351–369.
Samuels, K. (2006). *Rule of law reform in post-conflict countries: Operational initiatives and lessons learned*. Washington: World Bank, Conflict Prevention and Reconstruction.
Sargeant, E., Murphy, K., & Cherney, A. (2014). Ethnicity, trust and cooperation with police: Testing the dominance of the process-based model. *European Journal of Criminology, 11*(4), 500–524.
Smith, D. (2007). The foundations of legitimacy. In T. Tyler (Ed.), *Legitimacy and criminal justice: International perspectives* (pp. 30–58). New York, NY: Russell Sage.
Stahn, C. (2005). *Accountability and legitimacy in practice: Lawmaking by transitional administrations. [Manuscript]*. Leiden: University of Leiden.
Stan, L., & Nedelsky, N. (2013). *Encyclopedia of transitional justice*. Cambridge, UK: Cambridge University Press.
Stromseth, J. (2009). Justice on the ground: Can international criminal law courts strengthen domestic rule of law in post-conflict societies? *Hague Journal on the Rule of Law, 1*(1), 87–97.
Sztompka, P. (1993). Civilizational incompetence: The trap of post-communist societies. *Zeitschrift für Soziologie, 22*(1), 85–95.
Sztompka, P. (1996). Trust and emerging democracy: Lessons from Poland. *International Sociology, 11*(1), 37–62.
Teitel, R. (2002). *Transitional justice*. New York, NY: Oxford University Press.

United States Institute of Peace. (2013). *Truth commission digital collection.* Retrieved from http://www.usip.org/publications/truth-commission-digital-collection.

Wilson, J. M. (2006). Law and order in an emerging democracy: Lessons for the reconstruction of Kosovo's police and justice system. *Annals of the American Academy of Political and Social Science, 605*, 152–177.

Sentencing, Legitimacy, and Public Opinion

Julian V. Roberts and Mojca M. Plesničar

1 Introduction and Overview

The relationship between legitimacy and criminal justice has emerged as a central focus of empirical and theoretical scholarship. Much of this work has explored the ways that perceptions of legitimacy are shaped by contact with criminal justice professionals, notably the police (e.g., Tyler, 2007). The reason for this focus on policing is primarily empirical: the public are more likely to observe and have direct contact with the police; other criminal justice professionals remain hidden from public view, and personal contact is rare. The police are likely to have an influence over public perceptions of legitimacy to a degree not matched by other criminal justice professionals. Citizens presumably regard their contacts with the police as representative of the system more generally and the valence of these contacts (positive or negative) will color perceptions of the whole system. In contrast, the lack of direct contact with the courts or prisons means that public perceptions of the later stages of criminal process—criminal courts, parole boards—are more likely to be influenced by media reports. We shall return to the consequences of this reality later in this essay.

J.V. Roberts (✉)
Centre of Criminology, Oxford University, Manor Road Building, Manor Road, Oxford OX1 3UQ, UK
e-mail: julian.roberts@worc.ox.ac.uk

M.M. Plesničar
Institute of Criminology at the Faculty of Law Ljubljana, Poljanski nasip 2, 1000 Ljubljana, Slovenia
e-mail: mojca.plesnicar@pf.uni-lj.si

G. Meško, J. Tankebe (eds.), *Trust and Legitimacy in Criminal Justice*,
DOI 10.1007/978-3-319-09813-5_2

The concept of legitimacy has been defined and operationalized in many different ways, without a single consensual position emerging.[1] We offer no clear path through the dense forest of theories and concepts that have arisen in recent years; our focus here is more restricted. After some introductory discussion this essay focuses more narrowly upon the relationship between the sentencing regime and public perceptions of penal legitimacy. In discussing the latter we adopt Hinsch's (2008) label of "empirical legitimacy" to distinguish it from "normative legitimacy" (see also discussion in Hough, Jackson, & Bradford, 2013). Hough et al. (ibid.) propose three elements or "subcomponents" of empirical legitimacy: an obligation to obey; legality; and moral alignment. We focus on the third of these elements. Empirical legitimacy relates to community views of the legitimacy of sentencing; normative legitimacy concerns the extent to which a sentencing regime reflects and implements coherent moral principles. In this sense we are concerned with what Bottoms and Tankebe (2012) term "audience legitimacy"—recognizing that legitimacy also invokes multiple audiences or interests. Part I explores public attitudes to sentencing and the reasons why the public in many countries may perceive their sentencing system to *lack* legitimacy. Part II explores ways which we believe may enhance public perceptions of sentencing legitimacy. This includes the outline of what a "high legitimacy" sentencing regime would look like.

The argument may be summarized briefly as follows. In order to be perceived as legitimate (to achieve empirical legitimacy), a sentencing regime must be perceived to be: (a) clear and transparent; (b) consistent in application and therefore predictable; (c) sensitive to the input of all relevant parties; (d) grounded in sound principles. Clarity seems key: a system which lacks clarity is unlikely to generate empirical legitimacy. We illustrate the benefits of clarity in sentencing by reference to the way that two jurisdictions treat an important sentencing factor: sentence reductions for a guilty plea. In our view, some form of guidelines represents the best way of achieving the necessary levels of clarity and transparency. We also argue that a pan-European approach to sentencing may also result in higher levels of what we call "empirical legitimacy." Finally, on a more mundane level we argue that the sentencing system must be communicated to the public in an understandable fashion in order to avoid erroneous expectations. The mere existence of sound sentencing principles is insufficient to ensure a high degree of legitimacy.

2 Distinguishing Concepts

A number of related concepts are in play, including public confidence, legitimacy, and public evaluations of criminal justice. By *confidence* we refer to an expectation among the community that the criminal justice system (or specific criminal justice

[1] Indeed, a useful scholarly exercise would compile and critically examine the myriad definitions and components of legitimacy that have been proposed in recent years.

professionals such as police and judges) will perform their duties to an acceptable level of competence. *Legitimacy* appears to be a richer and more complex concept, encompassing different elements.

2.1 Public Confidence

This variable is measured by asking people how much confidence they have in various branches of criminal justice or different criminal justice professions. Results show highly variable responses both between and within branches and professions. The lack of direct contact and the reliance on media for information may explain why confidence in the courts has historically been much lower than confidence or trust in the police (Roberts & Hough, 2005).[2] It is hard for the public to have confidence in a system that is unfamiliar, and particularly when their limited information about sentencing is selective and often negative; media reports of sentencing usually highlight lenient sentences or decisions which are problematic in some respect, while the vast majority of cases remain unreported. This in turn generates public criticism of sentencers and sentencing.

The public themselves acknowledge that they are not well informed about sentencing: a nationwide survey in the UK in 2009 found that approximately three-quarters of the sample described themselves as "not informed about sentences given to people convicted of crimes" (Ipsos MORI, 2009). This lack of information—reflected in public levels of knowledge about sentencing and also in public ratings of their own knowledge levels—constitutes an important barrier to confidence and perceptions of legitimacy. The correlation between levels of information about sentencing and confidence in criminal justice is found in this same survey. Respondents who reported knowing less about sentencing also expressed less confidence in the criminal justice system as a whole. Further support for the knowledge–confidence relationship comes from the fact that almost half the respondents stated that knowing more about sentencing would increase their confidence in criminal justice (Ipsos MORI, 2009).

Negative community views of sentencing may have wider effects: The perceived legitimacy of the courts may well be fundamental to perceptions of the whole system. Although people have more contact with the police, the decisions of the courts at sentencing attract intense media attention; the sentencing decision represents the apex of the criminal process. The sentencing decision also has an intuitive appeal: While members of the general public may have trouble understanding complex legal issues such as evaluating culpability or the admissibility of evidence, determining sentence is perceived as rather straightforward. Most people form

---

[2] For example, a nationwide survey of the public in England and Wales found that approximately three-quarters of the public expressed confidence in the police, but only half had confidence in the courts (Roberts & Hough, 2005: Table 2.3).

views of the appropriateness of specific sentences quickly and with a high degree of confidence that their opinion is sound (Doob & Roberts, 1983).

Moreover, the moral element of legitimacy (Jackson et al., 2013) is also relevant, as a sentence deemed appropriate reaffirms one's moral alignment with the judicial process, while one perceived as too lenient (or too severe) undermines that relationship. In fact, if people perceive the courts to impose inappropriate sentences or to take into account the wrong factors, the legitimacy of the entire system may be called into question (Henham, 2012). Haveman (2006: 145) makes the point clearly when, writing of supranational sentencing he notes that "Expectations can make or break the success of the criminal law. These expectations have sometimes risen to incredible heights and their non-fulfilment has correspondingly led to bigger falls. In the long term this results in a huge legitimization problem."

Legitimacy is a related but distinct concept: an institution such as the judiciary may be seen as legitimate but people may still lack confidence in its performance. Thus the public in England and Wales regard the judiciary as a legitimate censuring authority: judges are perceived to be fair in the sense of dispensing justice without fear or favor and independent. Yet confidence in the courts may still be low on a number of dimensions. Empirical research sustains these variable public reactions. The courts are seen as being fair and independent yet also ineffective in controlling crime and responding to the needs of crime victims (MORI, 2003). Thus people express high confidence in the ability of the courts to dispense justice fairly, but low levels of confidence that the courts impose sentences which are effective in controlling crime (MORI, 2003).

Much of the literature on legitimacy discusses the issue through the lens of public perception—do the public regard the courts as a legitimate authority? For this reason, as noted, it is important to distinguish *normative* and *empirical* legitimacy. A sentencing regime is normatively legitimate if it punishes according to philosophically coherent principles and to the extent that these principles are faithfully applied by the courts. A system may well be empirically legitimate when in fact it lacks normative legitimacy. Similarly, a system may be coherent and principled, yet fail to attract the perception that sentencing is legitimate.

In this essay we are also interested in the contribution that sentencing makes to wider perceptions of penal legitimacy, namely the legitimacy of the criminal justice system. A number of ambitious claims have been made about the effects of the courts on legitimacy and compliance. For example, it has been argued that if sentencing is morally aligned with the views of the public, this will enhance compliance with the law and cooperation with the criminal justice system (e.g., Robinson, 2009). In this chapter we explore a much more modest question: what aspects of sentencing might enhance or undermine perceptions of legitimacy and levels of public confidence?

3 Sentencing and the Public: Some Empirical Findings

The empirical literature on public opinion and criminal justice is now substantial. However, no surveys of which we are aware have directly measured perceptions of the *legitimacy* of sentencing or the relative contribution that perceptions of sentencing make to overall views of criminal justice legitimacy. This constitutes an important priority for researchers. Respondents in a number of jurisdictions have been asked to express their level of confidence in the courts (and other branches of criminal justice), and from these we may draw some inferences about empirical legitimacy. As noted, although confidence and legitimacy reflect somewhat different concepts, if the public have confidence in the courts it is reasonable to assume that they regard the courts as taking appropriate, i.e., legitimate decisions.

The link between confidence in the courts and confidence in the criminal justice system as a whole emerges from a number of surveys. For example, Smith (2007) reports that perceptions of "consistency in sentencing" was the factor which most frequently came to mind when the British public were asked about their level of confidence in the criminal justice system. The nationwide survey reported by Smith also found that the two most important determinants of public confidence in criminal justice were "appropriate sentencing" and "an adequate police presence on the streets." Another national survey in Britain found that when asked to identify the "most important issue facing Britain when it comes to crime," sentencing was cited by the highest percentage of respondents (Duffy, Wake, Borrows, & Bremner, 2008). If sentencing is perceived to be so important, it seems reasonable to assume perceptions of sentencing will affect overall views of criminal justice. This would suggest that perceptions of sentencing are central to public confidence in criminal justice.

The beliefs and demands of the public with regard to sentences, often rooted in lack of information (Roberts & Hough, 2005), commonly exceed the options sentencers have at hand when deciding in actual cases. The public is typically only aware of one case at a time which enhances sympathy for the victim and antagonism towards the perpetrator. The systemic response to punitive demands is thus necessarily inadequate in that it hardly ever meets the level of punitiveness the public desires. The said seems true for most of Europe, with some notable exceptions in the Scandinavian countries (Pratt & Eriksson, 2013).[3]

[3] One notable exception was the response to the sentence imposed on the mass murderer Anders Breivik. In this case, the Norwegian public met the comparatively lenient sentence of 21 years imprisonment with seeming acceptance while the rest of the Western world was shocked that such an offence would not attract a sentence of life imprisonment without parole—the most punitive sanction available in EU jurisdictions. For the Norwegians, however, the sentence reaffirmed the legitimacy of the Court and the system as a whole, well captured in one survey respondent's words: "Don't let one terrorist take our rights." (in De Graaf, Van der Heide, Wanmaker, & Weggemans, 2013: 16)

3.1 Sentencing and Legitimacy

One way of approaching the issue is to ask what kind of sentencing regime might promote perceptions of legitimacy and inspire public confidence, and we shall attempt to sketch the outlines of such a regime later in this essay. First, however, we document the elements of contemporary sentencing which might *undermine* perceptions of legitimacy and drain public confidence in sentencing and criminal justice. The existing public opinion research offers some insight in this respect.

3.2 Analogy with an Unprincipled Taxation Regime

People are unlikely to express confidence in an organization or regime which is unfamiliar, and which takes decisions in a way that appears inscrutable. Consider a State taxation regime where the percentage of income tax deducted is determined by individual officials. When determining tax levels in individual cases, decision-makers in this jurisdiction apply vague criteria, many of which appear counter-intuitive. Imagine further that the officials are generally drawn from the social elite and are perceived to be unrepresentative of the wider society. The officials also benefit from wide discretion in their decisions, which do not appear subject to review by a higher authority. As a consequence, citizens have no clear idea of how much tax they will be required to pay, and little confidence that appropriate taxation rates are applied consistently across all affected individuals. How many taxpayers would consider such an arrangement or taxing authority to be legitimate? How much confidence would people repose in such a taxation regime? Would taxpayers be less inclined to report income for the purposes of being taxed?

There is a clear consequentialist parallel with criminal justice: if citizens perceive the tax laws to lack legitimacy they will likely be less inclined to honestly report taxable income. If members of the public perceive the justice system to lack legitimacy, they *may* also be less likely to cooperate by serving as jurors, witnesses or lay magistrates—although this is an empirically testable hypothesis rather than a documented finding. Sentencing is seen by many people in exactly this way, as is well documented by researchers.

Consider the following findings derived from surveys of the public drawing upon representative samples of respondents in multiple jurisdictions (e.g., Roberts & Hough, 2005). These misperceptions echo the features of a taxation regime which lacks perceived legitimacy:

- Sentencing is inconsistent and the outcomes unpredictable;
- Sentencing is biased towards protecting the interests of the offender at the expense of the interests of the crime victim;
- Sentencers are "out of touch with what ordinary people think" and courts consider inappropriate factors at sentencing;

- Sentences are too lenient, and the length of time an offender serves in custody bears little relation to the sentence imposed in court.

3.3 *Causes of Low Confidence in the Courts*

There are two principal causes of most of public perceptions and criticism of the courts.[4] First, the news media, particularly the tabloid media in western nations such as the UK, project a distorted image of sentencing practices in general, and the decisions of individual judges. There is probably little that can be done to change this state of affairs. Many sentencing decisions are reported in the news media, usually coupled with adverse commentaries. In contrast, stories about the exercise of discretion by prosecutors or police are far less likely to attract news media coverage—unless they are of an exceptional nature.[5] Second, the sentencing process in most western nations is often complex and confusing even to criminal justice professionals—imaging how baffling it must seem to laypersons.

The complexity of sentencing reflects the nature of the enterprise of legal punishment: it is impossible to achieve individualization or to reflect the many variables in play in sentencing with a simple scheme. "Three strikes" sentencing laws achieve simplicity—and may initially attract public support—but at the cost of principled sentencing. Determining how much time an offender sentenced to, say, 3 years imprisonment will serve in prison is challenging and dependent upon a number of variables. The public has little patience in penal matters and complicated release arrangements or sentencing for multiple offences resulting in concurrent and/or consecutive sentences generate public criticism for this reason. Most jurisdictions have created a wide array of penal sanctions for courts to impose, and the public is often confused about the nature and consequences of many disposals.

The indeterminacy of prison sentences in many jurisdictions is clearly one of the issues undermining public confidence in sentencing. In fact this is one of the causes of the abolition of discretionary conditional release from prison: it makes the

---

[4] Several of the public perceptions noted here are merely opinions expressed in response to questions without factual answers. However, in some cases they are more reasonably described as misperceptions, as when the public provide an inaccurate response to a factual question. One example of this involves sentencing trends. When asked to estimate the percentage of offenders convicted of common offences (such as robbery, burglary, or rape) who are sentenced to prison, most members of the public in all western nations in which surveys have been conducted significantly underestimate the actual custody rate (see Hough et al., 2013; Roberts & Hough, 2005).

[5] For example, when the police response results in the death of suspects as occurred in the shooting on the London underground in 2005 and in north London in 2011 or when in 2014 the Crown prosecution Service elected to prosecute three individuals found taking food from a refuse bin.

duration of time inside very hard to predict, even if the sentence is a determinate one with a clear date of closure.[6] Canada is an example of a common law jurisdiction with a sentencing regime which suffers from this problem of indeterminacy. An offender sentenced to 9 years imprisonment may be released as early as 18 months on day parole, and he may remain in the community for remainder of time on the sentence. On the other hand, if his applications for parole release are repeatedly denied he will leave prison after serving a full 6 years in prison. A small number of prisoners serving 9 year sentences will spend all 9 years inside prison, if their conduct in prison triggers an application by correctional authorities to detain beyond the two-thirds statutory release point. These arrangements, conceived to promote prisoners' rehabilitation and also to restrain the use of custody nevertheless undermine public confidence. Members of the public often discount terms of custody on the grounds that "he will be out in a few months." Similarly, most prisoners in England and Wales serve the first half of their custodial sentence in prison and the second half in the community. This leads people to interpret a 4 year sentence as simply a 2 year term.[7]

4 Promoting Public Confidence and Legitimacy at Sentencing

4.1 Role of Community Views: Direct Input?

How might the sentencing process contribute to, or enhance the legitimacy of the criminal justice system? One way of promoting perceptions of legitimacy might entail greater public involvement in the process. After all, people are unlikely to perceive a process as legitimate if they believe they have a stake in the process yet also feel totally excluded from participation. Several scholars have recently argued that greater democratization of punishment will bring benefits in terms of enhanced legitimacy. Bibas (2012) for example argues that reforms such as sentencing by juries, or public panels which review the decisions of criminal justice professionals such as police and prosecutors. Robinson (2009) advocates aligning sentencing practices with the views of the public because this will enhance the legitimacy of the criminal justice system and increase compliance with the law. Finally, other scholars have argued in favor of greater lay involvement in

[6] The very opposite solution to abolishing conditional release can be found in some European countries (e.g., Sweden, Finland, and Greece), where conditional release is mandatory after serving a given proportion of the sentence (Dünkel, Van Zyl Smit, & Padfield, 2010).

[7] Other causes of low confidence, and low empirical legitimacy would include: a failure to explain sentencing decisions; a perceived lack of engagement with the community; a failure to adequately consider the interests of crime victims and the use of sentencing factors opposed by the public. All these features are likely to undermine the perceived legitimacy of State punishment, i.e., empirical legitimacy.

sentencing with a view to promoting greater legitimacy (e.g., Dzur, 2013). In short, there is no shortage of critics who argue that the sentencing system should more directly reflect and incorporate public views.

These claims for more (or more direct) input may be seen as consistent with the notion of a "legitimacy deficit" identified by Bottoms and Tankebe (2012: 141) who note that "to be legitimate, power-holders must derive their authority from and act within the shared beliefs and values of a given society." Translated to sentencing this suggests that the values promoted by sentencing and the principles underpinning sentencing practices should be consistent with community values. If this is in fact what they mean, we would agree, but this does not necessarily justify direct public involvement in criminal justice or oversight of criminal justice decisions.

Our view is that while more direct public involvement (for example through sentencing by juries rather than professional judges) *may* enhance public perceptions of sentencing legitimacy, this remains a hypothesis rather than a demonstrable effect. Evidence is needed to demonstrate that perceptions of legitimacy are higher when the public play a more significant role in determining sentence. The few studies that have explored the link between the degree of public involvement and the level of perceived legitimacy offer little support for the proposition that greater public involvement enhances legitimacy. In fact, there is evidence that in certain jurisdictions at least, the public actually favor a judiciary which ignores public views and remains independent of what the community thinks.

For instance, in the Netherlands public opinion has been strongly punitive for decades while levels of public confidence in the courts have been high (see De Keijser, 2014; De Keijser & Elffers, 2009). The respondents who expressed dissatisfaction with levels of punishment imposed by judges also favored an independent and professional judiciary that maintains a certain distance from public opinion. De Keijser, Van Koppen, and Elffers (2007) asked respondents to rank order 10 essential traits of a criminal court judge. The three most favored were: "just," "impartial," and "independent." This finding indicates that even if the justice system fails to deliver what the public desires, its legitimacy is not necessarily affected—at least in the Netherlands, and possibly other countries too.

To summarize, we do not believe that sentencing policy and practice should be determined by public views in order to enhance the perceived legitimacy of the system. Sentencing requires complicated structures and potentially conflicting objectives and principles; as many scholars have pointed out, public opinion is an unreliable guide to punishment policies (e.g., Bagaric & Edney, 2004). Yet this does not mean that the sentencing process should isolate itself, creating a firewall between the community and the courts. Sentencing structures need to be as clear as possible and no more complex than necessary, much like in the previous analogy with the taxation system.

Returning to our analogy with the tax regime, perceptions of legitimacy in that domain are best promoted by creating a tax system which is clear and predictable and which reflects consensual views about the appropriate tax rates for different income levels as well as the appropriate grounds for tax credits. The experience in the UK and other western countries in recent years is illustrative. A number of features of the tax system have provoked widespread publicity, including the stratospheric annual bonuses awarded bankers in the City of London. These bonuses are sufficiently high, or are structured in ways that prevent the State from clawing back the high level of remuneration through taxation. In addition, multinational corporations construct elaborate accounting structures to avoid paying tax in jurisdictions with high corporate rates. These are examples of legal strategies and remuneration arrangements which nevertheless have brought domestic and international taxation laws into disrepute—they have undermined the legitimacy of the taxation system and also the governments responsible for administering these systems. In this sense they are legal yet not legitimate on some wider interpretation of the term "legitimacy."

4.2 *Structural Changes to Promote Legitimacy in Sentencing*

The analysis so far suggests that the structure of sentencing and the degree of empirical legitimacy in sentencing may be linked. The challenge for criminal justice is to devise and maintain a principled sentencing system which is perceived by the public to be legitimate, and which might in turn enhance perceptions of the wider criminal justice system. How might this be achieved? The minimal conditions of empirical legitimacy have been in place for many years: open courts; public proceedings; laws devised by elected representatives and so on. However, public perceptions of the legitimacy of sentencing may require more than these prerequisites. The sentencing process needs to ensure more than these minimal requirements.

One way of achieving the clarity and transparency which is essential to perceived legitimacy is through use of a more explicit sentencing regime. The traditional approach to sentencing in most jurisdictions has entailed a relatively loose set of statutory provisions which provide only the most general framework for an understanding of how courts sentence offenders. At the opposing end of the spectrum we can locate mandatory sentencing schemes which require courts to impose fixed sentences on all offenders convicted of a specific offence. Schemes of this kind maximize clarity, albeit at a significant cost in terms of individual justice.

4.2.1 Sentencing Guidelines

Sentencing guideline schemes represent a middle ground. Individualization is preserved by guideline schemes which specify ranges of sentence lengths (or sentencing options), yet sentences become at once clearer and more predictable. Guidelines make the sentencing criteria much clearer by clarifying the factors taken into account as well as the likely range of sentence that will be imposed. Guidelines come in many forms, some relatively rigid and detailed—such as those found in some US states. Others such as those proposed in New Zealand and already implemented in England are equally detailed but more flexible in application, allowing courts considerable discretion (see Ashworth & Roberts, 2013).

The judiciary often object that a relatively restrictive guideline scheme prevents a court from doing justice in individual cases—for example by preventing a court from giving sufficient weight to important mitigating factors. This may be true for some guidelines. Yet it is hard to contest the position that a clear and visible system of sentencing is more likely to be seen to be legitimate than one where sentencing decisions appear inscrutable or where a court imposes a sentence for reasons that are never fully explained. We can illustrate the utility of guidelines by reference to a specific issue, namely sentence discounts for a guilty plea. This issue is one which attracts public criticism, and which has the potential to undermine perceptions of legitimacy—if the public believe that the sentencing authority is rewarding offenders without justification.

Despite the benefits of plea-based sentence discounts, the public see little reason to reduce sentences in return for the defendant's cooperation (Dawes, Harvey, McIntosh, Nunney, & Phillips, 2011). Besides opposing the practice, most people also overestimate the magnitude of reductions accorded defendants who plead guilty, the same way that many overestimate the reduction in time served resulting from early release schemes from prison. Plea-based sentence reductions therefore represent a potential threat to public confidence and perceived legitimacy. Eliminating plea-based sentence reductions is neither practically feasible—the courts in most western jurisdictions would grind to a halt if the guilty plea rate dropped significantly following withdrawal of the incentive—nor desirable: defendants who acknowledge their guilt and who wish to take a stand against the offence should be rewarded. However, the practical implementation of such discounts is often inadequate and leads to undesirable consequences. The appropriate response to this issue is twofold: first, create a sentence discount regime that is transparent and predictable; second, ensure that the public are made aware of the benefits to the criminal justice system and victims/witnesses.

Sentence Reductions for a Guilty Plea

Most jurisdictions award sentence reductions to defendants who waive their right to trial and enter a plea of guilty although the magnitude of sentence reductions offered varies across different countries. Sentence reductions are offered to reward the defendant for having saved the State the time and expense of a prosecution and the victims and witnesses from having to testify. The justification for sentence discounts is seldom articulated for the public's benefit. For example, most common law countries lack sentencing guidelines which might specify why discounts are offered and how large they should be. The issue is even more complicated in those continental systems that mix adversarial and inquisitorial elements and proclaim principles such as the search for material truth and the individualization of punishment as guiding tenets of criminal process (Rauxloh, 2011; Thaman, 2007; Weigend, 2011). The conceptual conundrum those systems face is usually ignored by legislation and even European jurisdictions which have recently addressed the issue have brought little clarity or transparency to the issue.

This issue is one which has the clear potential to undermine public perceptions of legitimacy. Such an outcome has emerged in Slovenia, one of the most recent countries to introduce such reductions. As a result of adverse media coverage the Slovenian public was already highly skeptical of courts and the legal system. The introduction of sentencing discounts has led to public condemnation of the new reduction arrangements; people have repeatedly compared them to bargaining at a market. For example, in Slovenia, where discounts for guilty pleas (and plea bargaining) were introduced only as recently as 2012, the new legislation not only failed to provide a principled and nuanced system of reductions, the new provisions are so broad that even the prosecution felt the need to restrict them with an administrative act. The provision allows extensive reductions relative to the length of the sentence (see Appendix). Such a flexible solution was favored in order to offer additional incentives to plead guilty in a system that already offers rather extensive options for reducing the sentence and where sentences often linger at the bottom of the sentencing range. The criterion to sentence within those extremely broad ranges is supposedly the level of assistance offered by the offender to the criminal process (somewhat similar to the English system described below), but it is rather unclear as to how that assistance is measured or assessed.

In contrast to this relatively opaque (and unpredictable) arrangement, a guideline scheme would provide the necessary transparency. One such scheme is found in England and Wales where courts are bound to follow definitive sentencing guidelines. These apply to specific offences and also to generic sentencing issues—such as the reductions appropriate to defendants who plead guilty. The definitive guideline on plea-based sentence reductions notes the utilitarian justification for plea-based sentence reductions, namely that of saving court time and resources and sparing victims and witnesses from having to testify (Sentencing Guidelines Council, 2007).

In terms of the magnitude of reduction appropriate to defendants who enter a plea, if a guilty plea is entered at the first reasonable opportunity the recommended reduction is one-third. The size of the sentence reduction then diminishes the later the guilty plea is entered, and the defendant who changes his plea to guilty on the day the trial commences should receive a reduction of only 10 %. The arrangement is illustrated in Fig. 1 which is extracted from the published guideline.

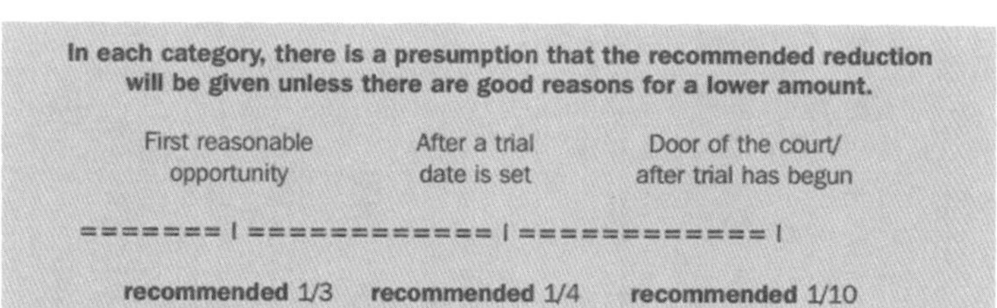

Fig. 1 Extract from Sentencing Guideline for Sentence Reductions for a Guilty Plea, England and Wales (Sentencing Guidelines Council, 2007)

Table 1 Empirical, Recommended and Expected Sentence Reductions, England and Wales, 2011 (Roberts, 2013)

	1/3 or greater	21–32 %	11–20 %	1–10 %	No reduction	Guideline recommended reduction
Early Plea cases	88 %	9 %	2 %	<.05 %	1 %	33 %
Intermediate cases	37 %	34 %	22 %	6 %	1 %	25 %
Late Plea cases	12 %	9 %	24 %	48 %	6 %	10 %

The impact of the guideline on judicial practice can clearly be seen in Table 1, which reveals that courts follow the guideline relatively closely. Thus the guideline (Fig. 1) recommends that offenders who entered a guilty plea early (i.e., at the first opportunity to do so), should receive a custodial sentence reduction of one third, and in almost all cases offenders in this category receive a reduction of this level (see Table 1).

The guideline is available on the Sentencing Council website and is prominently displayed in numerous publications. The use of a publicly facing guideline means that the public, victims, and indeed all interested parties can see (a) what the courts *should* be doing, and (b) what they *actually are* doing. This concordance between policy and judicial practice will surely help to promote perceptions of legitimacy. Absent a clear policy—and the evidence that the policy is followed in practice—the public is likely to form perceptions of sentencing founded upon misinformation.

A guideline system therefore offers much promise in terms of making sentencing more consistent and principled. In addition, by increasing the transparency of judicial decision-making—for an issue like plea based sentencing discounts, or the use of custody for different offences—a guideline scheme should contribute to enhancing public confidence and legitimacy. Of course, as with the link between moral alignment and compliance with the law, this hypothesis is susceptible of proof. It would be interesting to compare levels of public confidence or perceptions of legitimacy in jurisdictions with a transparent and predictable sentencing scheme and one where sentencing remains poorly understood and where the rules of application are known only to legal practitioners. This is another research priority.

Another way of promoting perceptions of sentencing legitimacy is to strengthen the international foundation on which domestic sentencing principles and practices rest.

4.2.2 Pan-European Sentencing?

Sentencing in specific jurisdictions has become increasingly influenced by international developments. This increased internationalization of criminal justice and sentencing has the potential to increase the empirical and normative legitimacy of the courts. Consider prosecutions at the International Criminal Court (ICC).

A defendant could be indicted in a domestic court for some crimes prosecuted at the ICC. However, we believe that the large number of jurisdictions which have accepted the jurisdiction of the ICC enhances the likelihood that prosecutions, convictions and sentences imposed in that tribunal will attract a degree of legitimacy in excess of what would have been possible in a domestic court.

In a recent essay, Van Zyl Smit (2013) discusses the relationship between legitimacy and the evolution of international standards for punishment. He notes the existence of three critical groups: scientific experts such as penologists who can contribute their expertise; nongovernmental organizations which promote particular values with which to infuse international standards; and national representatives to ensure that individual state voices influence the standards. Together with the approbation of elected legislators, these groups assure the legitimacy of the international standards.

Extrapolated to the context of sentencing we would argue that a pan-European "Model Sentencing Code" along the lines of the sentencing provisions contained in the Model Penal Code in the USA would enhance the legitimacy of sentencing within the European Union. The Model Penal Code is more than simply a compendium of "best practice"; it reflects the accretion of careful scholarship and consultation, and represents a more consensual approach to sentencing than can be found in any specific jurisdiction. In this respect it has the potential to contribute to both empirical and normative legitimacy. In Europe, to date at least, almost all jurisdictions have evolved their sentencing principles and practices with little or no apparent interest in regimes in other countries. Sentencing regimes vary widely across Europe. Sentencing in England and Wales—where courts follow detailed guidelines—is very different from sentencing on the continent. Within continental Europe regimes differ in many important respects.

An attempt at providing countries with general guidance has been made with the Council of Europe's Recommendation Consistency in Sentencing as far back as 1993, but in the 30 years since its adoption, little has changed in terms of harmonizing sentencing policies and practices across European countries. What we envision is more limited in territorial terms, as a Model European Sentencing Code would be limited to the EU countries. Some opposition would need to be overcome before such Code would be adopted. Of course, a more uniform approach towards sentencing might provoke resistance or opposition in specific jurisdictions. For instance, one justification for the existing insular approach is that sentencing is too culturally derived to allow principles and objectives of more universal application.

We would reject this view; while there may be significant cross-jurisdictional variation in perceptions of crime seriousness, levels of support for specific sanctions such as custody or punitiveness (e.g., Van Kesteren, 2009), it would be surprising if a principle as fundamental as proportionality was enthusiastically embraced in one country and rejected by residents of another. It would seem unlikely that a sentencing factor such as previous convictions was supported by residents of one European country yet opposed by residents of another jurisdiction. All sentencing systems face common challenges and deal with common dilemmas, yet solve them in different ways, for the most part not even considering a potentially better alternative implemented in a neighboring country. A more uniform approach towards solving them at the European level thus seems something not only feasible, but also helpful in terms of constructing a better sentencing system.

As noted, the Model Penal Code in the USA provides a "best practices" set of sentencing provisions. In addition to the harmonization of sentencing practices, a similar approach to sentencing in Europe would carry benefits in terms of public confidence and empirical legitimacy. If residents of any given country were aware that the general features of sentencing—if not levels of severity—derive from a cross-European framework, they may be more satisfied when reading of the decisions of their own courts. For example, a controversial practice like awarding plea-based sentencing discounts may be perceived as more legitimate if it is practiced across all European jurisdictions.

There is also an argument that there should be more consistency in sentencing principles and practices across Europe. Does it make sense for a European resident living in, say, the French town of Mauberge to be subject to different sentencing practices than fellow Europeans living just minutes away in neighboring Belgium? EU regulations apply to a vast range of public policies, even down to determining the size and shape of fruit sold at market. If the size of bananas is subject to European regulation,[8] why should sentencing regimes devolve to individual court systems?

4.2.3 Public Education, Consultation and Outreach

Finally, we turn to the practicalities of enhancing empirical legitimacy. Public legal education and consultation in the area of sentencing is rare. Most Ministries of Justice publish annual sentencing statistics which offer the interested reader some insight into sentencing practices, but few people are likely to even access these reports, let alone read them. Absent some clear and accessible information about sentencing from official sources, the public will naturally rely on media reports, which commonly over-represent extreme cases that fuel public criticism and confirm public skepticism. There is clearly a need for an independent authority to collect and disseminate information which would serve to inform the public and promote greater understanding of and confidence in the sentencing process, and ultimately the criminal justice system as a whole. This will in turn enhance empirical legitimacy. An important role, therefore, for a sentencing guidelines authority would be to disseminate information in an appropriate way. The three Australian Sentencing Councils, the English Council and those found in the USA all perform this important confidence-related function.

Related to the issue of information is the concept of public engagement. In the absence of a robust public engagement, the most principled sentencing

[8] EC Commission Number 2257/94 in effect since 1995 specifies minimum standards for specific quality classifications of bananas.

arrangements are unlikely to promote perceptions of legitimacy. For this reason it is important for a sentencing authority—be it a Council or Commission to perform a public legal education and consultation function. The Sentencing Advisory Council in the Australian state of Victoria is a good example of a body which disseminates information about the sentencing for the purposes of improving public knowledge. Similarly, in England and Wales, one of the Sentencing Council's statutory duties is to promote public understanding of the sentencing process.[9] It is less clear as to which body should carry that function in systems that do not have designated sentencing authorities, but the need for such engagement is no less present there.

Summary and Conclusion

To summarize, empirical legitimacy at sentencing would be enhanced by the following elements:

- A clear and comprehensive framework of sentencing accompanied by a system of guidelines;
- Sentencers perceived to be representative of the community and accountable for their decisions;
- Sentencing principles and practices are sensitive to the interests of the most affected parties such as crime victims;
- An independent sentencing authority (such as a sentencing council or commission) which disseminates information about sentencing and conducts public consultations;
- An active and ongoing research initiative to identify the specific areas of sentencing policy and practice which attract the greatest public criticism and which are most likely to undermine public perceptions of legitimacy. This would be allied to a continuing strategy to engage the public and promote better public understanding of sentencing.

To the extent that sentencing complies with these criteria it will be perceived as legitimate; to the extent that is departs from them it will undermine perceptions of legitimacy—both of the courts and the criminal justice system more generally.

A sentencing regime which inspires confidence and is perceived to be legitimate, may well contribute to wider and more global assessments of penal legitimacy. Put simply, a sentencing regime which is perceived to impose fair punishments consistently across all kinds of offenders creates the social context for a more positive public response to criminal justice.

We conclude by returning to the central question which began this chapter: how might a jurisdiction enhance the legitimacy of the sentencing process—and through this the legitimacy of the criminal justice system? In this essay

(continued)

[9] See http://sentencingcouncil.judiciary.gov.uk

we have argued that current sentencing regimes in most countries do little to enhance perceptions of legitimacy. Indeed, in many respects the absence of transparency and clarity may actively undermine public confidence and perceptions of legitimacy. A comprehensive yet flexible guideline scheme in which public consultation and outreach plays an important role offers considerable promise in terms of enhancing legitimacy from the perspective of the wider community.

To summarize, we draw the following conclusions. First, research has demonstrated that public perceptions of the legitimacy of criminal justice and levels of confidence in the criminal justice system are clearly affected by perceptions of sentencing and sentencers. The high media profile and intuitive resonance of sentencing explains this effect. Second, a number of characteristics of current sentencing practices undermine levels of confidence in sentencing and therefore perceptions of legitimacy. The exclusion of crime victims from the process, or the use of sentencing factors opposed by the public are both likely to lower public perceptions of legitimacy. Even if the public is very satisfied with the police, if the sentence ultimately imposed is either incomprehensible or at great odds with public views, people are unlikely to see the system as a whole as legitimate. It is therefore possible to identify the features of a "low legitimacy" sentencing scheme.

Equally, a high legitimacy scheme would be one in which incorporates a number of critical elements. We have argued that confidence and perceptions of legitimacy will be enhanced if sentencing is seen to be principled; predictable; fair and to reflect the interests of all parties (including the crime victim). Finally, we have advocated both a formal guidelines scheme as well as a Pan-European approach to sentencing as specific vehicles by which public confidence and perceptions of legitimacy in sentencing and criminal justice may be enhanced.

Acknowledgements We are grateful to Mike Hough and an anonymous reviewer for comments on an earlier draft of this essay, and also to participants at meetings held in Ljubljana and at the European Society of Criminology conference in Budapest

Appendix: Extract from the Criminal Code of the Republic of Slovenia

Article 51 (Limits to the Reduction of the Imprisonment Sentence), Paragraph 2

The sentence of an offender, who pleads guilty in accordance with the provisions of the statute on criminal procedure at his first hearing or who pleads guilty after reaching an agreement with the prosecution, may be reduced in accordance with the following:

1. if a prison sentence for a term of 10 or more years is prescribed as the lowest limit for a specific offence, such a limit may be lowered to 3 years of imprisonment
2. if a prison sentence for a term 3–10 years is prescribed as the lowest limit for a specific offence, such a limit may be lowered to 3 months of imprisonment;
3. if a prison sentence for a term of less than 3 years is prescribed as the lowest limit, such a limit may be lowered to 1 month of imprisonment;
4. if a prison sentence for a term of less than 1 year is prescribed as the lowest limit, a fine may be imposed in place of the prison sentence.

Article 58 (Suspension of sentence), Par 5

The sentence of an offender, who pleads guilty in accordance with the provisions of the statute on criminal procedure at his first hearing for an offence for which a suspended sentence may be applied or who pleads guilty for such offence after reaching an agreement with the prosecution, may also be suspended for offences requiring a term of no less than 5 years, when the offender has been sentenced to imprisonment of a term of 5 years, in which case the term of suspension is set to 10 years.

Article 68 (Conditions for Application of Judicial Admonition), Par 5

An offender, who pleads guilty in accordance with the provisions of the statute on criminal procedure at his first hearing for an offence for which a judicial admonition may be applied or who pleads guilty for such offence after reaching an agreement with the prosecution, may be also administered with a judicial admonition for offences requiring a term of imprisonment up to 3 years.

References

Ashworth, A., & Roberts, J. V. (2013). *Sentencing guidelines: Exploring the English experience*. Oxford: Oxford University Press.

Bagaric, M., & Edney, R. (2004). The sentencing advisory commission and the hope of smarter sentencing. *Current Issues in Criminal Justice, 16*(2), 125–139.

Bibas, S. (2012). *The machinery of criminal justice*. Oxford: Oxford University Press.

Bottoms, A., & Tankebe, J. (2012). Beyond procedural justice: A dialogic approach to legitimacy in criminal justice. *The Journal of Criminal Law and Criminology, 102*(1), 119–170.

Dawes, W., Harvey, P., McIntosh, B., Nunney, F., & Phillips, A. (2011). *Attitudes to guilty plea sentence reductions*. London: Sentencing Council of England and Wales.

De Graaf, B., Van der Heide, L., Wanmaker, S., & Weggemans, D. (2013). *The Anders Behring Breivik trial: Performing justice, defending democracy*. The Hague: The International Centre for Counter-Terroris. Retrieved from http://www.icct.nl/download/file/ICCT-De-Graaf-et-al-The-Anders-Behring-Breivik-Trial-August-2013.pdf.

De Keijser, J. W. (2014). Penal theory and popular opinion: The deficiencies of direct engagement. In J. Ryberg & J. V. Roberts (Eds.), *Popular punishment: On the normative significance of public opinion* (pp. 101–118). Oxford: Oxford University Press.

De Keijser, J. W., & Elffers, H. (2009). Public punitive attitudes: A threat to the legitimacy of the criminal justice system? In M. E. Oswald, S. Bieneck, & J. Hupfeld (Eds.), *Social psychology of punishment of crime* (pp. 55–74). Chichester: John Wiley & Sons.

De Keijser, J. W., Van Koppen, P. J., & Elffers, H. (2007). Bridging the gap between judges and the public? *Journal of Experimental Criminology, 3*(2), 131–161.
Doob, A., & Roberts, J. V. (1983). *Sentencing: An analysis of the public's view*. Ottawa: Department of Justice Canada.
Duffy, B., Wake, R., Burrows, T., & Bremner, P. (2008). *Closing the gaps: Crime and public perceptions*. London: Ipsos MORI.
Dünkel, F., Van Zyl Smit, D., & Padfield, N. (2010). Concluding thoughts. In N. Padfield, D. Van Zyl Smit, & F. Dünkel (Eds.), *Release from prison: European policy and practice* (pp. 395–444). Cullompton: Willan.
Dzur, A. (2013). *Punishment, participatory democracy and the jury*. New York: Oxford University Press.
Haveman, R. (2006). Supranational expectations of a punitive approach. In R. Haveman & O. Olusanya (Eds.), *Sentencing and sanctioning in supranational criminal law* (pp. 145–160). Antwerpen: Intersentia.
Henham, R. (2012). *Sentencing and the legitimacy of trial justice*. Abingdon: Routledge.
Hinsch, W. (2008). Legitimacy and justice. In J. Kuhnelt (Ed.), *Political legitimation without morality* (pp. 39–52). London: Springer.
Hough, M., Jackson, J., & Bradford, B. (2013). Legitimacy, trust and compliance: An empirical test of procedural justice theory using the European Social Survey. In J. Tankebe & A. Liebling (Eds.), *Legitimacy and criminal justice: An international exploration* (pp. 326–352). Oxford: Oxford University Press.
Ipsos MORI. (2009). *Sentencing – public attitudes survey*. London: Ipsos MORI.
Jackson, J., Kuha, J., Hough, M., Bradford, B., Hohl, K., & Gerber, M. (2013). *Trust and legitimacy across Europe: A FIDUCIA report on comparative public attitudes towards legal authority*. London: Birkbeck, FIDUCIA Project.
MORI. (2003). *Survey of public confidence in criminal justice*. London: MORI.
Pratt, J., & Eriksson, A. (2013). *Contrasts in punishment: An explanation of Anglophone excess and Nordic exceptionalism*. Abingdon: Routledge.
Rauxloh, R. (2011). Formalization of plea bargaining in Germany: Will the new legislation be able to square the circle? *Fordham International Law Journal, 34*(2), 296–331.
Roberts, J. V. (2013). Complying with sentencing guidelines: Latest findings from the Crown Court sentencing survey. In A. Ashworth & J. V. Roberts (Eds.), *Sentencing guidelines: Exploring the English model* (pp. 104–121). Oxford: Oxford University Press.
Roberts, J. V., & Hough, M. (2005). *Understanding public attitudes to criminal justice*. Buckingham: Open University Press.
Robinson, P. (2009). Empirical desert. In P. Robinson, S. Garvey, & K. Ferzan (Eds.), *Criminal law conversations* (pp. 29–38). Oxford: Oxford University Press.
Sentencing Guidelines Council. (2007). *Sentence reductions for a guilty plea: Definitive guideline*. London: Sentencing Council.
Smith, D. (2007). *Confidence in the criminal justice system: What lies beneath. Ministry of Justice Research Series 7/07*. London: Ministry of Justice.
Thaman, S. (2007). Plea-bargaining, negotiating confessions and consensual resolution of criminal cases. *Electronic Journal of Comparative Law, 11.3*. Retrieved from http://www.ejcl.org/113/article113-34.pdf.
Tyler, T. (2007). *Legitimacy and criminal justice: International perspectives*. New York: Russell Sage.
Van Kesteren, J. (2009). Public attitudes and sentencing policies across the world. *European Journal of Criminal Policy and Research, 15*(1–2), 25–46.
Van Zyl Smit, D. (2013). Legitimacy and the development of international standards for punishment. In J. Tankebe & A. Liebling (Eds.), *Legitimacy and criminal justice* (pp. 267–292). Oxford: Oxford University Press.
Weigend, T. (2011). Should we search for the truth, and who should do it? *North Carolina Journal of International Law and Commercial Regulation, 36*(2), 389.

Procedural Justice for Victims in an International Perspective

Jan van Dijk

1 Introduction

Most European countries have over the past decades made efforts to improve the treatment of crime victims by the authorities and to reduce risks of secondary victimization. To this end they have amended their legislation and issued guidelines for better treatment of crime victims by the police, prosecutors and the courts (Wemmers, 2012). In the European Union, a Framework Decision adopted in 2002, specifically obliged member states to assure a considerate reception of reporting victims by police and prosecutors, including the provision of adequate information. These obligations have now been extended and transposed into a binding EU Directive (Directive 2012/29/EU).

Much knowledge on the interactions between the police and victims of crime has been gained in the framework of national victimization surveys (Skogan, 1984). Questionnaires of such surveys as, for example the USA, British and Dutch victimization surveys, typically include sets of follow up questions to persons identified as victims about whether they have reported the incident to the police, reasons for doing so or not, and their satisfaction with the treatment received. These questions are also included in the standardized questionnaire of the International Crime Victimization Survey (Van Dijk, Van Kesteren, & Mayhew, 2014). The results of these surveys have been used to set performance targets for police forces and to monitor compliance with national or international standards for victim treatment (Van Dijk & Groenhuijsen, 2007).

On a parallel track the interactions between crime victims and police have been used to test theories of perceived justice such as Tyler's theory of procedural justice (Tyler, 2011). Such research explores the value of police using fair processes with

J. van Dijk (✉)
INTERVICT, University of Tilburg, Warandelaan 2, PO Box 90153, 5000 LE Tilburg, The Netherlands
e-mail: Jan.vanDijk@uvt.nl

G. Meško, J. Tankebe (eds.), *Trust and Legitimacy in Criminal Justice*,
DOI 10.1007/978-3-319-09813-5_3

victims of crime to enhance perceptions of the legitimacy of the police and people's willingness to subsequently report victimization and crime to the police and to abstain from offending. Seminal victimological research by Wemmers (1996) supports this argument. In the 1990 ties a package of reforms was introduced in the Netherlands to improve the treatment of crime victims by police and prosecutors, e.g., by instructing officials to be more helpful in giving information and securing compensation. These reforms were evaluated by Wemmers (1996) using a quasi-experimental design. She interviewed victims of assault and burglary in two test districts in the Netherlands where the reforms were implemented as a pilot and in two control districts where they were not. The first part of her study confirms that victims in the test condition were more satisfied with both the police and prosecutors. The victim-friendly reforms apparently had a positive impact upon the satisfaction of victims and on their opinions about police and prosecutors. Wemmers (ibid.) concludes that improved procedures for victims are highly appreciated by victims, regardless of concrete outcomes such as the arrest of the offender. In a secondary analysis of her data Wemmers (ibid.) tested Tyler's hypotheses regarding the favorable long term effects of perceived legitimacy on support for institutions, respect for the law and compliance. Her results confirm that victims, who have been treated well procedurally, are not just more satisfied with their treatment but have more regard for police and prosecution. They also feel more obliged to obey the law and to refrain from offending (measured with questions on self-reported offending). Her experimental findings, then, have unequivocally demonstrated that victim-friendly procedures enhance the perceived legitimacy of police and prosecution and, indirectly, contribute to the prevention of crime. Well-treated victims tend to be more law abiding.

The past years have witnessed a boom of studies on the procedural and outcome preferences of victims of different types of crime informed by Tyler's theory. A review of the literature confirmed the salience of procedural aspects of treatment by the police for victim satisfaction although not necessarily to the same extent for all categories of victims (Laxminarayan, Bosmans, Porter, & Sosa, 2013).

One of the most interesting comparative European research projects in criminology is the ongoing Euro-Justis Project (Hough & Sato, 2011). This large scale, multinational survey aims to examine the role of procedural justice policing in shaping legitimacy and cooperation/compliance with the police. It is informed by Tyler's procedural justice theory, tailored to policing (Tyler, 2011). The project' s central hypothesis is that if people trust criminal justice agencies, such as the police, they will regard them as a form of legitimate authority; they will then defer to this authority, obey the law and cooperate with the justice system, and abide by the law (Hough & Sato, 2011). In other words, fair treatment by the police or the courts yields public trust in criminal justice, which in turn consolidates the perceived legitimacy of these institutions and thus public cooperation and compliance with the law (Hough, Jackson, & Bradford, 2014). Results of a previous survey in England and Wales supported the argument by showing significant correlations between measures of trust in police, moral alignment with the police, willingness to cooperate with the police and compliance with the law (Jackson, Bradford, Stanko, & Hohl, 2012). A set of questions on relevant attitudes has been nested in the fifth sweep of the European

Social Survey conducted in 25 European countries and Israel in 2010. Hypotheses regarding the impact of procedural justice policing on support for the police and the law are now being explored using cross-sectional analysis.

Preliminary analyses support part of the argument by showing correlations between perceived fairness in policing and perceived legitimacy of the police across countries (Hough et al., 2014). The policy implications of these emerging results are far-reaching. According to the authors policing should be less focused on crime control through deterrence and more on building trust within communities through upholding standards of fairness and due process in interactions with citizens.

I am readily persuaded by the procedural justice concept of policing and look forward to future analyses of this European dataset. However, I was disappointed by the lack of standardized questions on victimization and the usual follow up questions to identified victims on reporting to the police and satisfaction with their treatment in the otherwise extensive Euro-Justis questionnaire.[1] The absence of these questions seems not to be just an oversight or the result of limited space. In one of their articles Hough et al. present their procedural justice model of policing as an alternative to the "crude discourse about crime control" (Hough, Jackson, Bradford, Myhill, & Quinton, 2010). The latter discourse is described by them as emphasizing deterrence, and offender bashing and a third element described as "greater responsiveness to the needs of victims" (ibid.). In the wake of Garland, the authors apparently construe the victims rights movement as a manifestation of penal populism (Garland, 2001). Whatever their considerations may have been, their Euro-Justis-project will, due to the lack of victim-directed questions, not shed light on how procedural justice for victims affects their attitudes towards institutions and the law. This seems a missed opportunity, given that citizens in many countries are more likely to have encounters with the police as victims than as suspects or in any other specific capacity.

For this reason I decided to revisit the findings of the ICVS, another large scale international survey on crime issues, with the purpose of exploring whether these lend support to the hypothesis that a better treatment of victims by the police results in more victim satisfaction and cooperation with the police. Although the ICVS has limited value for testing hypotheses on the role of procedural justice for crime victims—and was not designed for that purpose—the cross-national results seem, as we will show, to be largely in line with Tyler's hypothesis. In the discussion I will therefore argue for a readjustment of possible new rounds of the Euro-Justis-project. I will argue that crime victims should not be ignored in a procedural justice view of policing but rather be put at the center of it for both scientific and practical reasons. In a project meant to clarify the potential of legitimacy policing in Europe, questions on the treatment of victims seem indispensable.

[1] The Euro-Justis questionnaire includes one question asking whether respondents have in the course of the last 5 years been victimized by either a burglary or an assault. This catch all item does not meet the well-established standards of a victimization survey. Since victims are not asked whether they have reported the incident to the police, the results cannot be reliably used to examine the impact of police treatment of victims on their attitudes towards the police.

2 Results of the International Crime Victims Survey Revisited

Although the ICVS was, as said, never designed for this purpose, two hypotheses based on the procedural justice theory concerning crime victims, can be explored with ICVS results:

1. Crime victims will be more satisfied with their treatment by the police in countries where police forces are traditionally more democratically controlled and more inclined to render services to the public, including to victims of crime.
2. In countries where crime victims are more often satisfied with their treatment by the police, the percentages of victims of serious crimes reporting to the police will be higher.

The International Crime Victims Survey (ICVS) was initiated with the purpose of producing estimates of victimization that can be compared across countries. After the first round in 1989 the surveys were repeated in 1992, 1996, 2000 and 2004/2005. A modest repeat was conducted in 2010 in six European countries and Canada (Van Dijk, 2012). As in most national victimization surveys in Europe and elsewhere, respondents who have experienced one or more victimizations are asked whether they reported the incident to the police. Victims who had reported to the police types of crime with the most serious consequences for victims are asked whether they were satisfied with their treatment by the police. All respondents were asked to rate the effectiveness of their local police in controlling crime. The results of the ICVS on these issues have been duly reported elsewhere (e.g., Van Dijk, Van Kesteren, & Smit, 2008). Here we will revisit them to see whether they can shed light on the hypotheses mentioned above.

Similar to the Euro-Justis surveys, the ICVS allows analyses both at the aggregate and individual level. We will first focus on intercountry differences. In the ICVS country data classified according to global regions. This allows a comparison between North America, Central and Eastern Europe, Western Europe, Africa, Asia, Latin America, and Oceania (Australia and New Zealand). In some of the older publications comparisons were also made between developed, developing and transitional (ex-communist) countries. In Fig. 1 we present first the mean rates of the seven global geographical regions regarding satisfaction levels among reporting victims. These victim satisfaction rates can be seen as a proxy measure of trust in the police among a subset of the public.[2]

Among those who reported, less than half were satisfied with the way the police dealt with their case globally. Those least satisfied were the respondents from Eastern Europe. Within Europe satisfaction was, on average, lower in Eastern than in Central and Western Europe. This result confirms that police forces in ex-communist countries suffer from low legitimacy. Low satisfaction rates were

[2] Questions about the satisfaction of victims with their treatment by the police are the most commonly used measures in research to test Tyler's theory among crime victims (Laxminarayan et al., 2013).

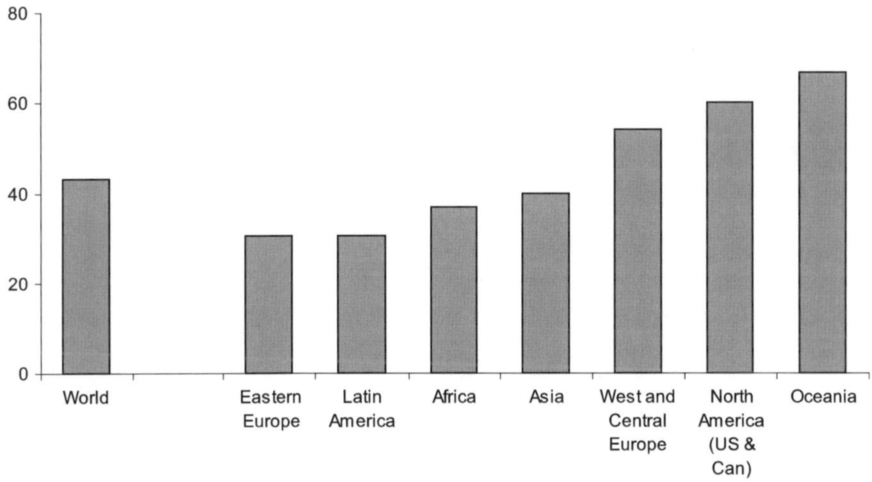

Fig. 1 Percentages of victims satisfied with the police after reporting serious crimes, in seven global regions in 1996–2000 (Van Dijk, 2008)

also found in Latin America/Caribbean, Africa and Asia. It is noteworthy that the satisfaction level among crime victims in Eastern Europe is even below that in the developing world. The country scores on victim satisfaction show that police forces in Anglo-Saxon countries including the UK (65 %) and in Northern Europe (Sweden 69 %) as well as in Australia and New Zealand (Oceania) provide the best services in the eyes of crime victims. These favorable rates are likely to boost perceived legitimacy of police forces in these countries. Among the old 15 member states of the EU, lowest rates are found in France, Italy and Greece. In Greece very few victims are satisfied with their treatment by the police (28 %). New members of the Union (Hungary, Poland, Estonia, and Bulgaria) as well as Turkey also show rates significantly below the European mean.

Hough et al. have formulated several hypotheses about the distribution of police trust or legitimacy across Europe. One of their expectations is that police forces in the social-democratic, Scandinavian countries will enjoy high levels of trust and that much lower levels will be found among formerly communist countries (Hough et al., 2014). The distribution of victim satisfaction in the ICVS datasets is roughly in line with the expectation of Hough et al. on the distribution of police legitimacy in Europe. By and large the distribution of victim satisfaction rates across regions and countries suggests that military-type or repressive type police forces such as those in Eastern Europe—and Latin America—perform less well in their interactions with crime victims than forces that have traditionally been more service-oriented such a police forces or services in Scandinavia and the UK. The latter seem better placed to provide procedural justice to crime victims.

We will now look into the second part of the hypotheses about the impact of normative policing on victims cooperation with the police. Does high satisfaction/legitimacy predict high cooperation with the police in the form of reporting criminal victimizations? Figure 2 presents reporting rates for any crime covered in the survey per global region.

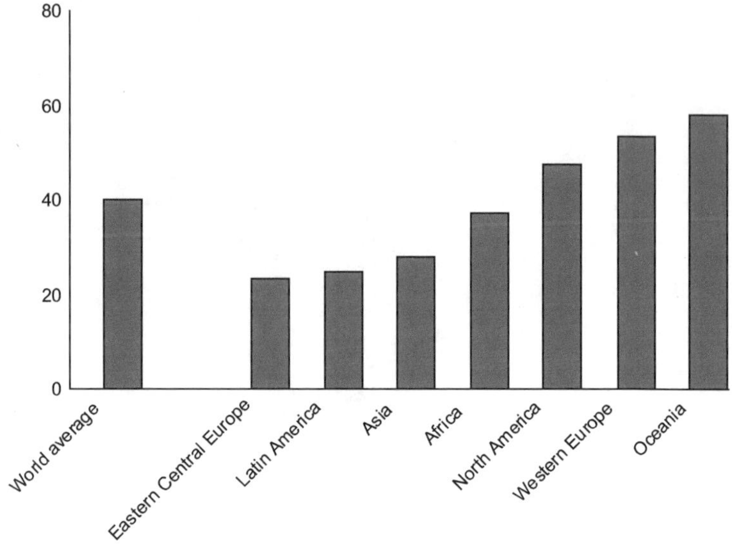

Fig. 2 Percentage of victims reporting any crime (Average reporting rates for nine types of crime: theft of car, theft from car, theft of motorcycle, theft of bicycle, burglary, robbery, theft of personal property, sexual offences and assault/threat.) to the police, by regions (Van Dijk, 2008)

Globally, less than half of conventional crimes are reported to the police (40 %). The rates of reporting to the police show considerable variation across world regions. In Western Europe, North America and Australia those experiencing victimizations are more likely to report to the police than those in other regions. The lowest reporting rates are found in Eastern and Central Europe and in Latin America. As the patterns in the two figures reveal, there is a strong correlation between regional levels of victim satisfaction and of overall victim reporting. In regions where smaller proportions are satisfied by their treatment by the police, fewer victims are prepared to report. Within Europe, the UK (59 %) and Sweden (58 %) stand out with comparatively high reporting rates. We also looked at the relationships between levels of satisfaction with the police per country and national rates of reporting to the police for nine types of crime. For all types of crime, the correlations between victim satisfaction and reporting at the country level were statistically significant. In the case of assault/threat, which is the least reported type of crime, the statistical correlation is fairly strong ($r = 0.47$; $n = 47$, $p < 0.05$).[3]

[3] Building on these ICVS results, the hypothesis can be formulated that victims will hold less favorable opinions of the police than non-victims in Eastern and Southern European countries because most of those who have reported to the police are likely to be dissatisfied with their treatment. In countries in North Western Europe these differences might be smaller, or altogether absent, because negative and positive experiences with the police will be more equally divided and offset each other in their diverging impact on opinions. As said, the lack of more and better questions on victimization and reporting of victims precludes a more pertinent examination of these relationships using the Euro-Justis dataset.

Goudriaan (2006), using data of the ICVS 2000, found in multilevel analyses that country level variables such as confidence in the competence of the police account for a substantial amount of the cross-country variation in reporting property crimes. In another secondary analysis of ICVS data, corruption experts found a strong, inverse correlation between the level of corruption in a country and the level of crime reporting, suggesting that victims in high corruption countries refrain from reporting out of mistrust in the integrity of the local police (Soares, 2005). In other words, the less competent and ethical the police are perceived to be, the less people are inclined to report their personal victimizations to them.

As explained in the introduction, the ICVS questionnaire, as most national victimization surveys, questions reporting victims about their main reasons for reporting and dissatisfied victims about the main reasons for their dissatisfaction. Some distinct regional patterns emerged. Victims of property crimes in developing and ex-communist countries mentioned much more often that they had sought the assistance of the police in the hope to recover their property than victims in developed countries (Van Dijk, 1999). These different motivations for reporting are mirrored in the reasons for dissatisfaction. In Asia, Latin America, Central and Eastern Europe and Africa dissatisfied victims of property crimes more often mentioned that the police did not recover their property and/or failed to arrest the offender (Van Dijk, 1999). In more affluent nations more victims are covered by insurance and this factor reduces their stake in successful investigations (Van Dijk, 1999). In the case of victims of non-property crimes victims in developing country did not show different responses from those in the developed countries. These victim-related, secondary results of the ICVS suggest that in the case of property offences victims in less affluent nations are more sensitive to outcome preferences such as arrests and restitution from the offender than victims in Western Europe and North America. From a procedural justice perspective this finding suggests that for victims of property crimes in poorer countries outcome preferences prevail over procedural preferences. This finding seems another example of what Laxminarayan (2012) calls the heterogeneity of crime victims.

ICVS data can, as said, also be analyzed at the level of individual respondents. Of special interest for the impact of normative policing is the question whether persons with negative experiences with the police will be less cooperative in future instances of personal victimization. In the ICVS data a distinction can be made between those who have over the past year been victimized once and those who have victimized more often (repeat victims). Repeat victims were found to be somewhat less inclined to report their last victimization to the police than others. If they did report, repeat victims tended to be less satisfied with their treatment by the police (Van Dijk, 2001). If they were dissatisfied the reason most frequently mentioned in the case of property crime was that the police failed to recover property or arrest the offender (Van Dijk, 2001). In addition, repeat victims were found to be on average more skeptical about the general effectiveness of the police in their neighborhood. Although these findings of a cross-sectional analysis do not prove causality, they are in line with the key hypothesis that bad treatment by the police fosters negative attitudes towards the police as well as non-cooperation.

They also suggest that for repeat victims, just as for victims in developing or transitional countries, outcome preferences are of special importance.

3 Discussion

By and large, the outcomes of our cross-sectional analyses of data on both country and individual level regarding satisfaction with the police, attitudes towards the police and reporting of crimes support the hypothesis that low perceived legitimacy reduces the willingness of victims to cooperate with the police. More specifically, they confirm that enhancing police legitimacy among crime victims is a challenge for police forces in the new member states of the European Union and in Southern Europe in particular. In these countries satisfaction and cooperation remain far below the average European level. Among victims of property offences in these countries, dissatisfaction might be especially difficult to improve since victims, for lack of other means to recoup losses, primarily seek outcomes such as the arrest of offenders and restitution of property. These outputs of criminal investigation might be harder to achieve than procedural ones.

Our review of older ICVS data suggests that the lack of questions in the Euro-Justis project of standardized items on victims is a missed opportunity indeed. The proven salience of treating crime victims better for building trust and legitimacy among the public seems to warrant the inclusion on a set of victimization items in any future version of the Euro-Justis survey. Such inclusion will allow an analysis of how variations in perceived legitimacy can be explained by different experiences of citizens in their capacity as victims. Such analysis will add an important new dimension to the cross-country comparisons envisaged by the Euro-Justis team.

The potential of victim-friendly policies for boosting legitimacy among the public at large seems considerable. As the ICVS has shown, over a 5 year period almost half of the world population is victimized by common crime once or more. Since roughly 40 % of these actual victims report their victimizations to the police, police forces in most countries come into contact with roughly 20 % of the public as reporting victims in 5 years. Life time prevalence of such encounters is hard to estimate, but probably half of the population in Western countries reports a crime at least once in a lifetime.

This ICVS-based estimate can be checked against findings from national surveys regarding recent contacts with the police. Several European victimization surveys have included questions on encounters with the police. In the Netherlands all respondents are asked whether they have had any contacts with the police over the past 12 months and for what reason (Centraal Bureau voor de Statistiek, 2012). One in three Dutch citizens had been in contact with their local police. The three main categories were law enforcement (fines, arrests, warnings etcetera), crime reporting and other (request for assistance, lost property, social chat). Of all contacts 38 % were related to the reporting of crimes. A recent survey in Chicago found even higher levels of interaction between police and citizens (Kruttschnitt &

Carbone-Lopez, 2009). Half of the citizens had had a personal encounter over the past year. The single most common encounter was reporting a crime (20 % of the population had done so). These results suggesting that between one in ten and one in five citizens report crimes to the police per year are similar to our estimations based on the victimization and reporting rates of the ICVS.

4 The Challenge at Hand

The knowledge that police forces have the opportunity to improve their perceived legitimacy among a large segment of the public every year by treating reporting victims better shows the potential of such policies. As discussed, the Dutch pilots with new guidelines for the treatment of victims evaluated by Wemmers (1996) have demonstrated that gains in victim satisfaction through improved services are indeed feasible. As Skogan (2005) found in Chicago, fair and respectful treatment during police-victim encounters is associated with higher satisfaction of victims and respect for the police. An experimental study in Greater Manchester, UK, confirmed that a brief training of police officers in victim-friendly behavior significantly improved victim satisfaction and respect for the police (Wheller, Quinton, Fildes, & Mills, 2013).

Although these national results are encouraging, it should not be assumed that improving satisfaction among crime victims can be achieved easily, and that victim reporting will automatically start rising once victim-friendly programs have formally been put in place. The ICVS has, as said, been repeated several times in a large sample of Western countries and so trend data about the levels of satisfaction among reporting crime victims are available for the period 1988–2005 or 2010. Contrary to expectations, rates of satisfaction among victims of serious crimes show a downward trend in many countries. Between 1996 and 2005 victim satisfaction went down in the USA, the UK, the Netherlands, Canada, and Sweden (Van Dijk & Groenhuijsen, 2007).[4] The ICVS was, as said repeated in 2010 in six Western countries (Canada, Denmark, Germany, the Netherlands, Sweden, and the UK) (Van Dijk, 2012). The results on satisfaction of victims with their treatment by the police confirm the downward trend over the past 10 years (Van Dijk, 2014). In Canada, the Netherlands, and the UK the mean satisfaction rate of the 2005/2010 surveys combined is significantly lower than the mean of 1996/2000. In Germany

[4] Nation-specific crime victim surveys in England/Wales and the Netherlands, using much larger samples, have also registered declines in satisfaction since 1995 (Allen, 2006; Centraal Bureau voor de Statistiek, 2006). In an overview of 25 years of the British Crime Survey Janson (2006: pp. 23) writes: "The BCS also asks victims how satisfied they were with the police. Victims' satisfaction with the way the police dealt with the matter decreased between 1994 and 2000, but has remained stable since." The Dutch victim satisfaction rate has also failed to move up after its drop around 2000. The level of satisfaction has remained below 60 % ever since (Centraal Bureau voor de Statistiek, 2012).

too victim satisfaction seems to have fallen rather than risen over the past 20 years. In Denmark and Sweden satisfaction among reporting victims appears to have remained stable. These results are counterintuitive since victim-friendly reception procedures are, as said, mandatory under EU legislation since 2002 and have been actively promoted in the six countries under scrutiny. The ICVS has also, independently from the other six surveys, been repeated in Estonia. Levels of satisfaction in Estonia in 2010 were still relatively very low. The Estonian results confirm that new EU members such as Estonia are still lagging far behind the older 15 members in reporting rates as well as in victim satisfaction (Van Dijk, 2012).[5] Although police forces in Central and Eastern Europe have undergone fundamental reforms upon entry into the Union, their interfaces with the public as reporting crime victims still leave much to be desired. ICVS-based surveys in Georgia, funded by the European Union, reveal a similar picture. Whereas levels of victimization and fear of crime have declined since 2005, both victim satisfaction and victim reporting remain far below the European mean (Van Dijk & Chanturia, 2012). Improving victim satisfaction seems to require more fundamental changes in policing than increasing instrumental performance. As discussed above, a complicating factor for poorer countries is that victims of property crimes report crimes with a view of recovering their property. Improvements in the procedural treatment of such victims may not lead to higher satisfaction.

The disappointing results in most European countries including those at the forefront of victim friendly reforms can be interpreted in different ways. One explanation is that victims are treated as professionally as before but that expectations among victims have been raised to the point that they can no longer be satisfied (Chandek & Porter, 1998). Police forces may ask victims whether they would want to be informed about the investigation. If subsequently no information is given, victims might be more upset than when the issue had not been raised at all. Another possible interpretation is that police forces have bureaucratized the reporting of crimes.[6] Thirdly, in countries, where special provisions for victims outside the police have been set up, police forces may feel that victim needs are duly met if a referral is made to such agencies. It seems striking in this respect that in Europe victims are more consistently satisfied with the police in countries where victim support outside the police hardly exists such as Denmark, France, Finland and Luxembourg. Police forces in the USA, the UK, and the Netherlands may be inclined to relegate victim support to existing, well-functioning outside agencies and to have cut back on their own victim services.

Whatever may be the reasons, that fewer victims are currently satisfied with their treatment by the police than 20 years ago should remind us that improving victim-

---

[5] Of the victims reporting a household burglary in Estonia only 31 % were satisfied with their treatment by the police.

[6] A factor behind the drop in satisfaction may the gradual increase of victims reporting by phone or via Internet. There is some evidence that in England/Wales victims who have no face-to-face contacts with the police are somewhat less satisfied (Allen, 2006).

based legitimacy is a daunting challenge. It should also remind us of the need to continue regular comparative surveys in Europe on victimization and on compliance with European legislation on victim reception and support. Such surveys, whether incorporated in the Euro-Justis project, or, preferably, as repeat of the ICVS in the EU (Van Dijk, Mayhew, Van Kesteren, Aebi, & Linde, 2010; Van Dijk, 2012), are indispensable for monitoring trends in the victim-based legitimacy of police forces in the European Union.

References

Allen, J, (Ed.) (2006). *Policing and the criminal justice system—Public confidence and perceptions: Findings from the 2004/2005 British Crime Survey*. Online report 07/06. Home Office. Retrieved from http://webarchive.nationalarchives.gov.uk/20100405140447/http:/www.homeoffice.gov.uk/rds/pdfs06/rdsolr0706.pdf.

Centraal Bureau voor de Statistiek. (2006). *Veiligheidsmonitor 2006* [Safety Monitor 2006]. Retrieved from http://www.cbs.nl/nl-NL/menu/themas/veiligheid-recht/publicaties/publicaties/archief/2006/2006-k00-pub.htm.

Centraal Bureau voor de Statistiek. (2012). *Veiligheidsmonitor 2012* [Safety Monitor 2012]. Retrieved from http://www.cbs.nl/nl-NL/menu/themas/veiligheid-recht/publicaties/publicaties/archief/2013/2013-veiligheidsmonitor-2012-pub.htm.

Chandek, M. S., & Porter, C. O. L. H. (1998). The efficacy of expectancy disconfirmation in explaining crime victim satisfaction with the police. *Police Quarterly, 1*(4), 21–40.

Directive 2012/29/EU of the European Parliament and of the Council of 25 October 2012. Establishing minimum standards on the rights, support and protection of victims of crime, and replacing Council Framework Decision 2001/220/JHA.

Garland, D. (2001). *The culture of control: Crime and social order in contemporary society*. Chicago, IL: University of Chicago Press.

Goudriaan, H. (2006). *Reporting crime: Effects of social context on the decision of victims to notify the police*. Doctoral dissertation, University Press (PhD Leiden University), Veenendaal.

Hough, M., Jackson, J., Bradford, B., Myhill, A., & Quinton, P. (2010). Procedural justice, trust, and institutional legitimacy. *Policing: A Journal of Policy and Practice, 4*(3), 203–210.

Hough, M., Jackson, J., & Bradford, B. (2014). Trust in justice and the legitimacy of legal authorities: Topline findings from a European comparative study. In S. Body-Gendrot, M. Hough, K. Kerezsi, R. Levy, & S. Snacken (Eds.), *The Routledge handbook of European criminology* (pp. 243–266). Milton Park: Routledge.

Hough, M., & Sato, M. (2011). *Trust in justice: Why it is important for criminal policy, and how it can be measured: Final report of the Euro-Justis project*. Helsinki: European Institute for Crime Prevention and Control.

Jackson, J., Bradford, B., Stanko, E. A., & Hohl, K. (2012). *Just authority? Trust in police in England and Wales*. London: Routledge.

Jansson, K. (2006). *British crime survey—Measuring crime for 25 years*. Retrieved from http://webarchive.nationalarchives.gov.uk/20110218135832/rds.homeoffice.gov.uk/rds/pdfs07/bcs25.pdf.

Kruttschnitt, C., & Carbone-Lopez, K. (2009). *Customer satisfaction: Crime victims' willingness to call the police*. Ideas in American Policing, no. 12. Police Foundation. Retrieved from http://www.policefoundation.org/sites/g/files/g798246/f/Kruttschnitt%20et%20al.%20%282009%29%20-%20Customer%20Satisfaction%20.pdf.

Laxminarayan, M. (2012). *The heterogeneity of crime victims: Variations in procedural and outcome preferences*. Nijmegen: Wolff's Legal Publishers.

Laxminarayan, M., Bosmans, M., Porter, M., & Sosa, L. (2013). Victim satisfaction with criminal justice: A systematic review. *Victims & Offenders, 8*(2), 119–147.

Skogan, W. G. (1984). Reporting crimes to the police: The status of world research. *Journal of Research in Crime and Delinquency, 21*(2), 113–137.

Skogan, W. (2005). Citizens satisfaction with police encounters. *Police Quarterly, 8*(3), 295–321.

Soares, R. (2005). Measuring corruption: Validating subjective surveys of perceptions. In *Global corruption report 2005* (pp. 289–291). Berlin: Transparency International.

Tyler, T. (2011). Trust and legitimacy: Policing in the USA and Europe. *European Journal of Criminology, 8*(4), 254–266.

Van Dijk, J. J. M. (1999). Criminal victimization and victim empowerment in an international perspective. In J. J. M. van Dijk, J. Wemmers, & R. van Kaam (Eds.), *Caring for crime victims: Selected proceedings of the 9th International Symposium on Victimology* (pp. 15–39). Monsey, NY: Criminal Justice Press.

Van Dijk, J. J. M. (2001). Attitudes of victims and repeat victims towards the police: Results of the international crime victims survey. In G. Farrell & K. Pease (Eds.), *Repeat victimization* (pp. 27–52). Monsey, NY: Criminal Justice Press.

Van Dijk, J. J. M. (2008). *The world of crime: Breaking the silence on problems of security, justice and development across the world.* Thousand Oaks, CA: Sage.

Van Dijk, J. J. M. (2012). The international crime victims survey: Latest results and prospects. *Newsletter European Society of Criminology, 11*(2), 24–33.

Van Dijk, J. J. M. (2014). Benchmarking satisfaction of victims with the police through survey research: A missed opportunity for the European Commission. In P. Schaefer & E. Weitenkamp (Eds.), *Establishing victimology: Festschrift for prof. dr. Gerd Kirschhoff* (pp. 117–126). Niederrhein: Hochschule Niederrhein.

Van Dijk, J. J. M., & Chanturia, T. (2012). *The remarkable case of Georgia.* Tbilisi: Gorbi Institute, Ministry of Justice Georgia.

Van Dijk, J. J. M., & Groenhuijsen, M. S. (2007). Benchmarking victim policies in the framework of European Union Law. In S. Walklate (Ed.), *Handbook of victims and victimology* (pp. 363–379). Cullompton: Willan.

Van Dijk, J. J. M., Mayhew, P., Van Kesteren, J. N., Aebi, M., & Linde, A. (2010). *Final report on the study on crime victimisation.* Tilburg: INTERVICT/Eurostat.

Van Dijk, J. J. M., Van Kesteren, J. N., & Mayhew, P. (2014). The international crime victims surveys: A retrospective. *International Review of Victimology, 20*(1), 49–69.

Van Dijk, J. J. M., Van Kesteren, J. N., & Smit, P. (2008). *Criminal victimization in international perspective: Key findings from the 2004-2005 ICVS and EU ICS.* Den Haag: Boom Legal Publishers.

Wemmers, J. (1996). *Victims in the criminal justice system.* Kugler (PhD Leiden University), Amsterdam.

Wemmers, J. (2012). Victims' rights are human rights: The importance of recognizing victims as persons. *Temida, 15*(2), 71–84.

Wheller, L., Quinton, P., Fildes, A., & Mills, A. (2013). *The greater Manchester Police procedural justice training experiment: The impact of communication skills training on officers and victims of crime.* London: College of Policing.

Empowering the Victims of Crime: A Real Goal of the Criminal Justice System or No More Than a Pipe Dream?

Witold Klaus, Konrad Buczkowski, and Paulina Wiktorska

1 Introduction

Zedner (2002: 447) describes the evolution of victimology as follows: "Victims now attract an unprecedented level of interest, both as a subject of criminological enquiry and as a focus of criminal justice policy. (...) Political pressure, too, has raised the victim's profile, ensuring that the needs of victims are recognized and that the services provided to them are seen as important. This has greatly expanded the role of compensation, provision of services, and information, and has allowed victims' interests to inform key decisions in the criminal justice process." But in the view of Walklate (2009) an entirely different process can be observed at present—victims are not viewed as individuals who have gone through particular ordeals and who need support, but merely as part of the backdrop of preventing and counteracting crime. Every member of the public is now seen as a potential victim. This shift in viewpoint has diverted the efforts of the public service from assisting individuals to fighting the common enemy of crime.

In this paper, we will try to show that the issue of protecting victims is making its way into the public debate in Poland but is being treated as a means to achieve specific political ends, and in no way implies that any real work is being done to ensure that individual victims are supported, apart from that required to meet Poland's international obligations (preferably construed as narrowly as possible). For politicians, "protecting victims of crime" is a catchphrase that vindicates introducing criminal legislation that is increasingly punitive and often unrelated to the actual needs and expectations of victims (cf. Garland, 2001: 143–144).[1]

[1] For more on punitiveness in Poland, see Klaus, Rzeplińska, and Woźniakowska-Fajst (2011).

W. Klaus (✉) • K. Buczkowski • P. Wiktorska
Institute of Legal Studies, Polish Academy of Sciences, Nowy Świat 72, Warsaw 00-330, Poland
e-mail: witold.klaus@gmail.com; k.buczkowski@inp.pan.pl; wiktorska.p@gmail.com

G. Meško, J. Tankebe (eds.), *Trust and Legitimacy in Criminal Justice*,
DOI 10.1007/978-3-319-09813-5_4

2 Protecting the Rights of Victims of Crime as Provided for in Polish Legislation

The Polish legal system has a range of statutes containing provisions on protecting victims of crime. Some of the most important are:

1. The Act of 6 June 1997 Criminal Code (CC) (Journal of Laws (J.L.) No. 88, Item 553 with amendments);
2. The Act of 6 June 1997 Criminal Procedure Code (J.L. No. 89, Item 555 with amendments);
3. The Act of 29 July 2005 on Countering Domestic Violence (J.L. No. 180, Item 1493 with amendments); and
4. The Act of 7 July 2005 on State Compensation for Victims of Selected Crimes (J.L. No. 169, Item 1415 with amendments).

These is the fundamental legislation designed to assist and support victims of crime by protecting their basic rights and making it possible for them to be at least partly compensated for the injury and damage they have sustained as a result of the offender's action(s).

The regulations in the Criminal Code and the Criminal Procedure Code accord with proposals adopted on the basis of EU legislation and the legislation of other European counties and other international regulations. Admittedly, in some cases, these were adopted as a result of EU member states endeavoring to implement similar legislative provisions and apply them in similar ways (Walkowiak, 2011). The following acts of international law are worth mentioning in this regard: UN Declaration of Basic Principles of Justice for Victims of Crime and Abuse of Power (Resolution 40/34), European Convention on the Compensation of Victims of Violent Crimes, Recommendation No. R(85)11 of the Committee of Ministers of the Council of Europe on the Position of the Victim in the Framework of Criminal Law, Recommendation No. R(87)21 on the Assistance to Victims and the Prevention of Victimisation, Council Framework Decision 2001/220/JHA on the standing victims in criminal proceedings, the European Parliament and the Council Directive 2012/29/EU of establishing minimum standards on the rights, support and protection of victims of crime and Council Directive 2004/80/EC relating to compensation to crime victims.

These have their counterparts in such criminal law provisions as the obligation to remedy damage and pay exemplary damages. The first of these is encapsulated in CC Art. 46 § 1, which relevantly provides that in the event of a conviction, the court may order, at a request of the aggrieved party of another party authorized in the order, the offender to partially or fully remedy any damage caused by the offence, or compensate for any injury. The second is encapsulated in CC Art 46 § 2, which relevantly provides that instead of the obligations set out in § 1, the court may order exemplary damages to be paid to the aggrieved party. Exemplary damages will be ordered up to 100,000 PLN (about 25,000 EUR). The provisions of the Criminal Procedure Code (CPC) include a series of regulations that enable people harmed by crime to defend their rights. While a detailed description is beyond the scope of this text, it is worth examining some of them by way of example. The main purpose of these regulations is to structure the proceedings in such a way that the interests of victims are taken into consideration (CPC Art. 2 § 1 Pt. 3). The most basic entitlement of a victim of crime (defined as "the injured party" in the Polish Criminal Procedure Code) is the right to detailed information on his/her rights and responsibilities. The victim is a party entitled to act in his/her own name and interests during preliminary proceedings (CPC Art. 299 § 1). He/she can have a lawyer represent him/her and can file motions for evidence throughout the trial and appeal the sentence.[2]

The Polish legal system, however, places special weight on the Act on Countering Domestic Violence and the Act on State Compensation for Victims of Selected Crimes to ensure that the rights of victims of crime are protected. From the time the Criminal Code of 1997 came into effect, i.e., since 1 September 1998, Art. 207 has been the only regulatory provision on domestic violence. This makes anyone "who mentally or physically mistreats a person close to him or her, or another person in a permanent or temporary state of dependence to the offender, a minor or a person who is vulnerable because of his or her mental or physical condition. Such person is liable to imprisonment for between 3 months and 5 years (Art. 207 § 1). If the act specified in § 1 is carried out with particular cruelty, the offender is liable to imprisonment for between one and 10 years (Art. 207 § 2). If the act specified in §§ 1 or 2 results in a suicide attempt by the afflicted party, the offender is liable to imprisonment for between 2 and 12 years (Art. 207 § 3)" liable for a penalty. It should be noted that other liability provisions of the Criminal Code may be applicable to domestic violence offenders as well, e.g., violation of bodily integrity (CC Art. 217), disturbance of the functioning of a bodily organ or disturbance to health (CC Art. 157), unlawful threat (CC Art. 190) and rape (CC Art. 197).

However, the provisions of the Criminal Code are not, and have never been, sufficient to ensure the safety of women and children, i.e., the victims of domestic violence, so in 2003, work began on a bill that would comprehensively resolve this issue. The resulting Act was modelled on Austrian legislation. The Act on Countering Domestic Violence was given assent on 29 July 2005 and is predicated on the following underlying assumptions: (1) domestic violence is a crime; (2) the state is responsible for preventing and punishing domestic violence; (3) the offender is liable for his/her actions; and (4) the victim has a right to safety. The Act stipulates that domestic violence is to be construed as isolated or repeated activity that wilfully and/or negligently infringes the rights of one or more family members and/or is detrimental to their personal wellbeing—especially when it endangers the

---

[2] The "Victims' Rights Charter" (www.elblag.policja.gov.pl/p_d_f/karta _praw_ofiary.pdf) is a Ministry of Justice initiative. Although it has no legal effect, the Charter lists the rights to which the victim is entitled, as well as information on the entities from whom or what they can be claimed.

lives and health of those persons, violates their dignity, bodily integrity and freedom (including sexual freedom), and injures their physical and/or mental health, and when it causes those affected by the violence to experience mental injury and suffering (Art. 2 Pt. 2).

The original wording of the Act, however, was mainly focused on highlighting the obligations of government agencies and local government bodies to implement measures to counter domestic violence and to initiate and support ventures aimed at raising social awareness of the causes and effects of domestic violence as already set out in other government Acts and documents. These bodies and agencies were not, however, assigned any new operational tasks.

As for ensuring the safety of victims of domestic violence, the Act imposed an obligation on people who, in the course of carrying out their official duties, suspected that a violent crime had been committed against family members to inform the police or the public prosecutor immediately (Art. 12). The Act additionally authorized the court, in the case of a conditional stay of criminal proceedings against someone accused of committing a violent crime or making an unlawful threat against a family member or in the case of a suspended sentence for someone convicted of such crimes, to specify the manner in which that person may make contact with the victim and/or prohibit that person from approaching the victim in certain specified circumstances (Art. 13).[3]

The Act gave the court another option to use against someone accused of committing a violent crime or making an unlawful threat against a family member in the event that the conditions for temporary arrest were met. Instead of this particular means of police supervision, the accused could be made to vacate premises jointly occupied with the victim within a period set down by the court and remain in a specified place (Art. 14). The accused could be further ordered to refrain from making contact with the victim in a specified manner.

NGOs were critical of regulations that enabled rulings to be made, prior to the sentencing stage, prohibiting contact and ordering the accused to vacate premises, being inserted into the Act, and called for a revision. In particular, there was a proposal to overhaul "conditional police supervision" (Spurek, 2012). These demands were factored into the amendments to the Act passed on 5 November 2009 and effective as of 6 August 2010 (J.L. No. 206, Item 1589).

Work began on the next tranche of (significantly broader) amendments to the Act on Countering Domestic Violence even before those just referred to had been completed. The amendments were passed by parliament in 2010 and effected a whole range of changes, not just in the wording of this act but in several others as well.[4] The preamble to the Act was changed so as to define domestic violence as a

[3] The authorisation of the court is given effect in imposing the obligation set out in CC Art. 72 § 1 Pt. 7a and Pt. 7b. This concerns the obligation to refrain from making contact with the victim or other persons in a specified manner or approaching the victim or other persons, as well as the obligation to vacate premises jointly occupied with the victim.

[4] Some of the most important changes include inserting a prohibition on parents and guardians administering corporal punishment to children into the Act of 25 February 1964—the Family and

violation of basic human rights, including the right to life and health and the right to have personal dignity respected, and to refer to the responsibility of the public authorities to ensure that the citizenry were treated equally and that their rights and freedoms were respected.

New provisions were added to the Act as well. These have to do with imposing an obligation on each municipality to set up an "interdisciplinary team" tasked with coordinating the activities of the various institutions and services that combat domestic violence with the participation of parole officers (obligatory) and prosecutors (optional) (Art. 9a-d). The Monitoring Team to Combat Domestic Violence was convened as a consultative body by the Minster responsible for social security matters. As Wiktorska (2013) points out, the convening of teams can only be regarded as a considerable achievement and one that enables different entities to work together to monitor problem situations while avoiding duplicating functions. In particular, it prevents victims and witnesses from being questioned several times, while minimizing the risk of secondary victimization. Moreover, the Act contains an article introducing a mandatory social obligation to report the commission of a violent domestic crime (Art. 12). Accordingly, anyone who witnesses domestic violence should notify the police, the public prosecutor or some other entity charged with combating domestic violence, and anyone who reasonably suspects that an indictable domestic violence offence has been committed during the course of his/her official and/or professional duties is obliged to inform the police or the public prosecutor immediately.

The 2010 revision introduced a new legal remedy where a person affected by the violence of another family member can petition the court to order that person to vacate jointly occupied premises in the event that his/her behavior has made joint habitation particularly onerous (Art. 11a). A ruling to vacate a residence is enforceable immediately it is handed down. Adopting this (previously called for) scheme should increase the protection of the rights of people affected by violence.

The most significant change, however, concerns the new Art. 12a, which provides for the removal of a child. This provision gives a social worker, assisted by a police officer, doctor, paramedic or nurse, the right to remove a child from its family and place it with another next-of-kin, i.e., one who does not cohabitate with the child, in a foster home, or in a round-the-clock educational care facility, if he/she reasonably believes there is a direct threat to the life or health of the child on account of domestic violence. The Act provides for short (24 h) time limits to notify the family court that a child has been removed and for parents and guardians to lodge a complaint. Such short time limits are justified on the grounds that ensuring the utmost protection of a minor outweighs the risk of making a bad decision under Art. 12a (Wiktorska, 2013).

Guardianship Code (J.L. No. 9, Item 59 with amendments). On the other hand, two new penal measures were inserted into the Criminal Code, constituting a milestone in safeguarding the rights of victims of domestic violence: (1) the option of ordering a prohibition on approaching specific people for 1–15 years; and (2) the option of ordering the vacation of premises occupied jointly with the victim for 1–10 years.

The last statute worthy of attention in protecting victims of crime is the Act on State Compensation for Victims of Selected Crimes. Work on this statute began as early as 1999 but was discontinued on the objection of the Minister of Finance, who refused to approve the creation of a special fund from which compensation would be paid. Work resumed a few years later. The Act was finally passed in 2005 under the pressure of having to introduce domestic regulations as a result of EU Directive 2004/80/WE. The State Compensation Act aims to even out the disparity between the offender and the victim by raising the status of the victim and by introducing remedies and procedures into criminal proceedings (and ancillary activities) that make it possible for the victim to pursue his/her legitimate rights and interests. Taking advantage of recognized entitlements, however, requires initiative, prior knowledge, and/or information on how to pursue legitimate claims (Niełaczna, 2007).

It has to be said that the Act only meets the bare minimum requirements in terms of granting financial support to victims of the most grievous crimes, including those where the victim is killed or who suffers grievous bodily harm or bodily injury or impairment to health. Compensation that cannot exceed 12,000 PLN (approx. 3,000 EUR) can in no way be considered just or genuine. Moreover, compensation payable to victims of such crimes only covers loss of earnings or other means of support, documented costs associated with medical treatment and rehabilitation, and funeral expenses.

The Compensation Act has been revised twice. The first revision, in 2008 (J.L. No. 96, Item 608) backdated the applicability of the provisions to 1 July 2005 (the Act became binding in September 2005). The second, in 2009 (J.L. No. 79, Item 665) made more substantial changes. Most importantly, the definition of "victim" in the Act was changed by removing the requirement that a violent crime be intentional. The new wording defines a victim as any natural person who has suffered death, grievous bodily harm or bodily injury or impairment to health as a result of a crime. As such, it includes unintentional crimes.[5] Compensation was extended to include the costs of medical treatment and rehabilitation.

The jurisdiction of the court competent to hear compensation cases was changed in order to make it easier for victims to obtain compensation. The Act originally granted jurisdiction to the regional court in the area in which the crime was committed. This arrangement could make it difficult, if not impossible, for victims to obtain compensation, especially when they resided a long way from the court. After the revision, the regional court of the place of residence of the person entitled to compensation (i.e., the victim) was given jurisdiction, unless this place of residence could not be determined, in which case the regional court of the area in which the crime was committed was given jurisdiction. As some entitled people were unable to appear in compensation cases (e.g., because they were dead or disabled as a result of the crime), the revised Act additionally granted the right to

[5] This change also brought about a change in the title of the Act by striking out the term "intentional."

lodge an application for compensation to the public prosecutor, who could then act in the interests of the victim. These changes were meant to improve the working of the Act in practice. Despite this, however, it is seldom applied (there is more detail on this in later chapters).

One more change in the Polish legal system should be noted. This concerns the revision of the Criminal Code in 2013 (J.L. 2013, Item 849), which introduced a change in the procedure for prosecuting rape (CC Art. 197), sexual intercourse with a person of limited soundness of mind (CC Art. 198) and coercing or pressuring a dependent person or a person in a critical situation into having sexual intercourse (CC Art. 199). The regulations that had been binding until then provided for prosecution on complaint of the injured party. This forced the victims of such crimes to lodge an application to prosecute the offender, which they often never did because for example they feared for their life after being threatened by the offender. These acts are now prosecuted ex officio. This is meant to ensure victims more effective legal protection than had previously been the case. The Criminal Procedure Code was also amended to restructure criminal procedure in cases concerning crimes against sexual freedom so as not to cause additional suffering to victims, especially minors. These changes had long been called for and, as such, can only be viewed positively. However, as they only came into effect in January 2014, it remains to be seen how they will work in practice.

3 Public Debate on Protecting Victims of Crime

3.1 General Observation

Legislative changes are usually accompanied by a broad public debate in which supporters and opponents argue their positions. Politicians, journalists, and experts and specialists from various academic fields all participate, and the views of ordinary citizens are canvassed. The issue of victims' rights—and procedural guarantees that they will be respected—has been quite topical in Poland over the last few years and has involved politicians, legal practitioners and even the general public. The victimological perspective of criminality is not popular and is often misunderstood by the Polish public. Far more attention is devoted to the perpetrators of crime, especially the most sensational crimes, which are blown up by the media. Many of our attitudes about victims of crime are deeply rooted in prejudices and stereotypes. As a society, we have a tendency to downplay the need to guarantee and genuinely respect the rights of victims, while stigmatizing and labelling them and frequently overstating their role in causing crime. This problem particularly concerns such crimes as violence towards close family members and rape. These provoke heated discussions that often betray a complete lack of understanding of the plight of victims.

3.2 Rape and Controversy on the Way It Has Been Prosecuted

The first examples worthy of examination in this context concern rape. The Polish regulations on rape are to be found in the criminal procedure of a case prosecuted on a complaint filed by the injured party, which was introduced into criminal code in 1932. This procedure occasionally appears in Polish procedural law. This depends on whether the injury party has to launch the prosecution by filing a complaint to the effect that a crime has been committed. The rationality of retaining this system has been discussed by politicians, legal practitioners and the public for many years. Those in favor of maintaining the status quo argue that it enables victims to safeguard their privacy and ensures that they can avoid the repeated pain and embarrassment of victimization as well as any feelings of shame. Opponents fear that "Poland is one of only a handful of countries to have embraced a system where rape is prosecuted on the filing of a complaint by the person injured by the crime. The explanation that the welfare of the victim is taken into account says a good deal about the attitude of the legislature and law enforcement agencies but does nothing to help the victim. This system might have been appropriate when it was adopted back in 1932, given the state of knowledge and the prevailing mentality at the time. But to support the position that prosecuting on a complaint filed by the injured party somehow protects the victim from shame and repeated victimization on the part of law enforcement agencies—effectively making them 'accessories' after the fact of rape—today, perpetuates and consolidates a patriarchal and sexist culture—including legal culture." (Płatek, 2011: 33)

Unfortunately, the view that rape victims often have provoked their attackers is still implicitly hold in Poland. Victims, especially women, are accused of being provocatively dressed and being in inappropriate areas, which it should be stressed, are most often public places with unrestricted access, such as parks, malls and city boulevards. A public statement made by the mayor of a Warsaw district in August 2013 especially caused a stir. After the rape of a woman in Kabacki Forest, he posted the following on Twitter: "A tragedy. I sympathize. Don't go running in deserted places alone after dark. Except, how could she run after dark?." (PAP, 2013). The Parliamentary Women's Group, whose members belong to various political parties, labelled the text scandalous in a special statement. These parliamentarians expressed their outrage as follows: "The mayor is suggesting that the victim herself is guilty and provoked the rape because she went running after 19:00! The Parliamentary Women's Group, as a mark of solidarity with the victim, strongly protests such a callous and thoughtless stigmatization of the woman and not the perpetrator of the rape. There is not, nor can there be, any condoning of rape! Time, place and gender are irrelevant. Mayor Guziała's statement is beyond the bounds of decency." (PAP, 2013) In response to the protest, the mayor defended himself by saying that he was expressing sympathy for the victim and simply questioning the rationality of practicing sports after dusk. He added that if feminists wanted to fight for women's rights, they should educate them on situations that might be risky for them. This is a classic example of subscribing to victim precipitation, a theory devised by Menachem Amir, whose study has been strongly criticized and dubbed "anti-victimological" (Amir, 1967; Jordan, 2013).

Public statements like that cited above cause a great deal of outrage and spark a lot of heated discussion. However, research shows that the level of awareness regarding rape and coercing or pressuring people into sexual intercourse is still very low in Poland. Most worrying is the persistence of the view that rape is not possible within a marriage or a de facto relationship. Sexologist Zbigniew Izdebski sees the fact that Polish people are brought up to feel embarrassed about sex instead of being educated on the topic as the main reason for this. The idea that wives exist to meet obligations, including that of having sexual intercourse with their husbands, whether they feel like it or not, is constantly instilled into women as part of their socialization. The studies cited on this topic find that one in three Polish women and more than one in two Polish men think that a woman has an obligation to engage in marital sex. The Centre for Public Opinion Research claims that 20 % of respondents simply answered that there is no such thing as rape in marriage. Even more worrying is that many of them were police officers (Szulc, 2013: 39). Joanna Piotrowska, President of the Feminoteka Foundation, an organization concerned with women's rights, says that "in the police force, the public prosecutor's office, the courts and during interviews, raped women are still being led to believe that they made the whole thing up, that there was no rape, and that they should be glad they have a temperamental husband" (Szulc, 2013: 39). "The media, the police, the courts, health services workers, and even psychologists, all too frequently perpetuate rape victim stereotypes. The belief that the woman is guilty, has done something wrong, and should be ashamed, remains very deeply rooted in our society." (Piotrowska & Synakiewicz, 2011:6) This is one reason why rape victims often decide against lodging a complaint.

The arguments raised by proponents of continuing to prosecute rape on complaints filed by victims are telling in this context. They obviously point out the possibility of avoiding any feelings of shame on the part of the victim. Having established a priori that the victim should feel ashamed, her refusal to do so is taken to mean that she is promiscuous and has most likely contributed to her own rape. That feelings of shame are precisely what should be expected from the perpetrator is not even considered. Feminist circles have long been calling to have rape prosecuted on an indictment issued by the public prosecutor instead of on a complaint filed by the victim, claiming that such a change is essential. A strong line of criticism has developed against retaining the prosecution of rape on complaint. The was based on the assumption that having to lodge an application would discourage victims from reporting this crime. The vast majority of crimes in Poland are prosecuted on an indictment issued by the public prosecutor. Law enforcement agencies institute and conduct proceedings ex officio. No one is proposing that victims of crimes such as robbery, theft, assault, counterfeiting, and bribery be given the option of deciding whether or not to launch prosecutions in the interests of their feelings of shame. An additional problem lies in the difficulties in understanding the differences between a private complaint procedure and a procedure on a complaint filed by the injured party. Private complaint procedure for such crimes as defamation and insult leaves the decision as to whether or not to launch criminal proceedings to the injured party. The injured party is additionally obliged to prepare and prosecute a private bill of indictment. Procedure on complaint, per contra, is restricted to ensuring that the right of the injured party to decide whether or not criminal proceedings are to be launched is honored. The proceedings themselves are conducted as per a procedure initiated by the public prosecutor. In practice, this means that preparing and prosecuting the indictment both lie within the jurisdiction of the public prosecutor (Gardocki, 2011: 60–61; Grzegorczyk & Tylman, 2003: 273–297).

Unfortunately, this distinction is not obvious given the low level of legal awareness in Poland and procedure on complaint is often equated with private complaint procedure. This often makes the victim additionally afraid that she will have to provide evidence for the court.

Police statistics for 2012 show that the number of proceedings initiated for rape was just over three times higher than for homicide and much lower than for other types of crime (cf. Table 1). Almost 2,000 rapes are reported in Poland every year. Victimological studies, however, provide grounds for estimating that the number of rapes actually committed exceed this by a factor of ten. Only around 200 sentences on average are handed down in rape cases every year and more than 60 % of cases are dismissed because the perpetrator cannot be identified. It is also alarming that the victim is usually nothing more than an evidentiary item during the trial and not an individual for whom support and assistance should be paramount (Borkowska & Płatek, 2011: 22).

A debate on the rights of rape victims and the mechanisms for protecting them eventually led to amendments being made to the Criminal Code and to the procedure on complaint and private complaint procedure for rape in 2013. The debate, however, has not died down. Only time will tell whether these legislative changes will change the way practitioners in the justice system work or have any effect on public opinion.

Table 1 Rape as opposed to other crimes—initiated and concluded proceedings

Type of crime	Initiated proceedings	Concluded proceedings
Homicide	566	582
Rape	1,786	1,432
Wilfully causing great suffering or serious injury to body or health	16,874	15,478
Economic crimes	82,328	141,483
Traffic offences	163,433	155,906

3.3 Domestic Violence as Seen by the Polish Public

The next example of a wide-ranging and controversial public debate concerned crimes of violence against close family members, the penalty for which is in Art. 207 of the Polish Criminal Code. As mentioned earlier, this is also covered by a separate Act on Countering Domestic Violence. As with rape, the victims of this crime are mostly women, although children are very often direct and indirect victims as well. Social stereotypes and the opinions of politicians on the need to protect victims are most clearly manifested in the work on amending the Act, described in the first part of the text. Despite the alarming pronouncements of NGOs, seconded by any number of experts involved in preventing and counteracting domestic violence, that the rights of victims needed to be strengthened and that, above all, victims needed to be guaranteed a real possibility of being separated from the offender, arguments that the amended Act would lead to an unacceptable level of state intrusion into the fabric of the family and its professed values and parenting mechanisms carried the day.

Prohibiting the hitting of children and making it possible for a police officer or social worker to remove a child from its family in the event of a direct threat to its life or health as a result of violence sparked the most heated social controversies ever shown in the media or manifested in street demonstrations. Parenting became an issue in which almost everybody became a self-appointed expert. Those against the prohibition on corporal punishment could be divided into those who saw it as useful and effective and those who did not really accept it but who nevertheless considered banning it pointless and ineffectual (MSU, 2008). The issue sparked a wide-ranging discussion. The addition of the following to the Family and Guardianship Code unleashed a barrage of criticism: "It shall be prohibited for individuals who execute parental authority or a guardianship or custody over a minor to resort to corporal punishments." The Ministry of Justice and the Legislative Council to the Prime Minister were against introducing the prohibition on striking children during the interdepartmental consultations on the amendments. In their view, the law in force at the time, which mandated that children be raised "by respecting their rights and dignity," was sufficient. The then Minister of Justice, Zbigniew Ćwiąkalski, said that "if a separate prohibition on striking children were introduced, we would do nothing else but look at formal complaints, which would then be used in divorce cases." The Commissioner for Civil Rights Protection, Janusz Kochanowski, added that, in his view, parents could punish children by spanking so long as they "did so lovingly." Roman Wieruszewski, Director of the Poznań Human Rights Centre, Polish Academy of Sciences, responded: "that the Commissioner, who should be upholding rights, would express himself this way is a sure sign that we need an explicitly worded prohibition" (Monkos, 2008).

It is worth mentioning that the original plan to insert the controversial provision prohibiting the physical punishment of children would also have prohibited "inflicting mental suffering and other forms of humiliation on children." These other provisions were quietly withdrawn behind the closed doors of parliamentary committee rooms without any heated discussions. Despite having finally been introduced into Polish law, the vigorously debated prohibition on striking children has made little practical difference. Research conducted in 2013 revealed that over 70 % of Poles were unaware that striking children had been legally proscribed since 2010. Spanking was accepted as an effective parenting tool by more than 60 % of respondents. Considerably more people admitted to not knowing about the legal prohibition on using physical force on children than had been the case in 2012. Only 29 % of those surveyed claimed to know this (8 percentage points less than in 2012) (Gawlik, 2013).

Inserting this provision into the Act on Countering Domestic Violence and delegated legislation created quite a firestorm. A lot of declarations and protests against this regulation were posted on Internet portals (Protest against the Act, 2010). Comments such as the following appeared on Internet forums: "Scandal. Won't be long before they'll be able to take them [children] away for the beliefs their parents are instilling in their children, (...) this is socialism also communism—they've always tried to smash the value that is the family, (...) this is not about helping the family, this is about wrecking the family. These thugs feel entitled to make decisions about us and we just shrug our shoulders (...) a scandal and a betrayal of the Nation" (Wybranowski, 2013). The media only publicized cases where the intervention of a police officer or social worker was controversial or completely unwarranted (Ula, 2013). Situations where removing a child from its family was necessarily and eliminated the threat to its life or health that existing violence was causing went unreported by the media and unnoticed by public opinion.

Signing the Convention on preventing and combating violence against women and domestic violence also aroused social misgivings. On the one hand, some argued for the necessity of strengthening the rights of women who had become victims of physical, mental and sexual abuse, usually at the hands of their partners. On the other hand, however, those against signing the Convention, and especially those aligned with right-wing, pro-Catholic political groups, argued that depriving women of their traditional roles as wives and mothers forced them to adopt "unhealthy" feminist attitudes. The lower house of the Polish parliament found it difficult to resolve the issue. The upshot was that Poland signed the Convention but did not ratify it. There were also dissenting voices in the Ministry of Justice. Deputy Minister Michał Królikowski warned against the "diktat of aggressive feminism" and demands that "threaten a radical social revolution" (Gąsior, 2014).

The parliamentary grouping "Stop ideologii gender" (Stop Gender Ideology), which proclaimed itself strongly opposed towards an ideology acknowledged as harmful and discriminatory, was formed against the backdrop of these discussions (Kania, 2014). There is a widespread view among that particular section of public opinion that "the Convention obliges [its signatories] to actively eradicate violence against women by means of offensive and aggressive changes to social and cultural norms, and the eradication of biases, customs, tradition, culture, religion and 'honor' based on a stereotypical model of the roles of men and women" (Trojanowska, 2013). Neither is there any shortage of contrary opinion to the effect that "The Convention of the Council of Europe on preventing and combating violence against women and domestic violence constitutes an important tool in the struggle against this behavior, contributes to victims of violence being better protected, and increases the rate of detection and punishment of this type of crime" (Ratyfikujmy Konwencję [...], 2013). These discussions on the need to ratify the convention led to an exchange on the topic of feminism, which frequently descended into irrationality and was characterized by a highly charged emotional atmosphere. The sociologist and rhetorician Jacek Wasilewski, observing that the word "feminist," had acquired the property of a "new insult" in public language, said that he did not find this surprising "as we generally consider ourselves very family oriented and declare this to be the value most important to us. The feminist is a threat because she tears down what we hold dear. When she is against domestic violence, she disturbs a harmonious arrangement in which nobody should meddle in our affairs and in which we all should bear our own cross. When she is in favor of equal rights, she disturbs a harmonious arrangement in which the man is the head and the woman the neck" (Wittenberg, 2013). Sylwia Chutnik, president of the MaMa Foundation and a feminists, believes that society too often forget that it is thanks to feminists having been active in Poland since the nineteenth century that women are now entitled to universal education and have the right to suffrage and employment when discussing this topic (Wittenberg, 2013).

After the constitutional and political changes in Poland in the 1990s political language, or to put it more broadly, the language of public debate, "became a counterpoint in which the alternation of roles of transmitter and receiver is one of the sources of the polyphony of texts, i.e. their variation in both form and content." Most statements on politics, rights and social problems, however, are directed towards the bulk consumer and the language resources they use are selected on the criterion of their persuasiveness. These statements are meant to induce people to do things or hold opinions compatible with the intentions of the broadcaster, to change their attitudes and behavior, and to adopt viewpoints and accept the value system pushed by the broadcaster (Kamińska-Szmaj, 2001: 7–8). The selected contexts of public debate designated above are concerned with making sure that victims of crime have real and effective protection mechanisms. They perfectly demonstrate that a solution that appears obvious and rational to one person may well be seen by another as a threat to his/her fundamental values. Discussion on the form the law should take is especially essential in a democratic country. However, this discussion seems to be characterized by too much populism and emotion and too few arguments based on facts and supported by studies.

4 How the Judicial Authorities Safeguard the Rights of Crime Victims in Poland

The legislative changes that have granted more rights to victims of crime and the public discourse that has accompanied their implementation were discussed in previous chapters. This chapter presents research findings that show how the police and the judicial system respect the rights of victims in practice. The legal consideration of the protected interests of the injured party is one of the purposes of criminal proceedings and is provided for in Art. 2 of the Polish Criminal Procedure Code. Whether this purpose has actually been fulfilled, however, is not clear. The chapter is divided into three parts. The first part describes how the rights of people harmed by crime are observed in criminal proceedings (in court and during preliminary proceedings). The second raises the problem of ensuring that these people are awarded damages and restitution for the injury they have suffered. The third focuses on two specific types of crime, viz. rape and intimate partner violence, and shows that victims are in fact not guaranteed protection on account of their gender. This would appear to be particularly relevant in light of the current debate in Poland on gender equality and ensuring that women are adequately protected.

4.1 The Rights of People Harmed by Crime in Criminal Proceedings

The provisions of the Polish Criminal Procedure Code give the impression that the procedural rights of victims are by and large generally safeguarded. A very different picture emerges, however, once we become acquainted with the way these provisions are applied in practice. The main thing to note is that victims are not overly active during proceedings—either at the preliminary stage or later in court. Unfortunately, there is a lack of statistical data on the number of victims who take an active part in criminal proceedings. Studies on this topic, which examine the record of criminal cases, have found that cases in which at least one victim has been active account for a mere 30 % of all relevant cases (Dudka & Artymiak, 2012: 62–64). Victims have mostly been involved as a source of evidence in preliminary proceedings, i.e., they have testified as witnesses summoned by the police or the public prosecutor, but have not otherwise been very actively involved. Only 5 % have submitted applications to have the investigating officers initiate further action and fewer than 2 % have reviewed the case file. Victims have only become more active when the prosecutor discontinued proceedings, in which case 20 % of those entitled to do so have lodged formal complaints (Dudka, 2006: 228–240). Victims mostly justify their passivity on the grounds that they do not know their rights (20 %), and that judicial bodies prevent their doing anything (20 %), that they do not have the time (12 %), and/or that they believe that any participation on their part would be futile (17 %). This ignorance on the part of victims should come as no surprise. Most are technically advised of their rights and entitlements, but this advice consists of excerpts from the applicable regulations, which are written in opaque legalese. They often only get to read the document and are not even given a copy. Only half those surveyed remember being advised of their rights. This means that the other half were only advised incidentally if at all. As many as two-thirds of those who were advised found the advice they were given either wholly or partially incomprehensible. People who have been victims of crime have the same opinion on the clarity of advice they were given regardless of whether it was furnished by the police, the public prosecutor or the court (Dudka, 2006: 254–260). The victim can therefore be said to be "merely an appendage to a criminal trial and not, as a general rule, a particularly welcome one. This is because he/she involves extra work, e.g. being notified of trial dates (...), the risk that the auxiliary prosecutor will drag out the proceedings (...). On the other hand, it is apparent that victims themselves are not particularly interested in taking part in proceedings and their knowledge, which could be their true function, is not all that great" (Dudka & Artymiak, 2012: 78–79).

The majority of passive victims (over 70 %) justify their inaction in court by saying that there is little they can achieve on their own without legal representation. The police convince them of this by arguing that effective action is not possible without the assistance of a lawyer (Dudka, 2006: 261–263). At the same time, studies show that even legal representation does not have much of an effect on safeguarding of the interests of the victim, as lawyers do very little (up to two-thirds of them do not participate in hearings) and the quality of the pleadings they draft is poor (Dudka & Artymiak, 2012: 65–70, 96).

The way the police and prosecutors behave towards victims is also problematic and leads to secondary victimization. The police inform them at the outset that their chances of finding the perpetrator(s) are minimal and discourage them from reporting a crime. Victimization studies show that up to 43 % of victims who have reported crimes to the police are dissatisfied with that institution (more than half the victims of crimes of aggression share this opinion). The rate of satisfaction of victims of serious crimes in Poland is far below the European average according to the International Crime Victims Survey (van Dijk, van Kesteren, & Smit, 2007: 113–116). The main charges are failure to find the perpetrators and recover lost property (60 %) and either not accepting crime reports or processing them in a dilatory manner (20 % overall and 25 % of robbery victims). As many as half the victims of assaults and robberies cite additional reasons for their critical appraisal of the police, e.g., rudeness, failing to ensure their safety, and taking too long to arrive (Marczewski, 2008).

The way the authorities treat victims as tools when carrying out functions connected with legal proceedings is another matter for concern. As mentioned above, victims are primarily viewed as a "source of evidence." As many as 95 % are therefore examined as witnesses—up to 15 % are examined several times in the course of a single preliminary hearing (several examinations have been conducted in less than 5 days in some cases).[6] Moreover, some functions amount to a violation of the victim's dignity. Placing the victim in the line-up with a suspect is actually

[6] In one case, the victim was examined 8 times as a witness, subjected to a medical examination, and made to participate in 3 line-ups with a witness and in 2 with a suspect. Moreover, a single examination of a rape victim is rare. Two are the norm and there are often three—and that is just in the preliminary proceedings (Dudka, 2012).

done quite frequently (occurring in 18 % of surveyed cases), although it should be kept to an absolute minimum, despite being legally permissible.[7] There have been cases where victims have been repeatedly subjected to medical examinations, professional psychologists have often participated in examinations of victims, and victims have been subjected to psychological examinations (the purpose of which have not been to support the victim but to assess his/her psychological state, intellectual development, and capacity to observe events) (Dudka, 2006: 229–230, 240–252).

Another problem, and one which is becoming increasingly apparent, is that of safeguarding the rights of victims in fast-track proceedings. The number of such proceedings has increased prodigiously in Poland over the last few years and more and more accused are being convicted without a hearing by voluntarily submitting to a penalty (during a trial in which the victim need not participate) or by negotiating a penalty with the prosecutor (in which case the victim can object to the sentence). Data furnished by the General Prosecutor show that from 1 January 2007 to 30 June 2013, prosecutors took advantage of the first option with almost 54 % of the indictments filed in court (the court allowed these applications in 82 % of cases) and 9.8 % of those convicted were convicted under the second option. Altogether, one of these two options was employed for 51 % of all convictions in Poland during this period.[8] At the same time, studies show that victims are only marginally involved in these proceedings. Of the 207,169 cases with negotiated convictions brought to court in 2010, victims were only involved in the proceedings of 119 (0.06 %) of them and only as a party in 42 (0.02 %). Of the 35,592 accused who voluntarily submitted to a penalty, victims were only involved in the cases of 292 of them (0.8 %) and only in 71 as a party (0.2 %). These studies show that even in cases where victims have some involvement in the proceedings, it is not significant. Moreover, victims have little say in the size of the penalty imposed by the court. Victims are understandably most interested in remedying and/or being compensated for the damage inflicted as a result of the crime (Gardocka, 2012). Given the data presented above, it should come as no surprise that the vast majority (86 %) are of the view that the accused has considerably more rights and a higher status than the victim in criminal proceedings. Moreover, as many as two-thirds do not consider the sentences handed down in their cases to have been just. The only people who have a positive opinion of the courts are those who have had the damage and/or injuries inflicted by the crime remedied or compensated by the offender through the proceedings (Dudka, 2006: 262–263).

---

[7] Such activities should be the exception—especially in the cases surveyed. Being subjected to examinations has become tantamount to illegal deprivation of freedom. Presumably, the trauma that such a crime causes the victim and his/her reluctance to meet the offender again are not trivial.

[8] Data from the General Prosecutor to the Deputy Marshall of the Senate dated 23 January 2013 (No. PG II P 070/1/13).

4.2 Ensuring That People Harmed by Crime Are Compensated for Damage or Injury

Apart from having the offender punished, victims, as one of the main reasons that criminal proceedings are conducted, are entitled to restitution in the form of having the damage and/or injury they have suffered repaired and/or remedied. This should therefore be one of the aims of the justice system as well. It is worth emphasizing that being made to remedy the damage inflicted on the victim is one of the punitive measures that can be imposed on the offender—either in lieu of or in addition to a penalty. There is a lack of data on imposing this measure in addition to a penalty, although it is very seldom imposed on its own (77 people in 1999–2012) (Błachnio-Parzych, 2009; Ministry of Justice, 2013).[9]

Criminal proceedings also give the victim the option of seeking damages from the offender (i.e., an "adhesion procedure"). There are, however, few such proceedings and their number has been steadily falling since 2005 (from over 8,371 cases in 2005 to 4,882 cases in 2010, i.e., 0.2 % of all criminal cases). Even when this procedure is invoked, the courts are more concerned with determining the proceedings quickly than they are with compensating the victim. This procedure has only been wholly or partly allowed in 47 % of cases (Dudka & Artymiak, 2012: 55, 98–100). Scholars are unanimous that this institution is "dying."

The victim's next option to be at least partly compensated for the consequences of a crime is to receive compensation from the state. This was only introduced in Poland in 2005 and the range of assistance available to victims is extraordinarily restrictive, both in terms of the formal requirements that have to be fulfilled and the paucity of support available (capped at approx. 3,000 EUR). These considerable restrictions and formalities, combined with a lack of any public awareness campaign,[10] have resulted in extraordinarily few applications for compensation being filed and as many as 73 % of those that have been filed have been disallowed (Łagodziński, 2011; Mazowiecka, 2012; Niełaczna, 2007) (Table 2).

The compensation awarded by the courts is paltry in the extreme. The average amount awarded in 2006–2009 was a meager 215 EUR. This obviously varies in particular cases—from 21 EUR to the 3,000 EUR maximum—but only two-thirds of compensation payouts exceed 230 EUR and one third 1,250 EUR. Amounts below 1,250 EUR have even been awarded when the victim has been killed. The highest awards of damages, viz. above 2,500 EUR, were paid to people who

[9] Although in the overwhelming majority of cases involving property damage, the offender repaired such damage either prior to judgement or by order of the court (together, this occurred in 94 % of cases) when the court ordered a conditional stay of proceedings (Jankowski, Momot, & Ważny, 2011: 32).

[10] The inordinately complicated form that has to be filed for compensation is also worth noting. This is incomprehensible to many victims. The courts have ordered applicants to put additional information in the form in 73 % of cases. This means that it must be completely incomprehensible to the public (Mazowiecka, 2012: 225).

Table 2 Cases for compensation for victims of crime 2006–2010 (Mazowiecka, 2012: 201)

	2006	2007	2008	2009	2010
Applications filed	329	251	148	164	161
Cases examined together, including:	232	272	174	135	175
Compensation allowed	45	60	26	29	43
Compensation disallowed	179	191	137	97	116

suffered grievous injury to health (two-thirds of victims in these cases). The legislature justified the restrictive compensation provisions by stating that this form of relief for victims would cost the state approx. 17,500,000 EUR annually. Actual payouts have been approx. 0.2 % of the projected amount (Łagodziński, 2011: 135; Mazowiecka, 2012: 278–279, 284–285).[11]

Judges and prosecutors who have applied the provisions of this legislation were asked for their assessment. The overwhelming majority regarded them as favorable to victims in claiming compensation and half of them did not find any shortcomings or irregularities. Sixty percent saw no need for the prosecutor to be involved in the proceedings and as many as 53 % did not see the need for the victim to have any legal representation either.[12] Judges also gave their opinion on what they believed was "just and appropriate compensation." They considered that it "should be credible and proportionate to the consequences of the damage or injury that has occurred," "appropriate to the physical and psychological suffering the victim has endured," "should compensate all costs" and should "cover all damages arising from the crime and compensate for pain and moral injury" (Niełaczna, 2007: 147–155). These are clearly reasonable desiderata that the parliament should take into consideration when amending this piece of legislation.

The way the Act on Compensation operates can generally be seen as the state's contribution to secondary victimization of crime victims. The provisions are drafted to severely restrict the number and categories of people entitled to relief, to impose a raft of onerous conditions (e.g., detailed documentation of medical expenditure, as only costs and loss of earnings can be reimbursed as compensation) and to significantly limit the maximum amount of compensation paid. As such they should be regarded as degrading for victims.[13] On top of that are the beggarly amounts of

---

[11] While Poland pays approx. 140,000 PLN p.a. in compensation, the Netherlands (to take one example) paid 12.7 million EUR to some 8,000 people in 2013 alone (Criminal Injuries [...], 2014). The amounts paid have been increasing every year since 1995 (Moolenaar, 2006: 31).

[12] Lawyers have seldom appeared in compensation cases. However, the courts have awarded the victim the monetary relief claimed in 68 % of the cases where they were present (Mazowiecka, 2012: 227–228).

[13] This has brought about enormous variation in the circumstances of victims. For example, wealthy people, who can afford a dental implant after losing a tooth as a result of a crime, will have their costs reimbursed, while poor people, who cannot meet these expenses upfront are left without any support. Some examples of the compensation that has been allowed in different cases: 2,525 vs. 86 EUR for having a tooth knocked out; 1,635 EUR for having two front teeth knocked out and sustaining a fractured skull; and 35 EUR for a disabled person who sustained multiple injuries, a fractured skull and a broken tooth (Mazowiecka, 2012: 323–325).

damages that are actually awarded. These can only be humiliating for victims. What needs to be borne in mind here is that this applies to victims of serious and extremely brutal crimes that have in most cases been committed wilfully and aggressively.

Studies on the way court proceedings are conducted also depict them as victimizing: protracted proceedings (court proceedings last 5–7 months on average and the longest case has taken 40 months);[14] victims being misinformed/deceived by the police and/or prosecutors as to the possibility of receiving compensation when the provisions make it patently clear that there is no entitlement thereto (e.g., because the deed in question was committed prior to the effective date of the provisions as set out in the Act); the justifications of court rulings (e.g., claiming that the victim suffered "too minor injuries" to merit relief); and allowing offenders to participate in the proceedings, even though the provisions expressly prohibit this. Two extreme cases of the dismal treatment meted out to victims by Polish courts are worth citing by way of example. In the first case, the victim was a girl who had undergone 3.5 months of intensive psychological treatment after being raped. The court first called experts to check whether her injuries were permanent and then refused to grant compensation. In the second case, a robbery victim, who was also undergoing psychiatric treatment, withdrew her application for compensation because she admitted that it would—as she put it in her application—"take too great a toll on her nerves" (Mazowiecka, 2012: 326).

Courts also impose a lot of conditions and obligations on victims during compensation proceedings. This concerns for example the requirement that damages for harm suffered be exacted from the offender. In some cases, courts have refused to award compensation on the grounds that victims have failed to exercise due diligence in doing so (some offenders were in prison at the time, which made exacting damages a nigh impossibility). Courts have sometimes additionally made victims pay the costs of the proceedings or have not exempted them. As an extreme example, a court in one particular case told a retired woman on a pension of approx. 170 EUR per month that she should have saved the money to pay for court proceedings (Mazowiecka, 2012: 239–247).

What all this shows is that Polish criminal procedure makes it virtually impossible for a victim to obtain damages from either the offender or the state. Victims of crime are pretty much left to fend for themselves when it comes to pursuing their claims and coping with trauma. It is worth adding that while many other countries are engaged in discussions on the effectiveness of elements of assistance and its availability for particular kinds of victims (cf. Zweig & Yahner, 2013), Poland does not offer victims any effective assistance of any kind provided by public institutions

[14] It has to be stressed that even in cases where applications are dismissed as unfounded by virtue of being inconsistent with the Act, these proceedings take 5 months on average and the longest has taken almost 30 months. Additional work is frequently demanded from victims in these proceedings, even though a declaration that their applications are unfounded would be extremely simple in most cases, as the provisions of the Act make this plain (Mazowiecka, 2012: 228 and foll.).

or financed by public money. Victims of crime can only obtain relief from NGO's, but there are very few that operate in this area and the assistance they provide is often inadequate as well. Most of those profiled are for victims of intimate partner violence and violence against women.

4.3 Protecting Women from Violence: Rape and Intimate Partner Violence

Protecting women from violence should be one of the main administrative functions of government. Unfortunately, this issue is viewed through a political and ideological prism in Poland, where upholding the family and the traditional role of women in society takes center stage. Ensuring that women crime victims are protected and supported is pushed into the background. Politicizing the issue has meant that public institutions fail to carry out the functions assigned to them and treat women as means to ends. It is worth emphasizing that while either gender can obviously be a victim of both types of crime, in the case of domestic violence "women are at disproportionate risk of serious victimization. Their risk of intimate-partner violence, sexual assault, and stalking are greater than those of men. They are also at greater risk of multiple types of victimization as well as recurrent violent victimization in relationships. (. . .) 22 % of all violent offenses against women were committed by intimates versus only 4 % of violence offenses against men" (Buzawa, 2013: 36). In the case of rape, women are four times more likely to become victims than men (O'Sullivan, 2013: 4–5). Gruszczyńska (2007) points out that 16.5 % of Polish women fall victim to some form of sexual violence during their lives.

One of the main problems with which women victims of intimate partner violence or rape have to contend is the attitude of judges towards punishing offenders. The penalties imposed betray a great deal of leniency on the part of the courts. Suspended sentences are ordered in over 82 % of intimate partner violence cases (cf. Table 3).[15] A suspended sentence implies that the offender is being tested and may be combined with the imposition of specified conditions.[16] The problem is, however, that the courts only respond in half the cases where these conditions are not met and only do so reluctantly, thereby evincing "the tireless efforts the courts make to avoid ordering prison sentences" (Budyn-Kulik, 2012: 26). The suspension is not revoked—even when another crime is committed or the conditions are

[15] This compares with 55.3 % of convicted robbers receiving prison terms and 44.5 % receiving suspended sentences in 2012.

[16] These obligations mainly consist of refraining from alcohol (95 % overall) and rarely involve protecting the victim. The court has imposed an obligation to "improve behaviour towards the victim and desist from quarrelling" in 42 % of cases but has only ordered an apology to the victim in 4 %, prohibited contact in 2.5 %, and ordered the offender to vacate jointly occupied premises and not approach the victim in 1 % (Budyn-Kulik, 2009: 50).

Table 3 Number of people convicted for rape and intimate partner violence compared with overall convictions in Poland in 2012 (Ministry of Justice, 2013)

	No. of people convicted	No. of prison terms	No. of prison terms not suspended		No. of suspended prison terms	
			No.	% of penalties	No.	% of penalties
Overall figure for all crimes	408,107	265,876	41,691	10.2	224,185	54.9
Rape	718	715	462	64.3	253	35.2
Intimate partner violence	12,388	11,730	1,522	12.3	10,205	82.4

otherwise seriously violated—for one in three offenders. The suspension is only ever revoked after the probation officer assigned to the case has submitted two or even three applications (Budyn-Kulik, 2009: 51). The offender is also given a suspended penalty in as many as one in three rape cases.

The leniency of the penalties imposed on offenders is another problem associated with the judiciary. Forty six percent of the custodial sentences handed down in intimate partner violence cases do not exceed 1 year (the median term) and 97 % do not exceed 3 years, even though this offence carries a maximum prison term of 5 years. The penalties for rape are more severe but still extraordinarily lenient considering they carry a maximum prison term of 12 years. Thirty seven percent do not exceed 3 years and 87 % do not exceed 5 years. Similarly lenient penalties have been handed down in human trafficking cases where the victims were women forced into prostitution. This offence carries a prison term of from 3 to 15 years. At the same time, in all the sentences not exceeding 5 years imprisonment given to all offenders in 1999–2009, 75 % of offenders were given a sentence of 3 years or less (the minimum penalty was given in 56 % of cases and extraordinarily lenient ones in 19 %). Penalties of this order of leniency are meted out "regardless of the circumstances of the case, regardless of whether the offender trafficked in one person or many people (there were 90-odd victims in one case), regardless of whether violence or deception was used, and regardless of whether the victims were raped" (Namysłowska-Gabrysiak, 2010: 86).

The foregoing considerations lead to the conclusion that, in practice, the Polish judiciary discriminates on the basis of gender and that its members do not give any priority to protecting women. The idea of "women's contribution" to rape—by their provocative attire, their behavior (including the very fact of drinking alcohol) and their location—seems to be embedded in the consciousness of judges and police officers. Victims are said to be "tiresome" and their credibility is often assessed by police officers ("she probably wanted a relationship but then had a change of heart" or "she couldn't have been raped by her husband or boyfriend'cos that's not rape")

(Grabowska, 2011; Zaduminska, 2006).[17] Somewhat different mechanisms are at work in the case of domestic violence. This is more about contemptuous disregard and refusing to interfere in private family matters (although the woman is defined as someone who provokes violence here too).

More than half the women who report violence to the police are dissatisfied with the way the matter is dealt with. The reaction of the police to domestic violence is often a put-on (the offender is detained briefly and given a cautionary interview). Eighteen percent of victims believe the police do nothing and only one in three respondents thought they ensured their protection (e.g., by detaining the offender). Experiences like these have led to as many as two-thirds of cases of violence against women not being formally reported.[18] The reason for this is the belief, held by almost a half of victims, that the police will do nothing to help them, together with the feelings of shame and embarrassment that go with being a victim of these sorts of crimes (Gruszczyńska, 2007: 115–125).

Women who report rape frequently find the experience a negative one. Neither the police nor the health services are equipped to ensure the dignity or comfort of the victim during activities connected with court proceedings (e.g., there are no suitable rooms or people to conduct interviews or medical examinations, showers, or changes of clothes). Rape victims are treated like any other victims (Grabowska, 2011). Police offers consider dissuading women from filing crime reports a form of support. As one said: "Why would a girl like that want that sort of reputation? She's better off not filing [a report]—for her own good" (Zaduminska, 2006: 20). This inability to understand that women crime victims have special needs is typical of the Polish justice system.

Although the law occasionally envisages special assistance, this is seldom provided in practice. Ordering the offender to vacate premises jointly occupied with the victim and prohibiting contact with her can be considered moribund remedies. They are ordered together in 3 % of cases on average (Wrona, 2011).

Victims report that being treated as objects by the justice system is a problem. "In the experience of women who have been through the mill of dealing with institutions and organizations, being treated as an object and not a person mainly manifests itself on three levels: (1) being denied any control over their own affairs; (2) having the credibility of their stories and the 'knowledge' of their own experience(s) challenged; and (3) having the principles of privacy and confidentiality disregarded" (Grabowska, 2011: 129). Many in the justice system consider themselves better qualified to determine what is and what is not in the best interests of victims. In their view, victims are emotionally unable to cope with making particular decisions. This happens from the moment their report is accepted (or rejected)

---

[17] Judges have made similar appraisals in cases of women victims of human trafficking, assessing their way of life prior to falling victim to this crime and using such terms to describe them as "goods," "prostitutes," "young ladies" and "people in search of adventure" (Koss-Goryszewska, 2013; Namysłowska-Gabrysiak, 2010).

[18] Barely 1 in 19 men who use violence against women were punished for it (Gruszczyńska, 2007: 119–120).

and continues right through the proceedings, with the victim often being denied any participation. Victims are made to feel like importunate supplicants. They are treated as objects during the proceedings. What matters is not them but the "case" (Grabowska, 2011: 180).

Conclusions and Discussion

Polish legal regulations concerning victims of crime seem to have been passed primarily to ensure that the country meets its international obligations, especially under EU law. It is because of this that compensation provisions have been enacted and rape prosecutions on complaint of the injured party have been repealed. Polish law can therefore be said to meet the minimum European requirements. However, it does not do the slightest bit more than that and has done absolutely nothing on its own initiative. The legislature was clearly not guided by the protection or welfare of the victim when enacting these new provisions (contrary to whatever official justifications were given) as the provisions themselves are sometimes structured in such a way as to lead to secondary victimization. By way of example, when issuing a restraining order prohibiting the offender from approaching the victim, the court can impose a range of conditions and restrictions on the victim, who should be given protection, not subjected to additional control. Moreover, the victim can be "punished" for violating these conditions by having the prohibition on the offender approaching her revoked (Bieńkowska, 2012).

The minimalist approach of the legislation is exacerbated by poor implementation by law enforcement, prosecutors and the judiciary. Many victims are dissatisfied by their treatment by the police. Information given to victims is often inadequate. Sentences of judges regarding victim compensation tend to be minimalist as well.

The standard of public debate on protecting victims of crime is no less a problem, being little more than an exercise in political point scoring while paying lip service to ensuring that victims are protected and supported. Victims are frequently objectified and blamed for contributing to crime. Moreover, a lot of arguments steeped in conservative ideology creep into these discussions as well, e.g., demands that women be protected from violence are decried as "aggressive feminist diktat."

As a society, we still approach victims of crime with a great deal of caution and distrust and forget that they are in need of protection and support. Instead of understanding, we look for their "specific complicity" in the crime and often accuse them of contributing to, or at least provoking it (blaming the victim). Most crimes cause fear and suffering and leave a feeling of powerlessness and inferiority in their wake. Those involving violence towards close relatives are especially painful to the victim. That is why we should be giving victims all the care and support we can, instead of protesting that institutional

(continued)

guarantees of their rights are breaking up families and violating our cultural autonomy.

The findings presented above show that the interests of victims are not given any priority in the Polish justice system. Victims are objectified and mainly viewed as a "source of evidence." Whatever they do is readily marginalized in criminal proceedings (as broadly understood). This convinces them that they are not in any position to defend their own interests. It is therefore not enough to say that nothing is being done to empower victims. The problem of the Polish justice system not ensuring that victims are treated as a person and not as an object has to be emphasized as well, as this has effectively vitiated their legal rights.

References

Amir, M. (1967). Victim precipitated forcible rape. *Journal of Criminology, Criminal Law and Police, 58*(4), 493–502.

Bieńkowska, E. (2012). Wiktymizacja wtórna – geneza, istota i rola w przekształcaniu polityki traktowania ofiar przestępstw [Secondary victimisation: Its origin, its essence and its role in reforming crime victim policies]. In L. Mazowiecka (Ed.), *Wiktymizacja wtórna – geneza, istota i rola w przekształcaniu polityki traktowania ofiar przestępstw [Secondary victimisation: Its origin, its essence and its role in reforming crime victim policies]* (pp. 53–79). Warsaw: Wolters Kluwer.

Błachnio-Parzych, A. (2009). Samoistny środek karny jako instrument racjonalnej polityki karnej [The independent penal measure as a rational penal policy tool]. In J. Jakubowska-Hara & J. Skupiński (Eds.), *Alternatywy pozbawienia wolności w polskiej polityce karnej [Alternatives to custodial sentences in Polish criminal policy]* (pp. 142–169). Warsaw: Wydawnictwo Naukowe Scholar.

Borkowska, O., & Płatek, M. (2011). Skala przestępstwa zgwałcenia w Polsce [The scale of rape in Poland]. In J. Piotrowska & A. Synakiewicz (Eds.), *Dość Milczenia. Przemoc seksualna wobec kobiet i problem gwałtu w Polsce [Enough silence: Sexual violence against women and the issue of rape in Poland]* (pp. 10–22). Warsaw: Fundacja Feminoteka.

Budyn-Kulik, M. (2009). *Przemoc w rodzinie – analiza wiktymologiczna oraz prawnokarne środki przeciwdziałania [Domestic violence: Victimological analysis and criminal law preventive measures]*. Warsaw: Instytut Wymiaru Sprawiedliwości.

Budyn-Kulik, M. (2012). *Oddziaływanie na sprawców przemocy w rodzinie przez sądy poprzez nakładanie obowiązku uczestnictwa w programach korekcyjno-edukacyjnych [The effect of court orders to participate in correctional and educational programs on domestic violence offenders]*. Warsaw: Instytut Wymiaru Sprawiedliwości.

Buzawa, E. S. (2013). Victims of domestic violence. In R. Davis, A. J. Lurigo, & S. Herman (Eds.), *Victims of crime* (pp. 29–56). Los Angeles: Sage.

Criminal Injuries Compensation Fund pays out € 12.7 million. (2014). Retrieved from http://www.government.nl/news/2014/03/17/criminal-injuries-compensation-fund-pays-out-12-7-million.html.

Dudka, K. (2006). *Skuteczność instrumentów ochrony praw pokrzywdzonych w postępowaniu przygotowawczym w świetle badań empirycznych [The effectiveness of legal measures to protect victims in preliminary proceedings in light of empirical studies]*. Lublin: Wydawnictwo UMCS.

Dudka, K. (2012). *Podstawy umorzenia i odmowy wszczęcia postępowania karnego w sprawach o przestępstwa zgwałcenia [Grounds for discontinuing and refusing to initiate criminal proceedings in rape cases]*. Warsaw: Instytut Wymiaru Sprawiedliwości.

Dudka, K., & Artymiak, G. (2012). *Sytuacja pokrzywdzonego w procesie karnym, ze szczególnym uwzględnieniem roli oskarżyciela posiłkowego i powoda cywilnego [The status of the victim in a criminal trial with a focus on the roles of auxiliary prosecutor and civil plaintiff]*. Warsaw: Instytut Wymiaru Sprawiedliwości.

Gardocka, T. (2012). *Skazanie bez rozprawy w kontekście praw pokrzywdzonego [Judgement without trial in the context of victims' rights]*. Warsaw: Instytut Wymiaru Sprawiedliwości.

Gardocki, L. (2011). *Prawo karne [Criminal law]*. Warsaw: C.H. BECK.

Garland, D. (2001). *The culture of control: Crime and social order in contemporary society*. Oxford: Oxford University Press.

Gąsior, M. (2014). *Pracuje w rządzie i przy episkopacie, napisał książkę z apb Hoserem [He works for the government and the episcopate, and wrote a book with abp. Hoser]*. Retrieved from http://natemat.pl/85903,pracuje-w-rzadzie-i-przy-episkopacie-napisal-ksiazke-z-abp-hoserem-kim-jest-wiceminister-sprawiedliwosci-michal-krolikowski.

Gawlik, P. (2013). Polacy nie zdaja sobie sprawy z zakazu bicia dzieci [Poles do not understand the prohibition on striking children]. *Gazeta Wyborcza*. Retrieved from http://wyborcza.pl/1,75478,14974844,Polacy_nie_zdaja_sobie_sprawy_z_zakazu_bicia_dzieci_.html.

Grabowska, M. (2011). Pomiędzy wiedzą a stereotypem: Instytucje publiczne i organizacje pomocowe wobec problemu gwałtu: Raport z badań [Between knowledge and stereotype: Public institutions and aid organisations on rape: Research report]. In J. Piotrowska & A. Synakiewicz (Eds.), *Dość milczenia: Przemoc seksualna wobec kobiet i problem gwałtu w Polsce [Enough silence: Sexual violence against women and the issue of rape in Poland]* (pp. 121–190). Warsaw: Fundacja Feminoteka.

Gruszczyńska, B. (2007). *Przemoc wobec kobiet w Polsce: Aspekty prawnokryminologiczne [Violence against women in Poland: Legal and criminological aspects]*. Warsaw: Wolters Kluwer.

Grzegorczyk, T., & Tylman, J. (2003). *Polskie Postępowanie karne [Polish criminal procedure]*. Warsaw: Lexis Nexis.

Jankowski, M., Momot, S., & Ważny, A. (2011). *Warunkowe umorzenie postępowania [Conditional stay of procedure]*. Warsaw: Instytut Wymiaru Sprawiedliwości.

Jordan, J. (2013). From victim to survivor – and from survivor to victim: Reconceptualising the survivor journey. *Sexual Abuse in Australia and New Zealand, 5*(2), 48–56.

Kamińska-Szmaj, I. (2001). *Słowa na wolności [Words at large]*. Wrocław: Wydawnictwo Europa.

Kania, S. (2014). *Kempa: nie dyskryminuję ideologii gender [Kempa: I do not discriminate against gender ideology]*. Retrieved from http://www.wprost.pl/ar/432321/Kempa-Nie-dyskryminuje-ideologii-gender/.

Klaus, W., Rzeplińska, I., & Woźniakowska-Fajst, D. (2011). Development of punitiveness in Poland. In H. Kury & E. Shea (Eds.), *Punitiveness: International developments* (pp. 245–268). Bochum: Universitaetsverlag Brockmeyer.

Koss-Goryszewska, M. (2013). Wizerunek ofiary handlu kobietami w krajowym orzecznictwie karnym na podstawie analizy wyroków w sprawach o handel ludźmi w latach 1997–2009 [The image of the victims of trafficking in women in Polish case law based on an analysis of the judgments in human trafficking cases 1997–2009]. *Archiwum Kryminologii, 35*, 156–187.

Łagodziński, S. (2011). Praktyka przyznawania świadczeń na podstawie ustawy z 7. 7. 2005 r. o państwowej kompensacie przysługującej ofiarom niektórych przestępstw [The practice of admitting testimony on the basis of the Act on state compensation for victims of selected crimes of 7 July 2005]. *Prawo w działaniu, 9*, 119–141.

Marczewski, M. (2008). Powody niezadowolenia ofiar z przyjęcia zgłoszenia przestępstwa [Why victims are dissatisfied with the reception they receive when they report a crime]. In A. Siemaszko (Ed.), *Geografia występku i strachu: Polskie Badanie Przestępczości '07 [Geography of crime and fear: Polish crime studies 2007]* (pp. 53–60). Warsaw: Instytut Wymiaru Sprawiedliwości.

Mazowiecka, L. (2012). *Państwowa kompensata dla ofiar przestępstw [State compensation for victims of crime]*. Warsaw: Wolters Kluwer.

Ministry of Justice. (2013). *Dorośli prawomocnie skazani wg rodzajów przestępstw i wymiaru kary w latach 2008–2012 [Finally sentenced adults by type of crime and size of penalty 2008–2012]*. Warsaw: Ministry of Justice. Retrieved from http://isws.ms.gov.pl/pl/baza-statystyczna/opracowania-wieloletnie/download,2577,1.html.

Monkos, A. (2008). Ćwiąkalski nie chce zakazu bicia dzieci [Ćwiąkalski does not want to prohibit the striking of children]. *Dziennik.pl*. Retrieved from http://wiadomosci.dziennik.pl/polityka/artykuly/134195,cwiakalski-nie-chce-zakazu-bicia-dzieci.html.

Moolenaar, D. (2006). *Expenditure on crime in the Netherlands*. The Haag: WODC. Retrieved from http://wodc.nl/onderzoeksdatabase/me2006-1-expenditure-on-crime-in-the-netherlands.aspx.

MSU. (2008). *Polacy podzieleni w kwestii bicia dzieci [Poles divided on the issue of striking children]*. Retrieved from http://wiadomosci.onet.pl/kraj/polacy-podzieleni-w-kwestii-bicia-dzieci/ttp02.

Namysłowska-Gabrysiak, B. (2010). *Analiza orzeczeń sądowych za lata 1999–2009 w sprawach dotyczących handlu ludźmi z art. 253 k.k. oraz wybranych losowo spraw z art. 204 § 4 k.k. [Analysis of judgments in human trafficking cases decided under CC Art. 253 and randomly selected cases decided under CC Art. 204 § 4 1999–2009]*. Warsaw: Instytut Wymiaru Sprawiedliwości.

Niełaczna, M. (2007). *Kompensata dla ofiar przestępstw – prawo a praktyka: Raport z monitoringu działania ustawy o państwowej kompensacie dla ofiar niektórych przestępstw umyślnych [Compensation for victims of crime – law and practice: Monitoring report on the working of the Act on state compensation for victims of selected crimes]*. Warsaw: Stowarzyszenie Interwencji Prawnej.

O'Sullivan, C. S. (2013). Sexual violence victimization of women, men, youth, and children. In R. Davis, A. J. Lurigo, & S. Herman (Eds.), *Victims of crime* (pp. 3–28). Los Angeles: Sage.

PAP. (2013). *Burza po wpisie Guziała o gwałcie na Kabatach [Storm over Guział's Kabaty rape comments]*. Retrieved from http://tvp.info/informacje/polska/burza-po-wpisie-guziala-o-gwalcie-na-kabatach/12308702.

Piotrowska, J., & Synakiewicz, A. (2011). Wstęp [Admission]. In J. Piotrowska & A. Synakiewicz (Eds.), *Dość Milczenia: Przemoc seksualna wobec kobiet i problem gwałtu w Polsce [Enough silence: Sexual violence against women and the issue of rape in Poland]* (pp. 4–9). Warsaw: Fundacja Feminoteka.

Płatek, M. (2011). Przestępstwo zgwałcenia w świetle prawa i perspektywy osób pokrzywdzonych [Rape as viewed by victims and the law]. In J. Piotrowska & A. Synakiewicz (Eds.), *Dość Milczenia: Przemoc seksualna wobec kobiet i problem gwałtu w Polsce [Enough silence: Sexual violence against women and the issue of rape in Poland]* (pp. 23–43). Warsaw: Fundacja Feminoteka.

Protest przeciw ustawie [Protest against statute]. (2010). Retrieved from https://pl-pl.facebook.com/pages/Protest-przeciw-ustawie-u%C5%82atwiaj%C4%85cej-urz%C4%99dnikom-odbieranie-dzieci-rodzinom/352958063948.

Ratyfikujmy Konwencję Rady Europy w sprawie zapobiegania i zwalczania przemocy wobec kobiet i przemocy domowej! – Petycja [Poland ratifies Convention on combating violence against women and domestic violence! Petition]. (2013). Retrieved from http://www.niebieskalinia.pl/4862-ratyfikujmy-konwencje-rady-europy-w-sprawie-zapobiegania-i-zwalczania-przemocy-wobec-kobiet-i-przemocy-domowej-petycja.

Spurek, S. (2012). *Komentarz do ustawy z dnia 10 czerwca 2010 r. o zmianie ustawy o przeciwdziałaniu przemocy w rodzinie oraz niektórych innych ustaw: Przeciwdziałanie przemocy w rodzinie: Komentarz [Commentary on the Act on changes to the Act on countering domestic violence and certain other acts: Countering domestic violence: commentary]*. Warsaw: Wolters Kluwer.

Szulc, A. (2013). Żona nie krzyczy [My wife doesn't shout]. *Newsweek Polska*, (40). Retrieved from http://polska.newsweek.pl/zona-nie-krzyczy-malzenstwo-gwalt-przemoc-maz-zona-newsweek-pl,artykuly,271465,1.html.
Trojanowska, M. (2013). *Konwencja Rady Europy o zapobieganiu i zwalczaniu przemocy wobec kobiet i przemocy domowej furtką do wprowadzenia gender? [Council of Europe Convention on violence against women and domestic violence paving the way for gender ideology?]*. Retrieved from http://www.fronda.pl/a/konwencji-rady-europy-o-zapobieganiu-i-zwalczaniu-przemocy-wobec-kobiet-i-przemocy-domowej-i-gender,31638.html.
Ula. (2013). *Odbieranie dzieci rodzicom – prawo i rzeczywistość [Removing children from their parents – the law and the reality]*. Retrieved from http://www.familie.pl/artykul/Odbieranie-dzieci-rodzicom-prawo-i-rzeczywistosc,6586,1.html.
van Dijk, J., van Kesteren, J., & Smit, P. (2007). *Criminal victimisation in international perspective: Key findings from the 2004–2005 ICVS and EU ICS*. Den Haag: WODC.
Walklate, S. (2009). Victims and the state. In R. Coleman, J. Sim, S. Tombs, & D. Whyte (Eds.), *State, power, crime* (pp. 174–184). London: Sage.
Walkowiak, W. (2011). Prawa ofiar przestępstw [The rights of victims of crime]. *Homines Hominibus, 7*, 115–126.
Wiktorska, P. (2013). Nowelizacja ustawy o przeciwdziałaniu przemocy w rodzinie – w kierunku racjonalizacji czy biurokracji [Reforming the Act on countering domestic violence – towards rationalisation or bureaucratisation]. In A. Rzeplinski, I. Rzeplinska, M. Niełaczna, & P. Wiktorska (Eds.), *Pozbawienie wolności – funkcje i koszty: Księga jubileuszowa Profesora Teodora Szymanowskiego [Custodial sentences – functions and costs: Volume in commemoration of professor Teodor Szymanowski]* (pp. 419–437). Warsaw: Wolters Kluwer.
Wittenberg, A. (2013). *Nowa polska obelga zastąpiła żyda, pedała, komunistę [New Polish insult replaces Jew, homo, communist]*. Retrieved from http://natemat.pl/31767,nowa-polska-obelga-feministka-zastapila-zyda-pedala-i-komuniste.
Wrona, G. (2011). Obowiązki nakładane na osoby skazane z art. 207 § 1 k.k. w orzecznictwie sądów rejonowych [Obligations imposed on people sentenced under CC Art. 207 § 1 in the regional courts]. *Archiwum Kryminologii, 33*, 213–226.
Wybranowski, W. (2013). Urzędnicy odbierają rodzinie dzieci [Officials remove children from family]. *Tygodnik Lisieckiego Dorzeczy.pl*. Retrieved from http://dorzeczy.pl/urzednicy-odbieraja-dzieci/.
Zaduminska, B. (2006). *Sytuacja ofiar zgwałcenia w postępowaniu przygotowawczym: Raport z monitoringu [Status of rape victims in preliminary proceedings: Monitoring report]*. Kraków. Retrieved from http://www.ekologiasztuka.pl/pdf/f0037zaduminska.pdf.
Zedner, L. (2002). Victims. In M. Maguire, R. Morgan, & R. Reiner (Eds.), *The Oxford handbook of criminology* (pp. 419–456). Oxford: Oxford University Press.
Zweig, J., & Yahner, J. (2013). Providing services to victims of crime. In R. Davis, A. J. Lurigo, & S. Herman (Eds.), *Victims of crime* (pp. 325–347). Los Angeles: Sage.

Is Legitimacy Police Property?

Paul Ponsaers

1 Introduction

This paper discusses the question of whether or not the problem of legitimacy is a problem that the police themselves can manage. The answer to this question seems obvious: the police have a problem with their legitimacy and should consequently gain public trust and confidence by increasing their effectiveness. Contrary to this position, this paper will argue that the police are not active agents in the construction on their own legitimacy. The paper starts with the classic Weberian sociological meaning of legitimacy by introducing the distinction between normative and empirical legitimacy. A remarkable geographical variability of empirical legitimacy is observed.

The introduction of Community (Oriented) Policing is presented as a police strategy to raise the effectiveness of the police and consequently of public confidence. Evaluation studies of COP do not give a satisfactory answer to this relationship. The paper will demonstrate that perceived *justice* is more important in the construction of confidence than perceived effectiveness, pointing to the prominent question of procedural justice in a Weberian sense.

Next, the paper develops the point of view that causal factors for the geographical variability are to be found in structural and individual characteristics of the inhabitants of territorial aggregates. These characteristics are hardly influenced by police strategies or actions. Again the observation is made that the police are not active agents of change of citizens' institutional trust. Trust seems to be tied to variations in social mechanisms that are beyond the reach of the police.

In this way the circle is complete. While police legitimacy is not police property, it are political decision makers who are responsible for the improvement of causal

P. Ponsaers (✉)
Faculty of Law, Research Unit Social Analysis of Security, Department of Penal Law & Criminology, Ghent University, Maïsstraat 110, 9000 Ghent, Belgium
e-mail: paul.ponsaers@ugent.be

G. Meško, J. Tankebe (eds.), *Trust and Legitimacy in Criminal Justice*,
DOI 10.1007/978-3-319-09813-5_5

factors that influence public confidence, institutional trust and ultimately police legitimacy. In conclusion, the paper returns to the Weberian meaning of police legitimacy, starting from the observation that the police are only a *refuge*, an intermediate stop because the police will never have the power to set the social injustice straight.

2 Back to Basics: The Concept of Legitimacy in Weber

Weber (1976) introduced the notion of legitimacy in social and political sciences. The starting point of his thinking lies in the question of how sustainable political power relations can be introduced and how they can stand firm. Weber asked himself why people submit themselves voluntarily to public authorities and how does this submission becomes sustainable? Some elements are essential in this Weberian thinking.

Legitimacy is bound for Weber to the exclusive domain of public authorities. Loader and Mulcahy (2003) stated that the police are not an enterprise or firm. They write: "The managerialization of the police is based on the assumption that in many respects police organizations do not differ from any other business organization. According to this view, police organizations should primarily be evaluated in terms of their output performance. However, in the long run and almost unnoticed, this may undermine the symbolic power of the police. In this sense the managerialization is a form of demythologization, which may erode the police legitimacy and authority." (Loader & Mulcahy, 2003: 291–292) In other words, in this logic the effectiveness of the public police can never be a consequence of its legitimacy or vice versa. Even when the public police are not effective in terms of performance, they can be legitimate.

Legitimacy is—in this classical meaning—attached to the voluntary subjection of citizens to the power of the state. This is the hard core meaning of legitimacy according to Weber. The recognition of legitimacy is an act of acceptance and implies the readiness to obey and to waive, to a large extent, the individual right and capacity to use violence. Weber pointed to institutions which were supported by a culture that molded these structures. Institutions are for Weber pillars for political order. The claim for legitimacy ("Anspruch") stems from a political system, and by institutions which function herein. It is only when this claim is recognized, honored, and validated by citizens that we can speak of legitimacy. Strong acceptance leads to solid legitimacy of the political system while weak acceptance can lead to (political) crisis. In other words: citizens can mistrust the police, but at the same time accept the legitimacy of the police. Both notions are of a different order and quality (Van Reenen, 2014).

Weber tried to find the causality of political and societal order. He was not interested in the daily variability of behavior, or the ever changing public opinion, but more precisely in the stability of phenomena. He tried to understand the shaping of a stable political order and thus of a stable society. He was interested in the predictability of behavior and consequently in the reasons why people submit themselves over a long period to political power and the subsequent obedience that results. Legitimacy functions thus on the long run and impacts the sustainability of relations, on the institutionalization of relations between citizens and public authorities. Notions as "trust" and "confidence" have another connotation: they are not sustainable and work in the short run. The attention for sustainability distinguishes Weber from other scholars (e.g., Jansen, Van den Brink, & Kneyber, 2012) who absorb variable performance indicators of public authorities into the problem of police legitimacy.

It is interesting to consider this in the context of law. Laws are strange phenomena. They are excellence expressions of the political will of the political class, bound to procedural demands. Once they are voted and confirmed, the obligation rests with the citizens to obey them. If necessary, obedience shall be enforced. This is the consequence of the model of *rational legitimacy* according to Weber. The strange thing is, however, that the political character of laws fades away once they are implemented, and they attain an objective and neutral character. The law exists and you have to behave according to the law. This is the way legitimacy works according to Weber. The political character disappears and is not recognized anymore. The acceptance of the political system, the expressions of the political will of this system and the belief in the rightness of it have the tendency to depoliticize and to make it a kind of self-evident and objective given.

The order which is created or changed by political acts of will is considered after a while as politically neutral, as self evident. An independent judge who adjudicates using these laws enforces this tendency. This is the way legitimacy works and this is the way power will speak for itself (Weber, 1976). Oomen (2005: 893) observes this mechanism in international relations: "A final factor explaining why the law (be it under the name of human rights or justice) became one of the main avenues of international engagement in the late 1990s, lies in the perceived characteristics of the law itself. Often deemed neutral, universal and above all a-political, the law seemingly has qualities that other forms of intervention (military, diplomatic) lack."

Legitimacy is also strongly linked to the acceptance of the monopoly of force and violence, of jurisprudence and the execution of sanctions by public authorities—more precisely the monopoly of *legitimate* physical violence (Weber, 1976). This also implies without any doubt the role of the police (enforcement, investigation). Also this monopoly is to a large extent a claim of power, until it is recognized and accepted by power subjects. It is because of the massive recognition of this monopoly position and the broad readiness within society to waive violence, and the willingness to comply, that legitimacy of political power becomes possible.

Force and violence become the specific means of the state and the legitimacy of this monopoly is essential for the functioning of (and in the name of) public authority (Van Reenen, 1979).

The broader this recognition, the more marginal the violence and resistance become against the state. This perspective on power and violence and the relation of the police with power and political legitimacy remain absent in the notion of "trust" or "mistrust." Different scholars argue that trust in police results from the conviction that the police will be there when you need them, that the police operate according to "good" motives, that the police act according to the "general interest" (Van der Veer, Van Sluis, Van de Walle, & Ringeling, 2013). That is without any doubt a beautiful wish, but this kind of assumption leaves precisely the essential element out of sight for a good understanding of the functioning of the police; more precisely the legitimacy of the monopoly of force and violence which is what precisely distinguishes the police from other public agencies.

3 Empirical Legitimacy and Geographical Variability

In line with this classic understanding of legitimacy, Hough, Jackson, and Bradford (2013), as Hinsch (2010) did before them, distinguish normative (or objective) legitimacy and empirical (and perceived) legitimacy. Normative legitimacy is present when authorities correspond to objective criteria, as for example the absence of corruption. Empirical legitimacy is based on the perceptions of citizens. In this sense, it is possible that the police do not enjoy empirical legitimacy, while the institution corresponds to the criteria of normative legitimacy in a democratic society. In this context it is important to note that only when a public institution enjoys empirical legitimacy, can it count on the support of the population, according to Hough, Jackson, Bradford, Myhill, and Quinton (2010).

Hough and his colleagues define legitimacy as "the recognition and justification of the right to exercise power and influence" (Hough et al., 2013: 1). This definition is in line with the definition by Beetham (1991), Tyler (2006b) and Jackson et al. (2012) who define legitimacy as the right to rule and the recognition by the ruled of that right. Thus, a legitimate authority does not only mean that citizens recognize the existence of and the right to enforce authority and to use power (Tyler 2006a, 2006b), but also that this right should be *justified* (Jackson et al., 2012). Authority will only be accepted by a citizen when he or she also believes in the righteousness of it.

This belief is based on the perception that the police and the citizens share the same values and norms ("moral alignment"), that the police act according to the law ("legality") and the degree that citizens submit voluntarily to the police as authority ("feeling the obligation to obey the police"). These are the three dimensions that Hough et al. (2013) are referring to in relation to the acceptance of the police as an authority.

Citizens obeying the police voluntarily show that they accept the authority of the police. Authority is not enforced, but accepted given the respect citizens have for the police as authority (Hinds & Murphy, 2007). Or to state it another way: citizens consider it their duty to obey the police even when they do not agree with the way the police are acting. Legitimate police thus means police that (1) are obeyed voluntarily by citizens, (2) act according to the law, and (3) share the same ideas as the citizens about values and norms in society.

The *European Social Survey* (ESS) contains attitudes, values, and opinions of inhabitants of more than 20 European countries and delivers an overview of their development. This paper brings ESS information together for all available editions, more precisely on a biannual basis from 2002 until 2012. The figures in Table 1 include only those countries which participated in all these editions. The question submitted to the respondents concerns the amount of perceived legitimacy ("confidence") they have in police, scored from 0 to 10. In the table only respondents with a high degree of confidence in police are included (scores 9 and 10).

Table 1 The evolution of confidence in police (European Social Survey, 2002, 2004, 2006, 2008, 2010, 2012; Norwegian Social Science Data Services, 2012)

	Strong confidence in police (%)					
	2002	2004	2006	2008	2010	2012
The Netherlands (NL)	4.3	3.8	3.5	5.7	5.1	5.1
Portugal (P)	6.2	5.7	6.4	6.5	5.5	6.9
Slovenia (SLO)	8.4	6.8	10.2	7.8	6.6	7.5
Belgium (BE)	6.1	5.8	5.9	7.8	6.2	7.9
Poland (PL)	7.2	5.8	7.3	7.8	6.7	8.3
Hungary (H)	9.5	7.8	12.5	5.7	7.6	9.2
Spain (S)	8.3	9.6	11.3	10.7	11.8	12.5
UK (GB)	13.8	12.5	11.9	14.1	14.0	15.7
Sweden (Z)	17.9	15.7	15.7	15.2	20.1	17.1
Ireland (I)	21.1	23.0	16.6	16.6	17.4	19.6
Germany (D)	17.8	14.9	17.1	20.7	20.0	19.9
Norway (N)	20.2	23.7	22.5	22.5	25.9	23.1
Switzerland (CH)	15.9	17.3	18.4	16.9	22.6	24.4
Denmark (DK)	39.7	42.5	39.2	35.1	34.7	42.6
Finland (FIN)	44.5	43.0	46.4	44.4	45.6	48.6

The table shows two striking things. On the one hand, we notice strong differences between the countries, while on the other hand we see that the variations over time for each of the countries are fairly marginal. In other words, confidence in police varies considerably between countries, but is stable over time. This geographical variability is very suggestive of a contextual interpretation.

4 COP: The relation Between Effectiveness and Confidence

One of the dominant contextual interpretations of this geographical variability of public confidence is the idea that it reflects to a certain extent the differences in effectiveness of police organizations in different countries (Bradford, Jackson, & Stanko, 2009; Jackson et al. 2012; Roberts & Hough, 2005; Tyler, 2006b). This is important, because only when a police force enjoys perceived public confidence, can it count on the support of the population (Hough et al., 2010), and this support is important in order to be effective (Fig. 1).

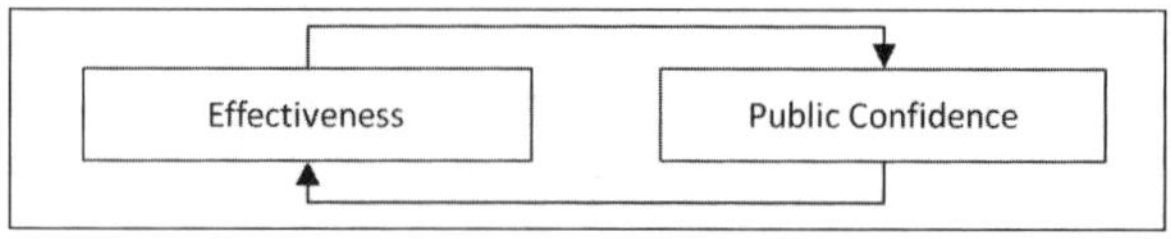

Fig. 1 The mutual relation between effectiveness of the police and public trust in the police

In line with this thinking, the police should gain public confidence to become more effective, and should also be effective to enjoy public confidence. Ultimately the solution for the problem lies in the hands of the police themselves as it is up to the force to remediate and break the vicious circle. Or, to state it briefly, the problem of public confidence is in this point of view police property and a preliminary necessity for the improvement of effectiveness.

This point of view was precisely to a large extent the reason why the police concluded in an impressive consensus the deficit of traditional police models (Bayley, 1994, 1998; Verhage & Ponsaers, 2013). The most important critiques on these traditional models, following evaluative academic research, were as follows: (1) The mere increase in the number of police officers is not an effective strategy to tackle crime or disorderly behavior. The quantitative assumption cannot resolve the necessary qualitative change of "how to do good policing" (Greene, 1998); (2) The police cannot prevent crime, and more generally, cannot function without the help of the population, which means that the population is much more than "the eyes and ears" of the police (Rosenbaum, 1998); (3) The classic tactics of traditional police models are too reactive, while they do not affect the circumstances that cause crime and disorder (Ponsaers, 2002); and (4) Police strategy is frequently too broad and is applied to different problems in one and the same way ("one size fits all"—Skogan, 1998). Observers have advocated for the need of "tailor-made responses" (Ponsaers, Tange, & Van Outrive, 2009; Verhage & Ponsaers, 2013).

All these critiques boil down to the conclusion that it is up to the police themselves to change strategy and functioning, in order to gain public confidence and become more effective.

The most important attempt for the transformation and reformation of policing in this sense, during the last decades was without any doubt the introduction of "Community (Oriented) Policing" (COP). The focus on COP studies during the 1990s led to the most influential books being studies on COP (Skogan & Harnett, 1996), while this focus continued in the early years of this century (Skogan, 2006). Without any doubt, this had a powerful and lasting effect on the image and the rhetorical capacity of the police themselves (Manning & Yursza Warfield, 2009). COP was in fact the promise or prophecy of a new form of policing, in which the police had to orient themselves to partnerships with the citizens and to the improvement of their effectiveness. COP was, from this standpoint, a working program for the police to solve the problem of weak public confidence, because an increase in effectiveness would lead to more confidence (Fig. 2).

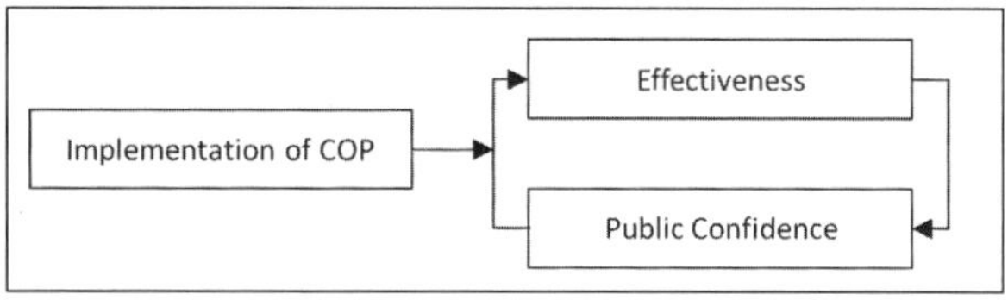

Fig. 2 The promise of the implementation of Community (Oriented) Policing

Despite this evolution, Eck and Rosenbaum observe: "There is no simple or commonly shared definition of community policing, either in theory or in practice." (Eck & Rosenbaum, 1994). Writing this, both authors suggest that COP over time became a container-notion. Bayley (1988: 225), who conducted a lot of research in different countries where COP was implemented, confirms this: "Despite the benefits claimed for community policing, programmatic implementation of it has been very uneven. Although widely, almost universally, said to be important, it means different things to different people (...) Community policing on the ground often seems less a program than a set of aspirations wrapped in a slogan."

After more than 20 years of promotion of this so-called police model (Ponsaers, 2001) by governments, foundations and leading universities, it is still not clear what effect it has on police practice (Brodeur, 1998). The results of evaluative research seem to be unimpressive and in some cases non-existent or immeasurable (Fielding, 1995; Greene, 2000). COP is stated to have little or no effect on the effectiveness of the police (Mastrofski & Greene, 1988; Weisburd & Braga, 2006). The most striking results were achieved in programs directed towards intensive problem solving strategies, focused on so-called "hot spots" (Bayley, 1994; Braga et al., 1999; Leigh, Read, & Tilley, 1996). The realization of results nevertheless seemed almost impossible while the police are confronted with problems they can never resolve (Brodeur, 1998). Also the frequently used programs of "neighborhood watch" resulted in limited effects on crime and effectiveness.

Despite this lack of impact in terms of effectiveness, COP tends to improve the contact between the police and the population. With a minimal use of compulsory measures, it was deemed possible to improve public confidence. But this coping strategy has only limited value, because those who are forced to stay in contact with the police (especially victims and offenders) seem to be precisely those who are mostly discontent with the functioning of the police (Fig. 3).

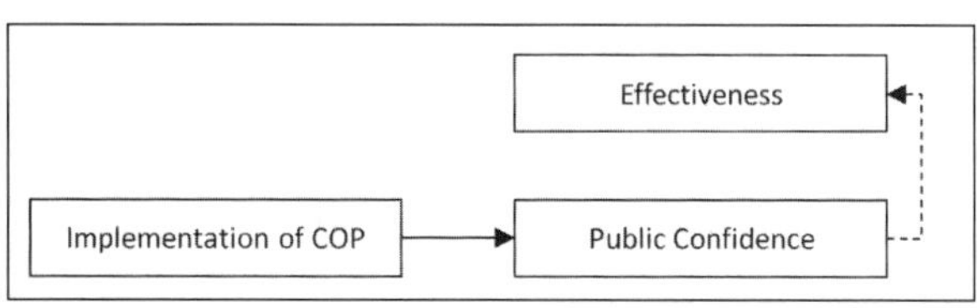

Fig. 3 The relation between COP and public trust, effectiveness

Nevertheless, COP programs seem to have a stronger impact on the improvement of public confidence and the image than on the effectiveness of the police. This was also demonstrated in research; the most important effect of the implementation of COP was found in the improvement of the confidence of the population towards the quality of the service rendered by the police to the public (Brodeur, 1998; Wycoff & Skogan, 1994). Moreover, it became clear that the improvement of the image of the police resulted in an intrinsic goal and was often misused to gain more (financial and personnel) facilities (Sacco, 1998).

Also neighborhood watch programs impacted the feelings of security and the communication is improving between the public and police. As a result of this, the public confidence in the police was reinforced and the job satisfaction of police officers was raised. But evaluative research demonstrated also that the majority of these initiatives were implemented in a defective way. It also became clear that the involvement of citizens in these initiatives, also in England, was weak (Bennett, 1990).

The difficulties in realizing a more intensive collaboration seem to be more serious than most advocates of COP expected. The empowerment of the public by means of a professional marketing strategy is certainly an interesting tool for the improvement of a more functional partnership between the police and the population. But the problems in mobilizing local inhabitants are often more structural in nature. In more deprived neighborhoods, the lack of collaboration by the public is often a result of feelings of despair and powerlessness, the fear of street gangs, and a deeply embedded mistrust and conflict with the police (Rosenbaum, 1998).

In the long run, according to advocates, COP would lead to a more or less important decrease in the number of emergency calls by the public (Brodeur, 1998). Instead, COP programs can have a regressive (instead of progressive) effect, while they are often directed towards the wrong target groups. Those groups within the population that are already organized succeed in using the police to their advantage, while the police feel comfortable in this part of society. In spite of this, research evoked that COP, by means of locally initiated consultations, structures the active participation of the population in problem identification and prioritizing. It gives a channel for external accountability for police performance. Often it became clear that the initiatives were directed towards the wrong territories and the target groups with the smallest needs (Skogan, 1998).

Some authors come to the conclusion that COP can have some effect on the perception of crime by the population and on the confidence in the quality of police care. Moreover, the feelings of insecurity seem to decrease, because of the increased visibility of the police in public spaces and the intensification of the interaction between the population and the police frequently lead to more confidence in the police service. COP seems to have an impact when neighborhood problems are tackled and on fear of crime. In any case, the results (in terms of effectiveness) of COP are not worse than traditional policing in the control of crime, but the results in tackling incivilities and feelings of insecurity in the communities are better (Greene, 1998).

Bayley (1994: 110), who did a lot of international comparative research on policing, concludes: “We don’t know if community policing works. Most of the time, a small effect can be detected, but sometimes also contradictory results. The best results can be observed in focused activities of problem oriented policing. It is not proven that citizens can act against insecurity in an effective way. Initiatives as ‘neighbourhood watch’ don’t have an effect on crime. Most of the time these initiatives work the best there were they are least needed and least where they are necessary. Nevertheless, most authors conclude that it is not the model that is failing, but in first instance the deficient implementation of it.”

The bottom-line of the implementation of COP is not that the strategy has failed. That would be an overstatement. COP has brought a lot of useful social side-effects in terms of external orientation, accountability, partnership, empowerment, and democratic weight. But the original promise, to break the vicious cycle of effectiveness/public confidence was not demonstrated until now.

Moreover, research has demonstrated (Hough et al., 2010; Tyler, 2003, 2006b, 2007, 2011; Van Damme, 2013) that perceived *justice* is more important in the construction of confidence than perceived effectiveness. In other words being treated honestly and respectfully by the police is more important for citizens than tackling problems in an effective way.

Two criteria seem to be important for the judgment of procedural justice. On the one hand, there is the quality of the process of decision making, on the other there is the quality of personal treatment. Citizens want to have the feeling that the police are treating them in an honest, neutral, and objective way. Also the extent to which citizens get the opportunity to explain their vision and behavior before the police make decisions seems important (Tyler & Fagan, 2008). Perceptions about procedural justice are to a large extent influenced by personal experiences. Bradford (2010: 2) states it in this context: “Personal contact is a key moment in the formation of opinions about the police. Individual encounters can create moments in which the legitimacy of the police is reinforced or undermined.”

Viewing our problem from this point of view, the police become again a constructor of perceived confidence, this time not from the angle of problem solving, but from a more Weberian point of view on the neutral position of the police in society.

5 The Causality of Public Mistrust Is Not Police Property

It is striking that the discussion about mistrust in different social (public) institutions appears within social sciences almost completely disconnected from the discussion about the implementation of COP and its consequences on effectiveness and public confidence. Again, research has indicated that there were strong geographical differences in cynicism about the police and penal law and in the lack of trust (Baumer, Rosenfeld, & Messner, 2003). Important differences in mistrust between countries, but also between cities, municipalities and neighborhoods were observed. Again this geographical variability was suggestive of a contextual interpretation; nevertheless this time the problem was tackled from another angle.

In this literature, it was no longer the police who were considered important active actors in the domain of solving the problem under study. Scholars have started to study causal background characteristics of the *population* of these differing geographical aggregates, which could explain the variability. Since the second half of the 1990s, the number of studies that have shown the detrimental influence of municipality level characteristics (cities and neighborhoods) for the citizens of these municipalities has slowly but surely grown (Sampson, Morenoff, & Gannon-Rawley, 2002). Consulting the literature about institutional mistrust, we observe a remarkably one-sided attention to the role of background characteristics such as vulnerability, social capital, feelings of discontent and mistrust. That is why no estimation can be made of the relative importance of each of these components in regard to mistrust (Fig. 4).

Fig. 4 The relation between trust and structural and individual characteristics

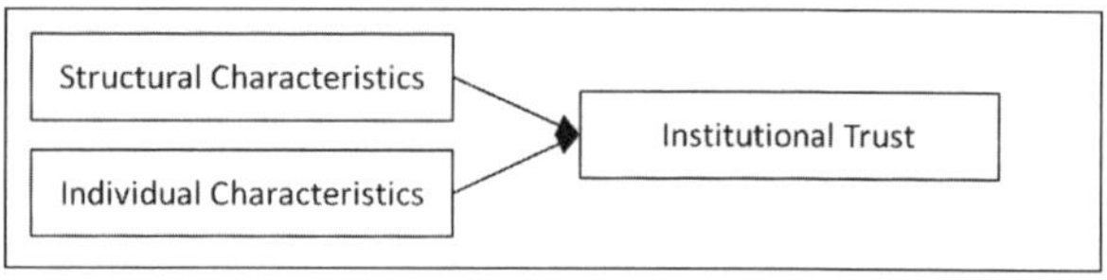

On the one hand, geographical differences were considered as a reflection of the differential composition of municipalities. On the other hand, these differences were understood as the consequence of environmental influence or contextual effect. Attention was paid to the role of collective efficacy, defined as social cohesion among neighbors combined with their willingness to intervene on behalf of the common good (Sampson, 2004). The concept of collective efficacy has been seen as one of the missing pieces of the social disorganization theory puzzle by many social scientists (Hardyns, 2010).

Social disorganization mechanisms were defined as the mechanisms or processes whereby the social structure of a residential area encourages crime. Thus, social disorganization could lead in this logic to greater concentrations of crime. In the field of criminology, Shaw and McKay (1942) were the first who empirically found an adverse effect of certain structural characteristics of a residential area such as higher degrees of urbanization and industrialization, economic disadvantage, residential mobility and ethnic heterogeneity on concentrations of crime. It is striking that the position or the strategy of the police was only marginally discussed in this literature, while crime was considered as a consequence of a multitude of geographical contextual factors that could explain the variations in crime as well as the variability in mistrust in public institutions such as the police. In these theoretical logics, the police were no longer active participants in the social construction of the security problem. Trust in the police, in other words, was no longer seen as police property.

Before the 1980s, the social disorganization theory was used exclusively to explain spatial variations in crime. Since the end of the 1980s, greater attention has been given to the interaction between the ecological context (residential area), the social (school, family) and individual (socio-demographic background characteristics and psychological attitudes) context. From then on, the geographical context has also been used to explain individual differences in crime-related characteristics such as fear of crime, differences in victimization and delinquent behavior. In their Chicago study, Sampson, Raudenbush, and Earls (1997) found that the degree of collective efficacy in a neighborhood is very closely related to concentrations of crime. It seems that collective efficacy is an important mediating mechanism which explains why area characteristics, which are seen as social disorganization mechanisms, lead to greater concentrations of crime. Neighborhoods with a high degree of collective efficacy seem to offer better resistance and are better able to stand up to all sorts of disorder.

Positive climate of social trust and solidarity go together with clearly defined shared values and norms and more informal social control and thus, less crime (Sunshine & Tyler, 2003). Accordingly, indicators for collective efficacy are informal social control and social trust, or mutual trust among members of a community, which are absolute conditions for fostering the willingness to intervene in the common interest of a community (Pauwels & Hardyns, 2009).

Both structural and social processes are at the basis of environmental concentrations of illegal disorder (Wikström & Dolmén, 2001). They all seem to play a part in the development of individuals' attitudes (Hardyns, 2010). It can be assumed that a low degree of collective efficacy goes together with high levels of mistrust in the criminal justice system. In other words, not only do social mechanisms in terms of geographical aggregates seem to be important, but also individual characteristics, for example social capital (Lin, 2001). Furthermore, personal resources (e.g., social networks) were also considered. According to Putnam (1993), social capital refers to the relationships between individuals (friends, neighbors, strangers) and social networks which results in convertible norms and trust in others. Not only Putnam, but also other scholars have pointed to the role of participation in organizations as a more formal aspect of social capital, referring to formal organizations such as cultural and social organizations, including voluntary organizations (Hooghe & Vanhoutte, 2011). Both participation in organizations and social ties have been argued to be important mechanisms in the explanation of individual differences in trust. More than ever, the problem of public mistrust has increasingly been considered as a social problem, resulting more from the active intervention or passive non-intervention of citizens and inhabitants, than of absent police officers (at least in the discussion).

Brehm and Rahn (1997) argued that social capital manifests itself in individuals as a tight reciprocal relationship between levels of civic engagement and interpersonal trust. "The more that citizens participate in their communities, the more that they learn to trust others; the greater trust that citizens hold for others, the more likely they are to participate" (Brehm & Rahn, 1997: 1002). Some scholars argue that a decline of social capital is likely to cause a loss of trust in political leadership and a loss of trust in the institutions of government (e.g., Norris, 1999; Pharr & Putnam, 2000). On the other hand, Newton (2001) argues that the relationship between social capital and institutional trust is moderate at best and therefore probably rather indirect.

Sociocultural values like ethnocentrism and anomia are supposed to have a negative effect on attitudes related to trust. Many studies have already pointed to the fact that general feelings of dissatisfaction with current society (or "discontent") are related to a decrease in trust in various institutions (e.g., McDill, 1961). People with high levels of discontent are supposed to be much more mistrusting.

He proposed that anomia, authoritarianism and ethnocentrism are all dimensions of what he called a "Negative Weltanschauung" (a negative worldview). Several studies of the factorial structure have empirically contradicted McDill's assumption of the *Negative Weltanschauung* (Lutterman & Middleton, 1970; Struening & Richardson, 1965). *Anomia* is often described as political powerlessness and has consequently been identified as a predictor of mistrust. This concept may be defined as an individual's feeling that he or she cannot affect the actions of the government, and that the "authoritative allocation of values for the society," which is at the heart of the political process, is not subject to his or her influence.

Ethnocentrism is a basic attitude expressing the belief that one's own ethnic group or one's own culture is superior to other ethnic groups or cultures, and that one's cultural standards can be applied in a universal manner. Ethnocentrism is closely related to other attitudinal indicators for racism, xenophobia, prejudice, mental closure, and more generally, to an authoritarian personality structure. Ethnocentrism is widely used in research on social and political attitudes because it is a very powerful and easily identifiable attitude that can be measured in a valid manner with a limited number of variables. While the relationship between ethnocentrism and levels of trust is not questioned in the empirical literature, the causal relationship is. Some authors (e.g., Meuleman & Billiet, 2005), have argued that levels of trust can explain individual differences of ethnocentrism. *Authoritarianism* is also strongly related to trust. While anomia and ethnocentrism are negatively related to trust, authoritarianism has been found to be positively related to governmental trust (Peterson, Doty, & Winter, 1993).

Some scholars discuss the relationships between these exogenous variables. From the social identity theory, anomia is argued to be causally prior to ethnocentrism (Scheepers, Felling, & Peters, 1992; Tajfel & Turner, 1979). The social identity theory suggests that an individual is in a permanent state of needing to assume a positive identity for himself or herself. This is done by identifying oneself with people who have perceived positive characteristics, the in-group, and contra-identifying with people who have perceived negative characteristics, the out-group. The link between anomia and ethnocentrism can be explained as follows: "...it may be argued that anomic people who are subject to powerlessness, meaninglessness and normlessness and who feel socially isolated, therefore have a strong urge to re-establish a positive identity by means of social identification, possibly accompanied by social contra-identification..." (Scheepers et al., 1992: 46). As we interpret this, we may conclude that the more an individual has anomic feelings, the more he or she has the urge to emphasize identification with the in-group and contra-identification with the out-group, which equates to ethnocentrism.

To summarize the argument of this part of this paper: an impressive amount of research has been done on the causality of institutional trust and geographical variability, pointing to a broad range of structural and individual characteristics of inhabitants. It is striking to observe that within this literature the position or the strategy of the police stays largely absent. The police are no longer considered the owners of the road to problem solving, as the active agents for social change.

In this literature, the causal mechanisms are to a large extent related to characteristics of the population within neighborhoods and municipalities and consequently a policy directed to raise institutional trust has to take these observations into account, and thus should be directed towards influencing social and individual causal factors of the population. It is remarkable that influencing these causal factors is far beyond the reach police institutions can have on social reality. It is clear that this is the domain of political decision making power on problems such as social cohesion, social efficacy, social capital, etc.

This thinking neglects the activism present in police strategy, but is probably a more realistic approach to social causality. The relationship between the efforts of police forces and institutional trust is simply weak and determined by a number of contextual factors. The quest of COP scholars, in search of the ultimate explanation for loss of mistrust of the police, seems to be in vain. The ultimate explanation can never lie in the functioning of the police themselves, at the most in a complex set of exogenous variables.

Conclusion

This paper began from the classic Weberian interpretation of police legitimacy. In this view, effectiveness of the public police can never be a consequence of their legitimacy or vice versa. Even when the public police are not effective in terms of performance, it can be legitimate from a Weberian point of view. Classic police legitimacy lies in the voluntary subjection of citizens to the power of the state. Legitimacy is strongly linked to the acceptance of the monopoly of force and violence, of jurisprudence and the execution of sanctions by public authorities—more precisely the monopoly of *legitimate* physical violence.

In line with this Weberian standpoint, we made the distinction in the second part of this paper between normative (or objective) and empirical (and perceived) legitimacy. Normative legitimacy is present when authorities correspond to objective criteria. In contrast, empirical legitimacy is based on the perceptions of citizens. We stressed that only when a public institution enjoys empirical legitimacy, can it count on the support of the population. We observed nevertheless a strong geographical variability in perceived legitimacy.

In the third part of this paper, we wondered if this variability reflects the differences in effectiveness of police organizations in different countries.

(continued)

This question was tackled by examining the results in terms of problem solving capacity (effectiveness) of COP, as a working program for the police to solve the problem of weak public confidence. The lack of dramatic impact in terms of effectiveness was demonstrated by means of several evaluation studies. We concluded that COP had several important social side-effects, but did not fulfil the promise of effective policing. The role of the police themselves in the construction of a more solid perceived legitimacy seemed to be very limited.

The criterion of effectiveness for legitimacy fits well with the growing culture of evidence based policy during the last decennia, exaggerating the importance of this tendency. The successive failures and deceptions in the realization of effectiveness, coinciding with the demise of the welfare state, illustrate the instability of this basis of legitimacy. Political power based on effectiveness is unstable power and is in fact a contradiction while the justification of this power is unstable. It is not less than the institutionalization of political crisis (Breuer, 1969).

Nevertheless, the possibilities in the domain of procedural justice were more important in relation to perceived legitimacy. Citizens want to have, first, the feeling that the police are treating them in an honest, neutral and objective way in a more Weberian sense. Here the police can take an active role again in shaping perceived legitimacy.

The last part of this paper discussed the literature on mistrust in different social (public) institutions. In this literature, it was no longer the police who were considered important active agents in the domain of solving the problem under study. Here we see that the variability of mistrust is explained by causal background characteristics of the population of geographical aggregates. It is striking that the position or the strategy of the police was only marginally discussed in this literature. The police are no longer considered as the owner of the road to problem solving, as the active actors for social change. Causal factors for institutional mistrust are beyond the reach of the police. It is clear that this is the domain of the political decision making power.

When the gaining and the maintenance of legitimacy is a specialty of the police, this means in the long run a politicization of the police. This kind of evolution is not desirable. Police are not specialized in political acting and have another function than the earning or the maintenance of legitimacy in a democratic context.

The police bring relief during social unrest, but are painfully aware, at the same time, that they do not have the political power to eradicate the causes of this unrest. The police stay dependent on politics in this sense. However, politicians do not have the power to always find the right answer to social problems. Nevertheless, social justice is considered to be a political ideal that must be pursued in the spirit of the age which at the same time is restricted by feasibility limits. Politics needs the police in this sense. The police must take care of the unrest that a failing government causes and channel it (Ponsaers & Devroe, 2012).

(continued)

When the political class does not have the power to offer radical answers, the police power will become its refuge. It is only a *refuge*, an intermediate stop because the police will never have the power to set the social injustice straight. In this sense, the citizen would rather worry about a weak democracy than about strong police force. The police become then a permanent power factor in failing democracies, a barricade that the political class can hide itself behind up until the moment that the police become a political factor on their own and democracy ceases to exist.

References

Baumer, E. P., Rosenfeld, R., & Messner, S. F. (2003). Explaining spatial variation in support for capital punishment: A multi-level analysis. *American Journal of Sociology, 108*(4), 844–875.

Bayley, D. (1988). Community policing: A report from the devil's advocate. In J. Greene & S. Mastrofski (Eds.), *Community policing: Rhetoric or reality?* (pp. 225–238). New York, NY: Preager.

Bayley, D. (1994). *Police for the future*. New York, NY: Oxford University Press.

Bayley, D. (1998). *What works in policing*. New York, NY: Oxford University Press.

Beetham, D. (1991). *The legitimation of power*. Palgrave: Macmillan.

Bennett, T. (1990). *Evaluating neighbourhood watch*. Aldershot: Gower.

Bradford, B. (2010). *The quality of police contact: Procedural justice concerns among victims of crime in London*. Retrieved from http://dx.doi.org/10.2139/ssrn.1596754.

Bradford, B., Jackson, J., & Stanko, B. (2009). Contact and confidence: Revisiting the impact of public encounters with the police. *Policing and Society, 19*(1), 20–46.

Braga, A. A., Weisburd, D. L., Waring, E. J., Greene Mazerolle, L., Spelman, W., & Gajewski, F. (1999). Problem-oriented policing in violent crime places: A randomized controlled experiment. *Criminology, 37*(3), 549–555.

Brehm, J., & Rahn, W. (1997). Individual-level evidence for the causes and consequences of social capital. *American Journal of Political Science, 41*(3), 999–1023.

Breuer, F. (1969). De legitimiteitsgronden van het gezag [Grounds for legitimacy of authority]. *Mens en Maatschappij, 44*(3), 197–214.

Brodeur, J.-P. (1998). Tailor-made policing: A conceptual investigation. In J.-P. Brodeur (Ed.), *How to recognize good policing: Problems and issues* (pp. 30–51). Thousand Oaks, CA: Sage.

Eck, J., & Rosenbaum, D. (1994). Effectiveness, equity, and efficiency in community policing. In D. Rosenbaum (Ed.), *The challenge of community policing: Testing the promises* (pp. 3–23). Thousand Oaks, CA: Sage.

European Social Survey [ESS]. (2002, 2004, 2006, 2008, 2010, 2012). London: ESS ERIC. Retrieved from http://www.europeansocialsurvey.org/data/round-index.html.

Fielding, N. (1995). *Community policing*. Oxford: Clarendon Press.

Greene, J. (1998). Evaluating planned change strategies in modern law enforcement, implementing community-based policing. In J.-P. Brodeur (Ed.), *How to recognize good policing: Problems and issues* (pp. 141–160). Thousand Oaks, CA: Sage.

Greene, J. (2000). Community policing in America: Changing the nature, structure, and function of the police. *Criminal Justice, 3*, 299–370.

Hardyns, W. (2010). Urbanisation, disorder, victimisation and fear of crime: An aggregate level analysis of 346 Belgian municipalities. In L. Pauwels, W. Hardyns, & M. Van de Velde (Eds.), *Social disorganisation, offending, fear and victimisation: Findings from Belgian studies on the urban context of crime* (pp. 161–175). The Hague: Boom Juridische Uitgevers.

Hinds, L., & Murphy, K. (2007). Public satisfaction with police: Using procedural justice to improve police legitimacy. *The Australian and New Zealand Journal of Criminology, 40*(1), 27–42.

Hinsch, W. (2010). Justice, legitimacy and constitutional rights. *Critical Review of International Social and Political Philosophy, 13*(1), 39–54.

Hooghe, M., & Vanhoutte, B. (2011). Subjective well-being and social capital in Belgian communities: The impact of community characteristics on subjective well being indicators in Belgium. *Social Indicators Research, 100*(1), 17–36.

Hough, M., Jackson, J., Bradford, B., Myhill, A., & Quinton, P. (2010). Procedural justice, trust and institutional legitimacy. *Policing: A journal of Policy and Practice, 4*(3), 203–210.

Hough, M., Jackson, J., & Bradford, B. (2013). Legitimacy, trust and compliance: An empirical test of procedural justice theory using the European Social Survey. In J. Tankebe & A. Liebling (Eds.), *Legitimacy and criminal justice: An international exploration* (pp. 246–265). Oxford: Oxford University Press.

Jackson, J., Bradford, B., Hough, M., Myhill, A., Quinton, P., & Tyler, T. R. (2012). Why do people comply with the law? Legitimacy and influence of legal institutions. *British Journal of Criminology, 52*(6), 1051–1071.

Jansen, T. G., Van den Brink, G., & Kneyber, R. (2012). Naar een legitieme, niet besmuikte gezagsuitoefening [Towards a legitimate, uncontested execution of authority]. In T. G. Jansen, G. V. D. Brink, & R. Kneyber (Eds.), *Gezagsdragers [Bearers of authority]* (pp. 296–317). Amsterdam: Boom.

Leigh, A., Read, T., & Tilley, N. (1996). *Problem-oriented policing: Brit pop*. Crime detection and prevention series, no. 75. London: Home Office.

Lin, N. (2001). *Social capital: A theory of social structure and action*. Cambridge: Cambridge University Press.

Loader, I., & Mulcahy, J. (2003). *Policing and the condition of England: Memory, politics and culture*. Oxford: Oxford University Press.

Lutterman, K. G., & Middleton, R. (1970). Authoritarianism, anomia, and prejudice. *Social Forces, 48*(4), 485–492.

Manning, P., & Yursza Warfield, G. (2009). Police research in the United States: An overview and an analysis. In P. Ponsaers, C. Tange, & L. Van Outrive (Eds.), *Insights on police: Quarter of a century research on police in Europe and the Anglo-Saxon world* (pp. 96–126). Brussels: Bruylant.

Mastrofski, S., & Greene, J. (1988). *Community policing: Rhetoric or reality?* New York, NY: Praeger.

McDill, L. E. (1961). Authoritarianism, prejudice, and socioeconomic status: An attempt at clarification. *Social Forces, 39*(3), 239–245.

Meuleman, B., & Billiet, J. (2005). Etnocentrisme in Vlaanderen: Opmars of afname? De evolutie van de perceptie van etnische dreiging tussen 1991 en 2004 en de relatie met institutioneel vertrouwen [Ethnocentrism in Flanders: Rise or decrease? The evolution of the perception of ethnic menace between 1991 and 2004 and the relation with institutional trust]. In *Vlaanderen gepeild [Surveying Flanders]* (pp. 37–60). Brussel: APS.

Newton, K. (2001). Trust, social capital, civil society and democracy. *International Political Sciences Review, 22*(2), 201–214.

Norris, P. (1999). *Critical citizens: Global support for democratic government*. Oxford: Oxford University Press.

Norwegian Social Science Data Services. (2012). *ESS5, 2010 Documentation report: The ESS data archive* (Ed. 2.1). Retrieved from http://ess.nsd.uib.nl/.

Oomen, B. (2005). Donor-driven justice and its discontents: The case of Rwanda. *Development and Change, 36*(5), 887–910.

Pauwels, L., & Hardyns, W. (2009). Measuring community (dis)organizational processes through key informant analysis. *European Journal of Criminology, 6*(5), 401–417.

Peterson, B. E., Doty, R. M., & Winter, D. G. (1993). Authoritarianism and attitudes toward contemporary social issues. *Personality and Social Psychology Bulletin, 19*(2), 174–184.
Pharr, S. J., & Putnam, R. D. (2000). *Disaffected democracies: What's troubling the trilateral countries?* Princeton, NJ: Princeton University Press.
Ponsaers, P. (2001). Reading about 'community (oriented) policing' and police models. *Policing: An International Journal of Police Strategies & Management, 24*(4), 470–496.
Ponsaers, P. (2002). On evaluating 'community (oriented) policing' through other police models. In T. Van den Broeck & C. H. Eliaerts (Eds.), *Evaluating community policing* (pp. 51–76). Brussels: Politeia.
Ponsaers, P., & Devroe, E. (2012). On how a failing government creates an intrusive police force. In E. Devroe, P. Ponsaers, L. Gunther Moor, J. Greene, L. Skinns, L. Bisschop, et al. (Eds.), *Tides and currents in police theories* (pp. 115–134). Antwerpen: Maklu.
Ponsaers, P., Tange, C., & Van Outrive, L. (Eds.). (2009). *Insights in police: Quarter of a century research on police in Europe and the Anglo-Saxon world.* Brussels: Bruylant.
Putnam, R. D. (1993). *Making democracy work: Civic traditions in modern Italy.* Princeton: Princeton University Press.
Roberts, J. V., & Hough, M. J. (2005). *Understanding public attitudes to criminal justice.* Berkshire: Open University Press.
Rosenbaum, D. (1998). The changing role of the police, assessing the current transition to community policing. In J.-P. Brodeur (Ed.), *How to recognize good policing: Problems and issues* (pp. 3–29). Thousand Oaks, CA: Sage.
Sacco, V. (1998). Evaluating Satisfaction. In J.-P. Brodeur (Ed.), *How to recognize good policing: Problems and issues* (pp. 123–137). Thousand Oaks, CA: Sage.
Sampson, R. J. (2004). Neighbourhood and community: Collective efficacy and community safety. *New Economy, 11*(2), 106–113.
Sampson, R. J., Morenoff, J. D., & Gannon-Rowley, T. (2002). Assessing neighborhood effects: Social processes and new directions in research. *Annual Review of Sociology, 28*, 443–478.
Sampson, R. J., Raudenbush, S., & Earls, F. (1997). Neighborhoods and violent crime: A multilevel study of collective efficacy. *Science, 277*(5328), 918–924.
Scheepers, P., Felling, A., & Peters, J. (1992). Ethnocentrism: Update of a classic theme and an empirical test. *Politics and the Individual, 2*(1), 43–60.
Shaw, C., & McKay, H. (1942). *Juvenile delinquency and urban areas.* Chicago, IL: University of Chicago Press.
Skogan, W. (1998). Community participation and community policing. In J.-P. Brodeur (Ed.), *How to recognize good policing: Problems and issues* (pp. 88–106). Thousand Oaks, CA: Sage.
Skogan, W. (2006). *Police and community in Chicago: A tale of three cities.* New York, NY: Oxford University Press.
Skogan, W., & Harnett, S. (1996). *Community policing: Chicago style.* New York, NY: Oxford University Press.
Struening, E. L., & Richardson, A. H. (1965). A factor analytical exploration of the alienation, anomia and authoritarian domain. *American Sociological Review, 30*(5), 768–777.
Sunshine, J., & Tyler, T. R. (2003). The role of procedural justice and legitimacy in shaping public support for policing. *Law and Society Review, 37*(3), 555–589.
Tajfel, H., & Turner, J. (1979). An integrative theory of intergroup conflict. In W. G. Austin & S. Worchel (Eds.), *The social psychology of intergroup relations* (pp. 7–24). Monterey, CA: Brooks/Cole.
Tyler, T. R. (2003). Procedural justice, legitimacy and the effective rule of law. *Crime & Justice, 30*, 283–357.
Tyler, T. R. (2006a). Psychological perspectives on legitimacy and legitimation. *Annual Review of Psychology, 57*, 375–400.
Tyler, T. R. (2006b). *Why people obey the law.* Princeton, NJ: Princeton University Press.

Tyler, T. R. (Ed.). (2007). *Legitimacy and criminal justice: International perspectives*. New York, NY: Russel Sage Foundation Press.
Tyler, T. R. (2011). *Why people cooperate: The role of social motivations*. Princeton, NJ: Princeton University Press.
Tyler, T. R., & Fagan, J. (2008). Why do people cooperate with the police? *Ohio Journal of Criminal Law, 6*(1), 231–275.
Van Damme, A. (2013). The roots and routes to compliance and citizen's cooperation with the Belgian police. *European Journal of Policing Studies, 1*(1), 39–62.
Van der Veer, L., Van Sluis, A., Van de Walle, S., & Ringeling, A. B. (2013). *Vertrouwen in de politie: Trends en verklaringen [Trust in police: Tendencies and explanations]*. Apeldoorn: Politie & Wetenschap, Reed Business.
Van Reenen, P. (1979). *Overheidsgeweld: Een sociologische studie van de dynamiek van het geweldsmonopolie [Violence of the state: A sociological study of the dynamic of the monopoly of violence]*. Doctoral dissertation, Erasmus Universiteit Rotterdam, Alphen a/d Rijn.
Van Reenen, P. (2014). De legitimiteit van de politie is haar zorg niet [Legitimacy is not the concern of the police]. In L. Gunther Moor, P. Ponsaers, M. De Vries, & M. Easton (Eds.), *Het Gezag van de Politie [The authority of the police]* (pp. 109–122). Antwerpen: Maklu.
Verhage, A., & Ponsaers, P. (2013). Community policing as a police strategy: Effects and future outlook. In EUCPN Secretariat (Ed.), *Community (oriented) policing in Europe: Concepts, theory and practice* (pp. 7–15). Brussels: European Crime Prevention Network.
Weber, M. (1976). *Wirtschaft und Gesellschaft*: *Grundriss der verstehenden Soziologie [Economy and society: An outline of interpretive sociology]* (5. rev. Aufl.) Tübingen: Mohr.
Weisburd, D., & Braga, A. (Eds.). (2006). *Police innovation*. Cambridge: Cambridge University Press.
Wikström, P. H., & Dolmén, L. (2001). Urbanisation, neighbourhood social integration, informal social control, minor social disorder, victimisation and fear of crime. *International Review of Victimology, 8*(2), 121–140.
Wycoff, M., & Skogan, W. (1994). Community policing in Madison: An analysis of implementation and impact. In D. Rosenbaum (Ed.), *The challenge of community policing: Testing the promises* (pp. 75–92). Thousand Oaks, CA: Sage.

Lost in Transition: Criminal Justice Reforms and the Crises of Legitimacy in Central and Eastern Europe

Benjamin Flander and Aleš Bučar Ručman

1 Introduction: "A Success Story": 20 Years Later

At the end of the 1980s, the European socialist countries[1] embarked upon a path of change, which signaled far-reaching social transformations. Gorbachev's Perestroika and Glasnost indicated a shift from the strict, closed, and restrictive Soviet policies, while signs of change could also be identified in other countries of the Eastern block and the Western Balkans. The list of movements and organizations calling for change was extensive. It included, among others, the Polish Solidarity (*Solidarność*); the civil society movements and changes in Yugoslavia and Slovenia (e.g., the establishment of the Council for the Protection of Human Rights and Fundamental Freedoms); the emergence of opposition parties (alliances) and the obvious national division within the Communist Party of Yugoslavia; the Civic Forum (*Občanské fórum*) in the Czech Republic; the Public Against Violence (*Verejnosť proti násiliu*) in Slovakia and Charter 77 (*Charta 77*) in both parts of

[1] Despite the fact that former socialist states are often analyzed and described as a homogenous group, there were numerous differences between them (Šelih, 2012: 5). Following its break from the Soviet influence in 1948, Yugoslav socialism chose its own path. It differed with respect to the workers' ownership of companies, the openness of Yugoslavia's borders to the West, the state-supported labor emigration to Western European countries, and the cooperation of its academics and scientists with the West. It also distinguished itself in terms of its key foreign policy aspect, since Yugoslavia, together with some other countries, tried to overcome the bipolar division of the World and was one of the initiators of the Non-Aligned Movement. Yugoslavia's reliance on the Eastern block was equal to its integration with the Western block. Despite the differences, however, the common characteristics of these countries should not be overlooked: they all had a single-party system and were characterized by restrictions and violations of political and civil rights, restrictions with respect to private property, and a closed internal market.

B. Flander (✉) • A.B. Ručman
Faculty of Criminal Justice and Security, University of Maribor, Kotnikova ulica 8, 1000 Ljubljana, Slovenia
e-mail: benjamin.flander@fvv.uni-mb.si; ales.bucar@fvv.uni-mb.si

G. Meško, J. Tankebe (eds.), *Trust and Legitimacy in Criminal Justice*,
DOI 10.1007/978-3-319-09813-5_6

Czechoslovakia; and the emergence of opposition parties in countries such as Bulgaria and Hungary. It was becoming obvious that the legitimacy of the communist power and its policies were being undermined and that it would be impossible to suppress people's aspirations for political freedom, progress, and the idealized material goods of the West, which were previously only available on the restricted black market. (Yugoslavia was again an exception, since its borders with Western states were open, which allowed its citizens to conduct shopping tourism in Italy and Austria.) Beck (1997: 100) describes all these changes as the success of bottom-up activities of the sub-political sphere in these countries. After all, they managed to overthrow governments and eventually defeat the system, which infiltrated all pores of society.

Transition suggested that it would be a story of success. It implied a classical narrative with a cruel beginning (repressive, totalitarian system), the main protagonist (Western democracy and capitalism), and a "happy-end." It soon became clear, however, that for the vast majority of the population the background of this success story eventually became sour and paved with new forms of deprivation, control, and structural violence and consequently with the shattering of the idealized image of democracy and capitalism. The wake up to reality was so much harsher, since the heralds of transition towards democracy put a strong emphasis exclusively on the grim aspects of the past, while the positive aspects of the former socioeconomic system (e.g., high level of social equality and social security), which, ironically, also contributed to greater social sensitivity in capitalist countries (Beck, 2003), were completely ignored. Šelih (2012: 6) asserts that the people desired "what seemed unachievable," i.e., to preserve the advantages of the former system, which they only became aware of once these were lost, and gain the benefits of the new system. They expected the preservation of social rights and the acquisition of political and economic advantages of the West, such as better quality of life measured mainly through their opportunities to access and possess consumer goods.

The transition of former socialist states must be seen in all its breadth and complexity. Transition was not "just another shift," but a deep transformation of the political, economic, social, and cultural value systems of these countries. Ideas and values, which exalted the importance of collective spirit, egalitarianism, socially owned property, solidarity, the subordinate nature of individuals, and modesty, were replaced by new values—individualism, egoism, materialism, and competitiveness. Šelih (2012) believes that out of all transitions undergone by European countries in the previous century, it was this particular transition that actually brought about "the Big Change" and generated the most far-reaching consequences. Therefore, it is understandable that this transition also transformed all key sub-systems of society and state.

Important changes brought about by the transition were related to property rights and the introduction of market economy. Stiglitz (2006: 37–39) observes that former socialist states implemented the privatization of state- or socially owned property (albeit with varying speed and in different scope), whereby they mostly followed advice provided by Western neoliberal economists from the World Bank, the International Monetary Fund (IMF), and the US Department of the Treasury, as well as Western academics. They advocated the "shock therapy" approach and were guided by the following principle: the privatization of all property must occur as swiftly as possible, since it will be the markets that will regulate and balance out all irregularities. Non-transparent privatization—which in numerous cases resulted in the theft of formerly collectively owned property—created a new class of oligarchs. "The new rich"—ambitious individuals and networks, which took advantage of this process—increased their wealth considerably, while other segments of society were excluded and found themselves on the brink of survival (Kossowska, Buczkowski, Klaus, Rzeplińska, & Woźniakowska-Fajst, 2012). The scope of transition and privatization of formerly socially owned property must be analyzed within the boundaries of political economy and understood as a form of primitive accumulation, i.e., "accumulation (which is) not the result of the capitalistic mode of production, but its starting point" (Marx, 1867/2012: 585). In order to establish a capitalist economy, it is necessary to provide "free" labor sellers and create new owners of the means of production (ibid: 586). And this is exactly what happened to transition countries. "Democratic" privatization in post-socialist states represented an outstandingly instant form of primitive accumulation, which spanned over several centuries in Western capitalist societies and also included violence, conquests, robberies, murders, and a vast international exploitation through the colonial system. Everything but a nice and peaceful process. Is it then even possible to expect a different ending of the story in former socialist states of Central and Eastern Europe (CEE)?[2]

Citizens of CEE countries were "liberated" from the social ownership of the means of production and the concurrent guarantees of their existence, which were—in some countries more than in others—provided by the socialist state. With the disintegration of internal markets, the emergence of global competition, privatization, reduced state interventions in the field of workers' rights, economic optimization (i.e., profit maximization) in companies, and the collapse of basic industries, citizens found themselves in a position, which was inconceivable or, paradoxically, even criminalized in former systems (e.g., in Hungary) (Lévay, 2012: 118). Many became a part of the legions of the unemployed. The former egalitarianism, one of the most essential attributes of socialist societies, literally dissolved overnight.[3] What emerged in its stead was "the growing gap between the

[2] Transition countries of Central and Eastern Europe, which are closely examined in this paper, include Bulgaria, the Czech Republic, Estonia, Hungary, Latvia, Lithuania, Poland, Romania, Slovakia, and Slovenia. These countries have been members of the European Union since 2004 or 2007.

[3] Data related to the Gini coefficient, i.e., the coefficient of internal (in-)equality with respect to the disposable income (and not in terms of wealth, where the divide is supposedly even greater), show that former socialist states very swiftly joined the group of countries with the highest level of internal inequality in the industrially developed world. In 2012, as many as 7 former socialist states were among the 13 EU member states where the inequality coefficient is higher than 0.300: Latvia (0.359), Bulgaria (0.336), Romania (0.332), Estonia (0.325), Lithuania (0.320), Poland (0.309),

few who were (often dubiously in moral terms) 'winners' and the more numerous group of those who became 'losers'" of transition (Šelih, 2012: 27).

The fact that the established principles of the so-called free market, which in practice represent the *de facto* principles of a selective free market, are not in the interest of the largest number of citizens and do not provide for an increase in their quality of life, but mainly fulfil the interests of the great speculative capital, became apparent in a very short period of time. By forging alliances with local businessmen and politicians, the fluid capital managed to take advantage of the situation by cooperating in the sale of state-owned property. Moreover, in light of Wallerstein's (2006) analysis of world systems, it is possible to observe that the capital (re-) created its own periphery in newly born capitalist states, where it has access to cheaper labor force found in the army of unemployed workers.[4] In transition countries, however, the growth of unemployment and fierce competition also became (one of) the mechanisms of informal control and subordination of the people. Finally, the proximity of cheaper labor force also affected workers' rights in the so-called old democracies. Instead of obliging employers to improve the conditions for less attractive jobs (through higher salaries and better working conditions), in these countries the issue is tackled by "importing" workers or "exporting" actual labor.

In the transition, global capital represented by Western retail chains, fashion and automotive industries, as well as other producers and dealers of consumer goods found its new habitat in former socialist states. The arrival of consumerism, which practically became a "new religion," is expressly indicated by the infinite number of shopping centers that appear on almost every corner today. Kanduč (2012), recognizing the control power of consumerism, argues that this is a type of social control, which has lured individuals into a trap represented by the vicious circle of heteronomous work and consumption. In his view, control powers of the capitalist system and the ideologically supported consumption (related to the internalization of dominant ideology, values, ideals, goals, and perspectives) are perhaps even stronger than control powers of former socialist systems. When compared with the new consumerist-capitalist socioeconomic system, the former system, according to Kanduč, was truly amateur in terms of social control.[5]

The misleading and false idea of transition as an exclusive herald of freedom is also present with respect to the performance of one of the key elements of Western

---

and Croatia (0.305). The group of countries where the coefficient amounts to up to 0.250—which is also the average value of Scandinavian countries (Sweden, Finland, Norway, and Iceland)—includes only two former socialist countries—Slovenia (0.237) and the Czech Republic (0.249)—while the group of countries where the coefficient ranges between 0.250 and 0.300 includes Slovakia (0.253) and Hungary (0.269) (Eurostat, 2013b).

[4] Perhaps this explains why the highest number of labor migrants to the UK in the last decade arrived exactly from EEC countries (Poland, Slovakia, and Lithuania) (UK Border Agency, 2008).

[5] For a comprehensive illustration of the entrapment of people from former post-communist societies in the web of consumerism and its hypnotic power, see, for example, the documentary film, *Český sen* (Czech Dream), made by students of the Czech Film Academy in 2004.

democracy—the mass media. It is true that the media in the socialist regime were controlled and subordinated to the interests of the communist party, though it is an illusion to think that capitalism and "democracy" brought their freedom. Following the transition period, the media adopted the same role that they have in the West, and profit maximization became their principal goal. In the "free new world," journalists, who once served socialist regimes, are forced to fight for their survival in the media market and serve the interests of capital regimes and consumerist-capitalist ideology. Sensational news about crime represent an important tool in this fight (Bučar Ručman, 2013; Kalin Golob & Poler Kovačič, 2005; Kossowska et al., 2012; Petrovec, 2003). In this respect new capitalist countries needed less than two decades to catch up with Western (mediated) culture. Conclusions of cultural criminology approach (see, for example, Ferrell & Sanders, 1995; Hayward & Young, 2004) argue that mass media present distorted picture of crime reality and influence the public perception of crime. Even more, they create specific cultural environment which reflects in the whole crime discourse and also influences on responses to crime, crime prevention strategies, and penal and control policies.

In the eyes of former socialist states and their citizens, human rights were an important factor contributing to the allure and legitimacy of the Western system. Since human rights were often violated in socialist states—the so-called negative freedom (Berlin, 1958/2002) of individuals was particularly under attack—people demanded change. In this context, one cannot deny the important achievements of transition; however, it is important to look into the background of this process. Human rights were implemented only within the boundaries of the Western (liberal) understanding of this concept and were strictly bound to the provision of minimum standards—and even these did not apply to everyone. By applying Galtung's (1969) distinction between direct and structural violence, it is possible to conclude that the liberal concept of human rights, which was introduced in new democracies, represents a mirror image of this concept in old democracies. It primarily provides for a (selective) security from subjective (direct) forms of violence while allowing and even promoting structural violence. In this sense, Žižek (2007: 16) sees something suspicious and symptomatic in the "old" and "new" societies' obsession to oppose all forms of subjective (direct) violence, as if these wished to obliterate from view other manifestations of systemic violence, which gradually became part of "normality" and the "normal" functioning of social structures.

One could argue that the fundamental characteristic of transition lies in the more or less uncritical appropriation of the Western political and economic model. The neoliberal economic and social policy (and practice) gradually became the dominant social ideology (and practice) of the CEE countries. As a part of transition from communism and socialism to democracy and capitalism, all countries in the region also underwent extensive reforms in their criminal justice systems. After the "promising" period in the first half of the 1990s, legislative reforms in CEE countries introduced measures that drove again their criminal justice systems towards a more extensive social control and greater penal repression. The following section aims to question the legitimacy of these reforms.

2 Questioning Legitimacy of Criminal Justice Systems in Transition Countries

In criminology and criminal justice studies, one comes across a large number of different theories of legitimacy. Widely recognized and popular are the so-called procedural theories, which are oriented towards questioning whether people express trust towards criminal justice authorities and, more specifically, whether (agents of) legal systems in general and criminal justice systems in particular treat citizens with proper respect for their integrity, liberty, privacy, and other human rights and fundamental freedoms. The premises of such theories were recently applied to produce certain new approaches, such as the concept of "dialogic legitimacy" (see Bottoms & Tankebe, 2012), which are aimed to advance the conceptual understanding of legitimacy by applying insights from wider social perspectives to criminal justice contexts. From the perspective of criminal justice reforms and social justice, the issue of legitimacy has also become an important topic within advanced critical criminological and criminal justice studies (see Arrigo, 1999). Taking into account some of the key concepts of these theories—no matter how problematic they might be—the principle aim of this chapter is to question the legitimacy of two decades of reforms and the current condition of criminal justice systems in transition countries. The legitimacy of criminal justice systems in these countries is addressed through critical assessment of trends in crime and crime policy, criminal law reforms, imprisonment, and trust in criminal justice institutions while considering the consequences of the capitalist globalization and transition processes in the region and in a given country.

2.1 *Trends and Alterations in Crime*

During the 1990s, all CEE countries experienced tremendous changes in the growth, nature, and pattern of crime.[6] A significant growth in crime was observed everywhere in the region regardless of the type of crime policy that individual countries pursued. Crime increased in countries such as Poland, where significant liberalization took place, but also in Romania or Bulgaria, where such a liberalizing

[6] The analysis of crime-related data and comparison of long-term crime rate trends in former socialist regimes raise several questions. The most obvious problem is related to the dubious quality of official statistical data on crime. In former authoritarian regimes, the monitoring and analyzing of this "universal and normal" social phenomenon (Durkheim, 1895/1982) was, at least in the core of pro-Soviet countries, considered a residue of the former capitalist society and a foreign object in socialism/communism. In some countries, the official data were filtered and distorted in different ways (see Gruszczyńska & Heiskanen, 2012: 85; Šelih, 2012: 8). In order to avoid these difficulties, we focus on crime trends observed in former socialist states in the period after transition.

tendency was much less evident, and in the Baltic states, where sentencing policies remained harsh and imprisonment rates high (Krajewski, 2004; Widacki, 2001).

A more detailed overview of statistical data related to crimes recorded by the police (Eurostat, 2013a) reveals that an increase in crime rates, which occurred at the beginning of the transition period and lasted until the end of the 1990s, was witnessed in all former socialist states, with the exception of Croatia and Slovakia. In Croatia, the trend of growing crime rates can be observed only from 1997 onwards, which coincides with the period after the end of war in 1995, while the number of criminal offences recorded by the police in Slovakia started to increase only after 1999. The trend of crime rates was characterized by a gradual multiannual growth. In some cases, the number of recorded crimes increased by more than 2.4 times when the peak figure is compared to the lowest number in the beginning of the 1990s. In Slovenia, the number of crimes rose from less than 45,000 to more than 90,000, in Poland from 850,000 to 1,466,000, and in Croatia from a little over 55,000 to more than 80,000. Following a decade of growth in recorded crimes, the observed trends differ, but most countries witnessed a stabilization of growth (e.g., in Estonia this occurred after 2000, in Slovenia after 2005, in Croatia after 2002, in Lithuania and Latvia after 2000) or even an initial decrease in crime followed by a stabilization and the preservation of relatively equal average annual values (e.g., in Bulgaria, the Czech Republic, Hungary, Poland). When compared with the statistical data from the very beginning of the transition period, the average values are significantly higher in all countries. Relatively similar trends can be observed when comparing these data with the trends in some "old democracies." These countries also saw an increase in crime recorded by the police in the mid-1990s, while the decrease and stabilization of this trend were observed in the last decade (e.g., in Austria, England, France, Italy, the Netherlands, Norway, Wales). It must not be ignored, however, that in 2010 former socialist states, which are now members of the EU, had an even smaller rate of recorded crimes than numerous old EU member states, if one considers the number of inhabitants in individual countries.[7]

In the process of democratic transition, post-socialist countries did not only experience changes related to the quantity of crime, but also differences in terms of the nature of crime. Krajewski's (2004: 379) description of the situation in Poland is almost identical to the one in Hungary, presented by Keresezi and Lévay (2008: 246–247). Both countries witnessed the emergence of organized and economic crime related to the privatization of formerly collectively owned property. Street crime became much more violent. New types of crime (armed robberies and drug-related crime), which were unheard of in the period before

[7] In comparison with some old EU member states, the rates of crime per 100,000 inhabitants in post-socialist countries are much lower: Romania 1.364; Sweden 1.467; Slovakia 1.756; Bulgaria 1.944; Lithuania 2.121; Latvia 2.273; the Czech Republic 2.983; Poland 3.016; Estonia 3607; Slovenia 4.372; Hungary 4.465; Italy 4.344; Spain 4.996; Austria 6.397; the Netherlands 7.195; Germany 7.253; Finland 8.066; Denmark 8.511; and Belgium 9.689 (calculated on the basis of Eurostat (2013c) data).

transition, also emerged. Juvenile delinquency, previously dominated by petty property offences, became more violent and grew in volume, too. Also, the use of illicit drugs with all its consequences, although not unknown under communism, emerged in a pattern fairly similar to that in the countries of Western Europe.

By the end of the 1990s, CEE countries observed a significant increase in recorded violent crimes (see, e.g., Bučar Ručman & Frangež, 2009; Dobryninas & Sakalauskas, 2011; Keresezi & Lévay, 2008; Lévay, 2012; Meško & Jere, 2012; Saar, 2004; Stamatel, 2012). This is true for all former communist countries in the EU, with the exception of Romania. In the past 5 years, however, the numbers of violent crimes have been decreasing. The only exception in this respect is Hungary, which experienced a 29.7 % increase in recorded violent crimes from 2007 to 2010.

Already in the 1980s and in the early post-communist period, most former communist countries experienced an increase in homicides, which ranged from 11 % in Romania up to a whopping 232 % in Estonia (Karstedt, 2003: 301–304; Stamatel, 2012: 158).[8] This trend began reversing in 1993 in all former communist countries, which are now members of the EU (see also Eurostat, 2013a). In 2010, Estonia saw 4.3 times fewer homicides than in 1994. In Latvia, their number was 3.4 times lower than in 1995. Bulgaria observed 3.2 times fewer homicides in the same period. In Poland and the Czech Republic, their number was 2 times lower than in 1993, while Romania recorded 1.8 times less homicides than in 1993. Despite the decrease in the number of homicides, one cannot ignore the fact that their share, compared with the number of inhabitants, is the highest in Europe (Slovenia is the only exception in this regard, as it records the lowest number of homicide per 100,000 inhabitants in the EU). Baltic states are at the very top of the scale among EU member states, as the numbers of homicides in Latvia, Estonia, and Lithuania are from two to four times higher than in other member states. As many as seven former communist states (the three Baltic states, Bulgaria, Romania, Slovakia, and Hungary) are among the first ten EU member states with the highest number of homicides per 100,000 inhabitants.

In terms of the types of crime, which mushroomed in the countries of Central and Eastern Europe in the period of transition, corruption holds a particularly important place. As illustratively described by Grozdanić and Martinović (2012), corruption

[8] Various authors provide different explanations for the growth of homicides and other highly violent crime rates in post-communist countries (see Dobryninas & Sakalauskas, 2011; Keresezi & Lévay, 2008; Salla, Ceccato, & Ahven, 2012). Karstedt (2003) links them to the absence of democratic culture and civil society combined with intensified pressure of neoliberal policies. We believe that the attempts to find explanations for the trends related to violent crime cannot be isolated from the analysis of changes in society, changes in the structure and numbers of other types of crime, as well as other negative social phenomena (e.g., lower social security and social rights, the position of socially marginalized groups). We agree with Šelih (2012: 27), who recalls that the scope of changes in CEE countries after the period of transition was extremely extensive and touched upon every segment of society, which is why changes in crime trends cannot be explained only from a single theoretical perspective.

became a peculiar "metaphor for societies in transition."[9] When embarking upon the path of transition, former socialist states were faced with new types of corruption, which was almost everywhere related to the privatization of the formerly socially owned property and the exploitation of the political and economic power by the social elites on one hand and the emergence of new organized crime groups on the other. In this context, Pływaczewski (2004) discusses the top-down organized crimes and corruption of corrupt public officials and politicians and bottom-up crimes of traditional criminal underworld. Dobovšek (2008) goes even further and states that in some cases it is possible to observe the acts of elite organized crime implemented through corruption, networking, and extortion, thus influencing the state's economy and policy. In some countries, corruption gained the dimensions of systemic and legal corruption. It became a part of established practices and activities carried out in new "democracies." Different authors (e.g., Cejp & Scheinost, 2012; Dobovšek, 2008; Grozdanić & Martinović, 2012; Jager, 2011; Nožina, 2004; Pływaczewski, 2004; Sajó, 2003) describe several types of top-down corruption in CEE states. These include criminal privatization, fixing of public tenders and other types of corruption with a purpose of appropriating public funds, cartel agreements and activities harming public funds, channeling of funds from healthy companies to other companies privately owned by the management, and asset-striping. Such types of corruption can be accompanied by the activities that harm the banking sector by channeling funds and awarding unsecured loans, and systemic corruption in the sphere of public procurement in the energy, health, and transport sectors.

Numerous cases of elite corruption committed by new local elites in former socialist states, whose members became global businesspeople, investors, and consumers of luxury goods overnight, are only rarely recorded by law enforcement institutions. There are several reasons for this. Despite the fact that such acts can be characterized as the most "unscrupulous robbery," as Grozdanić and Martinović (2012: 200) described privatization, they were actually legal in numerous cases. Furthermore, such activities were encouraged and implemented by the power holders—the political elite. Part of an answer to these developments lies in the fact that these countries, like their Western counterparts, and in the process of their transition to capitalist economy, witnessed the establishment of "informal networks" (Dobovšek & Meško, 2008) and "clientelistic structures" (Sajó, 2003). One must look deeper, however, into the background to obtain a comprehensive explanation. Such activities and conducts are integrated in the very nature of the capitalist system and "democracy" (Wallerstein, 2006), as well as in the "new" ideology, that was introduced to the CEE countries by the transformation process.

[9] According to the Transparency International (2013) data, the Corruption Perception Index in post-communist states is 1.5–1.9 times lower than in the best placed Northern and Western European states. One must not forget, however, that in comparison with numerous former socialist states (e.g., Croatia, the Czech Republic, Hungary, Lithuania, Poland, Slovakia, Slovenia), some "older" democracies and traditional capitalist states (e.g., Greece, Italy) hold a lower position on this scale.

By using a pinch of sarcasm, one could say that these processes merely mark another chapter of the "success" story of transition.

2.2 *Crime Policy and Criminal Law Reforms*

After the fall of communism, new laws dealing with the criminal justice system in the CEE countries were generally aimed at preventing the escalation of crime while at the same time guaranteeing the rule of law and limitation of state power through a variety of measures (Keresezi & Lévay, 2008; Šelih, 2012). While during the early years of transition the emphasis was placed on human rights guarantees[10] and the limitation of state power, the increase in crime had no significant influence on crime control policy. At least until the middle of 1990s, crime control issues, dominated by humanist criminologists and criminal justice experts, were not subject to intensive debate either among politicians or by the general public. As crime prevention policies remained reductionist and abolitionist, measures "in the name of law and order" were practically unknown in CEE countries.

Since the fall of the communist regime in 1989, Poland, for example, has attempted both to get rid of the Soviet inheritance and to introduce European/Western standards in criminal law and crime control policy. While the communist crime control policies had been notorious for their repressive character, the key factor in policy development after 1989 was to move away from it. Priority was given to the introduction of broad guarantees of due process and civil liberties together with substantive and procedural changes in the criminal law in order to anchor them in practice (Krajewski, 2004). Similarly, Slovenia also humanized and rationalized its criminal justice laws adopted during the socialist regime by focusing on the international principles and standards of the rule of law, due process, and human rights. Before its independence, when Slovenia was a socialist republic, the most severe penalties issued by the Penal Code included 20 years of imprisonment and capital punishment, which was considered an exceptional penalty. The country "on the sunny side of the Alps" became an abolitionist country in 1989 after the constitution was amended to prohibit the death penalty, although capital punishment had effectively already been abolished with the last execution carried out in 1957. The new democratic constitution (1991) stipulated that life is inviolable and that capital punishment is prohibited, while the Penal Code, which entered into force in 1995, preserved the 20-year imprisonment as the most severe penalty (Flander & Meško, 2010; Meško & Jere, 2012; Šelih, 2012). During the first years after transition, Hungary has also begun adapting its criminal justice legislation to the new pluralistic political system and to the demands of the concept of the

[10] It seems from today's perspective that the human rights agenda in the CEE countries gathered strength at the very moment when it was already losing its power in Western democracies (Šelih, 2012: 29).

"Rechtsstaat." The first change made to the penal law after the transformation of 1990 was the abolition of capital punishment (between 1980 and 1989, three death sentences were imposed and carried out on average per year). The 1993 reforms (e.g., amendments of the Penal Code), *inter alia*, decriminalized prostitution, lowered the minimum term of imprisonment from 3 months to 1 day, widened the framework of community sanctions, increased the power of judges at sentencing, and—for the first time in the history of Hungarian criminal law—introduced treatment instead of punishment for petty drug offenders (Keresezi & Lévay, 2008; Lévay, 2012).

The liberalizing tendency of the first wave of reforms was much less evident in countries such as Bulgaria, Lithuania, and Romania. In Lithuania, for instance, the criminal justice system did not start moving towards Western/European standards before the outset of the new millennium. Owing to sudden social, political, and economic changes during the first years of independence, this Baltic country was faced with a dramatic rise in crime rates and political elites responded to this trend by introducing harsh policies of crime control. These policies went so far that Nils Christie (in Dobryninas & Sakalauskas, 2011) described the criminal justice system of the early transition period in Lithuania as "a system that is still open to totalitarian scenarios." Nevertheless, significant changes in the criminal/penal law and criminal justice have been carried out in most transition countries. These countries, *inter alia*, ratified the European Convention on Human Rights and several other international instruments. The aim of these reforms was to make criminal law and crime policy a more legitimate and democratic instrument of formal social control. In line with this aim, the changes included important shifts in almost all segments of the criminal justice system.

In the vast majority of former communist countries, however, the second wave of reforms in the mid- and late-1990s changed these trends significantly. As crime became a matter of serious concern for politicians, the media, and the public,[11] and countries in transition became a place with an extremely high level of fear of crime, public attitudes towards crime and punishment changed and led to demands for stricter criminal laws, harsher penalties, and wider powers of the formal social control agencies (see below). Flander and Meško (2010) note that the early trend of limiting penal repression in Slovenia began shifting in 1999, when the Penal Code was amended, despite the opposition of the majority of penologists and legal experts to introduce the most severe penalty of 30-year imprisonment. Most of the criminal justice reforms, carried out by the right- and left-wing governments after 1998, have been introduced "in the name of law and order"—for the sake of

[11] While the importance of crime was played down in the socialist and early transition period, this was no longer the case during the mid-1990s. Šelih (2012) notes that in the second half of the 1990s, politicians, in general, and some, in particular, discovered that the slogan of "law and order" was a good tool for gaining votes—election strategies were designed and won on the basis of a principle that a politician promising to be "tough on crime" will get more support by the voters. The general punitive wave that began sweeping across Europe from the West slowly reached the CEE countries, too.

the effective suppression, detection, and prosecution of crime, on one hand, and preventing victimization, on the other. With the new Penal Code of 2008, a penalty of life imprisonment was adopted for the most serious crimes, such as genocide, crimes against humanity, and two or more counts of intentional murder. Flander and Meško (2010) claim that the trend towards more punitive laws and legislation giving "more effective" powers (such as "dataveillance" and *ante delictum* measures) to law enforcement agencies in Slovenia is also reflected in amendments introduced to the police and procedural criminal law, as well as to the various areas of legislation governing minor offences.

In Poland, efforts to reform crime policy and legislation during the second half of the 1990s also began to encounter serious obstacles, as political parties began to indulge in law-and-order rhetoric and experts started to lose their influence on shaping crime control policy and legislation. Krajewski (2004) states that the increasing fear of crime and penal populism began to play a central role in public discourse on criminal justice and resulted in a clear-cut tendency for recourse to punitive crime control policies and legislation. Krajewski (2004) also claims that in 2000, the conservative government openly expressed its desire to reverse all criminal law reforms implemented since 1989 and to return to a criminal justice policy exclusively oriented towards the reduction of crime through stricter law enforcement and criminal sanctions. The then-cabinet frequently referred to the "success" of the American penal policy, the positive effects of "mass imprisonment," and legislation and policies such as "three-strikes-and-you're-out" and "zero tolerance." In 2001, a parliamentary bill adopted provisions for the introduction of draconian penalties and limitations of certain due process guarantees. The enactment of this bill was prevented by a presidential veto. After a change of government in the autumn of 2001, the Polish parliament adopted reforms of substantive and procedural criminal law, which were far less radical than the rejected proposals. These reforms were aimed to simplify and speed up procedures and processes, but avoided the excesses of the previous proposals (Krajewski, 2004). A further transformation of the Polish criminal law was carried out with the 1997 Penal Code under the label of "internationalization" and approximation to the EU legislation (new types of offences were criminalized and jurisdiction over acts of a terrorist nature committed abroad was given to the Polish criminal courts). Due to the public discussion surrounding these reforms, significant changes occurred in the attitudes and opinions about penal affairs not only among the public and politicians, but also within criminal justice agencies. Even though the new criminal legislation has been described as excessively liberal and influenced by international standards, the courts clearly began to implement more restrictive sentencing policies (Krajewski, 2004; Nowak, 2013).

In Hungary, the trend of limiting penal repression was overturned with the criminal law reform of 1998. Keresezi and Lévay (2008) note that this reform was preceded by the first general election campaign in which public safety and crime control were considered as salient issues of party politics (in most of the election manifestos, the emphasis shifted from the limitations of criminal policy to the issue of efficiency). After winning the general election, the center-right

Hungarian Civic Party (FIDESZ) promised its voters "a tough response to crime" and introduced a law-and-order program that included, *inter alia*, tougher punishments, a proposal to introduce a mandatory life sentence without parole, and the concept of the "visible police" for deterring street crime offenders. As this was followed by an amendment to the Penal Code, the promises came true: life sentence without the possibility of parole was introduced in the Hungarian criminal law and the system of penal sanctions was generally made more severe (i.e., the minimum period of imprisonment was raised to 2 months). In addition, the amendment increased the role of criminal law in the social control of drug abuse.

The next comprehensive reform of the Penal Code was carried out in 2003, under the social-liberal coalition that was elected 1 year earlier. On the basis of this reform, the Hungarian criminal law once again, at least temporarily, became less repressive. The new government did not agree with the approach, which expected the mechanical imposition of severe punishment to produce an effective decrease in crime. With the reform of the Penal Code, which is partly still in force today, a much greater emphasis was placed on crime prevention. The developments in criminal justice policy under the social-liberal parties, which were in part induced to satisfy the demands of the European Union, also led to a proliferation of restorative justice measures, the creation of a uniform national probation service, and attempts to strengthen the inclusive features of crime control (Keresezi & Lévay, 2008). Finally, this trend changed course with the 2009 amendment to the penal law, which allowed stricter action against serious violent crimes and provided a higher standard of retribution and protection to victims through criminal law. In 2010, Viktor Orbán's right-wing conservative coalition adopted another amendment in the interest of improving public security. This amendment initiated the "three-strikes" rule, brought in harsher provisions on special and multiple recidivists, and limited the freedom of courts in determining sentence. According to Lévay (2012), these amendments referred to the dramatic increase in the number of serious violent crimes (i.e., homicides) in Hungary and were inspired by the "successful three strikes legislation in Slovakia and the USA."

To sum up, during the last 10 years, practically all countries in the region have moved away from liberalization and democratization efforts typical of the period immediately after 1989. Under the influence of global developments,[12] a stronger emphasis on safety and security became one of the most prominent goals of crime policy everywhere in the region. After a decade of criminal justice reforms, which followed Western standards, the notions of "risk society," "safety," and "effective crime control" became major paradigms in the CEE countries, similar to what had already occurred in older European democracies during the 1980s. While human

[12] Stimulated by the terrorist attacks on 11 September 2001, Western democracies experienced a tremendous turning point in their attitudes towards crime policy and justice. As crime and security issues started to dominate a large part of public debates in these countries, neoliberal and neoconservative "law-and-order" solutions to crime problems were adopted, which have increased the degree of punitiveness and lowered human rights standards that were taken for granted for decades.

rights guarantees for suspects, defendants, offenders, and prisoners lost their importance, the security of society at large, individual safety, and victims' rights have taken place as the most socially desirable goal (see Garland, 2001; Šelih, 2012). In CEE countries, reforms pushed the criminal justice systems towards greater repression and lower levels of legitimacy. This trend received new impetus after 2008, when the region was affected by the global economic and financial crisis.

2.3 Prison Rates

Punitive trends in crime policies and laws in the CEE countries are also seen in the increasing numbers of imprisoned population. In Europe, the number of imprisoned persons per 100,000 inhabitants in the past two decades increased the most in Russia (to almost 600) and in Baltic states (in Estonia and Latvia to almost 350 and in Lithuania to approximately 230). These are followed by the countries of Eastern Europe (the number of imprisoned persons in these countries ranges between 150 and 200 per 100,000 inhabitants) and the countries of "old Europe" (in the Netherlands, for instance, the number of prisoners in the past 25 years has increased approximately sixfold—from 20 to 130 prisoners per 100,000 inhabitants; in Spain, the increase was threefold—from 40 to 140 prisoners). Scandinavian countries can still pride themselves with the lowest share of imprisoned population, while Slovenia traditionally also belongs to the group of countries with the least prisoners (Aebi et al., 2010; Aebi & Delgrande, 2009).

The statistical data reveal that the CEE countries are at the very top of the scale in terms of the number of imprisoned population per 100,000 inhabitants in Europe. In Lithuania, for example, a dramatic rise in crime rates in the early 1990s was accompanied by a substantial growth in punitiveness. Between 1991 and 2002, the proportion of custodial sentences in the annual total of court-imposed punishments nearly doubled, rising from 27 to 47 %. At the same time, there was a dramatic drop in the use of community service penalties and fines, and legislative changes placed restrictions on the suspension of sentences (applied to previously unsentenced offenders and solely in cases of minor offences with no aggravating circumstances). Consequently, by 1999, the prison population in Lithuania reached 410 per 100,000 inhabitants—a rise from 248 in 1991 (Dobryninas & Sakalauskas, 2011). Following the introduction of provisions in the new Criminal Code to promote alternative sanctions and a large amnesty in 2000, with over 2,200 inmates being discharged from prison, the incarceration rate reduced significantly. According to Dobryninas and Sakalauskas (2011), the share of custodial sentences in the annual total of court-imposed punishments dropped to an average of 30 %, while the use of fines increased considerably. In 2007, fines accounted for a higher proportion of total court-imposed punishments than custodial sentences for the first time in the history of independent Lithuania. The prison population, however, started growing again in 2009, when Lithuania ranked second in Europe. The absolute annual number of released prisoners and the use of suspended sentences have undergone a decline in recent years (whereas 7,748 prisoners were released in 2003, only 3,191 were released in 2010). Similarly, the proportion of prisoners paroled early dropped from two-thirds of total releases in 2002 to a mere half in 2010. The majority of convicted prisoners are serving long-term sentences. In a large number of Lithuanian prisons, conditions remain poor, ranging from obsolete buildings with insufficient daylight to high humidity, despite repeated expressions of concern by parliamentary ombudsmen and representatives of the European Committee for the Prevention of Torture and Inhuman or Degrading Treatment or Punishment (Sakalauskas, 2005; Walmsley, 2003).

In Poland, a low crime rate (when compared with Western Europe) during the communist era was accompanied by an extremely high imprisonment rate: 235 imprisoned persons per 100,000 inhabitants during the 1960s, 235 during the 1970s, and 236 during the 1980s. According to Krajewski (2004), this rate was several times higher than imprisonment rates in any Western European country at the time, and even higher than the rate in the USA. During the 1990s, however, exactly the opposite was the case: much higher crime rates were accompanied by substantially lower imprisonment rates.[13] The rate dropped sharply after the fall of communism, reaching 120 prisoners per 100,000 inhabitants in 1990. At its lowest point in 1990, the imprisonment rate amounted to 42 % of its peak level in 1986. After 1990, the rate began to grow again for several years, but in 1994, it still amounted to only 56 % of its 1986 peak level. After some further decline in 1998, the rate rose again and in 2001 exceeded the 200 mark for the first time since the fall of communism. Krajewski (2004) argues that this amounted to a considerable step on the road towards a European "penal climate."

In Hungary, as in Poland, the beginning of the 1990s saw a general trend that led towards a steady decrease in the prison population. According to Keresezi and Lévay (2008), this was partly due to amnesties, decriminalization, and abolition of certain sanctions. This trend was reversed during the mid-1990s, when the prison population reached almost the same levels as that of the pre-transition era.

There was an overrepresentation of ethnic minorities within the prison system, as the total number of Roma inmates was approximately three times higher than that of inmates from other ethnicities. Prisons in Hungary were, according to Lévay (2012), regularly overcrowded, operating with twice the number of inmates for which they were originally designed. After the center-right government's amendment of the Criminal Code in 1998, the prison population rate continued to increase, but it stopped increasing after the liberal reforms of 2003 (these reforms were aimed at decreasing the rate of imprisonment and the prison population overall).

[13] During the 1980s, imprisonment accounted for 32 % of all sentences on average. After 1990, the role of imprisonment decreased significantly, and imprisonment accounted for only 12.2 % of all sentences by 1997. Despite a slight reversal of this trend at the end of the 1990s, custodial sentences constituted 16.5 % of all sanctions over that decade (Krajewski, 2004).

In contrast to other transition countries, Slovenia has traditionally had one of the lowest levels of prison population in the world (comparable to Scandinavian countries). In 2012, there were 69 prisoners per 100,000 inhabitants (Uprava za izvrševanje kazenskih sankcij, 2013). Nevertheless, the daily average number of prisoners in Slovenia has increased by over 26 % in the past 10 years. In spite of a relatively small average number of imprisoned persons per 100,000 inhabitants, prisons have been overcrowded (the occupancy of some prisons amounts to 120 %) and most of them are also situated in old buildings that are not suitable for the enforcement of custodial sentences. Flander and Meško (2013) report that the total number of prisoners, the number of newly admitted prisoners, and the number of prisoners in premises with stricter regime have also increased over the last 10 years. The majority of persons, however, were sentenced to relatively short prison sentences, and in 2012, for example, more alternative sentences were imposed than in the previous year. While in recent years the number of conditionally released prisoners has been decreasing, the number of recidivists and those who were released early remained at approximately the same level.

In his study of the links between the use of imprisonment in 30 European countries and factors, such as crime levels, the public fear of crime and public punitiveness, political structure and forms of democracy, trust in state/political institutions, income inequality, and investment in welfare programs, Lappi-Seppälä (2011) shows that, apart from a few exceptions, prisoner rates are largely unrelated to trends in reported crime across Europe (see also Sutton, 2004; Ruddell, 2005). Bulgaria, the Czech Republic, Estonia, Latvia, Lithuania, Poland, Romania, and Slovakia are former communist countries where the total reported crime correlates most inversely with imprisonment rates, though crimes related to lethal violence show a strong positive correlation. Similarly (with the exception of Slovenia, the Czech Republic, and Slovakia), the Baltic and CEE states are, according to Lappi-Seppälä (2011), regions where the association between the emergence of punitive policies and the scaling back of the welfare state has been the most intensive over the last decade.[14] Moreover, the CEE countries are also countries with the highest levels of incarceration and lowest public trust in police and other criminal justice institutions (see below). When examining associations between the fear of crime, public penal attitudes, and social tolerance, on one hand, and imprisonment rates, on the other, Lappi-Seppälä (2011) shows that transition countries in Central and Eastern European region are among European countries with the highest numbers of imprisoned persons, the highest levels of fear of crime, the highest scores of public punitiveness, and the lowest social tolerance.

[14] Lappi-Seppälä (2011) examined the association between the use of imprisonment and the impact of the following three welfare indicators: the fairness of income distribution measured by the Gini index, the level of social protection measured by public investments in welfare (both as a percentage of gross domestic product and as EURO per capita), and the general index of welfare and prosperity (published by the Legatum Institute).

2.4 (Dis)Trust in the Legal and Criminal Justice System

This subsection presents findings with respect to people's (dis)trust in the agents of legal and criminal justice systems of the transition countries in greater detail. The overview predominantly, albeit not exclusively, relies on the European Social Survey 2012 (ESS, 2012).

The analysis reveals certain differences with regard to "audience legitimacy" between six post-communist states included in the ESS (2012) (Bulgaria, the Czech Republic, Estonia, Poland, Slovakia, and Slovenia) and "older" European democracies (e.g., Denmark, Finland, Germany, Norway, and the UK). In transition countries, there is a larger share of respondents who do not have trust in the legal system than those who do (on a Likert scale with 11 stages where 0 stands for "no trust at all" and 11 means "complete trust," they selected answers with a value ranging from 0 to 4), while data from older democracies show quite the opposite. Estonia is the only exception in the first group of countries. The majority of respondents in Bulgaria (a whopping 34.6 %) and Slovenia (20.6 %) chose "no trust at all" out of all possible answers. This answer was also selected by approximately 11 % of respondents in Poland, the Czech Republic, and Slovakia. 81 % of respondents in Bulgaria, 71 % in Slovakia, 67 % in Slovenia, 61 % in Poland, 56 % in the Czech Republic, and 40 % in Estonia evaluated their trust in the legal system with a grade lower than 5. The trust in the legal system was graded between 6 and 11 by a mere 10 % of respondents in Bulgaria, 15 % in Slovakia, 18 % in Slovenia, 30 % in the Czech Republic, and 41 % in Estonia. "No trust at all" was rarely selected in Western EU countries (2.9 % in the UK, 3.1 % in Germany, and 4.6 % in Ireland) and scarcely ever in Scandinavian countries (0.5 % in Denmark and Finland, 0.9 % in Norway and 1.6 % in Sweden). In "older" democracies, the majority of respondents evaluated its trust in the legal system with grade 6 or higher, whereby their share ranges between 52 % in the UK and 85 % in Denmark, where as many as 13 % of respondents have complete trust in the legal system. The only exceptions among older EU member states are Portugal and Spain. In these two countries, the levels of trust in the legal system are closer to the ones in the group of transition countries than to the Western and Northern European states.

The data regarding the trust in police are different from the data regarding trust in the legal system. Even though transition countries and Western or Northern European countries achieve similar results on average, the level of trust in certain countries belonging to the first group (Bulgaria and partly Slovakia) is relatively low. The share of respondents, who have trust in police (grades between 6 and 11—complete trust), is larger than the share of respondents, who do not have trust in police (grades between 0—"no trust at all"—and 4), in all countries, with the exception of the aforementioned two. I must not be ignored, however, that the share of respondents, who have trust in police in Western and Northern European states, is significantly higher than their share in transition countries. Former socialist countries differ from other countries in the fact that most respondents in these countries selected a neutral grade, e.g., 5 (between 13 and 21 %), while respondents in Western and Northern countries mostly evaluated their trust in police with grade 8 (the UK, Germany, Norway, and Sweden) and even 9 in Finland. A completely different level of trust in police can be observed in Bulgaria, where the majority of respondents selected the answer "no trust at all" (22 %). 63 % of respondents in Bulgaria, 54 % in Slovakia, 39 % in the Czech Republic, 32 % in Poland and Slovenia, and 24 % in Estonia do not have any trust in police. The shares of distrust are significantly lower in Western and Northern European countries. In Scandinavian countries, 13 % of respondents in Sweden indicated that they do not have trust in police, 9 % in Norway, 5 % in Denmark, and 4 % in Finland. These countries also observe the highest levels of trust in police in Europe, since 74 % of respondents in Sweden, 83 % in Norway, 90 % in Denmark, and 93 % in Finland trust the police. In Western European countries, the levels of distrust are slightly higher (between 13 and 16 %), while the levels of trust are somewhat lower (between 73 and 77 %). Nevertheless, these shares are still much larger than in transition countries, where the trust in police was expressed by a mere 23 % of respondents in Bulgaria, 26 % in Slovakia, 42 % in the Czech Republic, 46 % in Poland, 49 % in Slovenia, and 57 % in Estonia.

Let us take a closer look at Poland and Lithuania, because the trust in criminal justice institutions in these two countries provides a good example for the general situation in the region. Krajewski (2004) claims that whereas in Poland the police have gone up in the public's estimation over the last few years, trust in the courts is significantly lower. In a 1993 survey, 54.7 % of Warsaw inhabitants trusted the courts, while in a national survey of 2002, as much as 29 % of Poles believed that the criminal courts' verdicts were unjust and 78 % of respondents believed that judges were not independent and were subject to undue influence in their rulings. Despite the low degree of trust, most respondents (59 %) said that if they had fallen victim to an unlawful act they would take it to court. The courts, as institutions protecting the rights of the individual, were rated second only to the Polish Ombudsman and ahead of the public prosecutor and the police. It is also worth noting that people who had dealings with the courts in recent years assessed them relatively positively—57 % of respondents were satisfied with their contacts with the courts (the courts came third in the public ranking of institutions of the justice system—ahead of the police). Krajewski (2004) believes that in Poland the media representation plays a key role in molding society's perception of how the police and other bodies of the justice system function. Information about the workings of the justice system is usually given a negative slant in the media, appearing alongside malfunctioning in the various justice bodies (e.g., prolonged court proceedings even in trivial cases, prisoners held on remand for unjustifiably long periods, rulings repeatedly overturned) and instances of corruption, drunken driving by judges, public prosecutors, and policemen, and private dealings by them with the criminal world.

Surveys, which have been conducted in Lithuania, showed that the level of public dissatisfaction with police performance has been found to be higher in Lithuania than in Western Europe, as well as Eastern and Central Europe. Dobryninas and Sakalauskas (2011), referring to Vilmorus, argue that it should be noted, however, that negative ratings of police performance in Lithuania have been dropping in recent years, and commercial survey research has shown public confidence in the police to have risen considerably, so that at the end of 2009, the proportion of people who trusted the police exceeded those who did not for the first time. In contrast, public trust in the judicial system has been declining. Between 2004 and 2011, the levels of trust fell from 24.2 % of respondents to 15.7 %, and levels of distrust rose from 33.8 to 43.1 %. According to Dobryninas and Sakalauskas (2011), it comes as no surprise that the level of public trust in the judicial system in Lithuania is one of the lowest in the EU. A mere 15 % of the Lithuanians surveyed expressed trust in the judicial system in 2009, compared with an EU average of 43 %.

Conclusions: Transition, Criminal Justice, and (the Crises of) Legitimacy

We believe that transition in post-socialist European countries can and shall not be understood as a social process of liberalization and democratization of former socialist states, which have more or less successfully escaped the iron clasp of totalitarianism. Instead, it must be understood in the context of a structural crisis of the global neoliberal postmodern capitalism, which is marked by the decline of the rule of law and democracy, e.g., by the crisis of legitimacy. If the transition was a success story, it was particularly successful in terms of transforming CEE countries into "normal" capitalist democracies. Countries in transition transformed from socialist to (small and medium sized) capitalist states while taking the role described by prominent sociologists as "weak states" (Bauman, 2008), "minimal states" (Beck, 2003: 15), and "subsidiary states" (Močnik, 2006). They have tended to compensate their subordination to large and powerful transnational corporations and fluid international capital by increasing their powers and control over the civil society, trade unions, and atomized citizens, and particularly over the marginalized groups of "others," who became easy targets of populist policies related to risks and threats. From this perspective, transition actually brought about a shift from the crisis of "democratic" socialism to the crisis of "capitalist" democracy (Kanduč, 2013: 618). In the process of uncritical imitation and application of Western capitalist ideology and policies stemming from it, they lost—or failed to create—their own identities and turned into Western-type "consumer democracies" (Bučar Ručman, 2011).

It is not surprising that following two decades of transition the situation in these countries, similarly to Western societies (see Bauman, 2002; Beck, 2003; Stiglitz, 2006; Wallerstein, 2006), is characterized by predatory economy, the domination of the interests of capital, the loss of sovereignty of nation states, and the accompanying crisis of legality, legitimacy, and rationality. Countries in transition became prisoners of "objective necessities" of

(continued)

neoliberal late capitalist economy, among which the demand for economic deregulation and the abolition of the interventionist (welfare) state seems to be the most prominent. If the previous system victimized population through direct and visible repression, the transition to capitalist democracy brought about a more refined and hidden victimization through structural violence. It appears that this also holds true for criminal justice reforms that occurred during the process of transition. The CEE countries experienced the transformation from an illegitimate communist-socialist criminal justice system into a democratic model of criminal justice pestered by the crisis of legitimacy. As the "promising" period of democratization ended in the middle of the 1990s, legislative reforms in CEE countries introduced measures that drove their criminal justice systems towards a more extensive social control and greater penal repression (e.g., towards lower levels of legitimacy), similar to those from the communist times. With a partial exception of some countries, the CEE has become a region where the rise in punitiveness, numbers of incarcerated, and levels of fear of crime on one hand, and the decrease of public trust in police and other criminal justice institutions as well as social tolerance on the other hand, have been the most intensive in Europe.

References

Aebi, M. F., Aubusson de Cavarlay, B., Barclay, G., Gruszczyńska, B., Harrendorf, S., Heiskanen, M., et al. (2010). *The European sourcebook of crime and criminal justice statistics—2010* (4th ed.). The Hague: Boom Juridische uitgevers.

Aebi, M., & Delgrande, N. (2009). *Council of Europe SPACE 1: 2007 Survey on prison populations: Document PC-CP (2009)*. Strasbourg: Council of Europe.

Arrigo, B. A. (1999). *Social justice/criminal justice: The maturation of critical theory in law, crime, and deviance*. Belmont: West/Wadsworth.

Bauman, Z. (2002). *Tekoča moderna [Liquid modernity]*. Ljubljana: Založba *Cf.

Bauman, Z. (2008). *Globalization: The human consequences*. Cambridge: Polity Press.

Beck, U. (1997). *The reinvention of politics: Rethinking modernity in the global social order*. Cambridge: Polity Press.

Beck, U. (2003). *Kaj je globalizacija? Zmote globalizma—odgovori na globalizacijo [What is globalization?]*. Ljubljana: Krtina.

Berlin, I. (1958/2002). Two concepts of liberty. In H. Hardy (Ed.), *Liberty* (pp. 166–217). New York, NY: Oxford University Press.

Bottoms, A., & Tankebe, J. (2012). Beyond procedural justice: A dialogic approach to legitimacy in criminal justice. *The Journal of Criminal Law & Criminology, 102*(1), 119–170.

Bučar Ručman, A. (2011). *Potrošniška demokracija: analiza politično—medijskega diskurza sodobnih »demokratičnih« družb [Consumer democracy: Analysis of political—media discourse of contemporary »democratic« societies]*. Ljubljana: Fakulteta za varnostne vede.

Bučar Ručman, A. (2013). Crime news discourse in Slovenia: Critical reflection two decades after transition to 'democracy'. *Crime, Law and Social Change, 59*(1), 21–37.

Bučar Ručman, A., & Frangež, D. (2009). Violence and Slovene society. *Varstvoslovje, 11*(1), 221–238.

Cejp, M., & Scheinost, M. (2012). Organized and economic crime: A common problem. In A. Šelih & A. Završnik (Eds.), *Crime and transition in Central and Eastern Europe* (pp. 157–178). New York, NY: Springer.
Dobovšek, B. (2008). Economic organized crime networks in emerging democracies. *International Journal of Social Economics, 35*(9/10), 679–690.
Dobovšek, B., & Meško, G. (2008). Informal networks in Slovenia: A blessing or a curse? *Problems of Post-Communism, 55*(2), 25–37.
Dobryninas, A., & Sakalauskas, G. (2011). Country survey: Criminology, crime and criminal justice in Lithuania. *European Journal of Criminology, 8*(5), 421–434.
Durkheim, E. (1895/1982). *The rules of sociological method and selected texts on sociology and its methods*. New York, NY: The Free Press.
European Social Survey [ESS]. (2012). *Round 6 Data. Data file edition 1.2. Norwegian Social Science Data Services, Norway—Data Archive and distributor of ESS data*. Retrieved from http://www.europeansocialsurvey.org/download.html?file=ESS6e01_1&y=2012.
Eurostat. (2013a). *Crime and criminal justice*. Retrieved from http://epp.eurostat.ec.europa.eu/portal/page/portal/crime/data/database.
Eurostat. (2013b). *Gini coefficient of equivalised disposable income*. Retrieved from http://epp.eurostat.ec.europa.eu/tgm/table.do?tab=table&language=en&pcode=tessi190.
Eurostat. (2013c). *Trends in crime and criminal justice, graphs and tables*. Retrieved from http://epp.eurostat.ec.europa.eu/statistics_explained/images/c/c4/SiF2013_Tables-and-graphs_07March13.xls.
Ferrell, J., & Sanders, C. (1995). Culture, crime and criminology. In J. Ferrell & C. Sanders (Eds.), *Cultural criminology* (pp. 3–21). Boston, MA: Northeastern University Press.
Flander, B., & Meško, G. (2010). 'Punitiveness' and penal trends in Slovenia: On the 'shady side of the Alps'? In H. Kury & E. Shea (Eds.), *Punitivity international developments* (pp. 227–249). Bochum: Universitätsverlag Brockmeyer.
Flander, B., & Meško, G. (2013). Punitivnost in kaznovalni populizem v Sloveniji [Punitiveness and penal populism in Slovenia]. *Revija za kriminalistiko in kriminologijo, 64*(4), 330–344.
Galtung, J. (1969). Violence, peace and peace research. *Journal of Peace Research, 6*(3), 167–191.
Garland, D. (2001). *The culture of control: Crime and social order in contemporary society*. Oxford: Oxford University Press.
Grozdanić, V., & Martinović, I. (2012). Corruption as a metaphor for societies in transition? In A. Šelih & A. Završnik (Eds.), *Crime and transition in Central and Eastern Europe* (pp. 179–204). New York, NY: Springer.
Gruszczyńska, B., & Heiskanen, M. (2012). Trends in police—recorded offences. *European Journal on Criminal Policy and Research, 18*(1), 83–102.
Hayward, K., & Young, J. (2004). Cultural criminology: Some notes on the script. *Theoretical Criminology, 8*(3), 259–273.
Jager, M. (2011). The politics of the Zemono Building Cartel on the sunny side of the Alps. In G. A. Antonopouos, M. Groenhuijsen, J. Harvey, & T. Kooijmans (Eds.), *Usual and unusual organising criminals in Europe and beyond* (pp. 105–118). Apeldorn: Maklu.
Kalin Golob, M., & Poler Kovačič, K. M. (2005). Med novinarskim stilom in etiko: senzacionalizem brez meja [Between journalism style and ethic: Sensationalism without borders]. *Družboslovne razprave, 31*(49/50), 289–303.
Kanduč, Z. (2012). Crime, class control, structural violence and social formations "in transition". In A. Šelih & A. Završnik (Eds.), *Crime and transition in Central and Eastern Europe* (pp. 253–276). New York, NY: Springer.
Kanduč, Z. (2013). *Politika, pravo, ekonomija in kriminal: kriminološke refleksije postmoderne družbe in culture [Politics, law, economy and crime: Criminological reflection of postmodern society and culture]*. Ljubljana: Inštitut za kriminologijo pri Pravni Fakulteti v Ljubljani.
Karstedt, S. (2003). Legacies of a culture of inequality: The Janus face of crime in post-communist countries. *Crime, Law and Social Change, 40*(2–3), 295–320.

Keresezi, K., & Lévay, M. (2008). Criminology, crime and criminal justice in Hungary. *European Journal of Criminology, 5*(2), 239–260.
Kossowska, A., Buczkowski, K., Klaus, W., Rzeplińska, I., & Woźniakowska-Fajst, D. (2012). Politicians, media, and society's perception of crime. In A. Šelih & A. Završnik (Eds.), *Crime and transition in Central and Eastern Europe* (pp. 37–63). New York, NY: Springer.
Krajewski, K. (2004). Crime and criminal justice in Poland. *European Journal of Criminology, 1* (3), 377–407.
Lappi-Seppälä, T. (2011). Explaining imprisonment in Europe. *European Journal of Criminology, 8*(4), 303–328.
Lévay, M. (2012). Penal policy, crime and political change. In A. Šelih & A. Završnik (Eds.), *Crime and transition in Central and Eastern Europe* (pp. 117–153). New York, NY: Springer.
Marx, K. (1867/2012). *Kapital, I. knjiga [Capital, Vol. I]*. Ljubljana: Sophia.
Meško, G., & Jere, M. (2012). Crime, criminal justice and criminology in Slovenia. *European Journal of Criminology, 9*(3), 323–334.
Močnik, R. (2006). *Svetovno gospodarstvo in revolucionarna politika [World economy and revolutionary politics]*. Ljubljana: Založba.
Nowak, C. (2013). The internationalization of the Polish criminal law: How the Polish criminal law changed under the influence of globalization. *Crime, Law and Social Chang, 59*(2), 139–156.
Nožina, M. (2004). The Czech Republic: A crossroads for organised crime. In C. Fijnaut & L. Paoli (Eds.), *Organised crime in Europe: Concept, patterns and control policies in the European Union and beyond* (pp. 467–498). Dordrecht: Springer.
Petrovec, D. (2003). *Mediji in nasilje: obseg in vpliv nasilja v medijih v Sloveniji [Violence in the media: The extent and the influence of violence in the media in Slovenia]*. Ljubljana: Mirovni inštitut.
Pływaczewski, E. W. (2004). Organized crime in Poland: Its development from "real socialism" to the present time. In C. Fijnaut & L. Paoli (Eds.), *Organised crime in Europe: Concept, patterns and control policies in the European Union and beyond* (pp. 467–498). Dordrecht: Springer.
Ruddell, R. (2005). Social disruption, state priorities, and minority threat: A cross-national study of imprisonment. *Punishment & Society: The International Journal of Penology, 7*(1), 7–28.
Saar, J. (2004). Crime, crime control and criminology in post-communist Estonia. *European Journal of Criminology, 1*(4), 505–531.
Sajó, A. (2003). From corruption to extortion: Conceptualization of post-communist corruption. *Crime, Law and Social Change, 40*(2–3), 171–194.
Sakalauskas, G. (2005). The rights of the persons with restricted freedom. In A. Cepas (Ed.), *Human rights in Lithuania* (pp. 304–331). Vilnius: UNDP, Law Institute.
Salla, J., Ceccato, V., & Ahven, A. (2012). Homicide in Estonia. In M. C. A. Liem & W. A. Pridemore (Eds.), *Handbook of European homicide research: Patterns, explanations, and country studies* (pp. 421–435). New York, NY: Springer.
Šelih, A. (2012). Crime and crime control in transition countries. In A. Šelih & A. Završnik (Eds.), *Crime and transition in Central and Eastern Europe* (pp. 3–34). New York, NY: Springer.
Stamatel, J. P. (2012). The effects of political, economic, and social changes on homicide in Eastern Europe. In M. Liem & W. A. Pridemore (Eds.), *Handbook of European homicide research* (pp. 155–170). New York, NY: Springer.
Stiglitz, E. J. (2006). *Making globalization work: The next step to global justice*. London: Penguin.
Sutton, J. (2004). The political economy of imprisonment in affluent Western democracies 1960–1990. *American Sociological Review, 69*(2), 170–189.
Transperency International (2013). *Corruption perception index*. Retrieved from http://files.transparency.org/content/download/700/3007/file/2013_CPIBrochure_EN.pdf
UK Border Agency. (2008). *Accession monitoring report, May 2004–September2008*. Retrieved from http://www.migrantsrights.org.uk/files/Accession_Monitoring_Report_may04sept08.pdf
Uprava za izvrševanje kazenskih sankcij [Prison Administration]. (2013). *Letno poročilo 2012 [Annual report 2012]*. Ljubljana: Ministrstvo za pravosodje, Uprava za izvrševanje kazenskih

sankcij. Retrieved from http://www.mp.gov.si/fileadmin/mp.gov.si/pageuploads/UIKS/Letna_porocila/LP_2012.pdf

Wallerstein, I. M. (2006). *Uvod v analizo svetovnih–sistemov [World system analysis: An introduction]*. Ljubljana: Založba *Cf.

Walmsley, R. (2003). *Further developments in the prison systems of Central and Eastern Europe: Achievements, problems and objectives*. Helsinki: HEUNI.

Widacki, J. (2001). Criminality in the Central and Eastern European countries in the period of transformation 1989–1999. In J. Widacki, M. Maczynski, & J. Czapska (Eds.), *Local community, public security: Central and Eastern European countries under transformation* (pp. 13–24). Warsaw: Instytut Spraw Publicznych.

Žižek, S. (2007). *Nasilje [Violence]*. Ljubljana: Društvo za teoretsko psihoanalizo.

Part II
Exploring Trust and Legitimacy in Police

Empirical Legitimacy as Two Connected Psychological States

Jonathan Jackson, Mike Hough, Ben Bradford, and Jouni Kuha

1 Introduction

Legitimacy is receiving a good deal of criminological attention. Typically conceived as the subjective state of mind of the policed (Bottoms & Tankebe, 2012; Jackson et al., 2011; Sunshine & Tyler, 2003; Tyler, 2006a, 2006b), legitimacy refers to people's beliefs about the right of justice institutions to hold power and influence. On the one hand, legitimacy is a response to an institution's claim to rightful authority. Legitimacy exists in the eyes of citizens partly when those citizens believe that the institution has a positive right to dictate appropriate behavior and when they feel that they have a corresponding duty to obey. On the other hand, legitimacy is a response to the claim that power is rightfully held and exercised. Legitimacy exists in the eyes of citizens partly when people believe that the institution acts in ways that accord with prevailing notions of appropriate moral conduct.

Legitimacy is important for two reasons. First, it reduces what Coicaud (2013: 40) calls the tension between power-holders and subordinates. When people believe that criminal justice institutions are legitimate, they recognize the system's authority to

J. Jackson (✉) • J. Kuha
Department of Methodology, London School of Economics, Houghton Street,
London WC2A 2AE, UK
e-mail: j.p.jackson@lse.ac.uk; j.kuha@lse.ac.uk

M. Hough
Institute for Criminal Policy Research, Birkbeck, University of London, 42 Store Street,
London WC1E 7DB, UK
e-mail: m.hough@bbk.ac.uk

B. Bradford
Centre for Criminology, University of Oxford, Manor Road Building, Manor Road,
Oxford OX1 3UQ, UK
e-mail: ben.bradford@crim.ox.ac.uk

G. Meško, J. Tankebe (eds.), *Trust and Legitimacy in Criminal Justice*,
DOI 10.1007/978-3-319-09813-5_7

determine the law, govern through the use of coercive force if necessary, punish those who act illegally, and expect cooperation and obedience, meaning that legal authorities no longer need to send costly signals of strength, suspicion and sanction in order to secure compliance (Hough, Jackson, & Bradford, 2013b, 2013c; Jackson, Bradford, Hough, et al., 2012; Jackson, Bradford, Stanko, & Hohl, 2012; Tyler, 2003, 2011b). Second, legitimacy places constraints on power. In the words of Coicaud (2013: 40): "... the whole purpose of legitimacy, of connecting power with legitimacy, is to put limits on the nature and exercise of power." If they are to be seen as legitimate in the eyes of the policed, the police must wield their authority in ways that accord with common "norms, values, beliefs and definitions" (Suchman, 1995: 574).

Research and legitimacy and legal authority is becoming increasingly international (see also Crawford & Hucklesby, 2012; Tankebe & Liebling, 2013; Tyler, 2007), with studies from across the world examining not just the factors that predict police legitimacy, but also the law-related behaviors that legitimacy seems to influence. Thus far, work has emerged from the USA (Gau & Brunson, 2010; Huq, Tyler, & Schulhofer, 2011a; Kane, 2005; Kirk & Matsuda, 2011; Papachristos, Meares, & Fagan, 2012; Reisig, Bratton, & Gertz, 2007; Sunshine & Tyler, 2003; Tyler & Jackson, 2014; Tyler & Wakslak, 2004; Tyler, Schulhofer, & Huq, 2010), the UK (Bradford, 2014; Hough, Jackson, Bradford, Myhill, & Quinton, 2010; Huq, Tyler, & Schulhofer, 2011b; Jackson, Huq, Bradford, & Tyler, 2013; Tankebe, 2013), Australia (Bradford, Murphy, & Jackson, 2014; Elliott, Thomas, & Ogloff, 2011; Mazerolle, Bennett, Antrobus, & Tyler, 2013; Murphy & Cherney, 2012; Sargeant, Murphy, & Cherney, 2014), Israel (Factor, Mahalel, Rafaeli, & Williams, 2013; Hasisi & Weisburd, 2011; Jonathan-Zamir & Harpaz, 2014; Jonathan-Zamir & Weisburd, 2013), and other countries (Bradford, Huq, Jackson, & Roberts, 2014; Dirikx & Van den Bulck, 2014; Kochel, Parks, & Mastrofski, 2013; Tankebe, 2009).

In this body of research, the dominant overarching explanatory framework is procedural justice theory. On this account, legal authorities build legitimacy by acting according to principles of procedural fairness (Dirikx & Van den Bulck, 2014; Hough et al., 2013b, 2013c; Mazerolle et al., 2013; Murphy, Tyler, & Curtis, 2009; Sunshine & Tyler, 2003; Tyler & Huo, 2002; Tyler, 2006a, 2006b). People's judgments about the extent to which legal authority is appropriate, proper, and valid are based in part on the degree to which individual justice agents wield their authority in fair and just ways; the exercise of authority via the application of fair process—treating people in ways that are recognized to be fair, respectful, and legal, and making fair and neutral decisions—strengthens the social bonds between individuals and authorities. Procedural justice encourages not just the belief that institutions have "a just, fair, and valid basis of legal authority" (in the words of Papachristos et al., 2012: 417) but also identification with the group that the authority represents (typically assumed to be the state or community), as well as the internalization of the belief that one should follow the rules of the group (Sunshine & Tyler, 2003; Tyler & Huo, 2002; Tyler & Jackson, 2014; Tyler, 2006b, 2011b).

In this chapter we contribute to ongoing debate about the meaning and measurement of police legitimacy (Gau, 2011; Jackson, Bradford, Hough, et al., 2012; Jackson, Bradford, Stanko, et al., 2012; Maguire & Johnson, 2010; Reisig et al., 2007; Tankebe, 2013; Tyler, 2006a, 2006b; Tyler & Jackson, 2013, 2014). We make the claim that legitimacy comprises two connected psychological states, where each is a way of processing and responding to an institution's claim to rightful authority (cf. Bottoms & Tankebe, 2012). First, power-holders make claims that they have the right to dictate, enforce and expect appropriate deferential behavior in the service of their mandate of maintaining social order and control. People process and respond to these claims, and to believe that the police are legitimate is partly to feel a positive duty to give up some of one's freedom to act when required to do so by a legitimate power-holder. Second, power-holders need moral validity in the eyes of citizens to legitimate their claims to rightful power. Their standing is in part premised on acting in accordance with prevailing norms of appropriate conduct. To believe that the police are legitimate is partly to judge that their actions are moral and justified. This accords with Suchman's (1995: 574) definition of legitimacy as "... a generalized perception or assumption that the actions of an entity are desirable, proper, or appropriate within some socially constructed system of norms, values, beliefs, and definitions."

To apply this definition in empirical research, we draw upon data from Round 5 of the European Social Survey (R5 ESS; see European Social Survey, 2011, 2012; Hough et al., 2013a, 2013b, 2013c; Jackson et al., 2011; Jackson, Kuha, et al., 2013). Fielded in 2010 and 2011, the R5 ESS collected data from national probability samples of 27 countries (Belgium, Bulgaria, Croatia, Cyprus, Czech Republic, Denmark, Estonia, Finland, France, Germany, Greece, Hungary, Ireland, Israel, Lithuania, the Netherlands, Norway, Poland, Portugal, Russian Federation, Slovakia, Slovenia, Spain, Sweden, Switzerland, the UK, and Ukraine). Inter alia, the module fielded questions on people's contact with the police, their trust in the effectiveness and fairness of the police and criminal courts, their beliefs about the legitimacy of the police and criminal courts, their willingness to cooperate with legal authorities and their compliance with the law. On the one hand, ESS R5 data allow social scientists to test instrumental and normative modes of compliance and cooperation in diverse social, legal and political contexts (Tyler, 2006a, 2006b, 2011a, 2011b). On the other hand, ESS R5 data can also contribute to conceptual and methodological discussions about the nature of public trust and institutional legitimacy.

The chapter proceeds as follows. First we consider Tyler's framework—and the ESS R5 data—in the context of Bottoms and Tankebe's (2012) dialogic account of police legitimacy. We then turn to empirical matters. Examining the dimensionality of the ESS R5 measures using the UK sample, a particular focus of our work is to assess where public beliefs about the lawfulness of the police fit into the conceptualization and measurement scheme. Is it appropriate to treat beliefs about the morality of the police and beliefs about the lawfulness of the police as one construct or as two constructs? We fit two statistical models. Both address different motivations to cooperate with the police and criminal courts. But in the first model we treat police legitimacy as a three-dimensional construct, while in the second model we treat police legitimacy as a two-dimensional construct. Finally, we consider legitimacy as a weighted sum of the two psychological states (cf. chapter 15 of Jackson, Bradford, Stanko, et al., 2012).

2 A Dialogic Account of Police Legitimacy

A key contribution of Bottoms and Tankebe (2012) is their account of the dynamic and interactive nature of legitimacy. From this perspective, legitimacy involves a claim to legitimacy from a power-holder and a corresponding audience assessment of and response to that claim. Because legitimacy is a dialogue between claims to power and a justification of those claims by public agreement, a complete analysis covers how power-holders make sense of their own power and authority (and how these self-beliefs shape subsequent behavior) and how subordinates process these claims to power and authority (and how this beliefs about legitimacy shape subsequent behavior).

Consider a street-stop, typically associated with policing policies like stop-and-search in the UK (or stop-and-frisk in the USA). The dynamic partly reflects the interplay between the officer's sense of authority and power (and his or her consequent actions) and the citizen's reception of the officer's claims to power and authority (and his or her consequent actions). Tyler (2011b) has called such an encounter a "teachable moment," in which the individual learns something about the law and legal authority and his or her status and value within some large, superordinate group. But as Bottoms and Tankebe (2013: 62) note, the encounter is also a "teachable moment" for the power-holder, because the officer learns something about his authority in the eyes of a member of the public. A full study of the dynamics of legitimacy in such an encounter would thus address both sides of the coin.

How does existing work on people's perceptions of police legitimacy fit into this account? In Tyler's research (for a recent methodology discussion, see Tyler & Jackson, 2013) "audience legitimacy" is typically measured as the combined belief that it is one's duty to obey the instructions of police officers (one grants legal institutions the authority to dictate appropriate behavior) and that the authorities have one's best interests at heart (one believes that the power is being exercised in ways that are normatively justified). Applied to a street-stop, the authority has made a claim about his or her right to make the stop, to question the individual, and to expect them to behave in certain ways. In turn the individual (implicitly or explicitly) makes sense of this claim, assessing whether the officer has honest and trustworthy intentions and whether one should defer to the officer. The constraint to power here is that legitimacy partly involves the assessment of the trustworthiness of the police (to take into account the interests of the citizens). Thus, to gain legitimate authority the officer cannot act in ways that communicate untrustworthy intentions.

Importantly, procedural justice theory predicts that the individual will view the officer's claims to legitimacy primarily through the lens of procedural fairness. Does the officer wield his or her authority in fair, just, and neutral ways? If the officer acts according to principles of procedural justice, then the individual will trust that the officer will take his or her interests into account when wielding their power and authority. That individual will also feel a positive duty to obey his or her instructions. Procedurally fair treatment and decision-making conveys value and status to the individual in question, which then strengthens social bonds and enhances police legitimacy (Tyler, 1997, 2006a). This legitimacy then flows into—or encourages—cooperation with police, compliance with the law, and other "pro-social" behaviors of the type that is crucial for the proper functioning of the police in a democracy.

2.1 Empirical Legitimacy as Consent and Moral Validity

The R5 ESS module conceptualizes people's perceptions of police legitimacy slightly differently (European Social Survey, 2011, 2012; Hough et al., 2013a, 2013b, 2013c; Jackson et al., 2011; Jackson, Kuha, et al., 2013). On this account, legitimacy is validated in the eyes of citizens not only when those citizens recognize the authority of the police and feel a corresponding duty of deference (consent) but also when individuals believe that police officers have an appropriate sense of right and wrong—more specifically that they share moral values with citizens—and that police officers act lawfully.

On the surface this may not seem very different to Tyler's (2006b) approach. But there are two departures worth noting. First, consent and felt obligation is assumed to be a separate (albeit connected) psychological state, distinct from judgments about the normative justifiability of power. Second, whereas Tyler's (2006b) index includes measures of generalized trust as a sense of the normative justifiability of power, we consider shared moral values and beliefs about lawfulness as central to normative justifiability in the eyes of citizens.

As in Tyler's (2006b) work, *felt obligation to obey* is central to our definition. A variety of processes and experiences—ranging from childhood socialization and cultural affiliations to individual encounters with police officers—lead people to internalize the value that they should obey the law and abide by the directives of justice officials (or not). This feeling, or set of motivations, is an important aspect of the empirical legitimacy of the police. People enter into a reciprocal-role relationship with police; the police officer is making a claim that he or she has the legitimate right to constrain behavior and impose obligations; and in turn the individual recognizes this right through authorization and consent. Believing that it is right to respect police directives subjectively precludes (or inhibits) the possibility of disobeying officers. Under such conditions, the authorization of actions by authorities carries automatic justification for them; legitimate authority is empowered to determine right and wrong behavior, and behavior becomes right or wrong because it is determined as such by the authority.

In addition, however, we treat legitimate authority and the judgment about the moral validity of power possession as separate, in the sense that they are different (but empirically correlated) psychological states. The R5 ESS module views this judgment through the lens of moral alignment, i.e., whether citizens believe that the police have an appropriate sense of right and wrong, where an appropriate sense of right and wrong means sharing their own moral values. Claims to legitimacy here partly reference a moral justification to power, whereby power-holders demonstrate that they exercise their power in ways that accord with prevailing norms of acceptable conduct, and citizens process these claims by assessing the moral values expressed by power-holders. We also assume that legality and lawfulness underpins moral validity. If the citizen in the encounter believes that the officer is abusing his or her power by using unjustified force or illegally stopping them (without due cause or reasonable suspicion), then this is a rejection of the officer's claim to legitimacy.

On this account, "legitimacy tames power" (in the words of Coicaud, 2013: 40) because power-holders need to act morally and lawfully in the eyes of citizens if they are to be seen as legitimate by those citizens. Applied to our hypothetical street-stop, the ESS definition assumes that authority and consent play one part in encouraging public acceptance of this use of police power (and the institution's right to exercise legitimate authority) and normative alignment and lawfulness plays another. Starting from the perspective of claims to authority and responses of consent, it is clear the officer making the stop is already also making a claim about his or her authority through the very fact that the stop has occurred; the officer may also demand to search the citizen or direct him or her to perform a certain action. To the extent that the citizen holds the police legitimate, they will willingly accept the right of the police to stop him or her, and willingly comply with the officer's directives because he or she authorizes the officer to intervene in people's lives and dictate appropriate behavior. Here, felt obligation reduces the tension between power-holders and subordinates, as Coicaud (2013) would say. It is important to note that the citizen may have other reasons for complying with the directives of the officer—most notably, fear of the consequences if they do not—but such reasons would neither rest on recognition of a legitimate power relationship nor help reproduce it.

We could go further here. It may be that the extent to which the officer believes in his or her authority and, perhaps, the extent to which he or she wields that authority in fair, just, and respectful ways (in accordance with principles of procedural justice), constitutes a claim in a particular moment—and more widely—to rightful authority. As a mode of behavior, procedural justice certainly underpins the ideology of policing in a country such as the UK, even if, in reality, police practice does not always live up to this ideal. When officers behave in procedurally fair ways they are making a claim to legitimacy—that the power vested in them is legitimate because it is wielded in appropriate ways, which is not to discount, of course, the idea that there may be other forms of behavior that also constitute a claim to legitimacy. In turn, the extent to which the citizen receives and processes these claims constitutes the psychological state of consent and authorization. For example, procedural injustice may reduce one's consent to the authority of the officer in that moment, and by extension perhaps to the institution, with the authority of the institution damaged by the officer not acting in ways that justify its power and role(s).

Police officers are, therefore, engaged in making implicit or explicit claims about the correctness of their power and role. This is a self-belief that their authority (and their exercise of authority) is morally justified—for example that they represent and enact justice and fairness, and that the social order and control that they help to shape accords with a generally shared sense of right and wrong. In the context of the encounter, the actions of the officer in part constitute a claim of moral correctness being made to the citizen; and the citizen receives, processes, and responds to these claims. If they believe that the officer is acting morally, the citizen comes to an implicit or explicit conclusion that the power of the institution is justified because of how it has been wielded. Crucially, if the police officer acted in accordance with principles of procedural justice, this communicates not just status and value to the citizen, but also a sense of ethical appropriateness. If the police officer did not, or did not appear to act, in accordance with principles of procedural justice, this communicates not just a lack of status and value, but also a sense of ethical inappropriateness.

3 Testing the Measurement Structure of Perceived Police Legitimacy

The latest edition of the R5 ESS data was released in December 2012. Thus far, our analysis of the ESS data has presented basic correlations between key constructs like trust in police effectiveness, trust in police procedural fairness, felt obligation to obey the police, moral alignment with the police, and beliefs about the lawfulness of the police (Hough et al., 2013a, 2013b, 2013c). We have also presented some more detailed modelling of people's willingness to cooperate with the police in the UK (European Social Survey, 2012; Hough et al., 2013c). The current analysis focuses in more detail on the measurement models of police legitimacy, with a specific focus on the UK.

Before we present the findings, however, we should detail the measures of perceived police legitimacy (Table 1). In the original bid for space in the ESS,[1]

[1] A little bit of history may be helpful. The R5 ESS module on "trust in justice" emerged out of an EU FP7-funded project entitled Euro-Justis, which ran from March 2008 to July 2011 (Hough & Sato, 2011). A key objective of Euro-Justis was to develop social indicators of public trust and institutional legitimacy. This involved careful methodological development work, in the form of cognitive interviews and a pilot survey in several countries. Parallel to the project Euro-Justis, we also made a successful bid for space in the ESS, drawing on the conceptual and methodological

Table 1 R5 ESS measures of perceived police legitimacy

Perceived legitimacy of the police: obligation to obey
Now some questions about your duty towards the police in [country]. To what extent is it your duty to . . .
(OBEY1) back the decisions made by the police even when you disagree with them?
(OBEY2) do what the police tell you even if you don't understand or agree with the reasons?
(OBEY3) do what the police tell you to do, even if you don't like how they treat you?
Use this card where 0 is not at all your duty and 10 is completely your duty.
Perceived legitimacy of the police: moral alignment
Please say to what extent you agree or disagree with each of the following statements about the police in [country]:
(MORALID1) The police generally have the same sense of right and wrong as I do.
(MORALID2) The police stand up for values that are important to people like me.
(MORALID3) I generally support how the police usually act.
Response alternatives: Agree strongly, agree, neither agree nor disagree, disagree, and disagree strongly [treated as categorical in the subsequent statistical analysis]
Perceived legitimacy of the police: corruption and legality of action
(LAWFUL1) How often would you say that the police in [country] take bribes?
Choose your answer from this card where 0 is never and 10 is always.
(LAWFUL2) The decisions and actions of the police are unduly influenced by pressure from political parties and politicians.
Response alternatives: Agree strongly, agree, neither agree nor disagree, disagree, and disagree strongly [treated as categorical in the subsequent statistical analysis]

perceived legitimacy was defined as a multidimensional concept involving consent, moral alignment, and lawfulness. Consent, moral alignment, and beliefs about the lawfulness of justice institutions were each conceived as reflective measurement tools. Each concept was regarded as a latent construct that is the cause of its appropriate measures and which exists independent of those measures (Borsboom, Mellenbergh, & Van Heerden, 2003). Variation in the latent variable is assumed to precede variation in the indicators. Statistical models like factor analysis and structural equation modelling (SEM) are used to represent such measurement. The measurement model for each concept typically specifies that its indicators are independent after conditioning on the latent variable.

Figures 1 and 2 show the findings from two fitted confirmatory factor analysis models of legitimacy. In the first (Fig. 1), legitimacy is specified as a three-factor construct, separately comprising beliefs about the morality of the police, beliefs

work of Euro-Justis (for the original proposal see http://www.europeansocialsurvey.org/docs/round5/questionnaire/ESS5_jackson_proposal.pdf). The formal process of ESS methodological development began in March 2009 (see Jackson et al., 2011), and throughout Euro-Justis and the ESS bid, a key focus was to conceptualize and operationalize empirical legitimacy as not just authorization but also normative justifiability of power. Others have since explored this distinction (e.g., Bottoms & Tankebe, 2012; Tankebe, 2013). But some key differences can be seen when it comes to operationalization. Compare Jackson et al. (2011) with Tankebe (2013), and for a commentary see Tyler and Jackson (2013).

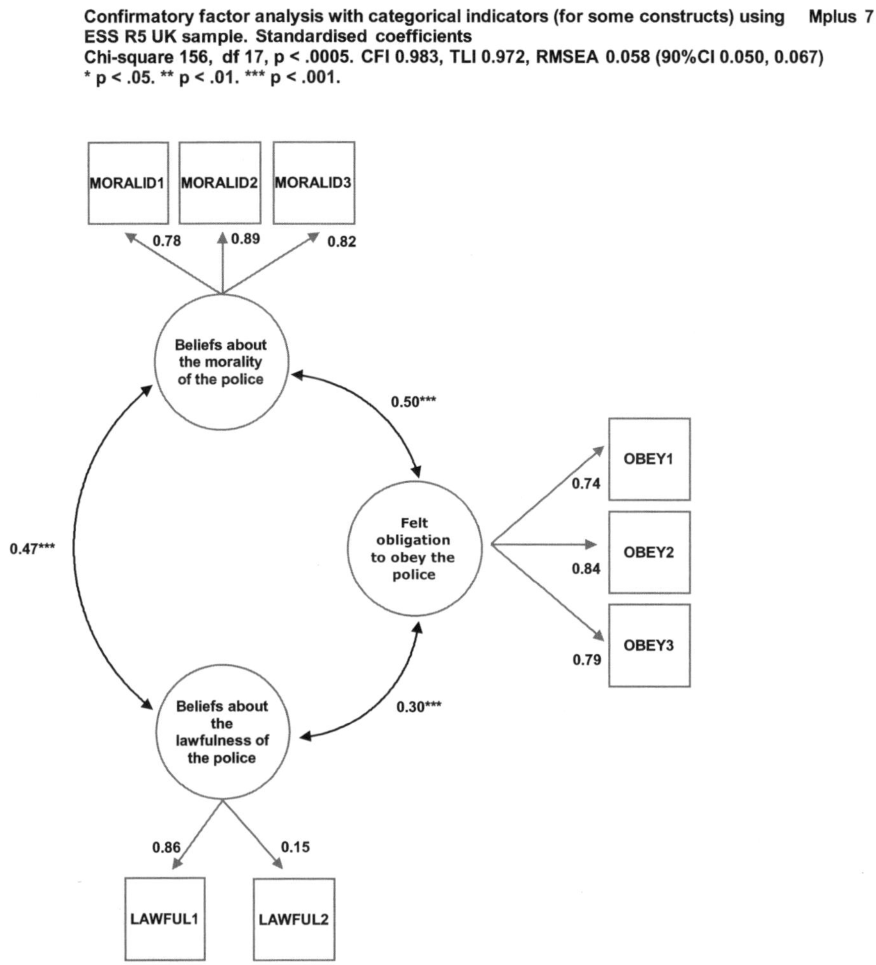

Fig. 1 Confirmatory factor analysis, 3 latent constructs

about the lawfulness of the police and felt obligation to obey the police. In the second (Fig. 2), legitimacy is specified as a two-factor construct, separately comprising beliefs about the morality and lawfulness of the police and felt obligation to obey the police. Note that both equally fit the data, in the sense that the approximate fit statistics for both models are acceptable.

Note also that LAWFUL2 (agree/disagree: *The decisions and actions of the police are unduly influenced by pressure from political parties and politicians*) has a low factor loading in both models. This suggests that the lawfulness aspect of police legitimacy was not measured as successfully as the other aspects of police legitimacy. The most likely explanation of this is that people think that believing that the "decisions and actions of the police are unduly influenced by pressure from

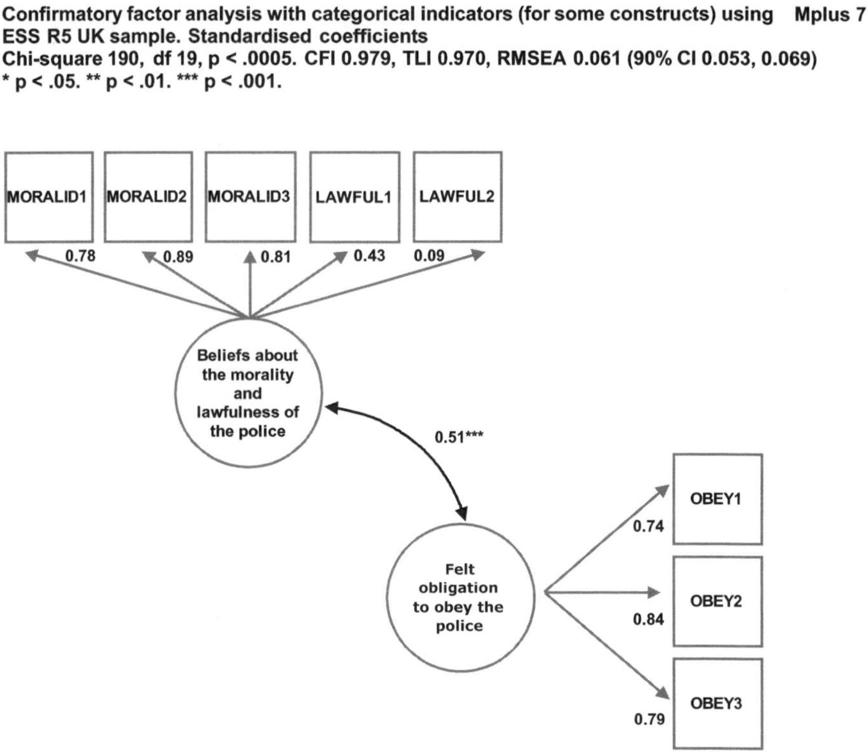

Fig. 2 Confirmatory factor analysis, 2 latent constructs

political parties and politicians"—political scientists would call this a particular form of "state capture," in which the ruling elite manipulate decision-making processes to their own advantage (see Hellman, Jones, & Kaufman, 2003)—is not corruption in the public eye, or at least not in the same way as taking bribes.

4 Why Do People Cooperate with the Police?

We next fit two structural equation models. Each predicts (on the right-hand side, see Fig. 3) respondent's self-assessed propensity to cooperate with police as one downstream potential outcome of legitimacy. In the first model we treat police legitimacy as a three-dimensional construct (see Fig. 4, overleaf). In the second model we treat police legitimacy as a two-dimensional construct (see Fig. 5, overleaf).

In each model we contrast instrumental and normative motivations to cooperate with the police (Huq et al., 2011a, 2011b; Jackson, Bradford, Hough, et al., 2012; Jackson, Bradford, Stanko, et al., 2012; Sunshine & Tyler, 2003; Tyler et al., 2010).

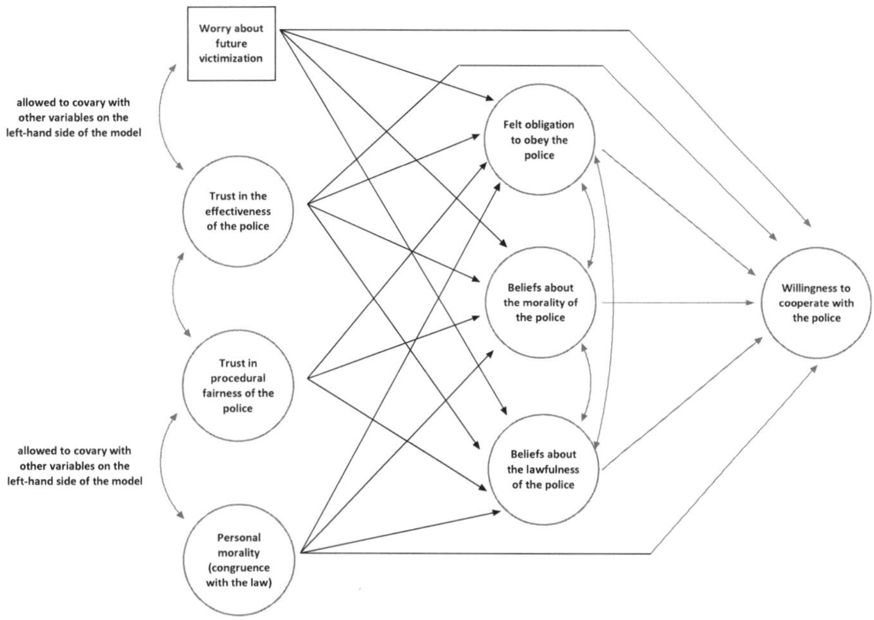

Fig. 3 Diagrammatic representation of the model to be fitted

An instrumental account posits that public cooperation is shaped by self-interest and material gains and losses; it follows that the police and criminal courts need to demonstrate effectiveness and generate a sense of safety if they are to guide law-related behavior. A normative account predicts that people cooperate because of morality, personal values and social connections; it follows that the police and criminal courts need to wield their power in fair ways and generate widespread commitment to the collective good. Being respectful to citizens and demonstrating legitimate authority encourages people to believe that cooperating with the police is *the right thing to do* (one accepts the right to the police to expect supportive behavior and one feels morally aligned with the police).

In order to examine people's willingness to cooperate with the police and criminal courts, the ESS R5 module asked respondents whether they would be willing to report a specific crime to the police, identify the culprits in questions, and give evidence in court. The following vignette and question/answer structure was used:

Now some questions about what you would do if you were the only witness to a crime. Imagine that you were out and saw someone push a man to the ground and steal his wallet.

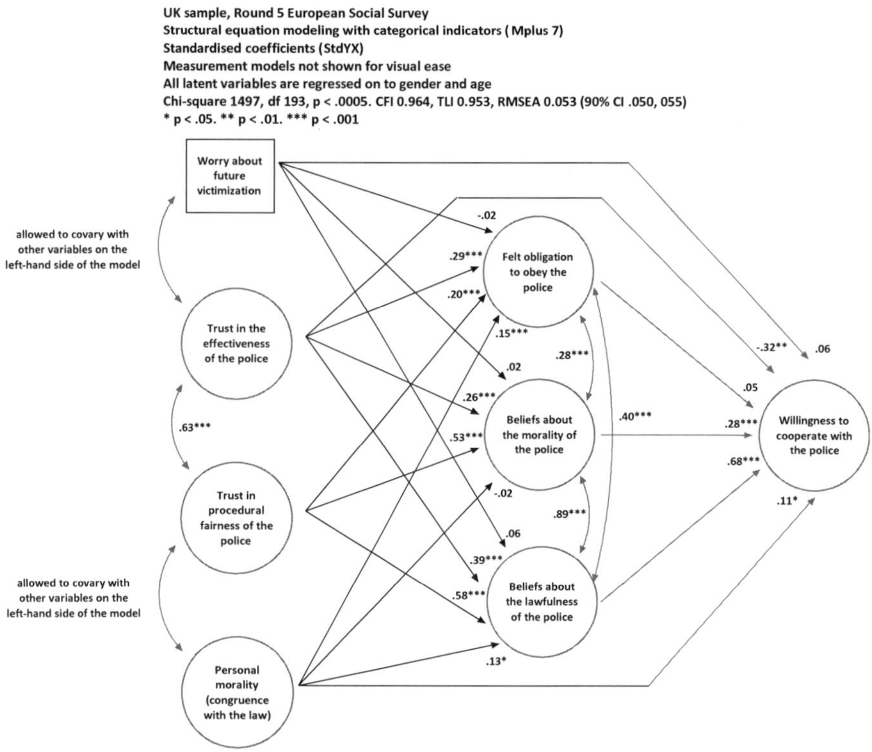

Fig. 4 Fitted model, where legitimacy is treated as three distinct constructs

- How likely would you be to call the police? Would you be ["not at all likely," "not very likely," "likely," or "very likely"?
- How willing would you be to identify the person who had done it? Would you "not at all willing," "not very willing," "willing," or "very willing"?
- And how willing would you be to give evidence in court against the accused? Would you "not at all willing," "not very willing," "willing," or "very willing"?

This measurement model was designed to reflect an underlying latent continuum: at the lower end a respondent is unlikely and unwilling to call upon and assist the criminal justice system in response to an indicative illegal act, while at the upper end a respondent is likely and willing to call upon and assist the criminal justice system in response to an indicative illegal act.

We have already outlined how police legitimacy was measured. Another normative motivation to cooperate is moral congruence with the law. The idea here is that people will cooperate with the police in part because they believe that the police are enforcing laws that they agree with. To help the police catch and convict a criminal may be partly driven by the need for *just deserts*: punishment restores balance.

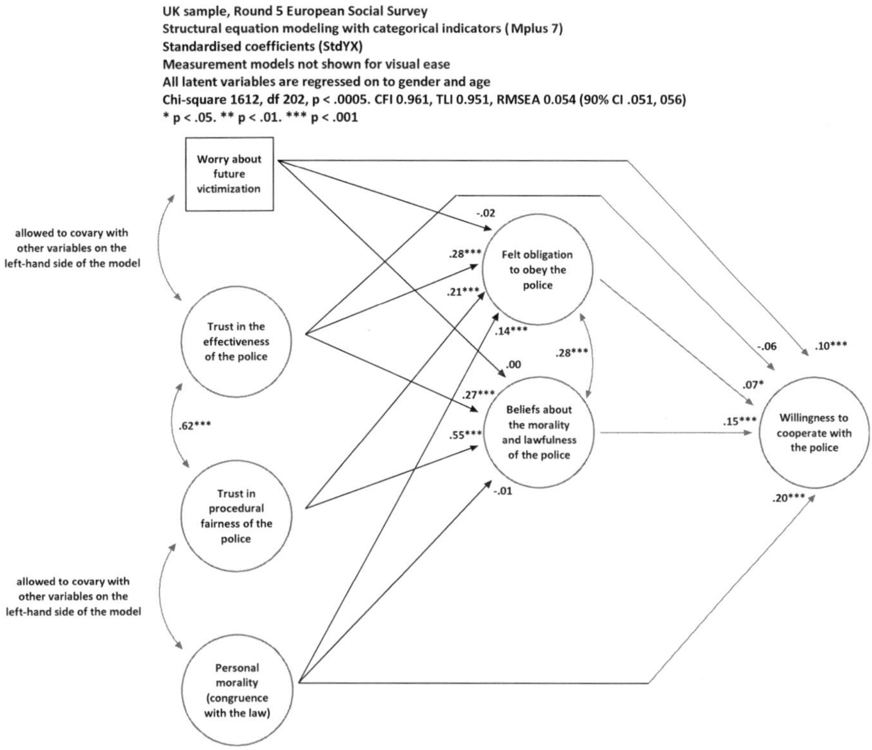

Fig. 5 Fitted model, where legitimacy is treated as two distinct constructs

Moral congruence with the law was measured by asking respondents whether they thought it was right or wrong to do each of the following three acts:

- . . . make an exaggerated or false insurance claim;
- . . . buy something you thought might be stolen; and
- . . . commit a traffic offence like speeding or crossing a red light.

These acts were chosen to represent so-called "everyday crimes" which straddle the line between more serious crimes and those which according to Karstedt and Farrall (2006: 1011) ". . . fall into a grey zone of legality and morality." In criminal terms, these are "low-level" behaviors that each of us may or may not be tempted by or engage in. The more people believe that these acts are immoral, the more likely they may be to call and assist the police as a response to someone pushing a man to the ground and stealing his wallet.

The two potential instrumental motivations center upon beliefs about the trustworthiness of the police to catch, deter, and respond to crime, and concerns about the personal risk of criminal victimization. Trust in police effectiveness was measured by asking respondents: "Based on what you have heard or your own experience, how successful do you think the police in this country are at . . .:"

- Preventing crimes where violence is used or threatened;
- Catching people who commit house burglaries; and
- How slowly or quickly police would arrive at the scene if a violent crime were to occur near your house.

Answers that respondents give to these questions can reasonably be assumed to reflect trust in police effectiveness. Trust is strategic, in that it involves specific and directed content, but it also involves unpredictability and risk. People do not know for sure whether the police would turn up quickly, but if they say that the police would arrive quickly, this is a positive expectation of behavior that mirrors the idea that the police take their interests into account. Conversely, if they say that the police would not arrive quickly, this is a negative expectation of behavior that mirrors the idea that the police would not take their interests into account.

Fear of crime was conceptualized as the frequency and impact of worry about becoming a victim of burglary and violent crime (for discussion about the meaning and measurement of fear of crime, see Farrall, Jackson, & Gray, 2009; Gray, Jackson, & Farrall, 2011). The ESS R5 measured fear of crime by asking respondents (Jackson & Kuha, 2014):

1. How often, if at all, do you worry about your home being burgled? with the response options "All or most of the time," "Some of the time," "Just occasionally," and "Never."
2. (If the answer to the first question was other than "Never"), Does this worry about your home being burgled have . . .
   - . . . a serious effect on the quality of your life
   - . . . some effect
   - . . . or no real effect on the quality of your life?

3. and 4. Two questions with similar wordings, but with "your home being burgled" replaced by "becoming a victim of violent crime."

Finally, procedural justice theory predicts that trust in the procedural fairness of the police is an important predictor of perceived police legitimacy. How was trust in the procedural fairness of the police measured? Trust is a belief about how police officers perform their roles (their intentions and competence to do what they are institutionally tasked to do) and one's positive expectations about how officers are expected to act. If one trusts the police, one believes that individual officers have the intentions and competence to perform the tasks inherent in their role (e.g., to be effective and fair). Trust in police procedural fairness was measured by respondents how often (from 1 = not at all often to 4 = very often) they think police in their country:

- Treat people with respect;
- Make fair and impartial decisions; and
- Explain their decisions and actions when asked.

Collectively, this measurement model captures three important dimensions of procedural justice. The first is treatment with respect and dignity, which is consistently one of the most important issues that concern people when they are dealing with authorities. When people feel demeaned or subjected to negative stereotypes, they view themselves as diminished as people and disrespected beyond what is appropriate when dealing with the law. Conversely, acknowledging people's rights and acting with courtesy leads them to feel fairly treated. The second is neutrality, which refers to making decisions based on the consistent application of rules based on proper procedure rather than on personal opinions or prejudices. The third is voice, which means providing opportunities for citizens to participate in decision making processes. Such opportunities for voice need not involve a formal or elaborate mechanism; studies of police street stops, for example, indicate that when officers provide people an opportunity to tell their side of the story before they take action, people are much more likely to feel fairly treated.

The first thing to do is to inspect the implications of treating police legitimacy as a two-dimensional (Fig. 4) or a three-dimensional construct (Fig. 5). The two models have essentially identical levels of goodness of fit. Furthermore, in the three factor model there is a high correlation ($r = .89$) between moral alignment and perceived lawfulness, which makes the predictors of cooperation unstable and difficult to tease apart. It also sheds doubt on the empirical distinctiveness of beliefs about the morality and lawfulness of the police. (Also note that the correlation between moral alignment and perceived lawfulness in the SEM is higher than in the CFA, now that we are adjusting for their joint predictors, most notably trust in police effectiveness and fairness). The belief that police officers share one's moral values overlaps so much with the belief that the police act lawfully and independently suggests that it is appropriate to treat them as one psychological state.

We thus proceed with the model presented in Fig. 5. First, worry about future victimization is a significant predictor of people's willingness to cooperate with the police. People who worry about burglary and physical attack are more likely say they would to call and assist the police and the courts. Conversely, people who are not worried about criminal victimization are less likely to cooperate with legal authorities, perhaps because they do not need legal authorities to reduce their material risk. This is an instrumental motivation, in that it reflects an image of policing centered on crime, risk and palpable police effectiveness. People's concerns about "what's in it for them?"—in the sense of calling the police, identifying the culprit and giving evidence in court—relate to the external promise of reducing criminal behavior and threat.

By contrast, trust in police effectiveness is not a significant predictor of cooperation. This is another instrumental motivation. One could hypothesize that if the police seem to be ineffective in fighting crime and supporting victims and witnesses, then people may conclude that there is little point in calling the police, identifying culprits and giving evidence in courts. Conversely, if people believe the police are effective they may be more willing to cooperate because of the concrete gains regarding crime, risk and punishment. Yet, in the ESS data at least, beliefs about the effectiveness of the police are not correlated with cooperation, adjusting for the other factors in the model.

Normative accounts shift the focus to morality and internalized social norms. Here, people will report a crime and give evidence in court because they believe that it is the right thing to do. Rather than being instrumentally based on incentives or sanctions, the motive to cooperate comes from morality, values and collective norms. We find that moral congruence with the law is an important predictor of cooperation, where moral congruence with the law refers to respondents' beliefs about the right or wrong of a number of "everyday crimes." The potential connection to people's willingness to cooperate with legal authorities lies in the moral correctness of the regulation of particular behavior, where people are motivated to report crimes and give evidence in court because to do so is to aid the regulation and punishment of what they believe to be wrongful acts. An individual harms society by rule-violations; criminal acts unbalance the scales of justice, and calling the police and identifying the culprit so they may be punished may restore this balance.

Finally, both aspects of perceived police legitimacy predict cooperation. As we described above, legitimacy is partly about authorization and consent. To cooperate may thus be to allow the police to dictate appropriate behavior and to expect supportive behavior; it may equally be about deference to the authority of the police and recognition of their right to claim authoritative command over the activities involved in "fighting crime." But legitimacy is also partly about believing that police officers have an appropriate sense of right and wrong. When people believe that the police act morally, this strengthens the moral value of cooperating with legal authorities. But it may also strengthen one's existing identification with the role of "law-abiding and morally upstanding citizen."

Kelman (2006) distinguishes between compliance (rule orientation), internalization (value orientation), and identification (role orientation). Applied to the current context, feeling an obligation to obey the police reflects the internalization that the police have the right to dictate appropriate behavior. By contrast, believing that the police share one's moral values helps to strengthen one's identification with the societal role of a "law-abiding and morally upstanding citizen" (Jackson, Bradford, Hough, et al., 2012). People accept a role relationship and they feel a corresponding need to meet the expectations of that role (Bradford, Murphy, & Jackson, 2014). Here, legitimacy helps to sustain societal roles, where authorities encourage the desire among citizens to nurture and sustain common identities and shared values. Part of this is a moral obligation to report crimes to the police, to identify culprits and to give evidence in court.

5 What Factors Predict Police Legitimacy?

Starting with beliefs about police morality and lawfulness, as represented in Fig. 3, we find that trust in police procedural fairness is a more important predictor than trust in police effectiveness. This supports procedural justice theory, in which the application of fair, respectful and neutral authority is said to generate the sense that the police have the right to dictate appropriate power and are acting according to appropriate moral and ethical standards. Numerous studies show how the exercise of authority via the application of fair process strengthens the social bonds between individuals and authorities (Sunshine & Tyler, 2003; Tyler, 2006b; Tyler & Huo, 2002). Individuals establish connections even in groups with only tenuous bases for group identification (Lind & Tyler, 1988; Mulford, Jackson, & Svedsater, 2008; Tajfel & Turner, 1986; Tyler & Lind, 1992); they are sensitive to signs and symbols that communicate information about their status and position within a group (De Cremer & Tyler, 2005); and how the police treat people communicates their status within the group that the police represent (Tyler & Blader, 2003), which has been jointly and variously characterized as the nation, state or community (Jackson & Bradford, 2009; Loader & Mulcahy, 2003; Reiner, 2010; Waddington, 1999).

Our findings suggest that when police treat individuals in procedurally fair ways (and can be trusted to do so) they indicate that they share and act on a set of values that individuals share and an impartial service to the law (see also European Social Survey, 2012; Hough et al., 2013a, 2013b, 2013c). Moral alignment with the police assists the process of transitioning goals or motives from the individual to the group, encouraging people to place greater emphasis on the outcomes of the group as a whole and to confer moral validity on the power and influence that the police hold (Blader & Tyler, 2009; Tajfel & Turner, 1986; Turner, 1974; Turner, Brown, & Tajfel, 1979; Tyler & Blader, 2003). Identifying with the group in these ways generates role and expectation involvement: people accept a reciprocal-role relationship (the law-abiding and upstanding citizen), they feel a corresponding need to meet the expectations of that role (Kelman, 2006), and they engage in reciprocal behaviors, such as cooperation with police officers.

However, trust in police effectiveness is a stronger predictor of felt obligation to obey than trust in police procedural fairness. The usual explanation for the strong association typically found between people's beliefs about the procedural fairness of the police and people's beliefs about the legitimacy of the police centers upon identification. What can we make of the link between beliefs about the effectiveness of the police and felt obligation to obey? It may be something to do with the object and purpose of police power. Trust in police effectiveness was measured by asking people whether they thought the police were successful at catching criminals and preventing crime, and whether they expected that the police would turn up quickly in an emergency. The relatively strong link between such judgments and felt obligation to obey the police suggests that people enter into the reciprocal-role relationship in part when they believe that the police are an effective agent of social order and control.

There are links here to a recent London-based study, which found that collective efficacy in a given neighborhood is strongly linked to residents' beliefs about police legitimacy (Jackson, Bradford, Stanko, et al., 2012). The interpretation given was that the police have the right to exercise legitimate authority in the eyes of local residents when a sense of order and control is achieved in the everyday. Because of the fit of the police to the activity of policing, the police organization may garner legitimacy from the extent to which the establishment and reproduction of normative social order is strong. People feel more obligated to obey officers when the local community seems well policed (and this means being policed by the informal social control mechanisms that regulate most conduct, rather than the formal policing that steps in when informal controls have failed) and are more likely to feel that the police share their values when the neighborhood seems orderly and well regulated. Conversely, they question police power and authority, and begin to doubt the desirability of conferring police power and authority in exchange for the regulation of social order, when they perceive wider processes of social ordering to be failing.

6 A Formative Measurement Model of Police Legitimacy

Finally, we briefly discuss the possibility of treating legitimacy as a formative construct. *Reflective* measurement tools, such as those already described, begin with a realist position that a given psychological construct exists. The task is then to *measure* it, by assigning appropriate numerical values to it, and we do this by first identifying behavioral indicators of the construct—e.g., appropriate survey measures for it. For the kinds of constructs considered here it is assumed that none of the indicators is a perfect measure of the construct, so several indicators are employed and the resulting data are modelled using latent variable techniques. In the context of police legitimacy, treating felt obligation and beliefs about the morality and lawfulness of police action as latent constructs, as we have done above, is an instance of such a reflective formulation.

Suppose now that we decide to take these two latent constructs and combine them into a single index of legitimacy. This index will then be a *formative* construct, in the sense that it is *defined* rather than measured by the calculation which forms it from its two components, here a weighted sum of them. From a conceptual point of view, doing so implies the pragmatic claim that the two psychological states which contribute to the index can be usefully aggregated, in that legitimacy is assumed to involve both consent and moral validity, and that both combine to generate positive motivations to act (e.g., call the police), positive constraints on police behavior, and positive ways to reduce the tension between power-holders and subordinates. We may then use the single formative measure to represent legitimacy in further analyses, for example as an explanatory variable for outcomes such as the willingness to cooperate with the police. A model which incorporates this idea is represented in Fig. 6, where "perceived police legitimacy" is the formative index. Here this is a depicted as an ellipse because as a combination of two latent variables it is also latent; it is nevertheless a well-defined quantity within the model, because its two components are themselves identified by their reflective measurement models.

The choice of *how* the components of a formative measure are aggregated can be made by the researcher in whatever way is substantively sensible and produces a

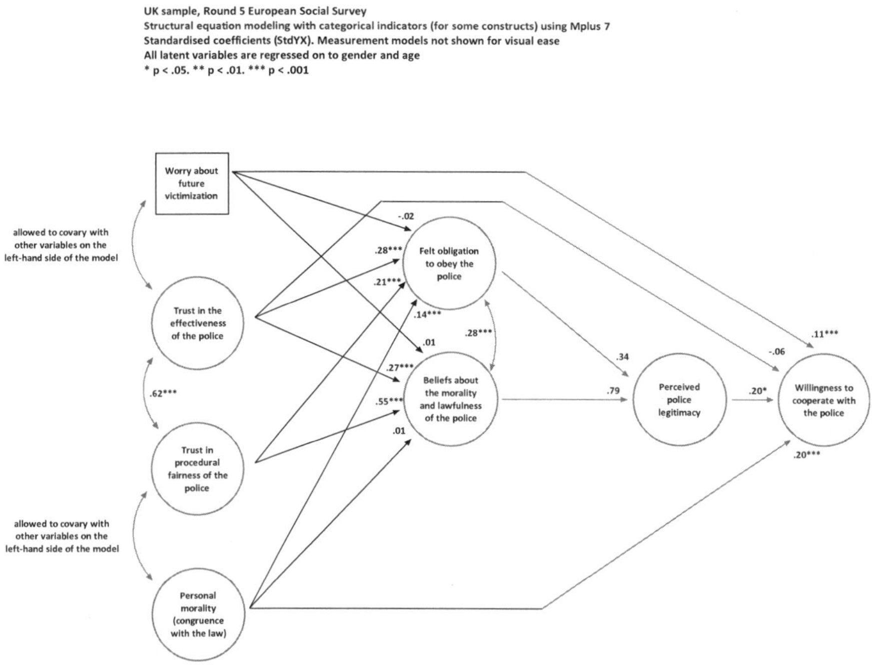

Fig. 6 Representation of a model where perceived police legitimacy is defined formatively, as a weighted sum of felt obligation to obey and beliefs about morality and lawfulness

measure which behaves well, e.g., as a predictor of other variables. In the example shown in Fig. 6, the weights of the two components of legitimacy have in fact been determined fully empirically, which means that the model is actually equivalent to the model in Fig. 5, just re-expressed to include the formative index of legitimacy as a separate variable. Here we see that the index is made up more by beliefs about the morality and lawfulness of the police than by felt obligation to obey the police, in that the former has a higher weight than the latter (the coefficients shown on the paths to perceived legitimacy in Fig. 6 are standardized regression coefficients, standardized by the implied standard deviations by the variables at each end of the path; in the unstandardized coefficients, the one for obligation to obey has been fixed at 1 and the one for morality and lawfulness estimated from the data). More generally, however, it is open to the researcher to weight these dimensions differently, for example by giving them equal weights in the index.

These results illustrate how legitimacy may be usefully seen as both a multidimensional construct *and* a single formative construct which in a sense combines the individual constructs.

Conclusions

In this chapter we have presented an argument, based on conceptual analysis, for specifying police legitimacy from the perspective of the policed as two connected psychological states. In line with Bottoms and Tankebe (2012), we argue that the claims of power-holders to legitimate authority are assessed by subordinates, and that these assessments involve consent (or not) and normative justification (or not). People hold the activity of the police up against their own moral judgments, and when they perceive congruence, they are motivated to consent to the role of a law-abiding citizen who actively supports justice institutions and to see the role and power of the police as morally justified (Jackson, Bradford, Hough, et al., 2012). Procedural justice seems to play an important part in this process, both as a mode of police behavior that encourages a sense of identification and shared group membership between police and public, and as a way of expressing a "morality" centered on values of fairness, equality, and respect that may transcend the moral content of individual laws or outcomes of police activity.

It is important to note, however, that procedural justice does not exhaust the foundations or precursors of police legitimacy. As shown above, and in other studies (Bradford, Murphy, & Jackson, 2014; Tankebe, 2009), the perceived effectiveness of the police can be an important predictor of legitimacy, possibly in similar ways to those outlined above—a police service that appears ineffective, for example, may be signaling that it does not share the values of citizens precisely because it is failing to live up to its proper role—or possibly in a more social contractarian sense. Moreover, there are likely to be other ways police might communicate a sense of shared values, some of which may be somewhat less normatively desirable than procedural justice (or indeed effectiveness). It does not seem unreasonable to suggest that to the extent "authoritarian" values are important to some people police may garner legitimacy among them by acting in ways that seem to reinforce such values. Equally, more negative forms of in-group solidarity may also be an important factor—some may look to the police to produce and protect exclusionary social formations, and legitimate it on this basis.

We take heart, however, from the seemingly near-universal importance of procedural justice (Bradford, 2014; Bradford, Murphy, & Jackson, 2014; Dirikx & Van den Bulck, 2014; Elliott et al., 2011; Gau & Brunson, 2010; Huq et al., 2011a, 2011b; Jackson, Bradford, Hough, et al., 2012; Jackson, Bradford, Stanko, et al., 2012; Jackson, Huq, et al. 2013; Jonathan-Zamir & Weisburd, 2013; Kochel et al., 2013; Mazerolle et al., 2013; Murphy & Cherney, 2012; Murphy et al., 2009; Reisig et al., 2007; Sargeant et al., in 2014; Sunshine & Tyler, 2003; Tyler, 2006b; Tyler & Jackson, 2014; Tyler et al., 2010). Whatever other factors may be in play, the evidence that procedural fairness is a vital precursor of legitimacy is strong. Our findings here serve as a small addition to this weight of evidence. In particular,

(continued)

we have presented the first evidence that it is appropriate to combine beliefs about the morality of the police and beliefs about the lawfulness of the police into one dimension of police legitimacy (the other dimension being felt obligation to obey), and we have considered the utility of pragmatically combining these two connected psychological states to produce a single index of perceived police legitimacy.

References

Blader, S., & Tyler, T. R. (2009). Testing and expanding the group engagement model. *Journal of Applied Psychology, 94*(4), 445–464.

Borsboom, D., Mellenbergh, G. J., & Van Heerden, J. (2003). The theoretical status of latent variables. *Psychological Review, 110*(2), 203–219.

Bottoms, A., & Tankebe, J. (2012). Beyond procedural justice: A dialogic approach to legitimacy in criminal justice. *Journal of Criminal Law and Criminology, 102*(1), 119–170.

Bottoms, A. E., & Tankebe, J. (2013). Voice Within: Power-holders' perspectives on authority and legitimacy. In J. Tankebe & A. Liebling (Eds.), *Legitimacy and criminal justice: An international exploration* (pp. 60–82). Oxford: Oxford University Press.

Bradford, B. (2014). Policing and social identity: Procedural justice, inclusion and cooperation between police and public. *Policing and Society, 24*(1), 22–43.

Bradford, B., Huq, A., Jackson, J., & Roberts, B. (2014). What price fairness when security is at stake? Police legitimacy in South Africa. *Regulation and Governance, 8*(2), 246–268.

Bradford, B., Murphy, K., & Jackson, J. (2014). Officers as mirrors: Policing, procedural justice and the (re)production of social identity. *British Journal of Criminology, 54*(4), 527–550.

Coicaud, J.-M. (2013). Crime, justice and legitimacy: A brief theoretical inquiry. In J. Tankebe & A. Liebling (Eds.), *Legitimacy and criminal justice: An international exploration* (pp. 37–59). Oxford: Oxford University Press.

Crawford, A., & Hucklesby, A. (Eds.). (2012). *Legitimacy and compliance in criminal justice*. London: Routledge.

De Cremer, D., & Tyler, T. R. (2005). Am I respected or not? Inclusion and reputation as issues in group membership. *Social Justice Research, 18*(2), 121–153.

Dirikx, A., & Van den Bulck, J. (2014). Media use and the process-based model for police cooperation: An integrative approach toward explaining adolescents' intentions to cooperate with the police. *British Journal of Criminology, 54*(2), 344–365.

Elliott, I., Thomas, S. D. M., & Ogloff, J. R. P. (2011). Procedural justice in contacts with the police: Testing a relational model of authority in a mixed methods study. *Psychology, Public Policy, and Law, 17*(4), 592–610.

European Social Survey. (2011). *Trust in justice: Topline findings from the European Social Survey*. Retrieved from http://www.europeansocialsurvey.org/docs/findings/ESS5_toplines_issue_1_trust_in_justice.pdf.

European Social Survey. (2012). *Policing by consent: Understanding the dynamics of police power and legitimacy*. Retrieved from http://www.europeansocialsurvey.org/docs/findings/ESS5_gb_toplines_policing_by_consent.pdf.

Factor, R., Mahalel, D., Rafaeli, A., & Williams, D. R. (2013). A social resistance perspective for delinquent behavior among non-dominant minority groups. *British Journal of Criminology, 53*(5), 784–804.

Farrall, S., Jackson, J., & Gray, E. (2009). *Social order and the fear of crime in contemporary times*. Oxford: Oxford University Press.

Gau, J. (2011). The convergent and discriminant validity of procedural justice and police legitimacy: An empirical test of core theoretical propositions. *Journal of Criminal Justice, 39*(6), 489–498.

Gau, J. M., & Brunson, R. K. (2010). Procedural justice and order maintenance policing: A study of inner city young men's perceptions of police legitimacy. *Justice Quarterly, 27*(2), 255–279.

Gray, E., Jackson, J., & Farrall, S. (2011). Feelings and functions in the fear of crime: Applying a new approach to victimisation insecurity. *British Journal of Criminology, 51*(1), 75–94.

Hasisi, B., & Weisburd, D. (2011). Going beyond ascribed identities: The importance of procedural justice in airport security screening in Israel. *Law and Society Review, 45*(4), 867–892.

Hellman, J. S., Jones, G., & Kaufman, D. (2003). Seize the state, seize the day: State capture, and influence in transition economies. *Journal of Comparative Economics, 31*(4), 751–773.

Hough, M., Jackson, J., Bradford, B., Myhill, A., & Quinton, P. (2010). Procedural justice, trust and institutional legitimacy. *Policing: A Journal of Policy and Practice, 4*(3), 203–210.

Hough, M., Jackson, J., & Bradford, B. (2013a). The drivers of police legitimacy: Some European research. *Journal of Policing, Intelligence and Counter Terrorism, 8*(2), 144–165.

Hough, M., Jackson, J., & Bradford, B. (2013b). The governance of criminal justice, legitimacy and trust. In S. Body-Gendrot, R. Lévy, M. Hough, S. Snacken, & K. Kerezsi (Eds.), *The Routledge handbook of European criminology* (pp. 243–265). Oxon: Routledge.

Hough, M., Jackson, J., & Bradford, B. (2013c). Legitimacy, trust and compliance: An empirical test of procedural justice theory using the European Social Survey. In J. Tankebe & A. Liebling (Eds.), *Legitimacy and criminal justice: An international exploration* (pp. 326–352). Oxford: Oxford University Press.

Hough, M., & Sato, M. (2011). *Trust in justice: Why it is important for criminal policy, and how it can be measured: Project report, Euro-Justis Project*. Helsinki. Retrieved from http://eprints.bbk.ac.uk/4507/

Huq, A. Z., Tyler, T. R., & Schulhofer, S. J. (2011a). How do the purposes and targets of policing influence the basis of public cooperation with law enforcement? *Psychology, Public Policy and Law, 17*(3), 419–450.

Huq, A. Z., Tyler, T. R., & Schulhofer, S. J. (2011b). Mechanisms for eliciting cooperation in counterterrorism policing: A study of British Muslims. *Journal of Empirical Legal Studies, 8* (4), 728–761.

Jackson, J., & Bradford, B. (2009). Crime, policing and social order: On the expressive nature of public confidence in policing. *British Journal of Sociology, 60*(3), 493–521.

Jackson, J., Bradford, B., Hough, M., Kuha, J., Stares, S. R., Widdop, S., et al. (2011). Developing European indicators of trust in justice. *European Journal of Criminology, 8*(4), 267–285.

Jackson, J., Bradford, B., Hough, M., Myhill, A., Quinton, P., & Tyler, T. R. (2012). Why do people comply with the law? Legitimacy and the influence of legal institutions. *British Journal of Criminology, 52*(6), 1051–1071.

Jackson, J., Bradford, B., Stanko, E. A., & Hohl, K. (2012). *Just authority? Trust in the police in England and Wales*. Oxon: Routledge.

Jackson, J., Huq, A., Bradford, B., & Tyler, T. R. (2013). Monopolizing force? Police legitimacy and public attitudes towards the acceptability of violence. *Psychology, Public Policy, and Law, 19*(4), 479–497.

Jackson, J., & Kuha, J. (2014). Worry about crime in a cross-national context: A model-supported method of measurement Using the European Social Survey. *Survey Research Methods, 8*(2), 109–126.

Jackson, J., Kuha, J., Hough, M., Bradford, B., Hohl, K., & Gerber, M. M. (2013). *Trust and legitimacy across Europe: A FIDUCIA report on comparative public attitudes towards legal authority*. Retrieved from http://dx.doi.org/10.2139/ssrn.2272975.

Jonathan-Zamir, T., & Harpaz, A. (2014). Police understanding of the foundations of their legitimacy in the eyes of the public: The case of commanding officers in the Israel National Police. *British Journal of Criminology, 54*(3), 469–489.

Jonathan-Zamir, T., & Weisburd, D. (2013). The effects of security threats on antecedents of police legitimacy: Findings from a quasi-experiment in Israel. *Journal of Research in Crime and Delinquency, 50*(1), 3–32.

Kane, R. J. (2005). Compromised police legitimacy as a predictor of violent crime in structurally disadvantaged communities. *Criminology, 43*(2), 469–498.

Karstedt, S., & Farrall, S. (2006). The moral economy of everyday crime: Markets, consumers and citizens. *British Journal of Criminology, 46*(6), 1011–1103.

Kelman, H. C. (2006). Interests, relationships, identities: Three central issues for individuals and groups in negotiating their social environment. *Annual Review of Psychology, 57*, 1–26.

Kirk, D. S., & Matsuda, M. (2011). Legal cynicism, collective efficacy, and the ecology of arrest. *Criminology, 49*(2), 443–472.

Kochel, T., Parks, R., & Mastrofski, S. (2013). Examining police effectiveness as a precursor to legitimacy and cooperation with police. *Justice Quarterly, 30*(5), 895–925.

Lind, E., & Tyler, T. (1988). *The social psychology of procedural justice*. New York: Plenum Press.

Loader, I., & Mulcahy, A. (2003). *Policing and the condition of England*. Oxford: Oxford University Press.

Maguire, E. R., & Johnson, D. (2010). Measuring public perceptions of the police. *Policing: An International Journal of Police Strategies and Management, 33*(4), 703–730.

Mazerolle, L., Bennett, S., Antrobus, E., & Tyler, T. R. (2013). Shaping citizen perceptions of police legitimacy: A randomized field trial of procedural justice. *Criminology, 51*(1), 33–63.

Mulford, M., Jackson, J., & Svedsater, H. (2008). Encouraging cooperation: Revisiting group identity and cooperative norm effects in prisoners' dilemma games. *Journal of Applied Social Psychology, 38*(12), 2964–2989.

Murphy, K., & Cherney, A. (2012). Understanding cooperation with police in a diverse society. *British Journal of Criminology, 52*(1), 181–201.

Murphy, K., Tyler, T. R., & Curtis, A. (2009). Nurturing regulatory compliance: Is procedural justice effective when people question the legitimacy of the law? *Regulation and Governance, 3*(1), 1–26.

Papachristos, A., Meares, T., & Fagan, J. (2012). Why do criminals obey the law? The influence of legitimacy and social networks on active gun offenders. *Journal of Criminal Law and Criminology, 102*(2), 397–439.

Reiner, R. (2010). *The politics of the police* (4th ed.). Oxford: Oxford University Press.

Reisig, M. D., Bratton, J., & Gertz, M. G. (2007). The construct validity and refinement of process-based policing measures. *Criminal Justice and Behaviour, 34*(8), 1005–1027.

Sargeant, E., Murphy, T., & Cherney, A. (2014). Ethnicity, trust and cooperation with police: Testing the dominance of the process-based model. *European Journal of Criminology*, 11(4), 500–524.

Suchman, M. C. (1995). Managing legitimacy: Strategic and institutional approaches. *Academy of Management Review, 20*(3), 571–610.

Sunshine, J., & Tyler, T. R. (2003). The role of procedural justice and legitimacy in public support for policing. *Law and Society Review, 37*(3), 513–548.

Tajfel, H., & Turner, J. C. (1986). The social identity theory of inter-group behavior. In S. Worchel & L. W. Austin (Eds.), *Psychology of intergroup relations* (pp. 276–293). Chicago: Nelson-Hall.

Tankebe, J. (2009). Public cooperation with the police in Ghana: Does procedural fairness matter? *Criminology, 47*(4), 1265–1293.

Tankebe, J. (2013). Viewing things differently: The dimensions of public perceptions of legitimacy. *Criminology, 51*(1), 103–135.

Tankebe, J., & Liebling, A. (Eds.). (2013). *Legitimacy and criminal justice: An international exploration*. Oxford: Oxford University Press.

Turner, V. (1974). *Dramas, fields, and metaphors: Symbolic action in human society*. Ithaca: Cornell University Press.

Turner, J. C., Brown, R. J., & Tajfel, H. (1979). Social comparison and group interest in ingroup favoritism. *European Journal of Social Psychology, 9*(2), 187–204.

Tyler, T. R. (1997). The psychology of legitimacy. *Personality and Social Psychology Review, 1*(4), 323–344.
Tyler, T. R. (2003). Procedural justice, legitimacy, and the effective rule of law. In M. Tonry (Ed.), *Crime and justice: A review of research* (Vol. 30, pp. 431–505). Chicago: University of Chicago Press.
Tyler, T. R. (2006a). Legitimacy and legitimation. *Annual Review of Psychology, 57*, 375–400.
Tyler, T. R. (2006b). *Why people obey the law*. New Haven: Yale University Press.
Tyler, T. R. (Ed.). (2007). *Legitimacy and criminal justice: International perspectives*. New York: Russell Sage Foundation.
Tyler, T. R. (2011a). Trust and legitimacy: Policing in the US and Europe. *European Journal of Criminology, 8*(4), 254–266.
Tyler, T. R. (2011b). *Why people cooperate: The role of social motivations*. Princeton: Princeton University Press.
Tyler, T. R., & Blader, S. L. (2003). The group engagement model: Procedural justice, social identity, and cooperative behavior. *Personality and Social Psychology Review, 7*(4), 349–361.
Tyler, T. R., & Huo, Y. J. (2002). *Trust in the law: Encouraging public cooperation with the police and courts*. New York: Russell-Sage Foundation.
Tyler, T. R., & Jackson, J. (2013). Future challenges in the study of legitimacy and criminal justice. In J. Tankebe & A. Liebling (Eds.), *Legitimacy and criminal justice: An international exploration* (pp. 83–104). Oxford: Oxford University Press.
Tyler, T. R., & Jackson, J. (2014). Popular legitimacy and the exercise of legal authority: Motivating compliance, cooperation and engagement. *Psychology, Public Policy, and Law, 20*(1), 78–95.
Tyler, T. R., & Lind, E. A. (1992). A relational model of authority in groups. *Advances in Experimental Social Psychology, 25*, 115–191.
Tyler, T. R., Schulhofer, S. J., & Huq, A. Z. (2010). Legitimacy and deterrence effects in counter-terrorism policing: A study of Muslim Americans. *Law and Society Review, 44*(2), 365–401.
Tyler, T. R., & Wakslak, C. J. (2004). Profiling and police legitimacy: Procedural justice, attributions of motive, and acceptance of police authority. *Criminology, 42*(2), 253–281.
Waddington, P. (1999). *Policing citizens: Authority and rights*. London: University College Press.

Assessing Validity of Different Legitimacy Constructs Applying Structural Equation Modeling

Jerneja Šifrer, Gorazd Meško, and Matevž Bren

1 Introduction

Legitimacy studies have been on the rise in criminological research and the importance of legitimacy as a strong predictor of compliance with the law is very well known, not only in studies pioneered by Tyler (2006) in the USA but also in European studies conducted within the last decade. Tyler and his colleagues argue that in the USA, legitimacy of the police and the courts depends centrally on fair and respectful treatment by justice personnel. Applying such theoretical work in the European area, the most important survey is European Commission FP7 project, JUSTIS, which involves the design and piloting of indicators of trust in justice (www.eurojustis.eu). The JUSTIS project dovetailed perfectly with Round 5 of the European Social Survey [ESS] (www.europeansocialsurvey.org). The module captured information on trust, legitimacy, cooperation and compliance in relation to criminal justice, and offers a groundbreaking and authoritative comparative study of public perceptions of justice (Jackson, Hough, Farrall, Aromaa, & de Keijser, 2009). One of the aims Jackson et al. (2009) emphasized was to develop a theoretical work about trust in criminal justice across most European jurisdictions.[1]

[1] For participating countries see http://www.europeansocialsurvey.org/index.php?option=com_content&view=article&id=322&Itemid=389

J. Šifrer (✉) • G. Meško • M. Bren
Faculty of Criminal Justice and Security, University of Maribor, Kotnikova 8, 1000 Ljubljana, Slovenia
e-mail: jerneja.sifrer@fvv.uni-mb.si; gorazd.mesko@fvv.uni-mb.si; matevz.bren@fvv.uni-mb.si

G. Meško, J. Tankebe (eds.), *Trust and Legitimacy in Criminal Justice*,
DOI 10.1007/978-3-319-09813-5_8

US and European studies (for example Bottoms & Tankebe, 2012; Hough, Jackson, & Bradford, 2012; Jackson, Hough, Bradford, Hohl, & Kuha, 2012; Reisig, Bratton, & Gertz, 2007; Reisig, Tankebe, & Meško, 2012; Sunshine & Tyler, 2003; Tyler, 2003, 2006) share the same findings: legitimacy is a strong predictor of compliance with the law, and public trust in the fairness of justice officials is a strong predictor of perceived legitimacy. In these surveys, samples were drawn from different populations; however, most of them were based on the general population and more banal types of law-violating behavior (such as unpaid parking tickets and excessive noise). Thus, while knowing why the average citizen obeys the law, the knowledge about populations most likely to commit serious violent crimes was not yet clear. Papachristos, Meares, and Fagan (2012) fill up that void by using a unique survey of active offenders in the Chicago Gun Project. They discovered that violent offenders who assess their experience with the police more positively are more likely to view the law as legitimate. The first attempt to test Tyler's theory in Slovenia (Reisig & Meško, 2009) was done on a sample of prisoners, and the findings showed that inmates who evaluate prison officers' use of authority as procedurally just, are less likely to report engaging in misconduct and are charged with violating fewer institutional rules. A similar survey was conducted by Reisig, Tankebe, and Meško (2012, 2014) on a sample of 683 young Slovenian adults. The results reveal that: (1) procedural justice judgments significantly shape individual perceptions of police legitimacy, and (2) perceived police legitimacy explains self-reported compliance with the law. The latest survey in Slovenia (and also Poland, Russia, Croatia, Bosnia & Herzegovina, Romania, Serbia and Macedonia) was conducted on a sample of law and criminal justice students (preliminary findings were first presented at the Cepol conference in Münster, Germany in September, 2013) (Meško, 2013), and the findings imply that law students in general question their willingness to comply with laws and cooperate with the police. Results also show that police authority and procedural justice are related to trust in the police in all countries and that police effectiveness is related to trust in the police only in Slovenia, Russia, Romania, Poland, Bosnia & Herzegovina and Croatia (Meško, 2013). The authors conclude that the police should strive primarily to improve their effectiveness, authority and procedural justice to increase levels of trust and legitimacy of policing in the respective countries.

In this chapter, the focus on police legitimacy is emphasized and, using Beetham's (1991) general definition of police legitimacy, which is the right for police to "rule" and the recognition by citizens of that right. Relationships between factors referring to public trust and fairness of justice officials (procedural justice, distributive fairness, trust in police (fairness), police authority, and police effectiveness) and different dimensions of police legitimacy (obligation to obey, trust in police, moral alignment and perceived legality) were our main focus. In addition, relationships between those dimensions referring police legitimacy, cooperation with police, and compliance with the law were also investigated.

In Slovenia, four different surveys on police legitimacy were conducted during the last 4 years. The most representative and important survey is, without doubt, Round 5 of the European Social Survey—specifically Trust in justice module (www.europeansocialsurvey.org). It was designed by Mike Hough, Jonathan Jackson, Ben Bradford (and colleagues), and carried out in 28 European countries (including Slovenia) in 2010–2011 on a total sample of almost 51,000. In the second survey in October 2011, Tyler's (2006) model on "why people obey the law" was tested in Slovenia. Tyler's questionnaire was translated and adopted regarding Slovenian legislation system and social circumstances; it was administered to students in four Slovenian faculties; the Faculty of Criminal Justice and Security and the Faculty of Organizational Sciences at the University of Maribor, and the Faculty of Arts and the Faculty of Law at the University of Ljubljana (Šifrer, 2013; Šifrer, Meško, & Bren, 2013). The purpose of this (pilot) survey was to check the questionnaire for its validity and reliability and to test Tyler's (2006) process-based model of policing. The third survey on legitimacy in Slovenia was conducted in November and December of 2011 among 683 young Slovene adults (18 years and older) who were enrolled in six high schools located in Maribor and Ljubljana, Slovenia (Reisig et al., 2012, 2014). The latter represents the pilot study for the next (fourth) survey also conducted by the Faculty of Criminal Justice and Security research team and partners. In autumn 2012 and spring 2013, it was administered to law students in eight Central and Eastern European countries Slovenia, Croatia, Bosnia & Herzegovina, Serbia, Former Yugoslav Republic of Macedonia, Romania, Poland and Russia (Meško, 2013). This survey explores several issues related to the legitimacy of policing in young democracies, i.e., post-communist countries in Central and Eastern Europe (Meško, Fields, Šifrer, & Eman, in press).

The main focus of this chapter is to find the model best fitting our data. The four collected datasets were analyzed employing SEM procedures to assess, evaluate and compare the validity of different legitimacy models in a way that the theoretical model is adjusted to the data (and not vice versa), which means adjusted to different cultural backgrounds. With this the legitimacy model adjusted to the Slovene cultural and socio-psychological background could be established. The analyses were performed in two steps: first the exploratory factor analyses were conducted with the SPSS to provide factors in line with the theoretical model and then the path analyses with AMOS to explore and find the best fitting of regression paths to the data. The results of preliminary factor analysis are presented in Appendices. The results of the SEM analyses are presented in Sect. 4 and are evaluated in Sect. 5.

2 Legitimacy, Public Trust and Fairness of Justice Officials, and Compliance

Generally speaking, legitimacy is the right to rule and the recognition by the ruled of that right (Bottoms & Tankebe, 2012). The key value that people hold is their widespread support for the legitimacy of the police—the belief that the police expect the public to follow the law and help combat crime, and that members of the public have an obligation to engage in cooperative behaviors (Tyler, 2004). If people trust the motives of authorities, feel that they are behaving neutrally, and feel treated with respect and dignity, they are more willing to voluntarily defer to authorities and obey their decisions (Tyler, 1997: 336). People are more willing to cooperate with legal authorities when they believe that those authorities are legitimate (Tyler, 2004). Legitimacy, on the one hand, involves the belief that police officers are trustworthy, honest and concerned about the well-being of the people they deal with. On the other, legitimacy involves the belief that police authority should be accepted and people should voluntarily defer to police decisions and directives. From this perspective, the police are legitimate if people defer to their decisions and follow their directives (Tyler, 2011). Based on this premise, much research has conceptualized legitimacy as a two-dimensional construct: obligation to obey the law and trust in police (Reisig et al., 2007, 2012; Sunshine & Tyler, 2003; Tyler, 2003, 2006). Meanwhile, Bottoms and Tankebe (2012) argue that the concept of perceived obligation to obey the law cannot be straightforwardly equated to legitimacy, and that both obligation and trust are conceptually distinct from legitimacy. Reisig et al. (2007) were among the first to assess the effects of legitimacy subscales (obligation to obey and trust in police) separately. Their conclusion was that combining the two legitimacy subscales (which the factor analysis revealed were unique constructs) produces misleading findings. This is an important finding given that Tyler (2006) has argued that perceived obligation to obey the law scales are the most direct way to measure legitimacy. Tankebe (2013: 106) feels that "the distinction between legitimacy and obligation is certainly not one of solely academic significance. Suppose that people feel an obligation to obey the police because of fear, a sense of powerlessness, or pragmatic acquiescence, but a police agency mistakes those feelings for widespread legitimacy". He argues that public assessments of police legitimacy should hinge on police lawfulness, police distributive justice, police procedural justice, and police effectiveness in the provision of security (ibid.).

Jackson et al. (2009) defined legitimacy as a multidimensional construct with three interlinked elements: the obligation to obey, moral alignment or normative justifiability, and perceived legality. Legitimacy is thus defined as an additive function of all three components. Citizens will view the police as more legitimate if they perceive police tactics as procedurally just; put simply, police will enjoy more legitimacy in the eyes of the public if they are perceived as making fair decisions and treating people respectfully (ibid.). Legitimacy is therefore strongly affected by citizens' belief that police treat them fairly (Meško & Klemenčič,

2007). Tyler (2006) distinguished between procedural justice and distributive fairness; procedural justice is focused on experiences that people have with legal authorities and it means that people care about fair and just procedures by which they arrived at outcomes which have to be fair and just. The latter is the domain of distributive fairness. The question that arises when talking about justice and fairness is do people distinguish between procedures (how decisions are made) and outcomes (what decisions are made) (Tyler, 2006). Tyler (ibid.) argued that those two concepts (distributive fairness and procedural justice) are distinct but not independent. Engel's (2005: 446) distinction regarding distributive and procedural justice is very similar: The concept of distributive justice implies that citizens are concerned about the fairness of outcomes, whereas the concept of procedural justice suggests that citizens are concerned with the fairness of the procedures used to achieve these outcomes.

Before Round 5 of the ESS began, Hough, Jackson, Bradford, Myhill, and Quinton (2010: 6) predicted that across Europe, trust in effectiveness would be a less powerful shaper of legitimacy than trust in fairness and shared values. They expected their measures of legitimacy to predict people's stated preparedness to comply with the law, and with their preparedness to cooperate with the police and courts. What the research of the ESS (trust in justice module) established are various linkages between trust in the police, police legitimacy, and consent to the rule of law (Hough, Jackson, & Bradford, 2013): if legal authorities (e.g., the police) are seen by the public to be unfair and disrespectful, this damages trust in them; low trust of legal authorities reduces their legitimacy, and the less legal authorities are seen as legitimate, the less the public will defer to their authority, resulting in reduced public commitment to the rule of law and preparedness to cooperate with police. Jackson et al. (2012: 207) also emphasized that legitimacy shapes law-related behavior; when people believe that the police and the legal system are legitimate, they recognize its power to determine proper behavior (they feel a sense of obligation to obey the police and the law) and they justify its power by feeling that the ethical and normative standpoints inherent in the system are aligned with their own. In this way legitimacy encourages people to obey the law and cooperate with legal authorities because they believe that it is the right thing to do. Changes in legitimacy will affect the degree to which people comply with laws in their everyday lives (Tyler, 2006). Concerned with people's compliance with institutional authority, procedural justice theories (Hough et al., 2010: 204) propose specific relationships between: (1) the treatment people receive at the hand of the police and justice officials, (2) the resultant trust that people have in institutions of justice, (3) the legitimacy people confer, as a consequence of this trust, on institutions of justice, (4) the authority that these institutions can then command when they are regarded as legitimate, and (5) people's consequent preparedness to obey the police, comply with the law and cooperate with justice.

Bottoms (2011: 90) proposed four main kinds of compliant behavior: (1) Instrumental/prudential compliance, based on self-interested calculations (about the potential costs and benefits of an offence or illegal act), (2) Normative compliance, based on a felt moral obligation, commitment or attachment (acceptance of/belief in norm; attachment leading to compliance; legitimacy), (3) Constraint-based compliance, derived from some form of constraint or coercion (the impact of obstructive strategies, such as locking up offenders to prevent their reoffending) (Hough et al., 2013), and (4) Compliance based on habit or routine.

In most US studies, support for the process-based model (established by Tyler, 2006) is confirmed; procedural justice judgments influence police legitimacy, which in turn shape compliance with the law (Sunshine & Tyler, 2003). Similarly, Reisig et al. (2007) discovered that police legitimacy predicts compliance with the law. In European studies, Hough et al. (2013) revealed significant effects of trust in police distributive fairness on compliance with the law via moral alignment, and that all three aspects of legitimacy (obligation to obey, moral alignment, perceived legality) are significant predictors of willingness to cooperate with police. Can similar effects be observed in Slovenia?

3 Methods

All four previously mentioned databases were used to empirically test legitimacy theory in Slovenia:[2] (1) *first model*: Trust in justice module of the European Social Survey (Round 5) (www.europeansocialsurvey.org); (2) *second model*: Test of Tyler's model on "why people obey the law" in Slovenia (Šifrer, 2013; Šifrer et al., 2013); (3) *third model*: Adult high school students survey—Slovenia (here and after High school students survey) (Reisig et al., 2012, 2014); and (4) *fourth model*: The study on law students about legitimacy in Slovenia (Meško, 2013; Meško et al., in press). In all these studies, the predictors of police legitimacy differ slightly but at their core they are practically the same (for example distributive justice, distributive fairness; trust in police and trust in police fairness), and latent variables are in the majority. Primarily, factor analyses (principal components method) were performed and factors (i.e., the new variables) were saved as weighted (weights were factor loadings) sums of measured variables that construct each factor.[3] According to this, path analysis of manifest variables are presented, since our aim is mainly focused on relationships between legitimacy, trust and compliance, and we adopted factors from their original surveys. Results of all factor analyses within each dataset are shown in Appendices 1, 2, 3 and 4. The tables present factors with their one-dimensional structures, factor loadings, total

---

[2] Here and after models are presented in a chronological sequence, from the first conducted (in 2010–2011) survey to the fourth (in 2012–2013).

[3] Variables which were not normally distributed were excluded (based on skewness and kurtosis statistics). In all used datasets, the variables of respondents' self-reporting on how often they broke the law were mostly the case.

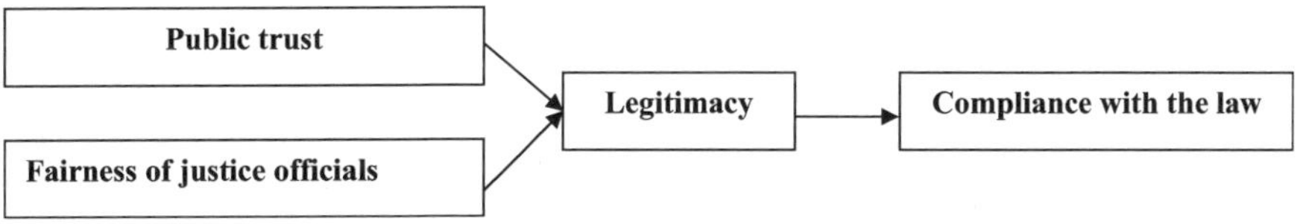

Fig. 1 Legitimacy as a mediator between justice and compliance

variances explained (var. in %), KMOs, Cronbach's alphas (α), and in cases where $\alpha < 0.6$ omegas (Ω[4]) are also computed.

Structural equation modelling as the assessment technique for a linear relationship between the dimensions with the emphasis on legitimacy the AMOS (22.0.0) was applied. For computing indirect effects and their 95 % confidence intervals the Bayesian estimation was used.

All four structural models were drawn and models were estimated with different fit indices, namely chi-square values (with corresponding degrees of freedom and the *p*-value of statistical significance), RMSEA (Root Mean Squared Error of Approximation), CFI (Comparative Fit Index), and TLI (Tucker-Lewis Index). With these selected indices, the recommendation of reporting the chi-square value (with corresponding degrees of freedom and the *p*-value), at least one absolute and one incremental index are met (Hair, Black, Babin, & Anderson, 2010). As previously mentioned, all the studies share the same findings: legitimacy is a strong predictor of compliance with the law and that public trust in the fairness of justice officials is a strong predictor of perceived legitimacy. These findings are presented with the path-diagram in Fig. 1.

The path-diagram in Fig. 1 presents the basis for our structural models. Nevertheless, not all four models provided the same results and the figure is not always represented in the empirical findings. All four structural models started with the model in Fig. 1, but in the SEM process they were modified to find the best fitting model of our data. We adopted, as Kaplan (2000) calls it, the "conventional" practice of SEM, and this conventional approach to structural equation modelling is generally practiced in the social and behavioral sciences. It is employed, as follows (Kaplan, 2000): (1) when available, a theory is presented (the structural equations represented in a path-diagram are seen as a one-to-one representation of the theory); (2) a sample is selected and measures are obtained on the sample; (3) this is followed by the estimation of the parameters of the model and the assessment of the goodness of fit of the model; and (4) at the end, the modifications of the model are performed if necessary. Typically, the last two stages are cyclical with the model continually being modified and evaluated in terms of goodness of fit until a decision is made that the model meets some standard of adequate fit.

---

[4] As shown by Cortina (1993) alpha is affected by the number of items, item intercorrelations, and dimensionality. That is why two other internal consistency coefficients (theta and omega) are introduced. Therefore, omega was computed, since it provides the highest estimate of reliability—that is the closest estimate to the true reliability of the measure (Carmines & Zeller, 1979).

4 Results

In this section, all four legitimacy (structural) models are presented, and for each model the goodness of fit is assessed with four goodness of fit indices (the chi-square value, RMSEA, CFI, and TLI), and the models are evaluated for direct and indirect effects on compliance. In some cases compliance was reversed in a way, that higher scores represent the higher compliance with the law. All four models differ with regard to the utilized dimensions of legitimacy. Dimensions are adopted according to specific model and are described at the very beginning of each section of the individual model, presented in addition.

4.1 First model: Trust in Justice Module of the European Social Survey (Round 5)[5]

Jackson et al. (2009) defined legitimacy as a multidimensional construct with three interlinked elements (see Appendix 1): the obligation to obey, moral alignment and perceived legality. According to Hough et al. (2013) legitimacy is thus defined as an additive function of all three dimensions, and to say that the police are legitimate is to say, for example, that people feel a positive duty to obey the police instructions, they feel aligned with the moral values of the police as an institution and they believe that police acts according to the law. The four factors, referring to various aspects of public trust and fairness of justice officials, are: (1) Procedural justice, (2) Police effectiveness, (3) Trust in police fairness, and (4) Distributive fairness. Cooperation (with the police) was measured on a 4-point scale ranging from 1—Not at all likely/Not at all willing to 4—Very likely/Very willing, and Compliance with the law was measured on a 5-point scale from 1—Five times or more to 5—Never. Survey respondents were asked to report the frequency with which they committed a variety of legal infractions within the past 5 years. Only the variable "How often have you committed a traffic offence like speeding or crossing a red light in the last five years?" is used in the analysis (due to the normal distribution) (see Appendix 1). Following Jackson's et al. (2009) definition, three models are presented on a sample of Slovenian citizens ($n = 1{,}403$) (Figs. 2, 3 and 4).

The "obligation" model (Fig. 2) fits the data well: the chi-square value is low ($\chi^2 = 6.514$), with Df = 7 and nonsignificant p-value ($p = 0.481$), and also other three reported indices RMSEA = 0.000, CFI = 1.000, and TLI = 1.004 confirm the goodness of fit. In Fig. 2, the highest predictor of Obligation to obey ($R^2 = 7$ %) is Trust in police fairness ($\beta = 0.22$; $p < 0.001$), followed by Police effectiveness ($\beta = 0.08$; $p < 0.01$). Trust in police fairness has also the highest influence ($\beta = -0.14$; $p < 0.001$) on Compliance with the law, followed by Police

[5] For more see: www.europeansocialsurvey.org/

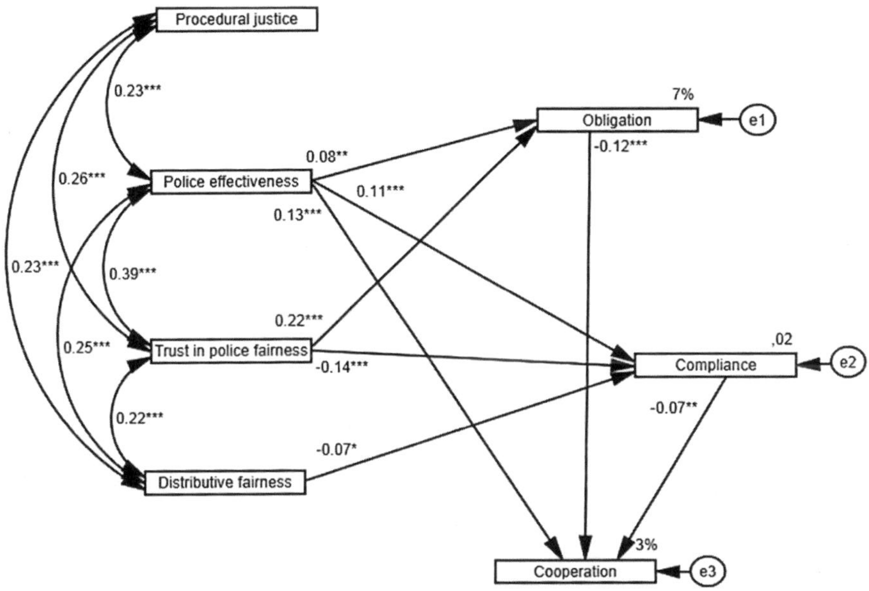

Fig. 2 Structural model of obligation, cooperation, and compliance (Trust in justice module of the European Social Survey—Round 5) (www.europeansocialsurvey.org/). ***$p < 0.001$; **$p < 0.01$; * $p < 0.05$. $\chi^2 = 6.514$; $p = 0.481$; Df = 7; CFI = 1.000; TLI = 1.004; RMSEA = 0.000. Standardized coefficients. *Obligation*: 0—Not at all my duty ... 10—Completely my duty; *Compliance*: 1—Five times or more... 5—Never; *Procedural justice*: 1—Very dissatisfied ... 5—Very satisfied; *Cooperation*: 1—Not at all likely/Not at all willing ... 4—Very likely/Very willing; *Police effectiveness*: 0—Extremely unsuccessful ... 10—Extremely successful; *Trust in police fairness*: 1—Not at all often ... 4—Very often; *Distributive fairness*: 1—Rich people treated worse, 2—Poor people treated worse, 3—Rich and poor treated equally

effectiveness ($\beta = 0.11$; $p < 0.001$), and Distributive fairness ($\beta = -0.07$; $p < 0.05$). The strongest predictor of Cooperation is Police effectiveness ($\beta = 0.13$; $p < 0.001$), followed by Obligation ($\beta = -0.12$; $p < 0.001$), and Compliance ($\beta = -0.07$; $p < 0.01$), and Compliance is also the mediator between Distributive fairness and Cooperation (indirect effect = 0.005; 95 % CI [0.00, 0.01]). Nevertheless, Obligation to obey does not affect the Compliance with the law and Procedural justice is also left out.

The "moral alignment" model (Fig. 3) also fits the data well: the chi-square value is low ($\chi^2 = 2.433$), with Df = 5 and nonsignificant p-value ($p = 0.787$), and also the other three reported indices RMSEA = 0.000, CFI = 1.000, and TLI = 1.023 confirm the goodness of fit. The highest predictor of Moral alignment ($R^2 = 17$ %) is again Trust in police fairness ($\beta = -0.18$; $p < 0.001$), followed by Procedural justice ($\beta = -0.17$; $p < 0.001$), Police effectiveness ($\beta = -0.17$; $p < 0.001$), and Distributive fairness ($\beta = -0.08$; $p < 0.01$)—see Fig. 3. Trust in police fairness has also the highest influence ($\beta = -0.16$; $p < 0.001$) on Compliance with the law, followed by Police effectiveness ($\beta = 0.08$; $p < 0.01$), and Distributive fairness ($\beta = -0.08$; $p < 0.01$). Moral alignment has the direct effect ($\beta = -0.13$;

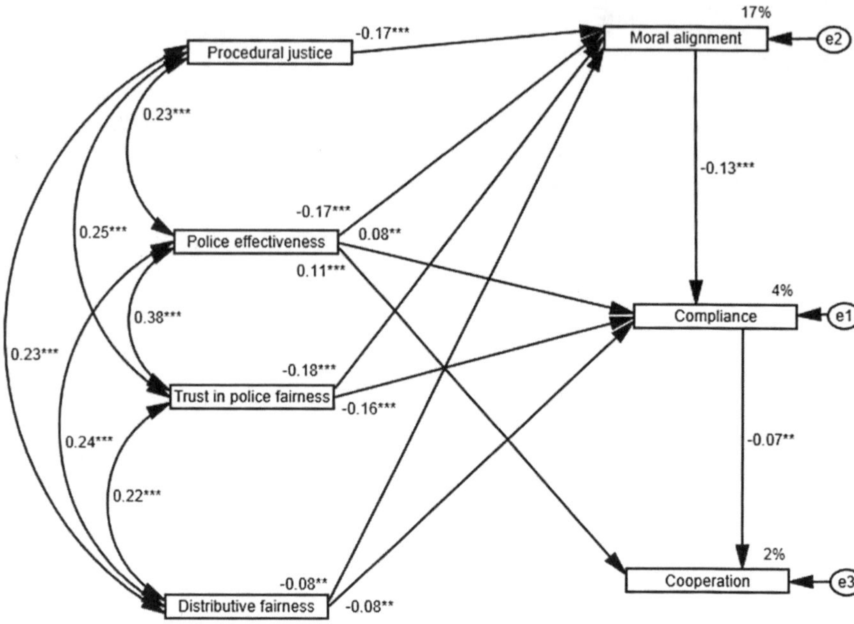

Fig. 3 Structural model of moral alignment, cooperation, and compliance (Trust in justice module of the European Social Survey—Round 5) (www.europeansocialsurvey.org/). $^{***}p < 0.001$; $^{**}p < 0.01$; $^{*}p < 0.05$. $\chi^2 = 2.433$; $p = 0.787$; Df = 5; CFI = 1.000; TLI = 1.023; RMSEA = 0.000. Standardized coefficients. *Moral alignment*: 1—Agree strongly … 5—Disagree strongly; *Compliance*: 1—Five times or more… 5—Never; *Procedural justice*: 1—Very dissatisfied … 5—Very satisfied; *Cooperation*: 1—Not at all likely/Not at all willing … 4—Very likely/Very willing; *Police effectiveness*: 0—Extremely unsuccessful … 10—Extremely successful; *Trust in police fairness*: 1—Not at all often … 4—Very often; *Distributive fairness*: 1—Rich people treated worse, 2—Poor people treated worse, 3—Rich and poor treated equally

$p < 0.001$) on Compliance with the law and it is, as such, the mediator between Trust in police fairness (indirect effect = 0.02; 95 % CI [0.01, 0.04]), Procedural justice (indirect effect = 0.02; 95 % CI [0.01, 0.04]), Police effectiveness (indirect effect = 0.02; 95 % CI [0.01, 0.04]), and Distributive fairness (indirect effect = 0.01; 95 % CI [0.003, 0.02]). Police effectiveness ($\beta = 0.11$; $p < 0.001$) and Compliance ($\beta = -0.07$; $p < 0.01$) have the direct effect on Cooperation, and Compliance is also the mediator between Moral alignment and Cooperation (indirect effect = 0.01; 95 % CI [0.002, 0.02]).

Here the "perceived legality" model (Fig. 4) also fits the data well: chi-square value is low ($\chi^2 = 8.459$), with Df = 6 and the nonsignificant p-value ($p = 0.206$) and also other three reported indices RMSEA = 0.017, CFI = 0.995, and TLI = 0.977 confirm the goodness of fit. The highest predictor of Perceived legality ($R^2 = 8$ %) is again Trust in police fairness ($\beta = -0.21$; $p < 0.001$), followed by Police effectiveness ($\beta = -0.13$; $p < 0.001$)—see Fig. 4. Trust in police fairness ($\beta = -0.12$; $p < 0.001$) and Police effectiveness ($\beta = 0.12$; $p < 0.001$) have the highest influence on Compliance with the law, followed by Distributive fairness

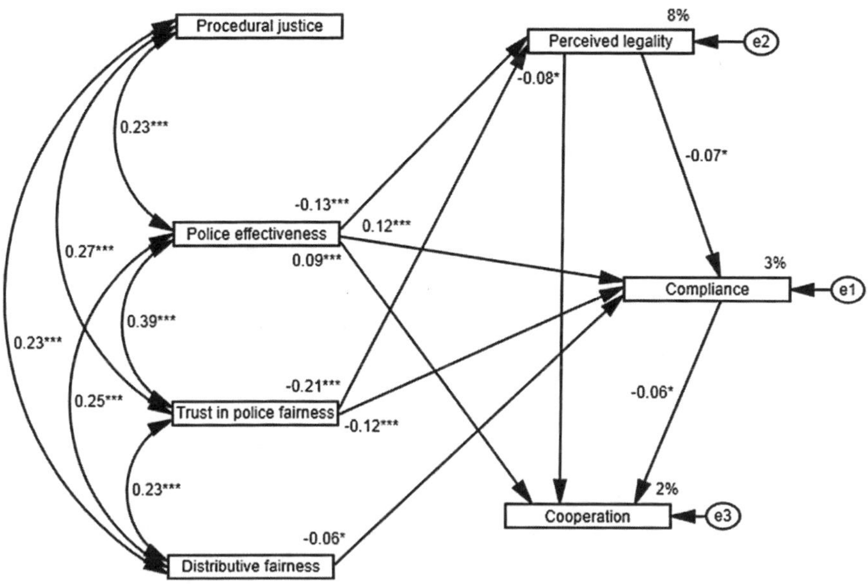

Fig. 4 Structural model of perceived legality, cooperation and compliance (Trust in justice module of the European Social Survey—Round 5) (www.europeansocialsurvey.org/). ***$p < 0.001$; **$p < 0.01$; *$p < 0.05$. $\chi^2 = 8.459$; $p = 0.206$; Df = 6; CFI = 0.995; TLI = 0.977; RMSEA = 0.017. Standardized coefficients. *Perceived legality*: 0—Never ... 10—Always; *Compliance*: 1—Five times or more... 5—Never; *Procedural justice*: 1—Very dissatisfied ... 5—Very satisfied; *Cooperation*: 1—Not at all likely/Not at all willing ... 4—Very likely/Very willing; *Police effectiveness*: 0—Extremely unsuccessful ... 10—Extremely successful; *Trust in police fairness*: 1—Not at all often ... 4—Very often; *Distributive fairness*: 1—Rich people treated worse, 2—Poor people treated worse, 3—Rich and poor treated equally

($\beta = -0.06$; $p < 0.05$). Police effectiveness ($\beta = 0.09$; $p < 0.001$) has the highest effect on Cooperation, followed by Perceived legality ($\beta = -0.08$; $p < 0.05$), and Compliance ($\beta = -0.06$; $p < 0.05$). Compliance with the law is also the mediator between Perceived legality and Cooperation (indirect effect = −0.005; 95 % CI [−0.01, 0.00]), and Distributive fairness and Cooperation (indirect effect = 0.004; 95 % CI [0.00, 0.01]).

4.2 Second Model: Test of Tyler's Model on "Why People Obey the Law" in Slovenia (Šifrer, 2013; Šifrer et al., 2013)

Our second model ($n = 479$) is based on Bottoms and Tankebe's (2012) arguments in which they emphasized that trust and legitimacy are not the same. It is not based on Tyler's (2006) model (as obligation to obey the law and support for legal

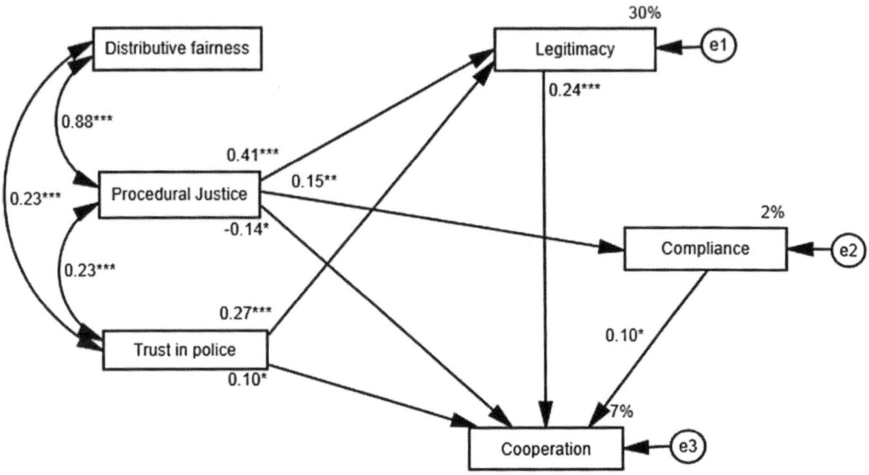

Fig. 5 Structural model of police legitimacy, cooperation and compliance (Test of Tyler's model on "why people obey the law" in Slovenia) (Šifrer, 2013; Šifrer et al., 2013). $^{***}p < 0.001$; $^{**}p < 0.01$; $^{*}p < 0.05$. $\chi^2 = 7.283$; $p = 0.200$; Df = 5; CFI = 0.997; TLI = 0.987; RMSEA = 0.031. Standardized coefficients. *Compliance*: 1—Very often ... 5—Never; *Legitimacy*: 1—Strongly disagree ... 5—Strongly agree; *Cooperation*, *Distributive fairness*, *Procedural justice*, *Trust in police*: 1—Very unlikely ... 5—Very likely

authorities), since it did not fit the data in a satisfactory level. Legitimacy is thus a one-dimensional construct of items (in majority of support of legal authorities), such as "I feel proud of the Slovenian police", "I feel that I should support the Slovenian police", "Police officers help citizens", for example. The three factors, referring to various aspects of public trust and fairness of justice officials, are: (1) Distributive fairness, (2) Procedural justice, and (3) Trust in police. Cooperation (with the police) was measured on a 5-point scale ranging from 1—Very unlikely to 5—Very likely. Compliance with the law was measured with respondents' self-reported assessments on how often they broke the law in the past year, on a 5-point scale ranging from 1—Very often to 5—Never. Survey respondents were asked to report the frequency with which they committed a variety of legal infractions, for example "How often have you driven over 130 km per hour on the highways?", "How often have you parked your car in violation of the law?", etc. (for all variables see Appendix 2). The model is presented in Fig. 5.

The model focusing on why people obey the law fits the data well: the chi-square value is low ($\chi^2 = 7.283$), with Df = 5 and nonsignificant p-value ($p = 0.200$), and also other three reported indices RMSEA = 0.031, CFI = 0.997, and TLI = 0.987 confirm the goodness of fit. In Fig. 5, the statistically significant standardized coefficients (betas (β)) show that the higher predictor of Police legitimacy ($R^2 = 30$ %) is Procedural justice ($\beta = 0.41$; $p < 0.001$), followed by Trust in police ($\beta = 0.27$; $p < 0.001$). Trust in police also has an indirect effect (0.06; 95 % CI [0.03, 0.1]) on Cooperation via Legitimacy. Distributive fairness does not affect Legitimacy nor Compliance or Cooperation directly, although it is highly correlated with Procedural justice ($r = 0.88$, $p < 0.001$). On the other hand, Procedural justice ($\beta = 0.15$; $p < 0.01$) has a direct effect on Compliance, and Cooperation ($\beta = -0.14$; $p < 0.05$).

4.3 *Third Model: High School Student Survey (Reisig et al., 2012, 2014)*

The High school student survey conducted among young Slovene adults in Maribor and Ljubljana ($n = 684$) (Reisig et al., 2012, 2014) followed studies of Tyler, Sunshine, and Reisig with co-workers (Reisig et al., 2007, 2012; Sunshine & Tyler, 2003; Tyler, 2003, 2006). They defined legitimacy as a two-dimensional construct: an obligation to obey and trust in the police. Some research (e.g., Reisig et al., 2012) operationalize police legitimacy by combining the obligation to obey items and the trust in police items into a single summate scale, nevertheless for the present study both dimensions were used separately. The four factors, referring to various aspects of public trust and fairness of justice officials, are: (1) Police authority, (2) Procedural justice, (3) Distributive fairness, and (4) (police) Effectiveness. Cooperation (with the police) was measured on a 4-point scale ranging from 1—Very unlikely to 4—Very likely. Compliance with the law was measured as respondents' self-reporting assessments on how often they broke the law in the past year, on a 4-point scale ranging from 1—Frequently to 4—Never. Respondents were asked to report the frequency with which they committed a variety of legal infractions such as "made a lot of noise at night", "illegally disposed of trash and litter", etc. (for all variables see Appendix 3). This model is presented in Fig. 6.

The third model also fits the data well: the chi-square value is low ($\chi^2 = 8.326$), with Df = 15 and nonsignificant p-value ($p = 0.910$). The other three reported indices RMSEA = 0.000, CFI = 1.000, and TLI = 1.008 also confirm the goodness of fit. The statistically significant standardized coefficients (betas (β)) show (see Fig. 6) that the higher predictor of Trust in police ($R^2 = 71$ %) is Procedural justice ($\beta = 0.59$; $p < 0.001$), followed by Police authority ($\beta = 0.25$; $p < 0.001$) and Effectiveness ($\beta = 0.10$; $p < 0.001$). Procedural justice is the only predictor of Obligation to obey ($\beta = 0.22$; $p < 0.001$; $R^2 = 13$ %). Distributive fairness is again highly correlated with Procedural justice ($r = 0.68$; $p < 0.001$) but it does not affect any of the dependent variables. In correspondence to our hypothesis (that legitimacy is a strong predictor of compliance) Trust in police has a statistical significant effect on Compliance with the law ($\beta = 0.27$; $p < 0.001$; $R^2 = 7$ %), but Obligation to obey does not. Trust in police has also effect on Obligation to obey ($\beta = 0.16$; $p < 0.05$) and Cooperation ($\beta = 0.15$; $p < 0.001$) (which is in other cases one of predictors). Trust in police is the mediator between:

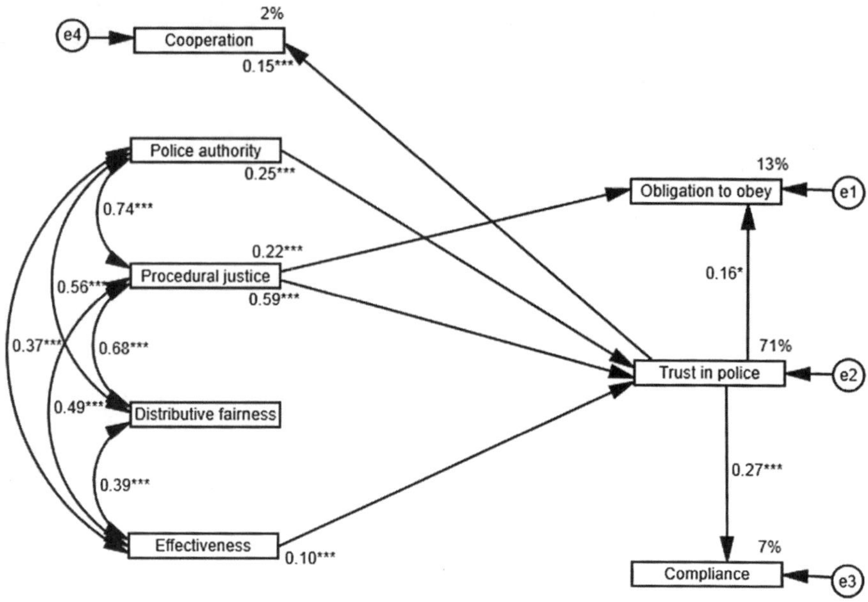

Fig. 6 Structural model of legitimacy (obligation and trust), cooperation and compliance (High school students survey) (Reisig et al., 2012, 2014). $***p < 0.001$; $*p < 0.05$. $\chi^2 = 8.326$; $p = 0.910$; Df = 15; CFI = 1.000; TLI = 1.008; RMSEA = 0.000. Standardized coefficients. *Compliance*: 1—Frequently ... 4—Never; *Obligation to obey*, *Trust in police*, *Police authority*, *Procedural justice*, *Distributive fairness*, *Effectiveness*: 1—Strongly disagree ... 4—Strongly agree; *Cooperation*: 1—Very unlikely ... 4—Very likely

- Police authority (indirect effect = 0.07; 95 % CI [0.05, 0.09]), Procedural justice (indirect effect = 0.16; 95 % CI [0.12, 0.21]) and Effectiveness (indirect effect = 0.03; 95 % CI [0.01, 0.04]) on the one hand and Compliance with the law on the other. These are the full mediations.
- Police authority (indirect effect = 0.04; 95 % CI [0.01, 0.07]), Procedural justice (indirect effect = 0.09; 95 % CI [0.02, 0.17]) and Effectiveness (indirect effect = 0.02; 95 % CI [0.003, 0.03]) on the one hand and Obligation to obey on the other. In the case of Police authority and Effectiveness they are the full mediations, and in the case of Procedural justice it is the partial mediation.
- Police authority (indirect effect = 0.04; 95 % CI [0.02, 0.06]), Procedural justice (indirect effect = 0.09; 95 % CI [0.04, 0.13]) and Effectiveness (indirect effect = 0.015; 95 % CI [0.01, 0.03]) on the one hand and Cooperation with the law on the other. These are the full mediations.

4.4 Fourth Model: The Study on Law Students about Legitimacy in Slovenia (Meško, 2013; Meško et al., in press)

The model of the study on law students about legitimacy in Slovenia (Meško, 2013; Meško et al., in press) is part of the international survey on crime and justice for university students of law and criminal justice and security (for the purpose of our study only Slovenian law students were selected, which is why the sample is relatively small [$n = 143$]). It also defined Legitimacy as Obligation to obey (item "You should accept police decisions because that is the proper or right thing to do") and Trust in police (items: "The police in my community are trustworthy" and "The police are usually honest") (see Appendix 4) but combined in one-dimensional Legitimacy. The five factors, referring to various aspects of public trust and fairness of justice officials are: (1) Trust in police, (2) Police authority, (3) Procedural justice, (4) Distributive justice, and (5) Police effectiveness. Cooperation (with the police) was measured on a 4-point scale ranging from 1—Not at all likely/Not at all willing to 4—Very likely/Very willing. The fourth model does not ask about compliance with the law, instead respondents were asked to assess how wrong (1—Not wrong, 2—Somewhat wrong, 3—Very wrong) it is, in their opinion, to commit a variety of legal infractions such as "made a lot of noise at night", "illegally disposed of trash and litter", etc. (factor Intentional compliance) (for all variables see Appendix 4). The model is presented in Fig. 7.

All reported indices confirm the goodness of fit of the fourth model: the chi-square value is low ($\chi^2 = 13.520$), with $Df = 14$ and nonsignificant p-value ($p = 0.486$), RMSEA = 0.000, CFI = 1.000, and TLI = 1.002. The statistically significant standardized coefficients (betas (β)) show that the higher predictor of Legitimacy ($R^2 = 67$ %) is Trust in police ($\beta = 0.68$; $p < 0.001$), followed by Police authority ($\beta = 0.19$; $p < 0.01$)—see Fig. 7. As such, Legitimacy is a mediator between Trust in police (indirect effect = 0.12; 95 % CI [0.01, 0.23]) and Police authority (indirect effect = 0.03; 95 % CI [0.001, 0.08]) on the one hand, and Intentional compliance on the other. Both Legitimacy and Intentional compliance are mediators of Trust in police and Cooperation (indirect effect = 0.03; 95 % CI [0.001, 0.08]), and Police authority and Cooperation (indirect effect = 0.01; 95 % CI [0.00, 0.03]). Legitimacy also influences the Cooperation via Intentional compliance (indirect effect = 0.05; 95 % CI [0.002, 0.11]). Procedural justice, Distributive justice and Police effectiveness do not influence Legitimacy nor Cooperation in this model. Nevertheless they do have quite high and significant correlations with Trust in police.

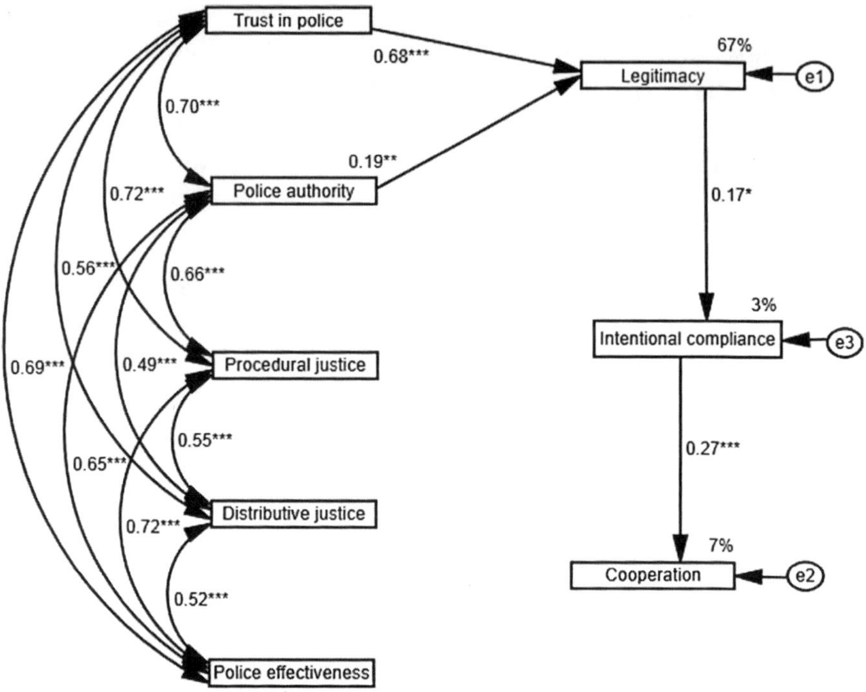

Fig. 7 Structural model of police legitimacy and cooperation (The study on law students about legitimacy in Slovenia) (Meško, 2013; Meško et al., in press). ***$p < 0.001$; **$p < 0.01$; *$p < 0.05$. $\chi^2 = 13.520$; $p = 0.486$; Df = 14; CFI = 1.000; TLI = 1.002; RMSEA = 0.000. Standardized coefficients. *Legitimacy*, *Trust in police*, *Police authority*, *Procedural justice*, *Distributive justice*, *Police effectiveness*: 1—Strongly disagree … 4—Strongly agree; *Intentional compliance*: 1—Not wrong … 3—Very wrong; *Cooperation*: 1—Very unlikely … 4—Very likely

5 Discussion

Discussions on legitimacy of legal authorities always led us to (more or less) the same conclusions: legitimacy is a strong predictor of compliance with the law, and trust in the police is an important factor in shaping people's sense of police legitimacy. Reisig et al. (2012) argued that Tyler's process-based model of regulation is challenged by the fact that most studies are conducted in the USA, leaving open the question of whether similar effects can be observed in countries with different historical and political contexts. Applying such theoretical work in the European area the most important survey is the European Commission FP7 project, JUSTIS, which dovetailed perfectly with Trust in justice module with Round 5 of the European Social Survey [ESS] (www.europeansocialsurvey.org). The aim of this project was to develop a theoretical work about trust in criminal justice across most European jurisdictions (Jackson et al., 2009).

In this paper, four legitimacy models of surveys conducted in Slovenia were verified using SEM: *first model*: Trust in justice module of the European Social Survey (Round 5) (www.europeansocialsurvey.org); *second model*: Test of Tyler's model on "why people obey the law" in Slovenia (Šifrer, 2013; Šifrer et al., 2013); *third model*: High school students survey (Reisig et al., 2012, 2014), and *fourth model*: The study on law students about legitimacy in Slovenia (Meško, 2013; Meško et al., in press). The findings within all four models showed clear and strong relationships between factors, referring to various aspects of public trust and fairness of justice officials and factors of various aspects of police legitimacy:

- In the first model, Trust in police fairness ($\beta = 0.22$; $p < 0.001$) was the strongest predictor of Obligation to obey (defined as the first dimension of legitimacy), Trust in police fairness ($\beta = -0.18$; $p < 0.001$)[6] was the strongest predictor of Moral alignment (defined as the second dimension of legitimacy), and Trust in police fairness ($\beta = -0.21$; $p < 0.001$) was the strongest predictor of Perceived legality (defined as the third dimension of legitimacy).
- In the second model, the strongest predictor of police Legitimacy was Procedural justice ($\beta = 0.41$; $p < 0.001$), followed by Trust in police ($\beta = 0.27$; $p < 0.001$).
- In the third model, the strongest predictor of Trust in police (defined as the first dimension of legitimacy) was Procedural justice ($\beta = 0.59$; $p < 0.001$), followed by Police authority ($\beta = 0.25$; $p < 0.001$), and Effectiveness ($\beta = 0.10$; $p < 0.001$). Procedural justice ($\beta = 0.22$; $p < 0.001$) was the only predictor of Obligation to obey (defined as the second dimension of legitimacy).
- In the fourth model, Trust in police ($\beta = 0.68$; $p < 0.001$) was again the strongest predictor of Legitimacy, followed by Police authority ($\beta = 0.19$; $p < 0.01$).

While these findings speak in support of our hypothesis—trust in police is an important factor in shaping people's sense of police legitimacy—legitimacy as a strong predictor of compliance is somewhat different.

In the first (ESS) model, Moral alignment ($\beta = -0.13$; $p < 0.001$) and Perceived legality ($\beta = -0.07$; $p < 0.05$) (defined as the dimensions of legitimacy) are significant predictors (direct effects) of Compliance, Obligation (defined as the dimension of legitimacy) is not. This is in of Hough et al.'s (2013) model where people who feel aligned with the values of the police (Moral alignment) tend to have a relatively low expected chance of buying stolen goods (in our case committing a traffic offence like speeding or crossing a red light), and people who believe that police officers take bribes (Perceived legality) are more likely to have bought stolen goods. Moral alignment is also a mediator between Procedural justice, Police effectiveness, Trust in police fairness, Distributive fairness on the one hand and

[6] Negative β, for example, determines that those who think that police generally treat people in Slovenia with respect more strongly believe that the police stand up for values that are important to people like them. In other words, those who have higher trust in police fairness feel more aligned with the moral values of the police as an institution.

Compliance on the other. Perceived legality is the mediator between Police effectiveness, Trust in police fairness on the one hand and Compliance on the other.

In the second model, Legitimacy did not predict Compliance. In the third model Trust in police (defined as the first dimension of legitimacy) predicted Compliance with the law ($\beta = 0.27$; $p < 0.001$) while Obligation to obey, defined as the second dimension of legitimacy, did not predict Compliance with the law. In the fourth model, Legitimacy predicted Intentional compliance ($\beta = 0.17$; $p < 0.05$).

Nevertheless, the R^2 was much lower when predicting Compliance with the law (2–7 %) than when predicting Legitimacy with factors referring to trust (e.g., 30 % in the second model, 67 % in the fourth model etc.).

When testing the models some indirect effects on Compliance with the law were found. The largest indirect effect (full mediation) has Procedural justice on Compliance via Trust in police defined as one dimension of legitimacy (indirect effect = 0.16; 95 % CI [0.12, 0.21]) in the third model. All other indirect effects were weak, and factors referring to trust had larger direct effects on Compliance with the law than did indirect effects via factors referring to the legitimacy. Therefore, to conclude that the first part of our hypothesis (legitimacy is a strong predictor of compliance with the law) is strongly supported would be exaggerating. And following Bottoms' (2011) proposed forms of compliant behavior (instrumental/prudential compliance, normative compliance, constraint-based compliance, and compliance based on habit or routine), there is much space left to continue this research.

We also tested people's willingness to cooperate with the police. According to Tyler (2004), people are more willing to cooperate with legal authorities when they believe that those authorities are legitimate. Our findings support this statement in the first model: Obligation ($\beta = -0.12$; $p < 0.001$) and Perceived legality ($\beta = -0.08$; $p < 0.05$) have significant effects on Cooperation. In the second model, Legitimacy influences the Cooperation ($\beta = 0.24$; $p < 0.001$), and in the third model, Trust in police ($\beta = 0.15$; $p < 0.001$) influences the Cooperation.

From our findings, it is clear that trust in police (fairness) is much stronger factor in predicting compliance with the law than legitimacy. Trust in police (fairness) is also the strongest predictor of legitimacy itself, which is in accordance with what Hough et al. (2010) found: trust in the police was an extremely powerful predictor of perceived legitimacy. And Hough et al. (2013) also discovered that social justice and fairness in the justice system are both likely to be preconditions for a well-regulated society.

Despite many formulations of legitimacy and different focus of its prediction in all four models and other US and European studies, the message is the same: relationships between dimensions of public trust and fairness of justice officials and dimensions of legitimacy are clear and strong; and among all dimensions of public trust and fairness of justice officials the trust in police (fairness) is of particular importance. It forms the strongest relationship with dimensions of legitimacy. Therefore, the most efficient way to improve legitimacy is to encourage people's trust in police with respectful, fair, and just treatment.

Appendix 1: Trust in Justice Module of the European Social Survey (Round 5) (www.europeansocialsurvey.org/) ($n = 1{,}403$)

Trust in justice module of Round 5 of the European Social Survey (www.europeansocialsurvey.org) was designed by Mike Hough, Jonathan Jackson, Ben Bradford (and colleagues), and carried out in 28 European countries (including Slovenia) in 2010–2011 on a total sample of almost 51,000. The survey involves strict random probability sampling, a minimum target response rate of 70 %, and rigorous translation protocols. The hour-long face-to-face interview includes questions on a variety of core topics repeated from previous rounds of the survey and also two modules developed for Round Five covering Trust in the Police and Courts and Work, Family and Wellbeing (the latter is a partial repeat of a module from Round 2). Each National Coordination team (in Slovenia: Faculty of Social Sciences, University of Ljubljana) is responsible for identifying a suitable sampling frame and producing a sample design suitable for implementation in their country. Sample in Slovenia must be representative of all persons aged 15 and over (no upper age limit) resident within private households, regardless of their nationality, citizenship or language. Sampling plan is based on two-stage stratified sampling driven out of Central register of population of Slovenia. First stage includes 12 regions and six types of villages, and in the second stage individuals are selected by strict random probability methods (15 persons per district). The sample size in Slovenia counts 1,403 citizens.

Factors	Factor loadings
Police effectiveness[a] (KMO = 0.500; var. = 84.5 %; $\alpha = 0.815$)	
How successful do you think the police are at catching people who commit house burglaries in Slovenia?	0.919
Based on what you have heard or your own experience how successful do you think the police are at preventing crimes in Slovenia where violence is used or threatened?	0.919
Trust in police fairness[b] (KMO = 0.500; var. = 82.8 %; $\alpha = 0.793$)	
Based on what you have heard or your own experience how often would you say the police generally treat people in Slovenia with respect?	0.910
About how often would you say that the police make fair, impartial decisions in the cases they deal with?	0.910
Cooperation[c] (KMO = 0.500; var. = 79.1 %; $\alpha = 0.735$)	
Imagine that you were out and saw someone push a man to the ground and steal his wallet. How likely would you be to call the police?	0.889
How willing would you be to identify the person who had done it?	0.889
Obligation[d] (KMO = 0.710; var. = 83.3 %; $\alpha = 0.899$)	
To what extent is it your duty to do what the police tell you even if you don't understand or agree with the reasons?	0.944

(continued)

Factors	Factor loadings
To what extent is it your duty to do what the police tell you to do, even if you don't like how they treat you?	0.929
To what extent is it your duty to back the decisions made by the police even when you disagree with them?	0.864
Moral alignment[e] (KMO = 0.688; var. = 71.0 %; $\alpha = 0.796$)	
The police stand up for values that are important to people like me.	0.881
The police generally have the same sense of right and wrong as I do.	0.845
I generally support how the police usually act.	0.804
Justice:[f] How dissatisfied or satisfied were you with the way the police treated you the last time you has been approached/stopped/contacted by the police for any reason in past 2 years	
Fairness:[g] When victims report crimes, do you think the police treat rich people worse, poor people worse, or are rich and poor treated equally?	
Legality:[h] How often would you say that the police in Slovenia take bribes?	
Compliance:[i] How often have you committed a traffic offence like speeding or crossing a red light in the last 5 years?	

[a] 0—Extremely unsuccessful ... 10—Extremely successful
[b] 1—Not at all often ... 4—Very often
[c] 1—Not at all likely/Not at all willing ... 4—Very likely/Very willing
[d] 0—Not at all my duty ... 10—Completely my duty
[e] 1—Agree strongly ... 5—Disagree strongly
[f] 1—Very dissatisfied ... 5—Very satisfied
[g] 1—Rich people treated worse, 2—Poor people treated worse, 3—Rich and poor treated equally
[h] 0—Never ... 10—Always
[i] 1—Five times or more ... 5—Never

Appendix 2: Test of Tyler's Model on "Why People Obey the Law" in Slovenia (Šifrer, 2013; Šifrer, Meško, & Bren, 2013) ($n = 479$)

Tyler's (2006) model on "why people obey the law" was tested in Slovenia in October 2011. Tyler's questionnaire was translated and adopted regarding Slovenian legislation system and social circumstances; data were gathered from the pencil-and-paper surveys administered to students of four preliminary chosen Slovenian faculties (covering different fields of social sciences), namely the Faculty of Criminal Justice and Security and the Faculty of Organizational Sciences at the University of Maribor, and the Faculty of Arts and the Faculty of Law at the University of Ljubljana. In the survey participated those students which attended lectures on the day that the questionnaires were given out at a given faculty. The participation was voluntary. The sample size counts 479 students of different gender, program and year of study.

Factors	Factor loadings
Compliance[a] (KMO = 0.608; var. = 53.3 %; $\alpha = 0.543$; $\Omega = 0.708$)	
How often have you driven over 130 km/h on the highways?	0.783
How often have you parked your car in violation of the law?	0.738
How often have you violated the law in the past year?	0.665
Legitimacy[b] (KMO = 0.893; var. = 56.3 %; $\alpha = 0.886$)	
I feel proud of the Slovenian police.	0.841
I have a great deal of respect for the Slovenian police.	0.799
Slovenian officers do their job professionally.	0.795
On the whole Slovenian police are honest.	0.764
I feel that I should support the Slovenian police.	0.760
Police officers help citizens.	0.689
Slovenian police always support people when they call them for assistance.	0.680
Slovenian police treat everyone equally.	0.654
Trust in police[b] (KMO = 0.592; var. = 51.5 %; $\alpha = 0.527$; $\Omega = 0.685$)	
The police should be allowed to stop people on the streets and require them to identify themselves.	0.776
The Slovenian police should be allowed to hold a person suspected of a serious crime until they get enough evidence to officially charge them.	0.743
Always (when possible) I attend any community meetings during which the police made a presentation.	0.625
Cooperation[c] (KMO = 0.611; var. = 52.0 %; $\alpha = 0.533$; $\Omega = 0.692$)	
How likely is it that you would call the police to report suspicious activity in your neighborhood?	0.764
How likely is it that you would call the police if you had a complaint against someone in your neighborhood?	0.704
How likely is it that you would call the police in an emergency?	0.693
Distributive fairness[b] (KMO = 0.788; var. = 66.9 %; $\alpha = 0.835$)	
The police were polite to me.	0.879
The police treated me very fairly.	0.845
The police showed concern for my rights.	0.809
It was important to me whether the police treated me in a fairly manner.	0.731
Procedural justice[b] (KMO = 0.952; var. = 60.0 %; $\alpha = 0.931$)	
I was very satisfied with the manner in which the police handled my problem.	0.875
When I think about the experience I feel pleased with the police.	0.873
The things the police did to deal with the problem were fair.	0.855
The police handled my problem in the expected manner (in a positive way).	0.838
When I think about the experience I feel angry at the police.	0.837
Overall, I was very satisfied with the outcome of the contact with the police.	0.796

(continued)

Factors	Factor loadings
I expect similar treatment in the future (in similar cases).	0.782
The police gave the problem enough attention.	0.730
The police officers gave me a great deal of opportunity to describe may point of view.	0.688
When I think about the experience I feel frustrated with the police.	0.600
The police officers got enough information to make good decisions in solving my problem.	0.577

[a]1—Very often . . . 5—Never
[b]1—Strongly disagree . . . 5—Strongly agree
[c]1—Very unlikely . . . 5—Very likely

Appendix 3: Adult High School Students Survey—Slovenia (Reisig, Tankebe, & Meško, 2012, 2014) ($n = 684$)

The survey on legitimacy in Slovenia was conducted in November and December of 2011 from pencil-and-paper surveys administered to 683 young Slovene adults (18 years and older) who were enrolled in six high schools located in Maribor and Ljubljana, Slovenia. These cities were selected because of the majority of the high schools in Slovenia are located in this two areas. Letters of requesting the permission to survey their students were sent to all of the high schools, and four in Ljubljana and two in Maribor granted it. Project managers travelled to each research site and administered surveys in classrooms. Participation of students was voluntary (Reisig et al., 2012, 2014). This survey represents the pilot study for the next (fourth) survey also conducted by the Faculty of Criminal Justice and Security research team and partners.

Factors	Factor loadings
Compliance[a] (KMO = 0.728; var. = 43.3 %; $\alpha = 0.663$)	
Made a lot of noise at night.	0.779
Drank alcohol in a place where you are not supposed to.	0.745
Illegally disposed of trash and litter.	0.616
Used marijuana or some other drug.	0.582
Broke traffic laws.	0.535
Obligation to obey[b] (KMO = 0.667; var. = 48.3 %; $\alpha = 0.635$)	
You should do what the police tell you to do even if you disagree.	0.787
You should accept police decisions even if you think they are wrong.	0.787
People like me have no choice but to obey the directives of the police.	0.616
You should accept police decisions because that is the proper or right thing to do.	0.560
Trust in police[b] (KMO = 0.859; var. = 50.1 %; $\alpha = 0.832$)	

(continued)

Factors	Factor loadings
I have confidence in the police.	0.799
I am proud of the police in this community.	0.799
The police in my community are trustworthy.	0.729
The police are usually honest.	0.689
People's basic rights are well protected by the police.	0.687
The police can be trusted to make decisions that are right for your community.	0.652
The police in this community are often dishonest (reversed score).	0.574
Police authority[b] (KMO = 0.701; var. = 50.5 %; $\alpha = 0.673$)	
When the police deal with people, they always behave according to the law.	0.730
If I were to talk to police officers in my community, I would find their values to be very similar to my own.	0.721
The police always obey the law.	0.707
The police act in ways that are consistent with my own moral values.	0.683
Cooperation[c] (KMO = 0.776; var. = 49.1 %; $\alpha = 0.733$)	
If the police were looking for witnesses in a case where someone's wallet was stolen, how likely would you be to volunteer information if you witnessed the theft?	0.789
How likely would you be to volunteer to serve as a witness in a criminal court case involving a crime that you witnessed?	0.763
Imagine that you were out and saw someone steal a wallet. How likely would you be to call the police?	0.669
How likely would you be to call the police if you saw someone break into a house or car?	0.669
Imagine you had evidence that someone bribed a government official. How likely would you be to report this behavior to the police?	0.596
Procedural justice[b] (KMO = 0.927; var. = 46.0 %; $\alpha = 0.867$)	
The police treat people fairly.	0.764
The police respect citizens' rights.	0.740
The police treat citizens with respect.	0.713
The police are courteous to citizens they come into contact with.	0.712
The police treat everyone with dignity.	0.708
The police make decisions to handle problems fairly.	0.695
The police follow through on their decisions and promises they make.	0.652
The police take time to listen to people.	0.639
The police make decisions based on the facts.	0.571
The police explain their decisions to the people they deal with.	0.555
Distributive fairness[b] (KMO = 0.605; var. = 59.4 %; $\alpha = 0.654$)	
The police enforce the law consistently when dealing with ALL people.	0.843
The police provide the same quality of service to all citizens.	0.799
The police make sure citizens receive the outcomes they deserve under the law.	0.657

(continued)

Factors	Factor loadings
Police effectiveness[b] (KMO = 0.761; var. = 49.9 %; $\alpha = 0.737$)	
The police are doing a good job preventing crime in my neighborhood.	0.794
The police do a good job maintaining order in my neighborhood.	0.784
There are not many instances of crime in my neighborhood.	0.704
Crime levels in my neighborhood have changed for the better in the last year.	0.663
I feel safe walking in my neighborhood at night.	0.560

[a]1—Frequently . . . 4—Never
[b]1—Strongly disagree . . . 4—Strongly agree
[c]1—Very unlikely . . . 4—Very likely

Appendix 4: The Study on Law Students about Legitimacy in Slovenia (Meško, 2013; Meško et al., in press) ($n = 143$)

A survey of law students with the Faculty of Criminal Justice and Security research team and partners was conducted in autumn 2012 and spring 2013. Law students were selected due to the nature of their studies (legal orientation), and a statement that they would also like to work in law enforcement or a criminal justice agency after graduation. The web-survey was administered in the respondent's native language to students in eight Central and Eastern European countries: Slovenia, Croatia, Bosnia & Herzegovina, Serbia, Former Yugoslav Republic of Macedonia, Romania, Poland and Russia. After preliminary tests, the survey was published on the web and the students were given a certain period of time in which to complete the survey online. The survey was accessible only to law students who received a web address and a specific code provided by their criminal law lecturer. The sample size counts 143 Slovenian students (and 1,848 in total) (Meško, 2013; Meško et al., in press).

Factors	Factor loadings
Legitimacy[a] (KMO = 0.633; var. = 63.0 %; $\alpha = 0.697$)	
The police in my community are trustworthy.	0.844
The police are usually honest.	0.837
You should accept police decisions because that is the proper or right thing to do.	0.691
Intentional compliance[b] (KMO = 0.630; var. = 41.5 %; $\alpha = 0.519$; $\Omega = 0.644$)	
In your opinion, how wrong is it for someone to make a lot of noise at night?	0.733
In your opinion, how wrong is it for someone to illegally dispose of trash and litter?	0.714
In your opinion, how wrong is it for someone to buy something you thought might be stolen?	0.591

(continued)

Factors	Factor loadings
In your opinion, how wrong is it for someone to break the traffic laws?	0.514
Police effectiveness[a] (KMO = 0.861; var. = 61.3 %; $\alpha = 0.873$)	
The police do a good job maintaining order in my neighborhood.	0.821
The police are always ready to provide satisfactory assistance to victims of crime.	0.811
The police are doing a good job preventing crime in my neighborhood.	0.796
The police respond promptly to calls about crime.	0.776
The police are always able to provide the assistance the public needs from them.	0.756
The police are doing well in controlling violent crime.	0.733
Distributive justice[a] (KMO = 0.669; var. = 68.4; $\alpha = 0.765$)	
The police enforce the law consistently when dealing with ALL people.	0.871
The police provide the same quality of service to all citizens.	0.837
The police provide better services to wealthier citizens (reversed score).	0.770
Procedural justice[a] (KMO = 0.912; var. = 56.6 %; $\alpha = 0.903$)	
The police treat people fairly.	0.821
The police treat citizens with respect.	0.820
The police respect citizens' rights.	0.800
The police are courteous to citizens they come into contact with.	0.789
The police make decisions to handle problems fairly.	0.750
The police take time to listen to people.	0.742
The police follow through on their decisions and promises they make.	0.695
The police make decisions based on the facts.	0.677
The police treat everyone with dignity.	0.658
Trust in police[a] (KMO = 0.868; var. = 67.0 %; $\alpha = 0.875$)	
The police can be trusted to make decisions that are right for your community.	0.855
I have confidence in the police.	0.821
The police in this community are often dishonest (reversed score).	0.811
I am proud of the police in this community.	0.809
People's basic rights are well protected by the police.	0.795
Police authority[a] (KMO = 0.690; var. = 63.5 %; $\alpha = 0.807$)	
The police act in ways that are consistent with my own moral values.	0.890
When the police deal with people, they always behave according to the law.	0.805
The police always obey the law.	0.756
If I were to talk to police officers in my community, I would find their values to be very similar to my own.	0.728
Cooperation[c] (KMO = 0.636; var. = 53.6 %; $\alpha = 0.706$)	
How likely would you be to volunteer to serve as a witness in a criminal court case involving a crime that you witnessed?	0.795
If the police were looking for witnesses in a case where someone's wallet was stolen, how likely would you be to volunteer information if you witnessed the theft?	0.764
Imagine that you were out and saw someone steal a wallet. How likely would you be to call the police?	0.694

(continued)

Factors	Factor loadings
Imagine you had evidence that someone bribed a government official. How likely would you be to report this behavior to the police?	0.668

[a]1—Strongly disagree ... 4—Strongly agree
[b]1—Not wrong ... 3—Very wrong
[c]1—Very unlikely ... 4—Very likely

References

Beetham, D. (1991). *The legitimation of power*. Houndmills: MacMillan.

Bottoms, A. (2011). Compliance and community penalties. In A. Bottoms, L. Gelsthorpe, & S. Rex (Eds.), *Community penalties: Change and challenges* (pp. 87–116). New York, NY: Routledge.

Bottoms, A., & Tankebe, J. (2012). Beyond procedural justice: A dialogic approach to legitimacy in criminal justice. *Journal of Criminal Law & Criminology, 102*(1), 119–170.

Carmines, E., & Zeller, R. (1979). *Reliability and validity assessment*. Beverly Hills, CA: Sage.

Cortina, J. M. (1993). What is coefficient alpha? An examination of theory and applications. *Journal of Applied Psychology, 78*(1), 98–104.

Engel, R. (2005). Citizens' perceptions of distributive and procedural injustice during traffic stops with police. *Journal of Research in Crime & Delinquency, 42*(4), 445–481.

Hair, J. F., Jr., Black, W. C., Babin, B. J., & Anderson, R. E. (2010). *Multivariate data analysis: A global perspective* (7th ed.). Upper Saddle River, NJ: Pearson Education.

Hough, M., Jackson, J., & Bradford, B. (2012). *Trust in justice and the legitimacy of legal authorities: Topline findings from a comparative European study*. Retrieved from http://fiduciaproject.eu/publication/8/trust-in-justice-and-the-legitimacy-of-legal-authorities-topline-findings-from-a-comparative-european.

Hough, M., Jackson, J., & Bradford, B. (2013). Legitimacy, trust and compliance: An empirical test of procedural justice theory using the European Social Survey. In J. Tankebe, & A. Liebling, (Eds.), *Legitimacy and criminal justice: An international exploration*. Oxford: Oxford University Press. Retrieved from http://papers.ssrn.com/sol3/papers.cfm?abstract_id=2234339.

Hough, M., Jackson, J., Bradford, B., Myhill, A., & Quinton, P. (2010). Procedural justice, trust and institutional legitimacy. *Policing: A Journal of Policy and Practice, 4*(3), 203–210.

Jackson, J., Hough, M., Bradford, B., Hohl, K., & Kuha, J. (2012). *Policing by consent: Understanding the dynamics of police power and legitimacy*. Retrieved from http://papers.ssrn.com/sol3/papers.cfm?abstract_id=2168702.

Jackson, J., Hough, M., Farrall, S., Aromaa, K., & de Keijser, J. (2009). *Question module design team (ESS Round 5) application form for new modules*. Retrieved from http://www.europeansocialsurvey.org/index.php?option=com_content&view=article&id=231&Itemid=360.

Kaplan, D. (2000). *Structural equation modelling: Foundations and extensions*. London: Sage.

Meško, G. (2013). *Perception of police legitimacy, trust in the police and legal cynicism in countries of Central and Eastern Europe—the results from a law student survey*. Paper presented at the Annual CEPOL European police research & science conference Policing civil societies in times of economic constraints, Münster, Germany, 11–13 September 2013.

Meško, G., Fields, C. B., Šifrer, J., & Eman, K. (in press). Understanding trust in police and legitimacy in Central Eastern Europe: The law student survey. *CEPOL Research and Science Bulletin*, 15 p.

Meško, G., & Klemenčič, G. (2007). Rebuilding legitimacy and police professionalism in an emerging democracy: The Slovenian experience. In V. T. R. Tyler (Ed.), *Legitimacy and criminal justice: International perspectives* (pp. 84–114). New York, NY: Russell Sage Foundation.

Papachristos, A. V., Meares, T. L., & Fagan, J. (2012). Why do criminals obey the law? The influence of legitimacy and social networks on active gun offenders. *Journal of Criminal Law & Criminology, 102*(2), 397–440.

Reisig, M. D., Bratton, J., & Gertz, M. G. (2007). The construct validity and refinement of process-based policing measures. *Criminal Justice and Behaviour, 34*(8), 1005–1028.

Reisig, M. D., & Meško, G. (2009). Procedural justice, legitimacy, and prisoner misconduct. *Psychology, Crime & Law, 15*(1), 41–59.

Reisig, M. D., Tankebe, J., & Meško, G. (2012). Procedural justice, police legitimacy, and public cooperation with the police among young Slovene adults. *Varstvoslovje, 14*(2), 41–59.

Reisig, M. D., Tankebe, J., & Meško, G. (2014). Compliance with the law in Slovenia: The role of procedural justice and police legitimacy. *European Journal on Criminal Policy and Research, 20*(2), 259–276.

Šifrer, J. (2013). *Metode merjenja zanesljivosti in veljavnosti konstrukta "mnenje državljanov o spoštovanju zakonov" [Reliability and validity methods of construct why people obey the law]* (Master thesis). Kranj: Fakulteta za organizacijske vede.

Šifrer, J., Meško, G., & Bren, M. (2013). Zakaj mladi spoštujejo zakone—Empirična izhodišča Tylerjeve teorije [Why young people obey the law—empirical backgrounds of the Tyler's theory]. *Varstvoslovje, 15*(1), 45–63.

Sunshine, J., & Tyler, T. R. (2003). The role of procedural justice and legitimacy in shaping public support for policing. *Law and Society Review, 37*(3), 513–548.

Tankebe, J. (2013). Viewing things differently: The dimensions of public perceptions of police legitimacy. *Criminology, 51*(1), 103–135.

Tyler, T. R. (1997). The psychology of legitimacy: A relational perspective on voluntary defence to authorities. *Personality and Social Psychology Review, 1*(4), 323–345.

Tyler, T. R. (2003). Procedural justice, legitimacy, and the effective rule of law. In M. Tonry (Ed.), *Crime and justice* (pp. 283–357). Chicago, IL: University of Chicago Press.

Tyler, T. R. (2004). Enhancing police legitimacy. *The ANNALS of the American Academy of Political and Social Science, 593*(1), 84–99. Retrieved from http://ann.sagepub.com/content/593/1/84

Tyler, T. R. (2006). *Why people obey the law*. Princeton, NJ: Princeton University Press.

Tyler, T. R. (2011). Trust and legitimacy: Policing in the USA and Europe. *European Journal of Criminology, 8*(4), 254–266.

Do We Trust Them? Public Opinion on Police Work in Plural Policing Environments in Central and Eastern Europe

Branko Lobnikar, Andrej Sotlar, and Maja Modic

1 Introduction

In contemporary societies, the police are often a source of controversy. However, regardless of how they are viewed or their role is carried out, the police form an important link between citizens and their government (Haberfeld, 1997). The main function of police—the provision of security—is one of the basic demands levied against the state by its society. In contemporary society, the focus ought to be on policing by consent rather than by the imposition and enforcement of regulations using superior force alone. As Haberfeld (1997) noted, the concept of police-community relations is not a new one for any democratic society. When Sir Robert Peel undertook reform of the London police with the Metropolitan Police Act of 1829, he emphasized that the police should work in cooperation with the people and officers should protect human rights, serve the needs, and earn the trust of the population they police. It is the same also in these days. Democratic policing is closely associated with the notions of legitimacy, professionalism, and accountability. Sustained legitimacy, skilled professionalism, and effective accountability must exist before policing can be considered democratic; and all three are interdependent. Professional behavior and accountability sustain legitimacy; accountability helps professionalize the police; legitimacy grants the police a necessary degree of professional autonomy (Caparini & Marenin, 2004). Authors emphasized that even a professional and accountable police force will not become legitimized if it fails in its major functions of maintaining order, neutrally enforcing laws, providing security, and protecting people in their persons and property without discrimination or bias. Tyler's (2011) model of social regulation puts

B. Lobnikar (✉) • A. Sotlar • M. Modic
Faculty of Criminal Justice and Security, University of Maribor, Kotnikova 8, Ljubljana 1000, Slovenia
e-mail: branko.lobnikar@fvv.uni-mb.si; andrej.sotlar@fvv.uni-mb.si; maja.modic@fvv.uni-mb.si

G. Meško, J. Tankebe (eds.), *Trust and Legitimacy in Criminal Justice*,
DOI 10.1007/978-3-319-09813-5_9

procedural justice and legitimacy center-stage. On the one hand police need to control population, but on the other hand, police need to win the "hearts and minds" of individuals through legitimate use of power.

According to Stenning (2009) the pluralization of policing has been noted in many countries during the last decades, but little has been written about how policing might be effectively governed and held accountable in the public interest in such an environment of plural provision. The state or public police are no longer perceived as the only bearer of the responsibility for providing safety; other public and private agencies are also perceived as important actors in the process of prevention and control of crime, disorder, and insecurity (Terpstra, 2008). These organizations, which might not have been primarily established for policing in a broader sense can be the following: the public prosecutor, the customs service, inspection services, intelligence-security services, judicial police, local policing bodies, private security companies, and private investigators (Sotlar & Meško, 2009). However, pluralization of policing is not the only trend in contemporary societies, traditional policing providers are going through changes as well. Bayley (2006) and Harris (2005) argued that police reforms have a dual character: on the one hand they seek to increase effectiveness (aiming at crime reduction, maintaining public order, etc.) and consequently provide (more) security; while on the other hand reforms seek to make police organizations more democratic and legitimate. Walsh and Conway (2011) argued that governance and accountability methods and processes have always served a range of objectives in policing. These include: legitimacy, the maintenance of democratic values, the protection of human rights, transparency, the promotion of force efficiency and discipline, and the enhancement of police; community relations which, in turn, can improve the capacity of police bodies to perform their functions.

Although there are many studies in the field of public confidence in authorities in the West, this is still not the case in the countries of Central and Eastern Europe. There is a lack of research in this field. Moreover governments and police forces lack awareness that their performance is based not only on the effective investigation of criminal offenses and maintenance of public order but also on the adoption, support, and trust that citizens show toward the police as well as toward other stakeholders of the expanding security/police community. The purpose of this chapter is to analyze existing research findings on public confidence in policing bodies from the countries of Central and Eastern Europe and to draw attention to gaps that still exist in this field that are typical for countries in transition.

2 Contemporary Forms of Policing in Central and Eastern Europe

In 2001 Ponsaers and Van Outrive (in Ponasers, 2001) summarized different policing models, and among others, the public–private policing model was described. According to the authors, the public–private model of policing can be understood as a reaction against both a too narrow and too traditional conception of police (and policing), and the neglect of new categories. Key notions within this police model are fragmentation, bifurcation, redistribution of police work, disintegration, interaction between police, consumerism, privatization, (un)safety, accountability, and the "new blue line" (Ponsaers, 2001: 487). The public–private model of policing rests on the notion that private and public police have gradually developed in conjunction with each other, so today's police model is not a characteristic of police organization, but rather a categorized allocation of certain police tasks (Ponasers, 2001). The notion of a private–public police model is well connected to the notion of plural policing. Plural policing is a process of transferring typical police activities to private security and other state and local police/security/supervisory organizations. Starting in the West, it gradually became a worldwide trend (Jones & Newburn, 2006). Many of these organizations were not set up to perform police duties but their tasks, and especially authorizations, defined them as "new police forces," be it at the state organizational level (e.g., customs, judiciary police, and financial police) or at the local/city level (e.g., city traffic wardens, private security firms, and private detectives). The least common denominator of all plural policing organizations is that all have authorizations that are greater than the duties of common citizens in the area of ensuring security (Button, 2007; Sotlar, 2010; Wakefield, 2005).

As part of the decentralization process of police and security functions we noticed a trend in developing city/local police or traffic wardens subordinated to mayors or local authorities. These forms of police organizations are right in the middle between state (public) police on one end of the spectrum, and private policing bodies on the other end of the continuum, exercising the main function of police—the provision of security—in local environments. In Poland, they primarily deal with ensuring public order and safety and supervising traffic (Czapska, 2013). In Hungary, The Hungarian Civil Guard, which is a totally civil organization of unarmed yet uniformed citizens, perform certain police tasks—predominantly protecting neighborhoods and patrolling in marked civil cars (Leyrer, 2013). In Slovenia, municipal wardens are responsible for ensuring public safety and public order in the municipality. In doing so, they ensure a safe and smooth traffic flow in residential areas; protect roads and the environment in villages and towns, as well as municipal roads outside settlements; provide safety of the municipal public transport, recreational and other public areas; protect public property, natural and cultural heritage, and maintain law and order (Sotlar, 2010).

Private security in the West was already developed in the past and then revived in the 1990s (Johnston, 1992). This can also be claimed for some Central European

Countries like Germany and Austria; however, in former socialist countries of CEE the changes in political, economic, and social systems enabled the emergence and expansion of the private security sector after the collapse of socialism in late 1980s and in the beginning of 1990s. Economic and financial crisis, starting in 2008, led to austerity measures in most of the countries in the region which affected the funding of police and other state organizations. As a consequence state police organizations were forced to redefine their work priorities and leave less demanding tasks to private security firms (Meško, Sotlar, & Lobnikar, 2014). State police officers in the Czech Republic and Serbia are outnumbered by private security officers; moreover, in Poland and Hungary the number of security officers is as much as twice and three times the number of police officers (Confederation of European Security Services [COESS], 2011). According to COESS (2011) data, the ratio between private security officers and police officers in some countries of Central and Eastern Europe is as follows:

- Austria: 0.73 security officer per 1 police officer;
- Bosnia and Herzegovina: 0.07 security officer per 1 police officer;
- The Czech Republic: 1.17 security officer per 1 police officer;
- Croatia: 0.78 security officer per 1 police officer;
- Germany: 0.49 security officer per 1 police officer;
- Hungary: 3.04 security officer per 1 police officer;
- Macedonia: 0.71security officer per 1 police officer;
- Serbia: 1.49 security officer per 1 police officer;
- Poland: 2.04 security officer per 1 police officer;
- Slovakia: 0.80 security officer per 1 police officer;
- Slovenia: 0.78 security officer per 1 police officer.

Meško et al. (2014) attribute these trends to economic and financial crisis, beginning in 2008, which led to austerity measures in almost every country of the region. It negatively influenced the budgets from which public police are funded, thus forcing them to make priorities in their work, "leaving" less demanding tasks and more room to private security firms.

Described trends indicate that regulated relationships between the police and private security organizations are of great importance (Meško et al., 2014). Despite the on-going debate and considerable research on plural policing, little has been said (written) about how policing should be effectively governed and held accountable in the public interest within "new" plural policing environment.

From an organizational standpoint, the police in Central and Eastern Europe are adopting several common characteristics, including democratization, accountability and legitimacy linked to citizens. In the last decade state police organizations in the region have accepted the fact that they have lost their monopolistic position in policing due to the development of plural policing. The pluralization of social control institutions, which encompasses state police organizations, local community police organizations, and private security organizations, has created competition in policing with individual police (state) organizations being forced to constantly prove themselves and justify their existence (Meško et al., 2014).

Public attitudes toward the police are fundamental for successful policing, since the police are dependent upon the people to report and provide information about crime and to testify as witnesses in court proceedings (McConville & Shepherd, 1992). However, the public is divided regarding their attitudes toward the police, which is problematic as it hinders the police from functioning effectively (Sunshine & Tyler, 2003).

Simplifying Tyler's (2011) considerable research on trust and legitimacy of policing, it should be emphasized that public opinion on police and their work shape citizens' behavior in reaction to the police. Therefore, it is important for the police to learn public opinion; moreover, it should become their key concern. Since security provisions in the last decades have become a concern of various state, local and private stakeholders, one can expect that interests of the public will at least partly shift from the public police to other security providers. Furthermore, increasing interests of the public leads to the questions of efficiency, responsibility and accountability on one side, as well as control over these plural policing bodies on the other. Every institution needs adequate public support in order to function successfully for the long term. Public support is usually measured by the public opinion polls. Since security and order are not provided only by public police, we can hypothesize that public opinion on other policing bodies should be of great importance and concern for competent authorities as well. Findings of some public opinion studies on police organizations will be presented in the next section.

3 Public Opinion on Policing in Central and Eastern Europe

The development of police and policing in Central and Eastern Europe is defined by political systems of the state and we can hypothesize a positive correlation between the level of legitimacy of the political state and the trust of police in the same country. In the post Second World War period, the undemocratic political regimes from Central and Eastern European countries were not perceived as legitimate, so it was the same for police organizations. It was typical of Central and Eastern European countries to have had the characteristics of the centralistic police whose primary purpose was to serve the governments of communist or socialist countries. Consequently, it is not surprising that police organizations were associated with quite a high level of illegitimacy or distrust amongst the citizens. Jenks (2004) finds that the Czech police did not regain the trust of the people even after the Velvet Revolution, which is also true of the East German police whose staff kept a negative attitude towards democratic changes. Also, as little as 12 % of East German citizens believed that their police were successful at preventing crime (Jobard, 2004). Not much was different with the Polish police (Kratcoski, 2000). To some extent, the only notable exception in public opinion on police in Central and Easter Europe were Slovenia and Croatia, the northernmost republics of ex-Yugoslavia. In these countries the militia staff actively participated in the independence processes and protected democratic processes with their activities, and subsequently during the transition from the socialist to the democratic society both countries enjoyed a high level of trust (Kovčo Vukadin, Borovec, & Ljubin Golub, 2013; Meško, Lobnikar, Jere, & Sotlar, 2013). However, even the police officers of these two countries were not highly respected in the times of former Yugoslavia. Kutnjak Ivkovich (2008) claimed that because of their arrogant and disrespectful attitude towards the citizens they were perceived as an uneducated, unprofessional and military led organization. In some countries the same bad image of police rests also in times after the democratization took place. Haberfeld (1997) reported that the image of the Polish Police after democratic changes in the beginning of the 1990s was of an understaffed, incompetent and fragmented force. Such an image certainly cannot promote effective cooperation between the force and the public. One might argue that this lack of competence and effectiveness would lead to feelings of empathy on the part of the public, which would eventually produce the desired outcome—citizen's cooperation, in order to achieve the long awaited consensus, at least as far as domestic peace is concerned. Unfortunately, it is a task extremely difficult to accomplish, since overall corruption, a high unemployment rate and economic chaos do not promote stability and consensus (Haberfeld, 1997). The author concluded that the Polish Police was not presently capable of protecting citizens' rights, serving the needs of the people or earning the trust of the population they police. The ability to function effectively is impeded by so many negative contributors that it is extremely unlikely that radical changes in people's perception of the police will take place in the near future. In Slovenia, Areh, Dobovšek, and Umek (2007) evaluated citizens' opinions of the quality of police procedures conducted in traffic stop encounters and traffic accidents. The findings show that police procedures were performed well, but not perfectly. In traffic stop encounters, citizens think that officers were polite, fair and understandable, but they failed to help drivers return to the flow of traffic and also did not inform people of their rights. In the case of traffic accidents, citizens were satisfied with the officers' tidiness and willingness to help. Several faults were found: citizens' satisfaction was lower with the officers' response time, officers frequently fail to inform drivers of their rights and female respondents believed their opinions were not given enough consideration.

Research findings indicate that personal interactions with police have a significant impact on citizens' general assessment of the police (Tyler & Fagan, 2008). While there is some debate over the effect of positive contacts with the police, researchers agree that unpleasant experiences tend to increase unfavorable opinions (Tyler, 2006). While one route to gaining public confidence in the police is treating people with dignity and fairness, another route may be offered by a neo-Durkheimian perspective (Zernova, 2012). As Sunshine and Tyler (2003) emphasized, citizens think about the police in ways that have to do with the values and norms that sustain social life and look to the police to protect and strengthen social values. When the community is seen as morally deteriorating, public satisfaction with the police may be affected negatively. So, public trust in policing is

Table 1 Levels of trust in police in Central and Eastern European countries (European Social Survey, 2008, 2010, 2012)

Country	Level of trust (mean)[a]	No trust at all (%)	ESS round (year)
Germany	6.84	1.4	2012
Austria	6.00	1.6	2008
Estonia	5.90	4.0	2012
Slovenia	5.38	6.3	2012
Hungary	5.34	4.0	2012
Poland	5.25	5.1	2012
Czech Republic	5.10	5.2	2012
The Republic of Kosovo	4.68	20.0	2010
Croatia	4.38	10.2	2010
Romania	4.35	13.1	2008
Slovak Republic	4.15	7.7	2012
Bulgaria	3.52	22.8	2012
Russian Federation	3.49	15.2	2012
Ukraine	2.48	27.3	2010

[a]Mean value on the scale ranging from 1 to 10, with higher values indicating higher level of trust

shaped by evaluations of the extent to which the police typify community morals and values (Sunshine & Tyler, 2003). The key to public support for the police is the view among members of the public that they share moral solidarity, or a set of common moral values, with the police.

In the Eurobarometer survey conducted in 2010 in 27 European Union Member States and four candidate countries[1] it was found that the majority (64 %) of Europeans still trust the police (European Commission, 2011). Questions regarding public trust in the police are also included in the European Social Survey. Recent available findings for Central and Eastern European countries are presented in Table 1.

It is evident from Table 1 that police enjoy the highest levels of trust in Germany, Austria, and Estonia. Results of recent surveys indicate that Germans hold the police in high esteem, even higher than some important organs of the constitutional democratic state—the federal government and federal parliament. The latest available results rank the police second after the federal constitutional court (Feltes, Marquardt, & Schwarz, 2013). Based on several national studies among citizens of Austria, Edelbacher and Norden (2013) noted that 70 % of the respondents expressed great confidence in the police, while in the confidence hierarchy of eight national institutions, the Police ranked second after the federal president. It is also worth noting that immigrants were more critical and expressed less confidence in the police than Austrian nationals. In both countries the percentage of people who had no trust in the police was low (1.4 and 1.6 %). According to the

[1] Four candidate countries in 2010: Croatia, the former Yugoslav Republic of Macedonia, Turkey, and Iceland.

recent Estonian public opinion poll 86 % of respondents trusted the police and Border Guard Board (Tabur, 2013); however, 4 % of respondents had no trust in police at all according to a recent European Social Survey (Table 1).

Slovenia, Hungary, Poland, and the Czech Republic represent the second group of countries, where levels of trust in police were above 5 on the scale ranging from 1 to 10, with higher values indicating higher levels of trust. According to Slovenian public opinion polls (Toš, 1999, 2004, 2009), public trust in the police varied greatly between 1991 and 2009. The level of trust in the police was the lowest in 1993, when only one-fifth of Slovenian citizens trusted the police. In 1994, almost sixty percent of respondents expressed trust in the police; however, in 1995 the level of trust declined again; less than one-third trusted the police. This trend continued until the year 2000, when more than one-half of respondents indicated a high level of trust in the police. It has been quite constant since with only minor deviations. The results of recent research on residents' opinion about the police (Meško, Sotlar, Lobnikar, Jere, & Tominc, 2012) illustrated that one third of respondents in Slovenia still fully trust the police. Furthermore, police enjoy the highest level of public trust compared to other members of the plural policing family: the mean value is 2.98 on the scale ranging from 1 to 5, with higher values indicating higher level of trust. Private security companies rank second after the police (2.87), followed by private detectives (2.76), municipal warden service (2.65), and inspection services (2.61) (Meško et al., 2012). As Leyrer (2013) reported, over the past 20 years public opinion on the police in Hungary remained consistently positive. Between 2003 and 2006 citizens exhibited higher level of trust in the police than in other armed services. Aggressive police response to anti-government protests in 2006 led to a significant decrease in public confidence in the police, while the other institutions maintained or even increased public support (Leyrer, 2013).

In their Police Development Strategy for 2005–2010 (National Police Headquarters, 2013), Polish police defined increasing social trust in the police as one of their strategic objectives. Walker (2009) reported that Polish police enjoyed high levels of trust—75 % of respondents trusted them, while the military was trusted by 84 % of the respondents and charity organizations by 80 % of the respondents. According to Czech Public opinion research center (Poll: Czechs trusted the military most, churches the least, 2013) 55 % of the respondents trusted the police, while the military (62 % of the respondents) and radio (58 % of the respondents) enjoyed the highest levels of public trust. At present, both military and police organizations enjoy considerably higher level of trust than in the second half of the 1990s.

The third group of countries, where the levels of trust in the police were between 4 and 5 on the scale ranging from 1 to 10, consisted of the Republic of Kosovo, Croatia, Romania, and the Slovak Republic. According to the results of Kosovo public opinion poll conducted in 2011, most respondents (78 %) had some or complete confidence in the Kosovo police, while 5.4 % of respondents had no confidence at all (Justice and the people, 2011). According to the European Social Survey results from 2010, there were an even higher percentage of people who did not trust the police—20 % (Table 1). In the 1990s, Croatian police enjoyed a high level of trust among citizens, because of their defensive role in the Homeland War. However, in the post-war period more negative attitudes and a lack of confidence in state institutions (including police) were generated by the processes of privatization and the advancement of individuals connected with the leading political structures. In the present, trust in the police is relatively high compared to the level of trust in other state institutions—only the Croatian armed forces enjoy higher level of trust among citizens (Kovčo Vukadin et al., 2013). According to the European Social Survey results from 2008, 13.1 % of Romanians did not trust the police at all.[2]

Police suffer from the lowest levels of trust in Bulgaria, the Russian Federation, and Ukraine (see Table 1). In Bulgaria, trust in police, as well as trust in courts, was low and has remained mostly unchanged over the last decade. In 2010, less than half of the respondents expressed favorable opinions on police performance (Center for the Study of Democracy, 2011). It is worth noting that on the European Union level, Bulgarian citizens are the least satisfied with the performance of the main government institutions (Center for the Study of Democracy, 2011). Sergevnin and Kovalyov (2013) pointed out that only 25–30 % of Russians trusted the police according to a series of surveys, conducted between 2004 and 2012. It was evident from the European Social Survey results (2012) that 15 % of the Russian respondents had no trust in police. It was also evident from Table 1 that in 2010, 27.3 % of Ukrainian respondents expressed no trust in the police at all, which was the highest level of distrust in the region (at least according to the European Social Survey database).

Data for some other countries of the region, which were not included in the European Social Survey, can be found in various sources. For instance, findings from the survey on trust in various institutions in Macedonia showed noticeable decreases in public confidence in the police—from 57.3 % in 2007, to 56.6 % in 2008 and 52.1 % in 2010. When compared to public trust in other institutions, police ranked third after the armed forces (62.9 % of the respondents expressed trust) and educational institutions (62.1 % of the respondents expressed trust) (Klekovski, Nuredinoska, & Stojanova, 2010). Recent research on citizens' attitudes about Montenegrin police showed that more than a half of respondents (54 %) mostly trusted the police and 14.2 % had complete trust in the police, while one quarter of respondents (24.8 %) mostly did not trust the police and 7 % had no trust in the police at all (Bešič, 2011). Recent research findings on public trust in various institutions indicate that almost half of the respondents (45 %) trusted the police, while 28 % of the respondents had no trust in the police and a quarter of respondents

[2] However, other available sources of data indicated even lower level of trust in the police. Andreescu and Keeling (2012) reported on findings of a public opinion poll conducted in 2010 on a representative sample, which showed that 66 % of respondents did not trust the police. When compared to 2008, the latest findings seemed even more unexpected since Romania joined the EU in 2007 and was together with Bulgaria under constant pressure and surveillance in order to strengthen the fight against organized crime and corruption. In fulfilling this goal, the police were expected to be one of the most important bodies.

were undecided (neither trust nor distrust). Serbian police ranked second after the church (trusted by 59 % of the respondents), followed by the armed forces (trusted by 44 % of the respondents) (Center for Free Elections and Democracy [CeSID], 2011).

In comparison with the growing body of research on public opinion and trust in public police, public interest in plural policing, as well as other aspects of the relationship between citizens and plural policing bodies, seems to be a rather under-researched field. While some opinion polls do include questions on trust in various institutions other than public police, these institutions are usually the following: government, parliament, constitutional court (Feltes et al., 2013), president of the state (Edelbacher & Norden, 2013), armed forces (CeSID, 2011; Klekovski et al., 2010; Poll: Czechs trust military most, church least, 2013; Walker, 2009), charity organizations (Walker, 2009), radio (Poll: Czechs trust military most, church least, 2013), educational institutions (Klekovski et al., 2010) and church (CeSID, 2011).

Recent research among Slovenian citizens and police officers on various aspects of local safety also addressed trust in plural policing institutions. The results show that the public police enjoy the highest level of public trust compared to other members of the plural policing family: mean value for police is 2.98 (on the scale ranging from 1 to 5, with higher values indicating higher level of trust), private security companies ranked second after the police with 2.87, followed by private detectives (mean 2.76), municipal warden service (mean 2.65), and inspection services (2.61). In contrast to previous research, these findings indicate that the responsibility for local safety provision is no longer perceived by the public as the sole monopoly of the police (Meško et al., 2012).

To the authors' knowledge, there is a lack of public interest and research on the relationship between citizens and plural policing bodies even outside the Central and Eastern Europe. Nalla and colleagues have conducted some research on public perceptions of private security guards in various parts of the world—specifically in the USA (Nalla & Heraux, 2003), Singapore (Nalla & Lim, 2003), and the Netherlands (Van Steden & Nalla, 2010). Nalla and Heraux (2003) commented that their first research project (conducted in USA) was inspired by previous research conducted by Shearing, Stenning, and Addario (1985), who interviewed Canadian citizens in 1985 to assess their views on private security personnel.

Conclusion

There are two prerequisites for successful policing: the legal operation of police organizations and an adequate level of legitimacy. Legality is a necessary but not sufficient condition for the success of a police organization. Police chiefs from Central and Eastern Europe know this from their own experience—after the democratization processes they have adapted the police legislation and assumed that the job is done. However, this was often not the case; successful policing requires an adequate level of legitimacy and consent of the

(continued)

public or in the words of British policing philosophy, policing by consent. One of the most utilized methods to assess trust and legitimacy of policing, and the one reviewed here, is through monitoring public opinion on police and their work. Without public trust and legitimacy, the police simply cannot function effectively. The results of public opinion surveys should therefore become a tool for everyday decision making as well as for strategic management of the police. Our analysis has shown that the study of public opinion on state police organizations has become more or less constant throughout Central and Eastern Europe. When comparing the results, it is evident that public opinion regarding the police is more negative in the countries which have less experience with the democratic tradition (e.g., Ukraine, Bulgaria, and Slovak Republic). These results present a serious challenge to police managers in these countries, especially as all police organizations in the region claim to comply with the principles of community policing, which is very difficult if not impossible with low levels of legitimacy and public support for police. As demonstrated by the body of research on the legitimacy of police organizations, public opinion is based on previous experiences that have a significant impact on one's future behavior (see, for example, Tyler, 2011). Therefore, monitoring public opinion about the police is not just the latest fad or a good public relations technique, but an essential tool for the successful management of the police.

Most of what has been written in this chapter about public opinion on the state police, increasingly applies also to the other institutions of the extended plural policing family. The fact is that the provision of security requires coordinated actions of several public (state and local) and private institutions operating within the plural model of policing. The results of public opinion on state police are often disregarded by the management of police organizations, while there is actually very little or no research data on the legitimacy of other policing institutions. We have demonstrated that people are more and more aware of the diversification of policing, but yet, the lack of serious scientific research on plural policing organizations from the public opinion point of view is obvious. Since the final result—ensuring safety—depends on all the institutions involved, even the excellent work of the state police cannot provide substantial results (any longer). A plural policing model requires a comprehensive approach to the study as well as management of policing, along with the consideration of community policing and problem oriented policing principles. Therefore, future public opinion surveys should focus also on local police organizations and/or municipal warden services, private security organizations, private investigators, and other members of diverse plural policing family.

References

Andreescu, V., & Keeling, D. G. (2012). Explaining the public distrust of police in the newest European Union countries. *International Journal of Police Science and Management, 14*(3), 219–245.

Areh, I., Dobovšek, B., & Umek, P. (2007). Citizens' opinions of police procedures. *Policing: An International Journal of Police Strategies & Management, 30*(4), 637–650.

Bayley, D. H. (2006). *Changing the guard: Developing democratic police abroad*. New York: Oxford University Press.

Bešič, M. (2011). *Attitudes of citizens of Montenegro on police and security issues*. OSCE Mission to Montenegro. Retrieved from http://www.osce.org/montenegro/81362.

Button, M. (2007). Assessing the regulation of private security across Europe. *European Journal of Criminology, 4*(1), 109–128.

Caparini, M., & Marenin, O. (2004). *Transforming police in Central and Eastern Europe: Process and progress*. Geneva: Geneva Centre for the Democratic Control of Armed Forces.

Center for Free Elections and Democracy [CeSID]. (2011). *Attitude of Serbia's citizens towards the police work*. Retrieved from http://www.mup.rs/cms/resursi.nsf/Public%20Opinion%20Research%202011.doc.

Center for the Study of Democracy. (2011). *Public trust in the criminal justice system – an instrument for penal policy assessment*. Sofia: CSD. Retrieved from http://www.csd.bg/artShow.php?id=15598.

Confederation of European Security Services [COESS]. (2011). *Private security services in Europe: Facts & figures 2011*. Retrieved from http://www.coess.eu/_Uploads/dbsAttachedFiles/Private_Security_Services_in_Europe-CoESS_Facts_and_Figures_2011%281%29.pdf.

Czapska, J. (2013). *Policje i strażemiejskie w Europie [Municipal policing in Europe]*. Krakow: Jagellonian University Press.

Edelbacher, M., & Norden, G. (2013). Policing in Austria: Development over the past twenty years, present state and future challenges. In G. Meško, C. B. Fields, B. Lobnikar, & A. Sotlar (Eds.), *Handbook on policing in Central and Eastern Europe* (pp. 15–31). New York: Springer.

European Commission. (2011). *Standard Eurobarometer 74: Public opinion in the European Union*. Retrieved from http://ec.europa.eu/public_opinion/archives/eb/eb74/eb74_publ_en.pdf.

European Social Survey. (2008). *Countries by round (year)*. Retrieved from http://www.europeansocialsurvey.org/data/country_index.html.

European Social Survey. (2010). *Countries by round (year)*. Retrieved from http://www.europeansocialsurvey.org/data/country_index.html.

European Social Survey. (2012). *Countries by round (year)*. Retrieved from http://www.europeansocialsurvey.org/data/country_index.html.

Feltes, T., Marquardt, U., & Schwarz, S. (2013). Policing in Germany: Developments in the last 20 years. In G. Meško, C. B. Fields, B. Lobnikar, & A. Sotlar (Eds.), *Handbook on policing in Central and Eastern Europe* (pp. 93–115). New York: Springer.

Haberfeld, M. R. (1997). Poland: "The police are not the public and the public are not the police": Transformation from militia to police. *Policing: An International Journal of Police Strategies & Management, 20*(4), 641–654.

Harris, F. (2005). *The role of capacity-building in police reform*. Pristina: Organization for Security and Cooperation in Europe. Retrieved from http://www.osce.org/kosovo/19789?download=true.

Jenks, D. (2004). The Czech police: Adopting democratic principles. In M. Caparini & O. Marenin (Eds.), *Transforming police in Central and Eastern Europe* (pp. 115–127). Münster: LIT.

Jobard, F. (2004). The lady vanishes: The silent disappearance of the GDR Police after 1989. In M. Caparini & O. Marenin (Eds.), *Transforming police in Central and Eastern Europe* (pp. 45–64). Münster: LIT.

Johnston, L. (1992). *Rebirth of private policing*. London: Routledge.
Jones, T., & Newburn, T. (2006). *Plural policing*. London: Routledge.
Justice and the people. (2011). *The justice and the people public opinion poll – Kosovo 2011*. Retrieved from http://www.justiceandthepeople.org/wp-content/uploads/First_Polling_Report_ENG.pdf.
Klekovski, S., Nuredinoska, E., & Stojanova, D. (2010). *Trust in Macedonia: General trust and trust in institutions trust in civil society knowledge and opinion about civil society organizations*. Skopje: Macedonian Center for International Cooperation. Retrieved from http://www.mcms.org.mk/images/docs/2011/trust-in-macedonia-2010.pdf.
Kovčo Vukadin, I., Borovec, K., & Ljubin Golub, T. (2013). Policing in Croatia: The main challenges on the path to democratic policing. In G. Meško, C. B. Fields, B. Lobnikar, & A. Sotlar (Eds.), *Handbook on policing in Central and Eastern Europe* (pp. 31–57). New York: Springer.
Kratcoski, P. C. (2000). Policing in democratic Societies: An historical overview. In D. K. Das & O. Marenin (Eds.), *Challenges of policing democracies: A world perspectives* (pp. 23–44). Amsterdam: Gordon and Breach Publishers.
Kutnjak Ivkovich, S. (2008). Comparative study of public support for the police. *International Criminal Justice Review, 18*(4), 406–434.
Leyrer, R. (2013). Finding the right path of policing In Hungary. In G. Meško, C. B. Fields, B. Lobnikar, & A. Sotlar (Eds.), *Handbook on policing in Central and Eastern Europe* (pp. 115–129). New York: Springer.
McConville, M., & Shepherd, D. (1992). *Watching police, watching communities*. London: Routledge.
Meško, G., Lobnikar, B., Jere, M., & Sotlar, A. (2013). Recent developments of policing in Slovenia. In G. Meško, C. B. Fields, B. Lobnikar, & A. Sotlar (Eds.), *Handbook on policing in Central and Eastern Europe* (pp. 263–286). New York: Springer.
Meško, G., Sotlar, A., Lobnikar, B., Jere, M., & Tominc, B. (2012). *Občutek ogroženosti in vloga policije pri zagotavljanju varnosti na lokalni ravni: CRP (V5-1038 A): poročilo ciljnega raziskovalnega projekta [Feelings of insecurity and the role of police in local safety provision]*. Ljubljana: Fakulteta za varnostne vede.
Meško, G., Sotlar, A., & Lobnikar, B. (2014). Policing in Central and Eastern Europe: Past, present, and future prospects. In M. D. Reisig & R. J. Kane (Eds.), *The Oxford handbook of police and policing* (pp. 606–622). Oxford: Oxford University Press.
Nalla, M. K., & Heraux, C. G. (2003). Assessing goals and functions of private police. *Journal of Criminal Justice, 31*(3), 237–247.
Nalla, M. K., & Lim, S. (2003). Students' perceptions of private police in Singapore. *Asian Policing, 1*(1), 27–47.
National Police Headquarters. (2013). *The Polish police's experiences focusing on strategic researches and building up the police strategy*. Retrieved from http://www.policja.pl/ftp/pliki/strategy.pdf.
Poll: Czechs trust military most, church least. (2013, March 28). *Prague daily monitor*. Retrieved from http://praguemonitor.com/2013/03/28/poll-czechs-trust-military-most-church-least.
Ponsaers, P. (2001). Reading about "community (oriented) policing" and police models. *Policing: An International Journal of Police Strategies & Management, 24*(4), 470–497.
Sergevnin, V., & Kovalyov, O. (2013). Policing in Russia. In G. Meško, C. B. Fields, B. Lobnikar, & A. Sotlar (Eds.), *Handbook on policing in Central and Eastern Europe* (pp. 191–217). New York: Springer.
Shearing, C. D., Stenning, P. C., & Addario, S. M. (1985). Public perceptions of private security. *Canadian Police College Journal, 9*(3), 225–253.
Sotlar, A. (2010). Private security in a plural policing environment in Slovenia. *Journal of Police Studies, 3*(16), 335–353.
Sotlar, A., & Meško, G. (2009). The relationship between the public and private security sectors in Slovenia: From coexistence towards partnership? *Varstvoslovje, 11*(2), 269–285.

Stenning, P. (2009). Governance and accountability in a plural policing environment: The story so far. *Policing: A Journal of Policy and Practice, 3*(1), 22–33.
Sunshine, J., & Tyler, T. (2003). The role of procedural justice and legitimacy in shaping public support for policing. *Law and Society Review, 37*(3), 513–547.
Tabur, L. (2013). Policing in Estonia: From police force to police service. In G. Meško, C. B. Fields, B. Lobnikar, & A. Sotlar (Eds.), *Handbook on policing in Central and Eastern Europe* (pp. 81–93). New York: Springer.
Terpstra, J. (2008). Police, local government, and citizens as participants in local security networks. *Police Practice and Research, 9*(3), 213–225.
Toš, N. (1999). *Vrednote v prehodu II: slovenskojavno mnenje 1990–1998 [Values in transition II: Slovene public opinion 1990–1998]*. Ljubljana: Fakulteta za družbene vede, Inštitut za družbene vede, Center za raziskovanje javnega mnenja.
Toš, N. (2004). *Vrednote v prehodu III: slovensko javnomnenje 1999–2004 [Values in transition III: Slovene public opinion 1999–2004]*. Ljubljana: Fakulteta za družbene vede, Inštitut za družbene vede, Center za raziskovanje javnega mnenja.
Toš, N. (2009). *Vrednote v prehodu IV: slovensko javno mnenje 2004–2009 [Values in transition IV: Slovene public opinion 2004–2009]*. Ljubljana: Fakulteta za družbene vede, Inštitut za družbene vede, Center za raziskovanje javnega mnenja.
Tyler, T. R. (2006). *Why people obey the law*. Princeton: Princeton University Press.
Tyler, T. (2011). Trust and legitimacy: Policing in the USA and Europe. *European Journal of Criminology, 8*(4), 254–266.
Tyler, T. R., & Fagan, J. (2008). Legitimacy and cooperation: Why do people help the police fight crime in their communities? *Ohio State Journal of Criminal Law, 6*(21), 231–275.
Van Steden, R., & Nalla, M. K. (2010). Citizen satisfaction with private security guards in the Netherlands: Perceptions of an ambiguous occupation. *European Journal of Criminology, 7*(3), 214–234.
Wakefield, A. (2005). The public surveillance functions of private security. *Surveillance and Society, 2*(4), 529–554.
Walker, T. E. (2009). *The distrust paradox: Trust and distrust in the Polish online press, cross-national data reports and public opinion surveys, 2002–2008* (Master thesis). Chapel Hill: University of North Carolina. Retrieved from https://cdr.lib.unc.edu/indexablecontent/uuid:10615342-c372-4fd1-ac0f-71850ef328c2.
Walsh, D. P. J., & Conway, V. (2011). Police governance and accountability: Overview of current issues. *Crime, Law and Social Change, 55*(2–3), 61–86.
Zernova, M. (2012). The public image of the contemporary Russian police: Impact of personal experiences of policing, wider social implications and the potential for change. *Policing: An International Journal of Police Strategies & Management, 35*(2), 216–230.

Trust in the German Police: Determinants and Consequences for Reporting Behavior

Nathalie Guzy and Helmut Hirtenlehner

1 Introduction

Legitimacy of the police is currently a booming topic. It has never stimulated more research than in recent years (Hough, Jackson, & Bradford, 2013a). In a narrow sense, empirical legitimacy refers to the right to rule and the recognition and acceptance of this right by the ruled (Bottoms & Tankebe, 2012; Hough, Jackson, & Bradford, 2014). Following Tyler (2006b: 27), the founder of procedural justice theory, legitimacy can be defined as "perceived obligation to comply with the directives of an authority" or, in brief, as "perceived obligation to obey." Already this narrow notion of legitimacy makes it clear that empirical legitimacy is a relational and attitudinal concept. So it is not astonishing that the legitimacy discussion in a broader sense covers all aspects of public trust in and views about the police (Tankebe, 2013), reaching out to "the extent to which authorities enjoy the public's support, allegiance, and confidence" (Tyler, 2006b: 28). From this latter perspective, "perceived obligation to obey" appears as a consequence of legitimacy, rather than as legitimacy itself. In some respect the question on the analytical distinction of trust and felt obligation to defer is an academic one: Both the theoretical and empirical literature on procedural justice theory stress the interweaving of public attitudes towards or confidence in the police and the perceived obligation to obey or cooperate (Bottoms & Tankebe, 2012; Hough et al., 2013a; Jackson et al., 2012; Tankebe, 2013; Tyler, 2006a, 2006b).

N. Guzy (✉)
Department of Police Crime Statistics, Criminology and Criminal Investigation Analysis, Federal Criminal Police Office, Bundeskriminalamt, 65173 Wiesbaden, Germany
e-mail: Nathalie.Guzy@bka.bund.de

H. Hirtenlehner (✉)
Centre for Criminology, Johannes Kepler University Linz, Altenberger Strasse 69, 4040 Linz, Austria
e-mail: Helmut.Hirtenlehner@jku.at

G. Meško, J. Tankebe (eds.), *Trust and Legitimacy in Criminal Justice*,
DOI 10.1007/978-3-319-09813-5_10

In this chapter, the emphasis is placed on public trust in the German police, its determinants, and its consequences for reporting behavior. The chapter starts with some macro-social considerations on cross-national differences in perceived legitimacy of the police within Europe and the array of country-level characteristics discussed as possible influencing factors. This section also provides the backdrop for situating the Germans' perception of their police within the wider European landscape and approaching the issue of East–West discrepancies in police legitimacy within a formerly divided country. At the heart of this work is a large-scale empirical study on public perceptions of the police in Germany. Data collected in the course of a nationwide victimization survey enables insights into the nature of public views about the police, some selected determining factors and the effects of trust in this institution on actual reporting behavior. The results of these analyses are interpreted in a procedural justice framework (Tyler & Huo, 2002).

2 Macro-Social Considerations: Cross-Country Differences in Attitudes Towards the Police and Their Determining Factors

The first section of the chapter is aimed at giving a snapshot of inner-European differences in police legitimacy and outlining some possible determinants of the corresponding divide, thereby locating Germany within the broader European context.

There is, without doubt, marked cross-national variation in the levels of trust in or perceived legitimacy of the police, even within Europe. Meanwhile we can draw on several cross-national studies to assess the extent and structure of these differences (Hough et al. 2013a, 2014; Hough, Jackson, & Bradford 2013b, Hough & Maffei, 2013; Kääriäinen, 2007, Kääriäinen & Sirén, 2011). The common database of these studies is the European Social Survey (ESS), a periodically conducted international survey program with more than 20 European nations among its participants (Jowell, Roberts, Fitzgerald, & Eva, 2007).[1] Although each wave of the ESS offers a global indicator of public trust in the police (Item B6: "Please tell me on a score from 0 to 10 how much you personally trust the police?" 0 = no trust at all; 10 = complete trust), most works make use of round 5 of the survey, which includes a special module on trust in criminal justice institutions. When relating the country-specific findings regarding views about the police to typologies of welfare regimes or political economies, as they are proposed by Esping-Andersen (1990), Arts and Gelissen (2002) or Cavadino and Dignan (2006, 2014), a general pattern evolves that can be described as follows: Citizens of the social-democratic welfare states Northern Europe's (e.g., Finland, Denmark) usually hold the most positive views about their police. They express the highest levels of confidence in and allegiance to this authority. The conservative corporatist welfare states Western

[1] Data can be obtained free of charge from the website www.europeansocialsurvey.org

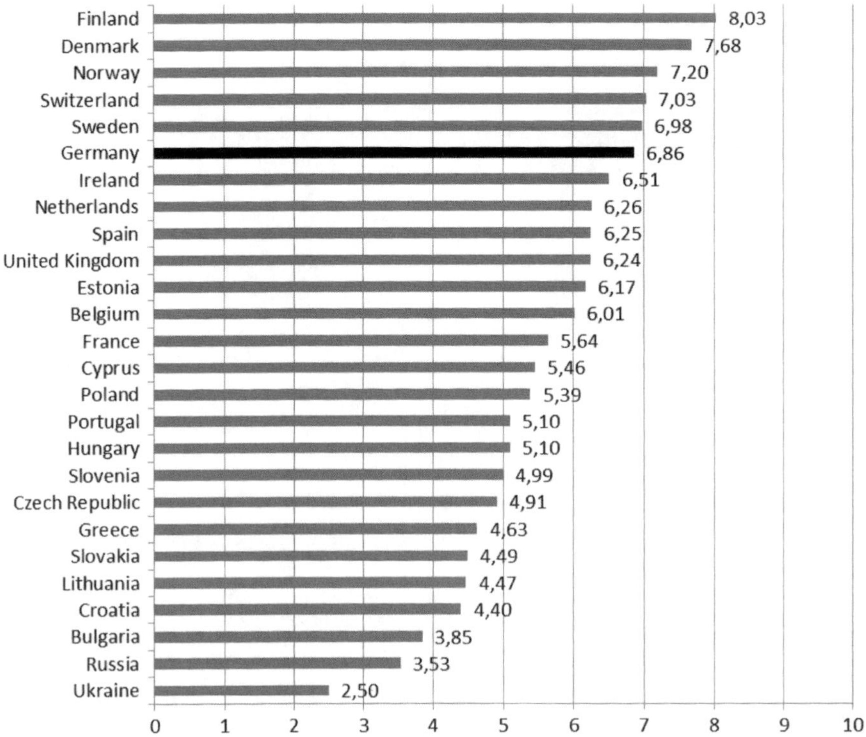

Fig. 1 Average trust in the police in European countries (Item B6 of ESS round 5, weighted data)

Europe's (e.g., Germany, Switzerland) rank next to the Nordic countries regarding trust in and acceptance of the police, tightly followed by liberal welfare states as the UK or Ireland. Support for the police decreases as we move south and east. The police of the rudimentary welfare states of Southern Europe (e.g., Portugal, Greece) suffers from considerably lower levels of trust and legitimacy. The bottom end of the scale is marked by the post-communist transformation societies of Eastern Europe. Respondents from the Eastern European countries (e.g., Russia, Ukraine) articulate the least favorable attitudes towards the police and also confer the least legitimacy on it.

Germany, a typical representative of the conservative corporatist welfare state (Esping-Andersen, 1990), usually ranks relatively high in these international comparisons. Independent of the employed measure of the attitudes towards this institution, German citizens tend to report high levels of confidence in and support for their police. This general finding is illustrated in Fig. 1, which gives the average scores of 26 European countries on the global indicator of public trust in the police

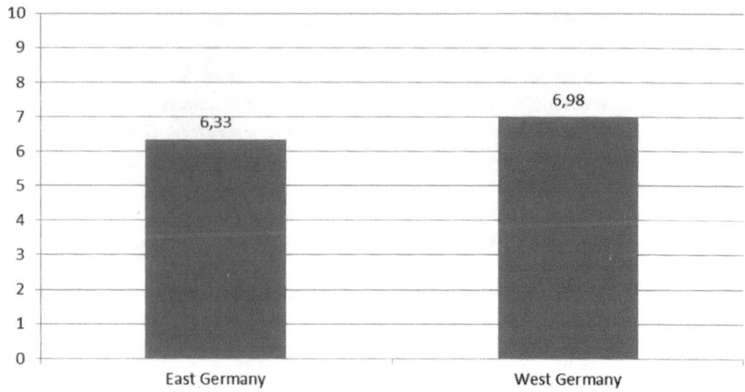

Fig. 2 Average trust in the police in East and West Germany (Item B6 of ESS round 5, weighted data)

as measured in the fifth round of the ESS in 2010/2011.[2] It is discernible that Germany ranks 6th out of 26, a position indicating a comparatively positive public stance towards this authority.

Since its reunification in 1990 Germany encompasses both the former Federal Republic of Germany (Western Germany) and the former German Democratic Republic (Eastern Germany). Figure 2 shows the mean levels of public trust in the police in the old and new federal states, again measured in terms of the global indicator provided by the fifth wave of the ESS. It can be seen that trust in the police is higher in Western than in Eastern Germany.[3] Inhabitants of the former German Democratic Republic tend to take a more critical stance towards this authority, which may be rooted in either the role of the police in the communist era or in experiences made with this institution in times around the upheaval.

Having established significant cross-national variation in the levels of public trust in or perceived legitimacy of the police, the logical next step is to investigate the determining factors of these differences. In the relevant literature several drivers of a nation's attitude towards its police are discussed. We give a brief overview here. Corruption among officials is assumed to undermine confidence in the police (Hough, Jackson, Bradford, Myhill, & Quinton, 2010; Kääriäinen, 2007; Karstedt, 2013, 2014). A lack of trust in political and governmental institutions in general is theorized to spread to the criminal justice system (Goldsmith, 2005; Hough et al., 2010; Kääriäinen, 2007). Higher levels of fear of crime are observed to be accompanied by less favorable views about the police (Hirtenlehner, Bacher, Oberwittler, & Hummelsheim, 2012; Kääriäinen, 2007; Kääriäinen & Sirén, 2011). A country's media culture seems to play an important role: Where the media deal with crime

[2] The country differences in public support for the police turn out to be highly significant (eta = 0.48; $p = 0.000$).

[3] The regional divide can withstand any form of significance testing (eta = 0.11; $p = 0.000$).

issues in a sensationalist, dramatizing and fatalistic manner, public distrust in crime-fighting authorities is fed (Boda & Szabo, 2011; Green, 2008a, 2008b; Surrette, 2007). Increased welfarism, expressed for instance by high social expenditures, is found to be associated with elevated trust in the police (Hirtenlehner et al., 2012; Kääriäinen, 2007; Lappi-Seppälä, 2008, 2014). Autocratic regimes are hypothesized to generate a more critical public attitude towards the police than democratic regimes, with established democracies being equipped with more institutional trust than developing or new ones (Goldsmith, 2005; Kääriäinen, 2007). Empirical evidence on this issue is scarce, however. In a seminal work, Karstedt (2013: 145) demonstrates that "democracies do not necessarily and by default enjoy higher levels of legitimacy (...) than non-democratic regimes." Some sorts of authoritarian or autocratic regimes seem to be capable of producing more confidence in the police than democracies, and it is in the nearly democratic state where resentments against the police are most likely to emerge.

Type of democracy can be related to confidence in the police also with reference to another classification of democratic regimes: Lijphart (1999) distinguishes between consensus and majoritarian (or conflict) democracies.

Majoritarian democracies tend to have two-party landscapes, a majority election system and, relative to the legislature, strong governments. Goal of the governing party is the monopolization of power and the exclusion of political competitors from all creative processes. The complete expulsion from policymaking drives opposition parties into radical confrontational strategies. They seek to gain power through intensive attacks on the competency and credibility of the governing party and its institutions. As Lappi-Seppälä (2008: 323) puts it, in such a political climate "the main project of the opposition is to talk up societal and political crises and to convince the public that there is an urgent need to remove the governing party from power." The omnipresent "crisis talk" and the permanent discrediting of the government and "its" authorities has, of course, effects on how the citizens think about state (and criminal justice) institutions. Nurtured additionally by a comparatively aggressive media culture, the constant attacks on the government's policy undermine public trust in the efficiency and reliability of a society's institutional apparatus—a process from which the police is not spared (Green, 2008a, 2008b; Lappi-Seppälä, 2008, 2014).[4]

Consensus democracies, on the other hand, are characterized by multi-party systems, frequent coalition or minority governments, strong parliaments and corporatist structures. Defining elements are a certain extent of power sharing and participation of political competitors in pivotal decision-making processes. The practiced negotiation and compromise orientation decreases the intensity of the political contest. When the opposition is granted a certain level of participation in real policy-making, this acts as a barrier to overly energetic and aggressive criticism

[4] In majoritarian democracies crime serves the opposition as a tool to discredit the work of the party in power (Green, 2008a, 2008b). It is exactly the scandalizing of the crime problem and the alleged incompetency of the police to solve it, which has negative consequences on public confidence in the police.

of the party in power. As a consequence, a societal crises discourse fails to appear in consensual systems, trust in public institutions remains intact and the police is not bothered with blatant legitimacy problems (Green, 2008a, 2008b; Lappi-Seppälä, 2008, 2014).[5]

The mechanisms outlined above suggest that not any single national characteristic alone is responsible for the intra-European legitimacy gap. It is, on the contrary, the interplay of several factors that appears to shape the level of public support for the police. This interplay may be best described in recourse to typologies of welfare regimes or political economies, as done by Hough et al. (2013a, 2013b, 2014). In this context additional insights can be gained from an empirical classification of European control landscapes. Hirtenlehner et al. (2012) demonstrate that national practices of handling social difference combine with public sentiments and mentalities to form coherent cultures of social control. Public trust in the police represents one element of these control cultures. A cluster analysis of 23 European countries that employs imprisonment rates, the de-commodification power of social welfare policy, trust in public institutions (among them several criminal justice institutions), fear of crime, und attitudes towards punishment as segmentation variables identifies three distinct regimes of governing social marginality: (1) an inclusive regime wherein generous welfare provision and little incarceration merge with low levels of fear of crime and limited support for harsh punishment, this all against the backdrop of considerable trust in public institutions; (2) an exclusionary regime characterized by modest welfare benefits and extensive imprisonment, wherein fear of crime, punitive attitudes and low confidence in state institutions are widespread; and (3) a hybrid regime in which inclusive and exclusionary elements form a fragile alliance. The inclusive regime is located predominantly in Scandinavia; the exclusionary regime can be found particularly in Eastern Europe. The utilized classification variables are also shown to be highly intercorrelated: Trust in public institutions (and with it confidence in the police) goes along with high de-commodification and low levels of fear of crime as well as little attitudinal and systemic punitivity.

3 Micro-Social Considerations: Determinants of Legitimacy and Their Consequences for Reporting Behavior

3.1 Trust in the Police, Police Legitimacy, and Public Cooperation: A Theoretical Embedding

Reporting behavior, a specific kind of public cooperation with the police, is subject to a complex individual decision-making process. Within the relevant literature,

[5] In this scheme Germany has to be classified as consensus democracy.

predominately three groups of influencing factors on reporting decisions are discussed: victim-specific, incident-specific and environment-specific characteristics (e.g., social capital). On the victim-specific level, several determinants are well established. These include sociodemographic variables like age, sex, income, and educational attainment (Baumer, 2002; Goudriaan, Witterbrood, & Nieuwbeerta, 2006; MacDonald, 2001), prior victimization experiences (Conaway & Lohr, 1994; Maguire, 1997), as well as several personal attributes, experiences and circumstances (MacDonald, 2001; Skogan, 1994; Tarling & Morris, 2010). With regard to the relevant personal attributes, victimization studies regularly demonstrate that—when asking people about the reasons for reporting a crime—the majority feels obliged to do so (Skogan, 1994; Tarling & Morris, 2010).

In the literature on trust in criminal justice institutions, the perceived duty to report a crime—or more general the belief to obey the rules and cooperate with authorities—is frequently discussed within the framework of "legitimacy." Differentiated from an instrumental (motive-based) model of policing which builds on the deterrence hypothesis and suggests that following the rules is influenced by self-interest and fear of punishment, a normative (process-based) model of policing emphasizes the concept of 'legitimacy' and argues that beliefs about the appropriateness and fairness of the police increase public cooperation by activating feelings of responsibility and obligation (Sunshine & Tyler, 2003; Tyler, 2006b; for an overview see Mazerolle, Bennet, Davis, Sargeant, & Manning, 2013).[6]

A legitimacy-based cooperation model has several advantages compared to an instrumental model because it is self-regulatory and does not depend on varying perceptions of sanction risk. "When people cooperate with the police and other legal actors because of norms or values they share with the law, their behavior may be linked more to intrinsic motivations and less to the influence of sanctions or incentives on behavior" (Tyler & Fagan, 2008: 236).

As already described above, subjective legitimacy refers to the "perceived obligation to comply with the directives of an authority" or rather the "perceived obligation to obey" (Tyler, 2006b: 27) and may thus be seen as related to trust in the police.[7] All aspects of trust in the police may function as a precondition for subjective legitimacy. In his most fundamental and best-known work, Tyler (2006b) identifies two distinct sources of police legitimacy: (1) satisfaction with police effectiveness and (2) trust in the procedural fairness of the police. These sources can be linked to an instrumental and a normative perspective of

[6] At this juncture it should be mentioned that there is a conceptual discussion whether cooperation with the police is an outcome of legitimacy or a constitutive part of it (Jackson & Bradford, 2010). In this work we draw on Tyler's notion that legitimacy represents a kind of belief and orientation that affects the citizen's behaviors.

[7] According to Hough et al. (2013a, 2013b), subjective or empirical legitimacy must be differentiated from objective or normative legitimacy. While the former refers to perceptions and attitudes of the governed (in the sense of acceptance and support), the latter addresses the question whether an institution meets certain external or substantive criteria.

legitimacy.[8] While the instrumental perspective of legitimacy (referring to the effectiveness of police work) relies on the belief that, if the police is recognized as being competent in handling crime, the public will support police activities and cooperate with this institution in order to increase its success, the normative (procedural justice) perspective of legitimacy draws on evaluations of the police's decision-making processes and places the emphasis on the quality and fairness of policemen's decision making and how the officers treat citizens in everyday encounters (Sunshine & Tyler, 2003; Tyler & Fagan, 2008). Closely tied to procedural justice considerations are public perceptions of the police's distributive fairness—i.e., whether this authority is distributing its services fairly across all social groups (Sunshine & Tyler, 2003).

Regarding the origins of trust in the police, a variety of predictors are discussed. Among them, personal experiences with the police play a particularly prominent role. It has repeatedly been shown that assessments of personal encounters with the police shape an individual's attitudes towards this authority, whereby unpleasant experiences seem to have a stronger effect than positive contacts (Rosenbaum, Schuck, Costello, Hawkins, & Ring, 2005; Tyler, 2006b; Tyler & Huo, 2002). In this context, both the type of police contact (self-initiated vs. police initiated) and the satisfaction with these encounters are assumed to exert a major influence (Kääriäinen, 2007; Rosenbaum et al., 2005; Schafer, Huebner, & Bynum, 2003).

Given this state of research, the relationship between experiences with and trust in police, legitimacy and reporting behavior appears to be straightforward: Based on their experiences with this authority, people develop (dis-)trust in the police. If the police is seen as trustworthy, it is also more likely to be seen as legitimate, which, in turn, fosters cooperation (e.g., reporting a crime) (Hough et al., 2010; Tyler & Huo, 2002).

Complexity, though, results from the fact that different dimensions of trust in the police may affect legitimacy and thus reporting behavior differently. Against this backdrop the focus of this article is on three components of trust in the police: effectiveness, distributive fairness and procedural fairness. Perceived effectiveness refers to the police's performance in fighting crime. Distribute fairness relates to the outcomes people receive, particularly to the fact whether different population groups are treated equally. Procedural fairness or justice describes "the fairness of the process employed to reach specific outcomes or decisions" (Tankebe, 2013: 111) and is often determined by the quality of the treatment of the individual in interactions with the police.

---

[8] With moral alignment with the police, Beetham (1991) refers to a further source of legitimacy. However, following Hough et al. (2010: 205), this approach can further be extended by the procedural justice model, in that "the sense of a shared moral position is communicated to citizens by the police through the quality of their behavior in specific interactions and in particular through their procedural fairness—or lack of it."

3.2 *Empirical Evidence*

3.2.1 Determinants of Trust in the Police and Police Legitimacy

Following Tyler's (2001) evaluation of several surveys testing his procedural justice theory, police legitimacy is obviously empirically related to both trust in the performance of the police and trust in the procedural fairness of the police. Thereby numerous studies indicate that the perceived procedural fairness of the police appears to be more important for legitimacy than the evaluation of police effectiveness (Jackson & Bradford, 2010; Lind & Tyler, 1988; Sparks, Bottom, & Hay, 1996; Sunshine & Tyler, 2003; Tyler, 2006b; Tyler & Fagan, 2008; Tyler & Huo, 2002). Complementary results show that negative evaluations of procedural fairness can undermine legitimacy, causing disobedience, resistance, and disrespect (Dai, Frank, & Sun, 2011; Fischer, Harb, Al-Sarraf, & Nashave, 2008; Mastrofski, Snipes, & Supina, 1996). Some studies, however, fail to support a relationship between trust in police effectiveness and police legitimacy or even found negative correlations (Jonathan-Zamir & Weisburd, 2009; Murphy, Hinds, & Fleming, 2008; Tyler, 2004).[9]

Looking at the evidence regarding the origins of trust in the police, a large body of research refers to a variety of influencing factors (Cheurprakobkit, 2000; Hawdon, Ryan, & Griffin, 2003; Tyler & Huo, 2002). Worth mentioning are media effects (Eschholz, Blackwell, Gertz, & Chiricos, 2002; Lasley, 1994), vicarious contacts with the police (Rosenbaum et al., 2005), victimization experiences (Hurst & Frank, 2000; Payne & Gainey, 2007), as well as several sociodemographic variables like age, education, and migration background (Decker, 1981; Schafer et al., 2003; Weitzer & Tuch, 2005).

One of the best established predictors of attitudes towards the police, one that often exhibits the greatest explanatory power, is the assessment of personal encounters with the police (for an overview see Rosenbaum et al., 2005; Schafer et al., 2003). The majority of studies found negative, dissatisfactory experiences in the course of personal contacts with the police fostering negative attitudes towards this institution, while positive and satisfactory experiences increase support for the police (Bartsch & Cheurprakobkit, 2004; Kääriäinen, 2007). Perceptions of officers' courteousness, helpfulness and fairness when personally dealing with them have repeatedly been proven to impact on citizens' general attitudes towards the police (Skogan, 2005; Tewksbury & West, 2001; Tyler, 2006b; Tyler & Huo, 2002). Results furthermore indicate that negative experiences tend to have a greater effect than positive ones and that already a single negative experience can have a

[9] Following Tankebe (2007), these results might be explained by cultural differences. In a study in Ghana Tankebe found police effectiveness to be the main determinant of police cooperation, probably because in countries which are exposed to high crime levels, police effectiveness becomes more important than the procedural fairness of the police. Tyler and Huo (2002) found similar results in their Californian study in which procedural justice played a less important role for minority than for majority groups.

deteriorating impact on opinions about the police (Frank, Smith, & Novak, 2005; Jackson et al., 2011; Weitzer & Tuch, 2005). Besides this, it is well known that police contacts, which are initiated by the respondents, are typically assessed more positively than police-initiated encounters (Decker, 1981; Skogan, 2005; Tyler & Huo, 2002).

3.2.2 Consequences of Legitimacy and Trust in the Police on Reporting Decisions

So far, numerous studies have found that trust in the police and police legitimacy encourage compliance and cooperation (for an overview see Eisner & Nivette, 2013; Mazerolle et al., 2013; Tyler & Fagan, 2008). This brief literature review concentrates on cooperation with the police. Mastrofski et al. (1996) as well as McCluskey, Mastrofski, and Parks (1999), among others, show that citizens are significantly more likely to comply with a request when the police treat them fair and with respect. Works of Tyler corroborate a relationship between trust in the police or police legitimacy and self-reported willingness to report a crime (Sunshine & Tyler, 2003; Tyler & Fagan, 2008; Tyler & Huo, 2002). In a study by Bradford and Jackson (2010), citizens' perceptions of procedural fairness and effectiveness of the police were associated with the probability of cooperation (again in terms of self-reported willingness), although procedural justice seems to exert the greater influence. Similarly, Reisig and Lloyd (2009) found the willingness to report crimes or suspicious activities to the police being dependent on legitimacy, which is fed by perceptions of procedural justice (see also Murphy et al., 2008). Moreover, a variety of studies confirm a connection between trust in the distributive fairness of the police and intended reporting behavior (Reisig, Bratton, & Gertz, 2007; Sunshine & Tyler, 2003; Tyler & Fagan, 2008). Nevertheless, the effects of the latter appear to be weaker than the effect of procedural justice (Sunshine & Tyler, 2003). It must also be mentioned, however, that a few studies cannot establish significant associations between trust in the police and reporting behavior (Goudriaan, Lynch, & Nieuwbeerta, 2004; Hickman & Simpson, 2003; Kääriäinen & Sirén, 2011).

4 Research Question

This study aims to investigate the determinants and consequences of several dimensions of trust in the police. Levels of public support for the police are set out for Germany altogether as well as for the Eastern and Western parts of the country separately. With regard to the determinants of trust in the police, the focus will be on one of the most salient and frequently discussed predictors, namely the nature and

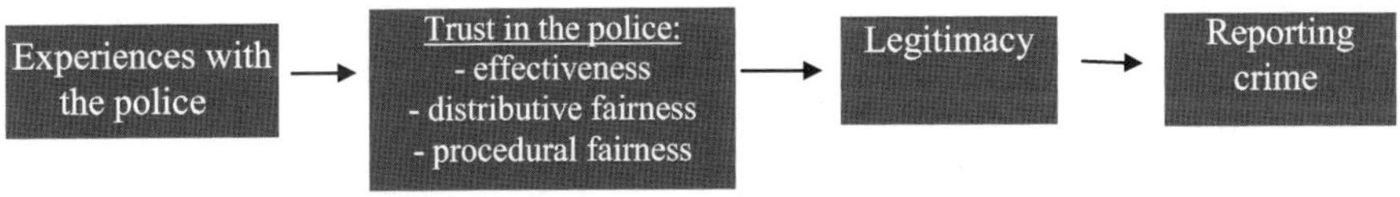

Fig. 3 Theoretical model

quality of one's personal experiences with the police. Thereby we address not only the fact of whether or not police contact has occurred, but also whether the contact was police- or self-initiated and how this contact was assessed. When it comes to the consequences of trust in the police, the emphasis is placed on victims' actual reporting behaviors. Unlike the majority of the available studies, which draw on mere intentions to report a crime, this work tackles the relationship between trust in the police and factual crime reporting. The analysis is guided by the theoretical model displayed in Fig. 3. This model serves as the backdrop to study which kind of police experiences has the greatest influence on trust in the police and which dimension of trust in police exerts the most significant influence on reporting behavior.

5 Methodology

Database of the present study is a computer-assisted telephone survey (CATI) on victimization experiences, reporting behaviors, fear of crime and crime-related attitudes. The study was part of a research project called "Monitoring Security in Germany" (acronym: Barometer Security in Germany "BaSiD") which was funded by the German Ministry of Education and Research and run by the Federal Criminal Police Office in close cooperation with the Max Plank Institute for Foreign and International Criminal Law.

Target population were all residents of Germany older than 16 years of age speaking either German, Turkish, or Russian (if they lived in private households and were accessible by telephone). A stratified random sample, comprising about 35,000 persons, was generated by Randomized Digit Dialing. The survey was conducted in 2012.[10] Respondents were contacted by landline as well as by mobile telephones. In order to achieve an appropriate choice of persons with migration background, a sub-sample was created by using onomastic sampling procedures. The questionnaire, which was available in German, Turkish, and Russian, was structured in modules, which means that parts of the questionnaire were only provided to subsamples. The overall response rate was 22 %.

Questions about experiences with and attitudes towards the police were mainly collected within the module 6 called "Crime-related attitudes." This module was presented to a sub-sample of 2,100 persons selected at random from the overall

[10] The data collection was realized by the social research institute "Infas."

sample. Information on the type of experiences with the police and the satisfaction with these police-encounters was collected within this module. An exception is "overall trust in the police" which was part of the main questionnaire and thus provided to the full sample of 35,000 persons.

Four indicators of trust in police were employed:[11]

(a) Trust in the effectiveness of the police ("How well do the local police work in controlling crime? Very good/quite good/quite bad/very bad?").
(b) Trust in the distributive fairness of the police ("When victims report crimes, do you think the local police treat rich people worse, poor people worse, or are rich and poor people treated equally?").
(c) Trust in the procedural fairness of the police ("What do you think how often do the police use more force than is legally or situationally warranted? Very often, often, sometimes, seldom, never.").
(d) Overall trust in the police ("Please tell me on a score from 0 to 10 how much you personally trust the police. 0 means you do not trust the police at all, 10 means you have complete trust.").

Reporting behavior was operationalized by first determining whether the respondent had been the victim of one of several crimes (burglary, theft, robbery, assault, fraud, credit card abuse) within the last 12 months. If the respondent had fallen victim to at least one of these crimes in the reference period, it was investigated whether or not the police was informed about this event. Thereby a person was classified as having reported a crime to the police if at least one of the experienced victimizations became known to the police.[12]

Satisfaction with the police was measured by asking whether or not the respondent had had contact with this authority within the last 12 months preceding the survey and how satisfied he or she was with the last police encounter (very satisfied/quite satisfied/quite dissatisfied/very dissatisfied).

Unfortunately the questionnaire does not include a direct measure of legitimacy in the narrow sense, so the analysis has to focus on the relationships between the available indicators of trust in the police and reporting behavior. As our pivotal variables (satisfaction with police encounters, trust in the police and reporting behavior) refer to different sub-populations—namely persons with police contact ($n = 618$), all respondents provided with module 6 ($n = 2{,}100$) and participants of module 6 who were victimized during the last 12 months ($n = 346$)—the analysis is conducted in three separated steps. We start with descriptive findings on the distribution of trust in the police in Germany. Then we turn to the determinants of confidence in the police (focusing on the effects of experiences with this institution). After this we study the consequences of trust in the police for actual reporting behavior.

[11] At this juncture, it should be mentioned that the employed items do not measure distributive and procedural fairness extensively. For this, multiple-item measures would be necessary. Such an approach, however, was not realizable here due to restrictions of space in the questionnaire.

[12] In total, 5,832 persons (15.6 % of the overall sample) reported being a victim. 38.1 % of the victims filed at least one complaint.

All analyses are based on weighted data. The employed weights reflect a combination of design-weighting and redressment.[13]

6 Results

6.1 Trust in the German police

As illustrated in Figs. 4, 5, 6, and 7, the German police enjoy high levels of public trust: About 87 % of the respondents assess the police as at least good in controlling crime and only 12 % expect the police to use more force than is legally or situationally warranted. Judgments about the distributive fairness of the police are more divided: three out of ten respondents believe that the police would treat a rich and a poor person unequally (most often treating the poorer person worse). In terms of the 11 point scale to assess general trust in the police, more than half of the respondents (52 %) opt for value greater equal 8.

Looking at the differences between East and West Germany, it can be seen that, with the exception of trust in procedural fairness, the Western states are characterized by slightly higher levels of trust in the police than the Eastern states.[14] The most pronounced divide can be found in terms of overall trust.

Table 1 gives the results of a series of logistic regression analyses on dichotomized trust in the police.[15] The multivariate models indicate that the East–West differences are significant only in the case of overall trust[16] (this after controlling for other variables like sex, age, education, migration background,[17] income, victimization, and police contact).

Apart from the partial trust advantage in the Western states, another finding deserves attention: personal victimization experience is fairly consistently associated with reduced trust in the police. Previous victimization—or the police's handling of the incident—has apparently the potential to decrease public support for this institution. This observation paves the way for a more thorough examination of the relationship between police contact and public trust in the affected authority.

---

[13] The post-stratification was based on a generalized regression estimator calculated from following variables: sex, age, education, employment status, migration background, household size, federal state, and size of domicile.

[14] When comparing East and West Germany, it must be noted that the survey only asked in which federal state the respondent currently lives. The respondent may, however, have grown up in another federal state, a fact that tends to blur differences between East and West Germany.

[15] For the nature of the dichotomization see footnote 18.

[16] Bivariate correlation analyses with the untransformed trust measures provide substantively identical results.

[17] This includes all immigrants to the present territory of the Federal Republic of Germany after 1949 as well as all foreigners born in Germany and all individuals born as Germans in Germany with a least one immigrant parent or one parent born as a foreigner in Germany.

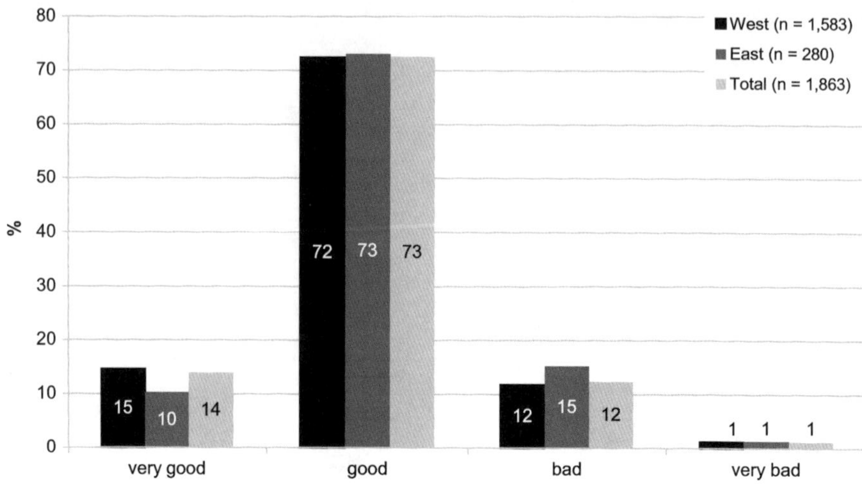

Fig. 4 Trust in the effectiveness of the police (*How well do the local police work in controlling crime?*)

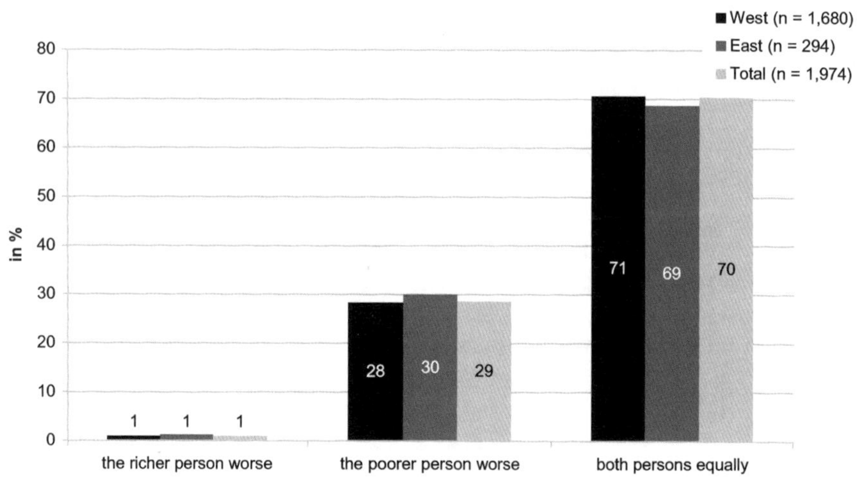

Fig. 5 Trust in the distributive fairness of the police (*When victims report crimes, do you think the local police treat rich people worse, poor people worse, or are rich and poor people treated equally?*)

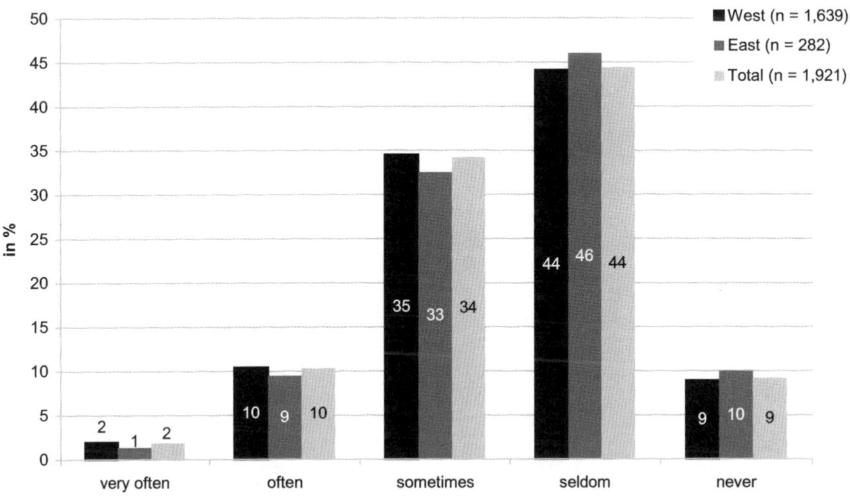

Fig. 6 Trust in the procedural fairness of the police (*What do you think how often do the police use more force than is legally or situationally warranted? Very often, often, sometimes, seldom, never*)

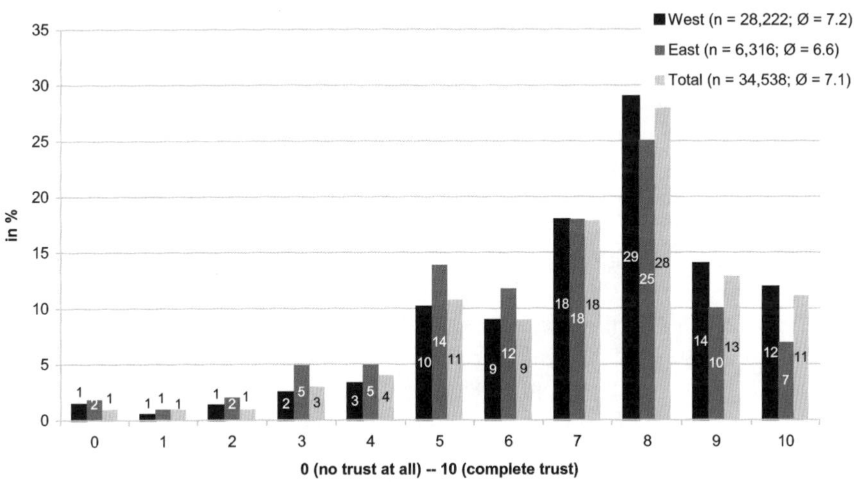

Fig. 7 Overall trust in the police (*Please tell me on a score of 0–10 how much you personally trust the police. 0 means you do not trust the police at all, 10 means you have complete trust*)

Table 1 Results of logistic regression models for trust in the police

	Trust in effectiveness	Trust in distributive fairness	Trust in procedural fairness	Overall trust
	$n = 1{,}748$	$n = 1{,}853$	$n = 1{,}802$	$n = 1{,}907$
	Odds ratio			
Age	0.996*	0.995	1.008	0.990*
Sex (female)	1.089	1.418*	0.692*	1.131
Education (A level)	1.263*	1.038	1.068	1.130
Migration background	1.376	1.290	0.843	0.829
Income 1,000 > 2,000 EUR[a]	1.226	1.339	0.978	0.613*
Income 2,000 > 3,000 EUR[a]	0.930	1.794*	0.991	0.633*
Income 3,000+ EUR[a]	0.990	1.558	1.602	0.722
East Germany	0.741	0.851	1.221	0.513**
Police contact	0.794	0.968	0.927	0.604**
Victimization experiences (within the last 5 years)	0.470**	0.621**	0.848	0.605**

*$p < 0.05$; **$p < 0.01$; ***$p < 0.001$
[a]Reference category: Income < 1,000 EUR

6.2 Determinants of Trust in the Police

With regard to the determinants of trust in the police it can be seen from Table 2 that whether or not the respondent had an encounter with the police during the last 12 months exerts a significant influence only on his or her overall trust in this institution.[18] Here, personal experience with the police decreases trust in the authority. While 54 % of the respondents without a police contact show a high level of overall trust, the same applies only to 43 % of the respondents with police encounters. Contrary to this, trust in the effectiveness as well as the distributive and procedural fairness of the police is not significantly shaped by police contacts themselves. These findings remain stable after controlling for sociodemography (age, sex, education, migration background, and income), victimization experiences, and domicile in East or West Germany (see Table 1).

A more notable effect of experiences with the police appears when drawing on the assessment of police encounters (Table 3). With the exception of perceptions related to the distributive fairness of the police, a general picture emerges according to which persons who were (very or quite) satisfied with their last police contact believe the police to be more trustworthy than persons who were dissatisfied. While

[18] For the following tables, the diverse measures of trust in the police were dichotomized. Tables 2, 3, and 4 report the following percentages: trust in the effectiveness of the police: doing a very good/quite good job; trust in the distributive fairness: treating both persons equally; trust in the procedural fairness: using never/seldom more force than is warranted; overall trust: values greater equal 8).

Table 2 Trust in the police by police contact

Police contact within the last 12 months	Trust in effectiveness	Trust in distributive fairness	Trust in procedural fairness	Overall trust
	in %			
Yes ($n=552$)	84.9	70.9	53.0	42.6
No ($n=1{,}346$)	87.5	70.2	54.6	54.0
Correlation coefficient (r)	−0.034	0.006	−0.015	−0.104**

*$p<0.05$; **$p<0.01$; ***$p<0.001$

Table 3 Trust in the police by satisfaction with police contact

Satisfaction with last police contact	Trust in effectiveness	Trust in distributive fairness	Trust in procedural fairness	Overall trust
	in %			
Satisfied ($n=477$)	87.5	71.3	55.6	50.8
Dissatisfied ($n=73$)	73.2	69.0	42.6	8.6
Correlation coefficient (r)	0.153	0.020	0.105	0.338***

*$p<0.05$; **$p<0.01$; ***$p<0.001$

Table 4 Trust in the police by type of police contact

Type of police contact	Trust in effectiveness	Trust in distributive fairness	Trust in procedural fairness	Overall trust
	in %			
Police-initiated contact ($n=71$)	90.4	75.2	55.9	40.2
Self-initiated contact ($n=351$)	86.4	74.4	54.1	51.0
Correlation coefficient (r)	0.046	0.007	0.014	−0.085

*$p<0.05$; **$p<0.01$; ***$p<0.001$

88 % of the satisfied persons think that the police is effective in controlling crime and 56 % expect the police using never or seldom more force than is situational and legally allowed, this is only the case for 73 % (trust in police effectiveness) and 43 % (trust in procedural fairness) of the respondents with unsatisfactory police contacts. However, due to small sample sizes within module 6 of the survey, statistically significant differences can only be demonstrated for the overall trust measure: 51 % of the persons who were satisfied and only 9 % of those who were dissatisfied with their last police contact show a high level of trust.

The reason for the police contact does not seem to play a major role in shaping trust in the police (Table 4). Whether the last encounter with the police was police-initiated or self-initiated affects none of our measures of trust in the police significantly. Slight, but insignificant differences are discernible for overall trust—with self-initiated contacts being accompanied by elevated trust compared to police-initiated encounters.

6.3 *Consequences of Trust in the Police for Reporting Behavior*

Figure 8 illustrates the percentage of crimes reported to the police for varying levels and measures of trust in the police. It is apparent that in disaccord with the hypothesized relationship between trust and reporting behavior (namely that trust in the police increases the likelihood of reporting a crime), persons who were identified to have a high level of trust show either identical or even lower reporting rates than respondents with low trust in the police. While for overall trust as well as trust in procedural fairness reporting rates are the same for persons with either high or low levels of trust, persons with elevated trust in the distributive fairness or effectiveness of the police tend to report crimes less often than their less trusting counterparts.

These results, which are also backed by multivariate logit models incorporating various socio-demographic characteristics (see Table 5) are surprising both from a theoretical point of view and in the light of the current state of research. While the willingness to report a crime has been shown in other works to depend on police legitimacy or trust in this institution, studies barely draw on actual reporting behaviors. When analyzing real—and thus past—reporting decisions, the temporal ordering of the variables becomes critical. This is the case here: Trust in the police was determined at the time of the survey, reporting behavior refers to the last 12 months preceding the survey. From this it follows that the causal ordering of the involved concepts may have to be reversed, thereby rendering negative associations

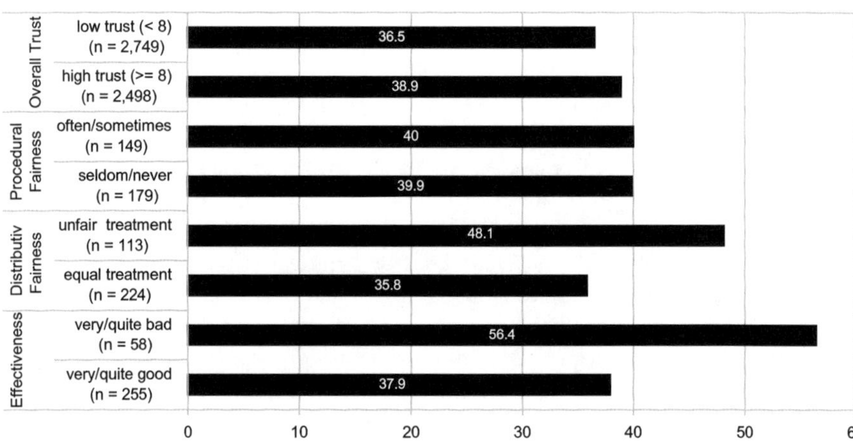

Fig. 8 Reporting rates by trust in the police

Table 5 Results of hierarchical logistic regression models for reporting behavior

	Reporting behavior	Reporting behavior	Reporting behavior
Odds ratio [*KHB Coefficient*]			
	Model 1 ($n = 313$)	Model 2 ($n = 293$)	Model 3 ($n = 293$)
Effectiveness	0.472(*) [*−0.941*(*)]	0.389* [*−0.1.042**]	0.621 [*−0.426*]
Age		0.981(*)	0.990
Sex (female)		1.928(*)	2.082(*)
Education (A level)		0.924	1.270
Migration background		0.487	0.645
1,000 > 2,000[a]		1.019	1.414
2,000 > 3,000[a]		0.524	0.607
3,000+[a]		1.387	1.676
East Germany		1.374	1.493
Unsatisfactory police contact			7.241**
	Model 1 ($n = 337$)	Model 2 ($n = 315$)	Model 3 ($n = 315$)
Distributive fairness	0.603 [*−0.092*]	0.511(*) [*−0.182*(*)]	0.538 [*−0.025*]
Age		0.979*	0.983
Sex (female)		1.787	1.798
Education (A level)		1.085	1.512
Migration background		0.434(*)	0.400(*)
1,000 > 2,000[a]		1.186	1.528
2,000 > 3,000[a]		0.557	0.659
3,000+[a]		1.167	1.109
East Germany		1.629	1.693
Unsatisfactory police contact			3.423*
	Model 1 ($n = 328$)	Model 2 ($n = 306$)	Model 3 ($n = 306$)
Procedural fairness	0.996 [*0.233*]	1.017 [*0.131*]	0.983 [*0.037*]
Age		0.983(*)	0.986
Sex (female)		1.549	1.556
Education (A level)		0.972	1.343
Migration background		0.433(*)	0.407(*)
1,000 > 2,000[a]		0.908	1.148
2,000 > 3,000[a]		0.491	0.580
3,000+[a]		0.927	0.891
East Germany		1.478	1.555
Unsatisfactory police contact			3.266*

(continued)

Table 5 (continued)

	Reporting behavior	Reporting behavior	Reporting behavior
Odds ratio [*KHB Coefficient*]			
	Model 1 ($n = 5{,}247$)	Model 2 ($n = 4{,}834$)	Model 3 ($n = 4{,}834$)
Overall trust	1.110 [*−0.219*]	1.116 [*−0.231*]	1.682***[*0.283*] ***
Age		1.003	1.008*
Sex (female)		1.004	1.005
Education (A level)		0.987**	1.163
Migration background		0.694	0.617**
1,000 > 2,000[a]		1.013	0.998
2,000 > 3,000[a]		0.983	1.099
3,000+[a]		1.096	1.109
East Germany		0.962	1.074
Unsatisfactory police contact			71.011***

(*)$p < 0.1$; *$p < 0.05$; **$p < 0.01$; ***$p < 0.001$
[a]Reference category: Income < 1,000 EUR

equally plausible. As reporting a crime implies a contact with the police, which is itself subject to evaluations, it becomes possible that personal reporting experiences go together with reduced trust in the police. It may be that experiences when reporting a crime (mediated by evaluations of the reporting process and/or the according police behaviors) shape (in our case seemingly erode) trust in the police.

Such a conclusion is supported by analyses investigating people who were dissatisfied with a reporting process at least once in the last 12 months.[19] About a third (32 %) of the victims who reported a crime to the police turned out to be very or quite discontent with this experience. These dissatisfied people exhibit considerably lower levels of trust in the police than persons without any police contacts during the reference period (Table 6). Apart from the procedural fairness item, all measures of trust in the police indicate that unsatisfactory reporting experiences are suited to undermine trust in this authority.

The already addressed hierarchical logistic regression models on actual reporting behavior (Table 5) point in the same direction. While the effect of trust

[19] To avoid misunderstandings, it should be noted that these persons ("dissatisfied with the reporting process") are not identical with the persons who were determined in the preceding section as "dissatisfied with their last police contact." The former group is much smaller than the latter one. While we draw here on respondents who got victimized within the last 12 months and made negative experiences with the crime-reporting process (i.e., victims who answered the question "How satisfied have you been with the way the police handled the incident?" with "quite dissatisfied" or "very dissatisfied"), in the previous section we referred to the overall assessment of the last police encounter.

Table 6 Trust in the police by satisfaction with the reporting process

	Trust in effectiveness in %	Trust in distributive fairness	Trust in procedural fairness	Overall trust
Dissatisfied with reporting process ($n = 30$)[a]	34.4	49.3	51.1	25.3
No police contact ($n = 1,346$)	87.5	70.2	54.6	54.0
Correlation coefficient (r)	−0.221*	−0.070	−0.011	−0.226***

(*)$p < 0.1$; *$p < 0.05$; **$p < 0.01$; ***$p < 0.001$
[a]For overall trust: $n = 569$

in the police on reporting behavior is initially either negative or not significant for all dimensions of trust (both in models without any control variables and in models controlling for several sociodemographic characteristics), the effect coefficients are clearly reduced—in one case even reverse—after adjusting for the existence of unsatisfactory police encounters. This suggests that unpleasant experiences with this institution are at least partly responsible for the unexpected association.[20] In the case of overall trust in the police the at first negative effect of this measure on reporting behavior even turns around and achieves—as theoretically assumed—a highly significant positive value. The KHB logit coefficients[21] increase from −0.219 (trust-only model) or −0.231 (second model controlling for sociodemographic variables) up to + 0.283 ($p < 0.001$). This suggests that a high level of overall trust in the police elevates the probability of reporting a crime. Similar effects can, however, not be demonstrated for the other dimensions of trust in the police.

Furthermore, the logit models demonstrate that experience with at least one unsatisfactory police contact is positively linked to the probability of having reported a crime to the police. Once again, this significant association should not be misinterpreted in the sense of bad experiences with the police raising the readiness to report. The positive connection is equally compatible with the notion

[20] For analytic purposes—and also owing to small cell counts—the variable "unsatisfactory police contacts" is not restricted to unpleasant experiences during a reporting process but comprises all sorts of negative experiences with this institution. We rely again on the overall assessment of the last police contact here. This operationalization makes sense from a substantive point of view, as we aim to control for general interdependencies between satisfaction with police encounters and trust in this authority.

[21] In order to compare logit coefficients between nested models we rely on a method proposed by Karlson, Holm, and Breen (2012). This so-called KHB method isolates and eliminates the rescaling effect always inherent in a logit coefficient when adding a new predictor to a model. Consequently, the logit coefficients of a predictor variable possess the same scale in both models and can thus be compared in terms of their magnitude. For further details see Karlson et al. (2012) and Kohler, Karlson, and Holm (2011). In this regard, special thanks are directed to Prof. Dr. Ulrich Kohler who provided us with the Stata syntax for calculating multi-step hierarchical logit models displaying logit coefficients adjusted for the aforementioned rescaling effects.

that previous reporting experiences were unpleasant and unsatisfactory. Here, "unsatisfactory police contact" should primarily be regarded as a control variable, enabling an identification of the net relationship between trust in the police and reporting practice. The fact that, after partialling out the effects of negative experiences with the police, the global measure of trust in the police begins to correlate significantly and positively with the reporting likelihood corroborates the argument that unsatisfactory experiences in the course of actual reporting processes may blur the connection between police legitimacy and reporting behavior in cross-sectional surveys. This finding is also obtained in separate analyses for the Eastern and Western federal states, whereby overall trust appears to exert a somewhat greater influence in Eastern Germany.[22]

7 Discussion

The purpose of this chapter was to explore the interrelationships between citizens' personal experiences with the police, their trust in this institution and their actual reporting behaviors. Inspired by Tyler's (2006b) procedural justice theory it is assumed that personal encounters with the police (depending on the type and assessment of the contact) play a critical role in shaping judgments about this authority, which in turn have consequences for future reporting decisions. This catalogue of hypotheses was tested using data from a large-scale German victimization survey conducted in 2012, which contained several measures of trust in the police. The full sample included approximately 35,000 respondents from both the old and the new federal states. Some analyses could, however, only be conducted for a subsample of 2,100 persons.

First of all, the study brought to the fore that Germany exhibits a high level of public trust in the police. Citizens' trust in this institution appears to be slightly higher in Western than in Eastern Germany. This divide may be rooted in either the role of the East German police in the communist era, where the police was seen as a politically steered agency devoted to keeping citizens under surveillance and defending communism, or in experiences made with this institution in the course of the upheaval. Lower levels of public support for the police in the new federal states are compatible with the general observation that established democracies are characterized by higher police legitimacy than developing democracies (Karstedt, 2013).

Concerning the factors determining trust in the police, it could be shown that having had contact with officers in the last year only affects overall trust in the police, with respondents reporting personal contact experience being less likely to trust the police. Taking the concrete assessment of personal encounters into consideration, it becomes clear that unsatisfactory contact undermines trust in this

[22] The corresponding odds ratio's amount to 4.054*** for East and 1.473*** for West Germany.

institution. The less satisfied respondents were with their last police contact, the more critical their stance towards this authority becomes.

The relationship between experiences with and trust in the police is mirrored by the connection between trust and actual reporting behaviors. While the available theoretical and empirical literature suggests that public confidence in the police increases victims' intentions to report crimes (Tyler & Fagan, 2008; Tyler & Huo, 2002), at first sight our findings provide indication of a zero or negative association between these concepts. Lower levels of trust in the police are accompanied by either identical or even higher reporting rates. From a theoretical point of view, it seems, of course, highly unlikely that low trust in the police leads to an elevated probability of reporting a crime.

Key to the resolution of this contraction is the operationalization of reporting decisions. While previous studies usually measured reporting behavior in terms of the self-reported willingness to inform the police of crimes or suspicious behaviors, this study draws explicitly on actual—and thus past—reporting behavior. With that, a serious methodological problem becomes apparent. Cross-sectional victimization surveys, as they are implemented in many countries, imply that attitudes towards the police are determined at the time of the interview, while the measurement of personal reporting behaviors refers to a specific reference period preceding the survey. From this it follows that the causal ordering of the concepts becomes critical and may have to be reversed. As a consequence, negative correlations between trust and cooperation become substantively plausible. It may be that previous reporting experiences mediated by assessments of the corresponding police contacts (or subjective appraisals of the results of the reporting process) affect trust in the police. Such an argument is well compatible with procedural justice theory. Here, several detail findings support an interpretation in this direction. Respondents who were dissatisfied with a previous reporting process articulate less trust in the police than people who had no encounter with the police at all. The most pronounced differences in reporting rates are found when the sample is split by assessments of the effectiveness of police work. In multivariate analyses, controlling for the effects of unsatisfactory police contacts, the negative effects of trust in the police on reporting behavior are reduced to insignificance or, in the case of overall trust, the trust measure even begins to exert a significantly positive influence.[23]

On balance, data gained from cross-sectional victimization surveys is subject to pitfalls complicating the study of the interweaving between trust in the police and factual reporting practice. As these data do not meet the requirements to analyze the exact causal ordering of the concepts, one can only speculate on the concrete nature of the underlying cause-and-effects relationship. In cross-sectional studies, associations between support for the police and reporting behavior may reflect either cooperation-stimulating effects of trust or trust-reducing effects of prior reporting experiences. Both processes may also cancel each other out, bringing about a null

[23] The observation that victims, compared to non-victims, report lower trust in the police also speaks for this interpretation.

correlation between the concepts. To separate the aforementioned effects, repeated measurements and thus longitudinal research designs are indispensable. With this chapter, we hope to contribute to the stimulation of a corresponding longitudinal research agenda.

Apart from the purely cross-sectional nature, the present study is limited also in terms of the measurement of some key concepts. The questionnaire captured only a selection of the various subcomponents of public trust in the police, and this only with singe-item measures. Information on the perceived obligation to obey is missing completely. It is for future work to refine our findings with better and more comprehensive measures.

References

Arts, W., & Gelissen, J. (2002). Three worlds of welfare capitalism or more? A state-of-the-art report. *Journal of European Social Policy, 12*(2), 137–158.

Bartsch, R., & Cheurprakobkit, S. (2004). The effects of amount of contact, contact expectation, and experience with police on attitudes toward police. *Journal of Police and Criminal Psychology, 19*(1), 58–70.

Baumer, E. P. (2002). Neighbourhood disadvantage and police notification by victims of violence. *Criminology, 40*(3), 579–616.

Beetham, D. (1991). *The legitimation of power*. London: Macmillan.

Boda, Z., & Szabo, G. (2011). The media and attitudes towards crime and the justice system: A qualitative approach. *European Journal of Criminology, 8*(4), 329–342.

Bottoms, A., & Tankebe, J. (2012). Beyond procedural justice: A dialogic approach to legitimacy in criminal justice. *Journal of Criminal Law and Criminology, 102*(1), 119–170.

Bradford, B., & Jackson, J. (2010). *Cooperating with the police: Social control and the reproduction of police legitimacy*. Retrieved from http://ssrn.com/abstract=1640958.

Cavadino, M., & Dignan, J. (2006). *Penal systems: A comparative approach*. London: Sage.

Cavadino, M., & Dignan, J. (2014). Political economy and penal systems. In S. Body-Gendrot, M. Hough, K. Kerezsi, R. Levy, & S. Snacken (Eds.), *The Routledge handbook of European criminology* (pp. 280–294). New York, NY: Routledge.

Cheurprakobkit, S. (2000). Police-citizen contact and police performance: Attitudinal differences between Hispanics and non-Hispanics. *Journal of Criminal Justice, 28*(4), 325–336.

Conaway, M. R., & Lohr, S. L. (1994). A longitudinal analysis of factors associated with reporting violent crimes to the police. *Journal of Quantitative Criminology, 10*(1), 23–39.

Dai, M., Frank, J., & Sun, I. (2011). Procedural justice during police-citizen encounters: The effects of process-based policing on citizen compliance and demeanor. *Journal of Criminal Justice, 39*(2), 159–168.

Decker, S. (1981). Citizen attitudes towards the police: A review of past finding and suggestions for future policy. *Journal of Police Science and Administration, 9*(1), 80–87.

Eisner, M., & Nivette, A. (2013). Does low legitimacy cause crime? A review of the evidence. In J. Tankebe & A. Liebling (Eds.), *Legitimacy and criminal justice: An international exploration* (pp. 308–325). Oxford: Oxford University Press.

Eschholz, S., Blackwell, B., Gertz, M., & Chiricos, T. (2002). Race and attitudes toward the police: Assessing the effects of watching 'reality' police programs. *Journal of Criminal Justice, 30*(4), 327–341.

Esping-Andersen, G. (1990). *The three worlds of welfare capitalism*. Cambridge: Polity Press.

Fischer, R., Harb, C., Al-Sarraf, S., & Nashave, O. (2008). Support for resistance among Iraqi students: An exploratory study. *Basic and Applied Social Psychology, 30*(2), 167–175.

Frank, J., Smith, B. V., & Novak, K. J. (2005). Exploring the basis of citizens' attitudes toward the police. *Police Quarterly, 8*(2), 206–228.
Goldsmith, A. (2005). Police reform and the problem of trust. *Theoretical Criminology, 9*(4), 443–470.
Goudriaan, H., Lynch, J. P., & Nieuwbeerta, P. (2004). Reporting to the police in western nations: A theoretical analysis of the effects of social context. *Justice Quarterly, 21*(4), 933–969.
Goudriaan, H., Witterbrood, K., & Nieuwbeerta, P. (2006). Neighbourhood characteristics and reporting crime. *British Journal of Criminology, 46*(4), 719–742.
Green, D. (2008a). Political culture and incentives to penal populism. In H. Kury (Ed.), *Fear of crime—Punitivity. New developments in theory and research* (pp. 251–276). Bochum: Brockmeyer.
Green, D. (2008b). *When children kill children: Penal populism and political culture*. Oxford: Oxford University Press.
Hawdon, J. E., Ryan, J., & Griffin, S. P. (2003). Policing tactics and perceptions of police legitimacy. *Police Quarterly, 6*(4), 469–491.
Hickman, L. J., & Simpson, S. (2003). Fair treatment or preferred outcome? The impact of police behavior on victim reports. *Law & Society Review, 37*(3), 607–634.
Hirtenlehner, H., Bacher, J., Oberwittler, D., & Hummelsheim, D. (2012). Strategien der Bearbeitung sozialer Marginalität: Eine empirische Klassifikation europäischer Kontrollregime [Strategies of dealing with social marginality: An empirical classification of European control regimes]. *Soziale Welt, 63*(3), 191–212.
Hough, M., Jackson, J., Bradford, B., Myhill, A., & Quinton, P. (2010). Procedural justice, trust, and institutional legitimacy. *Policing: A Journal of Policy and Practice, 4*(3), 203–210.
Hough, M., Jackson, J., & Bradford, B. (2013a). Legitimacy, trust, and compliance: An empirical test of procedural justice theory using the European Social Survey. In J. Tankebe & A. Liebling (Eds.), *Legitimacy and criminal justice: An international exploration* (pp. 326–352). Oxford: Oxford University Press.
Hough, M., Jackson, J., & Bradford, B. (2013b). The drivers of police legitimacy: Some European research. *Journal of Policing, Intelligence and Counter Terrorism, 8*(2), 144–165.
Hough, M., Jackson, J., & Bradford, B. (2014). Trust in justice and the legitimacy of legal authorities: Topline findings from a European comparative study. In S. Body-Gendrot, M. Hough, K. Kerezsi, R. Levy, & S. Snacken (Eds.), *The Routledge handbook of European criminology* (pp. 243–265). New York, NY: Routledge.
Hough, M., & Maffei, S. (2013). Trust in justice: Thinking about legitimacy. *Criminology in Europe: Newsletter of the European Society of Criminology*, 12(2), 4–10.
Hurst, Y. G., & Frank, J. (2000). How kids view cops: The nature of juvenile attitudes toward the police. *Journal of Criminal Justice, 28*(3), 189–203.
Jackson, J., & Bradford, B. (2010). What is trust and confidence in police? *Policing: A Journal of Policy and Practice, 4*(3), 241–248.
Jackson, J., Bradford, B., Hough, M., Kuha, J., Stares, S., & Widdop, S. (2011). Developing European indicators of trust in justice. *European Journal of Criminology, 8*(4), 267–285.
Jackson, J., Bradford, B., Hough, M., Myhill, A., Quinton, P., & Tyler, T. (2012). Why do people comply with the law? Legitimacy and the influence of legal institutions. *British Journal of Criminology, 52*(6), 1051–1071.
Jonathan-Zamir, T., & Weisburd, D. (2009). The effects of security threats on antecedents of police legitimacy: Findings from a quasi-experiment in Israel. *Journal of Research in Crime and Delinquency, 50*(1), 3–32.
Jowell, R., Roberts, C., Fitzgerald, R., & Eva, G. (2007). *Measuring attitudes cross-nationally: Lessons from the European Social Survey*. London: Sage.
Kääriäinen, J. T. (2007). Trust in the police in 16 European countries: A multilevel analysis. *European Journal of Criminology, 4*(4), 409–435.
Kääriäinen, J. T., & Sirén, R. (2011). Trust in the police, generalized trust and reporting crime. *European Journal of Criminology, 8*(1), 65–81.

Karlson, B. S., Holm, A., & Breen, R. (2012). Comparing regression coefficients between same-sample nested models using logit and probit: A new method. *Sociological Methodology, 42*(1), 286–313.

Karstedt, S. (2013). Trusting authorities: Legitimacy, trust, and collaboration in non-democratic countries. In J. Tankebe & A. Liebling (Eds.), *Legitimacy and criminal justice: An international exploration* (pp. 127–156). Oxford: Oxford University Press.

Karstedt, S. (2014). State crime: The European experience. In S. Body-Gendrot, M. Hough, K. Kerezsi, R. Levy, & S. Snacken (Eds.), *The Routledge handbook of European criminology* (pp. 125–153). New York, NY: Routledge.

Kohler, U., Karlson, K. B., & Holm, A. (2011). Comparing coefficients of nested nonlinear probability models. *Stata Journal, 11*(3), 420–438.

Lappi-Seppälä, T. (2008). Trust, welfare, and political culture: Explaining differences in national penal policies. In M. Tonry (Ed.), *Crime and justice: A review of research* (Vol. 37, pp. 313–387). Chicago: University of Chicago Press.

Lappi-Seppälä, T. (2014). Imprisonment and penal demands: Exploring the dimensions and drivers of systematic and attitudinal punitivity. In S. Body-Gendrot, M. Hough, K. Kerezsi, R. Levy, & S. Snacken (Eds.), *The Routledge handbook of European criminology* (pp. 295–336). New York, NY: Routledge.

Lasley, J. (1994). The impact of the Rodney King incident on citizens' attitude toward the police. *Policing and Society, 3*(4), 245–255.

Lijphart, A. (1999). *Patterns of democracy: Government forms and performance in 36 countries.* New Haven, CT: Yale University Press.

Lind, E. A., & Tyler, T. (1988). *The social psychology of procedural justice*. New York, NY: Plenum Press.

MacDonald, Z. (2001). Revisiting the dark figure: A micro-econometric analysis of the under-reporting of property crime and its implication. *British Journal of Criminology, 41*(1), 127–149.

Maguire, M. (1997). Crime statistics, patterns and trends: Changing perceptions and their implication. In M. Maguire, R. Morgan, & R. Reiner (Eds.), *The Oxford handbook of Criminology* (pp. 135–188). Oxford: Clarendon.

Mastrofski, S. D., Snipes, J. B., & Supina, A. E. (1996). Compliance on demand: The public's response to specific police requests. *Journal of Research in Crime and Delinquency, 33*(3), 269–305.

Mazerolle, L., Bennet, S., Davis, J., Sargeant, E., & Manning, M. (2013). Procedural justice and police legitimacy: A systematic review of the research evidence. *Journal of Experimental Criminology, 9*(3), 245–274.

McCluskey, J. D., Mastrofski, S. D., & Parks, R. B. (1999). To acquiesce or rebel: Predicting citizen compliance with police requests. *Police Quarterly, 2*(4), 389–416.

Murphy, K., Hinds, L., & Fleming, J. (2008). Encouraging public cooperation and support for police. *Policing & Society, 18*(2), 136–201.

Payne, B., & Gainey, R. R. (2007). Attitudes about the police and neighborhood safety in disadvantaged neighborhood: The influence of criminal victimization and perceptions of a drug problem. *Criminal Justice Review, 32*(2), 142–155.

Reisig, M. D., Bratton, J., & Gertz, M. (2007). The construct validity and refinement of process-based policing measures. *Criminal Justice and Behavior, 34*(9), 1005–1028.

Reisig, M. D., & Lloyd, C. (2009). Procedural justice, police legitimacy, and helping the police fight crime: Results from a survey of Jamaican adolescents. *Police Quarterly, 12*(1), 42–62.

Rosenbaum, D. P., Schuck, A. M., Costello, S. K., Hawkins, D. F., & Ring, M. (2005). Attitudes toward police: The effects of direct and vicarious experiences. *Police Quarterly, 8*(3), 343–365.

Schafer, J., Huebner, B. M., & Bynum, T. S. (2003). Citizen perceptions of police services: Race, neighborhood context, and community policing. *Police Quarterly, 6*(4), 440–468.

Skogan, W. (1994). *Contacts between police and public: Findings from the 1992 British Crime Survey*. Home Office Research Study No. 134. London: Home Office.
Skogan, W. (2005). Citizen satisfaction with police encounters. *Police Quarterly, 8*(3), 298–321.
Sparks, R., Bottom, A., & Hay, W. (1996). *Prison and the problem of order*. Oxford: Clarendon.
Sunshine, J., & Tyler, T. (2003). The role of procedural justice and legitimacy in shaping public support for policing. *Law & Society Review, 37*(3), 513–547.
Surrette, R. (2007). *Media, crime, and criminal justice: Images, realities, and policies*. Belmont: Thomson Wadsworth.
Tankebe, J. (2007). *Policing and legitimacy in a post-colonial democracy: A theoretical and empirical study of Ghana*. Doctoral dissertation, University of Cambridge, Cambridge.
Tankebe, J. (2013). Viewing things differently: The dimensions of public perceptions of legitimacy. *Criminology, 51*(1), 103–135.
Tarling, R., & Morris, K. (2010). Reporting crime to the police. *British Journal of Criminology, 50*(3), 474–490.
Tewksbury, R., & West, A. (2001). Crime victims and satisfaction with police services: An assessment in one urban community. *The Justice Professional, 14*(4), 271–285.
Tyler, T. (2001). Public trust and confidence in legal authorities: What do majority and minority group members want from legal authorities? *Behavioral Sciences and the Law, 19*(2), 215–235.
Tyler, T. (2004). Enhancing police legitimacy. *The Annals of the American Academy of Political and Social Science, 593*(1), 84–99.
Tyler, T. (2006a). Psychological perspectives on legitimacy and legitimation. *Annual Review of Psychology, 57*(1), 375–400.
Tyler, T. (2006b). *Why people obey the law*. Princeton, NJ: Princeton University Press.
Tyler, T., & Fagan, J. (2008). Legitimacy and cooperation: Why do people help the police fight crime in their communities? *Ohio State Journal of Criminal Law, 6*(1), 231–275.
Tyler, T., & Huo, Y. (2002). *Trust in the law: Encouraging public cooperation with the police and courts*. New York, NY: Russell Sage.
Weitzer, R., & Tuch, S. A. (2005). Determinants of public satisfaction with the police. *Police Quarterly, 8*(3), 279–297.

Legitimacy of Policing in Central and Eastern Europe: Results from a Cross-National Law Student Survey

Gorazd Meško and Katja Eman

1 Introduction

> Legitimacy (or "the right to exercise power") is now an established concept in criminological analysis, especially in relation to policing. (Tankebe, 2013: 103)

Even in 1997 Tyler (1997) asked "Why people view group authorities as legitimate and voluntarily defer to them?" In doing so, he contrasted two theories about legitimacy: (1) resource-based theories (instrumental models),[1] and (2) identification based theories (relational model) (Lind & Tyler, 1988: 221–222).[2] Tyler (1990) is convinced that legitimacy is very important in these relations because the feeling of perceived obligation as part of legitimacy leads to voluntary deferential behavior. If the authorities wish to be effective in maintaining order, they must be able to influence the behavior of group members (Tyler & Lind, 1992), whereby people as members of groups often internalize their feelings of obligation to obey group rules and group leader's decisions (Tyler, 1997: 323). If people within

[1] Resource-based models actually suggest that people should react to their experiences with authorities, focusing on instrumental aspects of the experience. "The resource-based model develops from realistic group conflict and social exchange theories and links legitimacy to the favourability of the resources that individuals receive from groups and group authorities. Resource-based models link the evaluation of rules and authorities to (a) resources received in the past or expected in the future; (b) task competence; (c) people's judgments about the likely future behaviour of others); (d) outcome fairness, procedural justice, and judgments about investments in group membership." (Tyler, 1997: 324).

[2] Relational model is identity based and thereby links legitimacy to people's concerns about their social identity. The model builds on social identity theory, believing that that "people draw information about their identities from their group memberships" (Tyler, 1997: 325).

G. Meško (✉) • K. Eman
Faculty of Criminal Justice and Security, University of Maribor, Kotnikova 8, 1000 Ljubljana, Slovenia
e-mail: gorazd.mesko@fvv.uni-mb.si; katja.eman@fvv.uni-mb.si

G. Meško, J. Tankebe (eds.), *Trust and Legitimacy in Criminal Justice*,
DOI 10.1007/978-3-319-09813-5_11

organized groups believe that authorities and rules are legitimate, they will voluntarily accept and obey them. Research confirms the existence of relational (e.g., "authorities draw an important part of their legitimacy from their social relationship with group members" (Tyler, 1997: 323)) and instrumental component to legitimacy.

Similar to Tyler's discussion in 1997, the aim of the present study is to find out: "Why young people—law students in South-Eastern Europe—view police authority as legitimate and if they/why they voluntarily defer to them?" The secondary question is: are there important differences between the law students in countries of South and Eastern Europe?

For example, Hinds and Murphy (2007: 28) believe that police legitimacy presents a form of institutional legitimacy and a social value learned in childhood. Children learn from others the acceptance and the extent to which people are willing to accept the police authority. This is important, as stressed by Tyler and Darley (2000), because in the process of child's growing up (especially adolescence period), the gained experiences shape their judgments regarding police legitimacy. This actually means, as emphasized by Reiss (1971), that even actions of just one individual police officer can have a crucial impact on people's opinion about police legitimacy—these actions can either enhance or lower people's judgments, especially young adolescents that live in the contemporary society, daily facing social, economic, and political challenges. In addition to the above-mentioned reasons, student demonstrations in Slovenia in 2010 (Škrinjar, 2010), and the specific field of study that enables the possible employment in the criminal justice system in the future, lead us to the question "Do young law students in South-Eastern Europe view police authority as legitimate and why?"

In addition to the spatial placement in the area of South Eastern Europe, the reason for conducting a study in this part of Europe is to compare our research results with the findings of the previous surveys on legitimacy and youth perception in this area, such as the project Euro Justice (Hough & Sato, 2011), and the European Social Survey (Jackson et al., 2011).

Corkin (2008: 359) emphasizes in the debates on legitimacy and relations between science and legitimacy "scientists are to provide reasoned, factual analysis and justify their input; whereas the institutions are to enjoy discretion to meld the scientists' contribution with relevant lay voices." Following Corkin (2008), the primary focus of this chapter is young people's perception of police legitimacy in the countries of South Eastern Europe. Sections 3 and 4 present the theoretical basis for the research on youth perceptions of police and legitimacy in specific countries of South-Eastern Europe. The following section focuses on their attitudes towards the police and criminal justice, followed by the results of the conducted study. The authors believe that understanding of (police) legitimacy is necessary to test and discuss how law students behave towards the police and why they do (or do not) cooperate with them. The discussion begins at the theoretical groundwork—the concept of legitimacy.

2 The General Concept of Legitimacy

"The legitimacy of legal authorities—in particular the police—is central to the state's ability to function in a normatively justifiable and effective manner." (Bradford, Huq, Jackson, & Roberts, 2013: 1). Thus public perception of legitimacy is determined by perceptions of procedural fairness that are influenced by comparisons of observed outcomes with moral mandates (Skitka & Houston, 2001: 305).

Legitimacy could be described as a central concept in procedural justice theory (Hough, Jackson, Bradford, Myhill, & Quinton, 2010: 204), and thereby it is a composition of different elements (i.e., rules, appropriate beliefs, relevant actions, etc.). If these elements are present, people believe in the legitimacy of power (Beetham, 1991a: 43). The comprehension of legitimacy as a multidimensional phenomenon enables scientists to distinguish different ways in which power is (non)legitimate (Beetham, 1993). Therefore, one of the remaining crucial questions is: "What shapes police legitimacy?" From the discussion about legitimacy in the era of Greek philosophers and Aristotle through today, various factors influenced the development of the concept of legitimacy and its correlates. These factors were (Jackson & Bradford, 2010: 6): the history and development (i.e., changing) of police legitimacy; changing values and expectations of society; changed and still changing police service and with it close related police culture; increasing crime after the Second World War; (mass) media coverage of daily events; and rising public awareness. Jackson and Bradford (2010) are convinced that in contemporary changing society with rapid political, economic and social shifts, trust and confidence in the police represent the key link between police and society.

The aforementioned reasons together with the fact that traditionally observation of public trust is part of the public opinion pools, represent one part of the reason that study of legitimacy became interesting for criminologists and other researchers toward in the end of the last century and remains a "hot topic" currently as well. The second reason for studies on legitimacy and its correlates is the belief that there is a difference between Western (Reisig & Lloyd, 2009; Sunshine & Tyler, 2003; Tankebe, 2008; Tyler & Fagan, 2008) and Eastern cultures (Hinds & Murphy, 2007; Jonathan-Zamir & Weisburd, 2013; Reisig & Meško, 2009; Šifrer, Meško, & Bren, 2013). The typical phenomenon in Eastern countries is the discovery that the effectiveness of the police is more important than legitimacy and all its correlates. For example, a study of victims, conducted by Dvoršek, Maver, and Meško (2006), showed that property crime victims were satisfied with police officers that have been effective and caught the perpetrator (police effectiveness), even if they behaved a little bit awkwardly (e.g., rude, rough) rather than polite and friendly (procedural justice). Nevertheless, it is possible to discuss tests of Western models in the environment where the study on legitimacy largely has been the subject of philosophical debates and part of the sociology of law (Igličar, 2013). Furthermore, the initial attempts empirically verify legitimacy and the factors that influence on the perception of legitimacy is another reason for studies on legitimacy.

The project Euro Justice (Hough & Sato, 2011) and the European Social Survey (Jackson et al., 2011) tested perceptions of (police) legitimacy and showed that contact with police officers is a key predictor of people's trust judgments, where significant variation in the proportion experiencing a police-initiated contact was detected across the 20 countries. In Finland, people reported the highest rates of police-initiated contact and in Bulgaria the lowest. Respondents were asked to evaluate their contact(s) with the police, and the results show that Israelis, Russians, and Hungarians were least satisfied, while people in Sweden, Norway, Finland, Denmark, and Belgium were most satisfied. The authors conclude that there is no necessary connection between the number of the contacts people have with the police and levels of satisfaction with the police. For example, Sweden and Finland have high rates of contact and high levels of satisfaction; while Switzerland has a high level of contact but a lower level of satisfaction. In the case of the trust in the police, results indicate that opinions of procedural fairness of the police vary widely across Europe. People in Israel, the Russian Federation, and Bulgaria have the most negative opinion about the way in which the police treat people, while in Denmark, Finland, Norway, and Spain citizens have the most positive opinion. Furthermore, people least trust to the police in Russia, Israel, Bulgaria, Portugal, and Poland (Jackson et al., 2011: 4–5).

The last part of the survey focused on perceived legitimacy of justice systems. This concept was divided to three dimensions: (1) obligation to obey the police; (2) moral alignment with the police; and (3) perceptions of the legality of the police. The findings suggest that "countries with a relatively strong sense that the police share a common moral framework with its people also tend to have a populace who feel a relatively strong duty to obey police directives" (Jackson et al., 2011: 7). For example, in Israel, Hungary and the Czech Republic, people reported relatively low levels of moral alignment but higher levels of felt obligation. Views about the probity of the police and courts are similar within the countries. A comparison between the countries show that public perceptions of corruption in the criminal justice system is low in Scandinavian and Northern European countries, but much higher in ex-Communist countries (Jackson et al., 2011: 7–8). Finally, the authors concluded that people in the Nordic countries report the highest levels of trust in their police and courts and believe that their institutions are legitimate holders of power and authority. On the contrary, citizens in the Eastern and sometimes Southern European countries report lower level of trust in authorities. In addition, trust and legitimacy have a multi-dimensional nature. The authors assume that trust is revealed by public assessments of the trustworthiness of institutions along three dimensions: effectiveness, procedural fairness, and distributive fairness. Likewise, legitimacy is revealed by citizens' consent to power and their sense of the normative justifiability of power. Finally, Hough, Jackson, and Bradford (2013b: 243) emphasize that there is strong support between different European countries based on the connection between trust in the police and people's perceptions of the police legitimacy. The analysis revealed patterns of relationship across country between two dimensions: trust in the police and perceived legitimacy of the police; therefore it can be concluded that trust in police and belief in their fairness are very important factors of police legitimacy in the European space (Hough et al., 2013b: 259). The pattern revealing that Nordic countries trust police the most and believe that they are legitimate holders of the given power and authority, and that Eastern (sometimes Southern Eastern) countries trust the least is actually not surprising (Hough et al., 2013b: 263). In additional analyses, Hough, Jackson, and Bradford (2013a) found that compliance with the law and cooperation with the police (or authority in general) are consequences of the legitimacy. They identified four significant predictors: (1) instrumental compliance; (2) morality of the act; (3) moral alignment with the police; and (4) perceived lawfulness of the police and criminal courts.

Furthermore, Reisig, Tankebe, and Meško (2012) conducted an analysis of legitimacy, procedural justice, and public cooperation with the police among young Slovene adults and thereby tested various research hypotheses derived from the process-based model of policing. They used cross-sectional data from pencil-and-paper surveys administered to 683 individuals 18 years and older enrolled in six high schools in Ljubljana and Maribor. Results showed that there is a strong correlation between procedural justice and police legitimacy, and that the latter influences public cooperation—the authors identified low level of willingness to help and cooperate with the police among young adults in Slovenia. As such, police legitimacy plays very important role in the legitimation process of the legal authorities.

3 Police Legitimacy

The issue of legitimacy relates to no other state institution more directly than the police. The fact is that the police, in their daily pursuit of legitimacy, are forever entangled in more or less conflicting understandings of their relationship with citizens. Herbert (2006: 481) emphasizes that concerning legitimacy, police represent both the majesty and potential tyranny of state authority and is "the most visible reminder of the state's coercive power."

In the field of police legitimacy there are specific articulations that are crucial in the relationship between the police and citizens. Herbert (2006) discusses three modes of the police–citizen (or state–society) relation: *subservience* (the main task of modern police organizations is "to protect and to serve" which leads to the conclusion that "the police are always considered under the sway of citizen influence" (Herbert, 2006: 484)), *separation* (despite the daily contact and police responsiveness to calls of the citizens, police departments accept a collectively reinforced distinction between police officers and citizens (liberal legal order, police culture, etc.)—police officers see themselves as autonomous and authoritative agents, pretty distinct from the citizenry (Herbert, 2006: 486)) and *generativity* (society is generated by the state, through its policies, epistemologies and its moralities and all this often includes the police (Herbert, 2006: 489)). The author directly observed everyday police practices in Seattle. Based on the above explained modes of police–citizen relations, Herbert (2006) analyzed two fields: the procedural justice model and community policing, with the aim to address important contemporary approaches that can improve the standing of the police in this contemporary (risk) society. He concluded that there is no simple solution for enhancing police legitimacy, because while all aforementioned modes of the state–society relationship possess power, normative conflict between both groups is inevitable. For example, experiences with community policing show that not every effort to increase police responsiveness is successful. Therefore, Herbert (2006) believes that it is important to take into consideration what role citizens actually wish the police to play in improving communities. He concludes that we need to accept "the inevitability of an on-going political struggle over the police–community relation . . . the politics of police legitimacy will remain perpetually tangled" (Herbert, 2006: 500–501). Therefore, we agree that *in modern, democratic societies, police legitimacy rests on public consent* (Hinds & Murphy, 2007: 30).

Jackson and Bradford (2010: 5) describe legitimacy as "public perception of police conformity to a set of rules, of public perceptions of the justifiability of those rules, and the expressed consent of the public" and divide it into: (1) *high-level legitimacy* (i.e., originates from a so-called deep connection between individuals and the legal or social control systems round them), and (2) *low-level legitimacy* (i.e., operates almost immediately at an everyday level, such as police official procedures). Based upon the above classification of legitimacy, Jackson and Bradford (2010: 6) describe police legitimacy as a dynamic process; originating from deeply entrenched structures of power, but being experienced and tested through daily experiences.

Hinds and Murphy (2007: 27) studied the effects of procedural justice and police legitimacy on public satisfaction with the police in Australia. The research showed that "people who believe police use procedural justice when they exercise their authority are more likely to view police as legitimate, and in turn are more satisfied with police services." Legitimacy was the strongest predictor of satisfaction with the police in Australia. Moreover, the study confirms the importance of public opinion about fair and effective policing; the more positive opinions about the police people have, the more they believe in their use of procedural justice and find it legitimate. Results indicated that police performance had almost as strong impact on police legitimacy as procedural justice (Hinds & Murphy, 2007: 31, 36). Hinds and Murphy (2007) concluded that views about police and its legitimacy have an important impact on general public satisfaction with police. In other words, "people who view police as more legitimate are more likely to be satisfied with police services" (Hinds & Murphy, 2007: 39).

As new approaches to policing, focused on police legitimacy, public compliance with the law, acceptance of police authority and cooperation with the police in responding to crime, began to develop, Tyler (2011) emphasized their value, especially the connection between trust and legitimacy. He acknowledges that the professionalization of police forces has influenced the growth of the quality of policing, but public support for the police, known as "trust and confidence" in the police, must also be taken into consideration, especially factors that shape public views about police legitimacy:

> If public trust and confidence in the police are not linked to objective performance, the nature of trust and confidence needs to be addressed as a distinct question in and of itself. The issue is: 'What is the basis of perceived police legitimacy?' Understanding how public views about police legitimacy form and change can provide us with a new framework through which to evaluate policing policies and practices. (Tyler, 2011: 255)

Tyler (2011: 258) believes that the manner and quality of a police officer's performance and attitude towards those involved in legal procedures has an important impact on public opinion and people's feelings about the police. For this reason, the police must implement policies that encourage an approach to communities in which public views are central, thus focusing on the way that people evaluate the police and police actions. Tyler (2011: 263) is certain that these public views shape how people behave in reaction to the police.

Tankebe (2008: 8) analyzed the procedural fairness conception of police legitimacy and pointed out that its theoretical framework is too limited to constitute the basis for any legitimacy-based model of policing. Tyler and Blader (2000) presented a "two component model" of procedural fairness ("the quality of decision-making" and "the quality of interpersonal treatment"). In addition, Tyler and Lind's (1992: 75) group-value model, with three central elements: social standing, neutrality and trust, seem to have an important impact on attitudes towards authority. More recently, Tyler (2003) presented a process-based model of regulation, based on the belief that "views about legitimacy are rooted in the judgment that the police and the courts are acting fairly when they deal with community residents" (Tyler, 2003: 286).

Tankebe (2008) emphasizes that all presented models need to be expanded and must include other crucial variables such as the role of police self-legitimating activities in shaping treatment of the public by the police. In his opinion, inappropriate approaches to legitimacy and with it related concepts represents a danger of making false promises to police forces if specific socio-political realities are overlooked (Tankebe, 2008: 17). The author goes even further in his critique: "Procedural fairness, and by extension police legitimacy, must be pursued as something of intrinsic value, a good in and of itself; treating people fairly should not be an issue of choice contingent simply on demonstrable evidence of the facilitation of the task of the police in maintaining order." (Tankebe, 2008: 8)

Public trust in policing is important and needed because of its influence on attitudes towards and public cooperation with justice. Furthermore, public trust in justice has an important impact on institutional legitimacy and public compliance with the law. Jackson, Bradford, Hough, and Murray (2012: 30) define police legitimacy as "obligation to obey and moral alignment" and link it to legal legitimacy, cynicism, and compliance with the law.

A normative concept of legitimacy sets out "objective" criteria, according to which an authority or institution is legitimate, not because of the subjective state of mind of those it governs, but because the arrangement meets certain substantive requirements (usually requirements of justice and rationality). In addition, any normative conception of legitimacy needs to describe why meeting these criteria confers authority on norms, institutions, or persons. Why do the criteria generate morally binding rules? Empirical legitimacy means stating that people believe an arrangement to be right and just. Normative legitimacy means substantive recognition that the truth (or validity) of these arrangements is right and just (Jackson, Bradford, Hough, Myhill, et al., 2012: 48–49).

Bradford, Jackson, and Hough (2013) presented a model of policing based on procedural justice theory[3] and theory about policing by consent. The origin was Tyler's (2006a, 2006b) argument that "if the normative route to compliance with the law can be achieved, it is likely to be more durable and less costly than the coercive route that requires a credible deterrent threat" (discussed in Bradford, Jackson, et al., 2013: 80). The model predicts that if police officers treat people with respect and dignity, a basis for fair decision-making processes is created, allowing police officers to have a voice in the interaction. This communication must reflect officers' respectful behavior and messages of status and worth to the individual concerned. Furthermore, in this way police officers show people that the power they have in the process is balanced and that they are acting in accordance with values of legality and propriety. Sunshine and Tyler (2003) described such behavior as a "procedurally fair way" that leads to the belief that the police are legitimate and that their power is justified (Bradford, Jackson, et al., 2013: 82). The authors conclude that police should invest more in policies that clearly promote procedural fairness as a core aspect of police work. Police leaders need to explain clearly that "improvements in trust and legitimacy have to be earned, and not simply claimed" (Bradford, Jackson, et al., 2013: 95). Nevertheless, police officers need to retain a certain degree of distance from individuals to be able efficiently and fairly resolve conflicts in the communities.

For the purpose of this paper, legitimacy is understood as a composite variable consisting of trust and obligation to obey the police.[4] Understanding the correlates of legitimacy is important for the further discussion and interpretation of the research results; therefore, police authority, police effectiveness, procedural and distributive justice, and cooperation with the police, obligation to obey the police, legal compliance, deterrence, legal cynicism, and moral credibility are discussed in the following sections of the chapter.

---

[3] "Procedural justice promotes internalisation of the idea that one should obey the police and strengthens people's identification with the moral group that the police represent, and this translates into feeling that (a) one has a duty to allow the police to dictate appropriate behaviour, and (b) the police operate within appropriate ethical or normative frameworks." (Jackson in Bradford, Jackson et al., 2013: 82)

[4] How perceived legitimacy (of police) is measured and assessed? It involves two domains: (1) the belief that police officers are trustworthy, honest and care about the citizens and their well-being; and (2) the belief that police authority ought to be accepted by public and that people voluntarily obey and follow police decisions and orders. In other words, "the police are legitimate if people defer to their decisions and follow their directives" (Tyler, 2011: 256).

4 On Legitimacy and Its Correlates

Legitimacy is more than merely an excuse for seeking and maintaining power. Legitimacy is also the justification of the power, known also as "moral alignment" between individuals and the criminal justice system they use. For this reason, when considering legitimacy, researchers should regard a normative, ideological, or moral element of legitimacy. Moreover, the fact that legitimacy is based on an expression of commonly shared values should not be ignored; therefore Jackson (2010: 10–11) based his framework of the legitimacy on the cognition that *"individual confers legitimacy on the justice system when that individual feels: (a) an obligation to obey the authority (b) that the authority expresses shared morals; and (c) that the justice system follows its own internal rules."*

4.1 Police Authority and Moral Alignment

Authority is described as a "legitimate power" given to the police or other agency, whereby this power derives from their position and command. Police authority constitutes "an aspect of power relations and a means of power in its own right" (Beetham, 1991b: 49). Jackson and Bradford (2010: 1) argue that the legitimacy of the police force is one of the crucial conditions for justifiable use of state power, whereby legitimacy represents the foundation of police authority (Tyler, 2006a). The authority of the police originates from relations between authorities (e.g., government) and subordinates (e.g., people) in society or social groups, whereby Jackson, Bradford, Stanko, and Hohl (2013: 152) emphasize that actually "identification with the authority generates the belief that the police are justified in expecting feelings of obligation and responsibility from citizens."

Tyler and Wakslak (2004: 253) conducted a study on police legitimacy and acceptance of police authority, which confirmed the procedural justice hypothesis stating that "the fairness with which the police exercise their authority influences whether members of the public view the police as profiling." Furthermore, judgments about police profiling are associated with the level of public support for the police.

Jackson (2010) emphasizes that legitimacy is more than merely an excuse for power. It is also the justification of the power, known also as "moral alignment" between individuals and the criminal justice system they use. For this reason, when considering legitimacy, researchers have to pay attention to a normative, ideological or moral element of legitimacy. Besides, the fact that legitimacy is based on expression of common shared values should not be ignored; therefore Jackson (2010: 10–11) based his framework of the legitimacy on the cognition that *"individual confers legitimacy on the justice system when that individual feels: (a) an obligation to obey the authority; (b) that the authority expresses shared morals; and (c) that the justice system follows its own internal rules."*

Jackson, Bradford, Hough, and Murray (2012: 30) define police legitimacy as "obligation to obey and moral alignment" and link it to legal legitimacy, cynicism, and compliance with the law. Thus Jackson and Bradford (2010: 3) emphasize that police are legitimate when the public feels obligated to obey them and their orders. According to the Hinsch's (2008) normative concept of legitimacy, the individual's decision to accept the power of police authority and to accept the justification of that power cannot be ignored. In other words, moral alignment between people and the criminal system is set in the forefront of the discussion. Jackson and Bradford (2010: 3) explain this situation with the following words: *"If one follows this criteria then judgments among individuals about the legitimacy of an institution must be based to some degree on assessments of the congruence between its goals, practices and behaviors and their own."*

4.2 Police Effectiveness

In studies about police legitimacy, researchers usually try to detect the reasons for why and how police effectiveness can be increased and at the same time crime and disorder are reduced (Hinds & Murphy, 2007). They analyzed previous studies on police legitimacy (Sunshine & Tyler, 2003; Tyler, 1990, 2004; Tyler & Huo, 2002) and concluded that "evaluations of police legitimacy are based on people's views about the way police treat them, independent of people's views about how well police perform their job" (Hinds & Murphy, 2007: 29). In addition, when people believe that the acts of a legal authority are legitimate, they are more willing to cooperate with the authority (i.e., compliance behavior) accept their decisions with more satisfaction.

As discussed below, the term legitimacy has, from the procedural justice aspect, been defined as "the belief that authorities do their job well (i.e. are effective) and are entitled to be obeyed," which means that "people feel that they ought to defer to legitimate decisions and rules, and follow them voluntarily out of obligation rather than out of fear of punishment or anticipation of reward" (Murphy, Tyler, & Curtis, 2009: 2).

4.3 Procedural Justice

Procedural justice can be described as the perceived fairness in the decision-making legal procedure led by those with legal authority (Murphy et al., 2009; Tyler, 2006a). Tyler (1997) stresses that procedural justice is effective in shaping compliance behavior due to its positive impact on the perceived legitimacy of an authority. In other words, citizens who believe that they have been fairly treated by an authority regard its authority status as more legitimate. Murphy et al. (2009: 2) emphasize that studies on procedural justice consistently ascertained that "people and organizations are much more likely to obey the law and accept decisions made by authorities when they feel that the decision-making procedures are fair, respectful, and impartial" (Murphy, 2005; Tyler, 2006a; Winter & May, 2001). In addition, Feldman and Lobel (2008) add that people report crime or other wrongdoing to an authority more than in the past when they were treated fairly.

Tyler and colleagues (Lind & Tyler, 1988; Sunshine & Tyler, 2003; Tyler, 1990, 2006b) established that respectful treatment, neutral procedures and trustworthiness of authorities in the criminal justice process are the most integral factors of procedural justice. Goodman-Delahunty (2010: 407) emphasizes that trust remains the key variable of procedural justice and compliance with the law. Furthermore, trust in the police positively relates to legitimacy and legal compliance (Goodman-Delahunty, 2010; Reisig, Bratton, & Gertz, 2007; Tyler, 2006a). In addition, Thibaut and Walker (1975) stressed that the theory on interpersonal relations provides insight into the understanding of the execution of police procedures and thereby appearing to effectively deliver policing skills. The authors named it "procedural fairness," now more often known as "procedural justice." When following the procedural fairness effect, we have to keep in mind that citizens care more about the treatment they receive in criminal justice procedures than the outcome, which would be favorable for them (Goodman-Delahunty, 2010; Meško & Umek, 2002; Tyler & Huo, 2002).

4.4 Distributive Justice

According to distributive justice theories, people compare the outcomes of conflicts to standards of what is deserved (Tyler, 2012: 358). Different conflicts can be solved in various ways, and when people that are involved in social interactions with others realize that they cannot resolve conflicts by themselves, they search for other possibilities, most often help and support of the authorities. Thibaut and Walker (1975) believe that the assistance of authorities is a good idea because they have two desirable attributes—neutrality and expertise due to specialized training or experience with conflicts—that make them more capable to resolve conflicts. The authors believe that a "neutral authority can establish a fair outcome" (Tyler, 2012: 363). In addition, they can use more complex and therefore more effective distributive justice rules. Tyler (2012) agrees that authorities use neutrality and expertise to craft needed justice based solutions, but wonders if those solutions will be accepted. When making justice-based decisions in the process of resolving conflicts and accepting justice rules, authorities need to be able to "get acceptance for their decisions both among the parties involved and people more generally" (Tyler, 2012: 366). Similarly, when we discuss the process of punishment, "it is equally important that all parties—victim, offender, observers—feel that justice is done" (Tyler, 2012: 367). Therefore, the authorities need to have in mind when they make decisions and try to achieve justice, that it is really important how they "make their decisions legitimate to all the parties to a conflict" (Tyler,

2012: 367), so that they are accepted. In general, people fulfil the need to create shared principles of justice and then use them as a tool for cooperation and to solve conflicts.[5]

4.5 Cooperation

Dealing with the question of a possible relationship between justice and cooperation, Tyler (2012: 355) emphasizes that justice facilitates effective cooperation and enables social coordination in superior levels. In general, people fulfil the need to create shared principles of justice and then they use them as tools for cooperation and to solve conflicts. Tyler (2012: 373) is convinced that "these forms of justice encourage the resolution of interpersonal conflicts, support the legitimation of authorities, and facilitate the viability of institutions."

In surveys about citizens' attitudes toward the police and cooperation with them, researchers found the following (Carr, Napolitano, & Keating, 2007: 448): (1) African American populations are less likely trust police than whites; (2) white people are more favorably disposed to the police (Gallup, 1999; Harris, 1999; Jacob, 1971); (3) the attitude of the Hispanic population towards the police varies but they are more favorable when compared to African Americans and less than whites (Carter, 1985; Lasley, 1994); (4) the attitude towards police varies with age (Campbell & Schuman, 1972; Jesilow, Meyer, & Namazzi, 1995; Sullivan, Dunham, & Alpert, 1987); and (5) the contact, cooperation, and satisfaction with the police is dependent on prior interaction and experience in dealing with police procedures (Hagan, Shedd, & Payne, 2005; Rusinko, Johnson, & Hornung, 1978).

Hough et al. (2010: 208–209) tested procedural justice theory in the UK, and established that public trust in policing is needed due to two reasons: (1) because it can result in public cooperation with justice, and (2) because it builds institutional legitimacy. Survey results showed a similar situation in public compliance with the law and commitment to the rule of law in the English environment. The authors emphasize that police legitimacy is a powerful predictor of compliance with the law because of the impact of personal morality and with it legal cynicism. The general conclusion is that if the police treat people unfairly, legitimacy suffers and people become cynical, not only about police and legal systems of justice but also about human nature generally.[6]

---

[5] Tyler (2012: 373) is convinced that "these forms of justice encourage the resolution of interpersonal conflicts, support the legitimation of authorities, and facilitate the viability of institutions."

[6] "Without the cooperation of the public, policing in developed democracies would become essentially unworkable. Acts of cooperation may also serve to cement the relationship between police and public and promote the view that addressing crime is a collaborative process and not just about delivering services." (Hough et al., 2010: 207)

4.6 Moral Credibility

The Police are powerfully linked to the law, therefore their unfairness "undermines the feeling that the law defines appropriate behavior" (Jackson, Bradford, Hough, Myhill, et al., 2012: 1062). Police abuse of power and wielding their authority in unfair ways can negatively affect the sense of obligation to obey the authority (i.e., police) directives and, as stressed by Hough et al. (2010), to people's perception of "moral authority and therefore the moral right of the law to dictate appropriate behavior." Such behavior of the police or other authorities, breaking the generally accepted social norms, can generate powerful cynicism, justified with the well-known saying: "if the police can behave however they please, and ignore the rules, so can I." On the other hand, if the police perform their authority using fair procedures, they influence the sense of normative commitment to the police and enhance people's compliance with the law (Jackson, Bradford, Hough, Myhill, et al., 2012: 1063).

The public perception of legitimacy is determined by perceptions of procedural fairness that is influenced by comparisons of observed outcomes with moral mandates (Skitka & Houston, 2001: 305) generally known as moral credibility of the police officers.

4.7 Deterrence

"Rooted in conceptions of free will, deterrence is concerned with how sanction threats and the imposition of sanctions inhibit criminal activity from occurring in society at large (in the case of general deterrence) and with the persistence of crime among offenders (in the case of specific deterrence)." (Piquero, Paternoster, Pogarsky, & Loughran, 2011: 337) Sanctions deter future crime to the extent that punishment is certain, almost immediate, and harsh enough to outweigh the benefit that was obtained with the commission of crime. Thus, deterrence is a "perceptually based phenomenon or a social psychological theory" (Piquero et al., 2011: 337), because it is expected that people (e.g., potential offenders) must be acquainted with the possible threat of being sanctioned for the crime to actually be affected by them.

Social Organization Theory focuses on environment (i.e., places) and not people; therefore, Meares (2000: 391) argues that its explanation of crime persistence sometimes does not specify the content of the norms, values, and ideas that go together with compliance. Due to the fact that voluntary compliance with the law is governed much more by norm-based reasons than by instrumental ones, the "policies that harness norms, as opposed to those policies that attempt to achieve compliance by targeting the consequences of failing to obey, will produce useful crime policy" (Meares, 2000: 392). According to deterrence theory and with it closely related criminal justice policy, punishment is used for compliance and to deter future criminal activity. On the one hand, prior studies established that punishment actually weakens compliance or it depends on moderating factors, and on the other, punishment has little or no effect on compliance. Analysis revealed that individual's responses to deterrent threats and the imposition of punishment can sometimes vary in not only expected but also in unexpected ways—individual differences (e.g., social bonds, morality, discount rate, impulsivity, social network position, decision-making competence) and situational differences (e.g., emotions, alcohol/drug use) (Piquero et al., 2011: 356).

4.8 Obligation to Obey, Legal Compliance, and Legal Cynicism

"Authorities can rely on citizens' internal motives for self-control rather than risking the cost, danger, and alienation associated with using actual force or the threat of force. Equally, internal moral drivers to obey the law and cooperate with the system may be *more powerful* than an external set of rules involving deterrent threat. These internal moral drivers may be fundamentally linked to the perceived legitimacy of the justice system. Such legitimacy is—according to Tyler—the obligation to obey police authority and is, as outlined above, separate to personal morality." (Jackson & Bradford, 2010: 6–7) Public compliance with the law and obeying legal authorities can be crucial for maintaining social order in general. Jackson and Bradford (2010: 1–2) emphasize three important aspects of legitimacy in policing: (1) legitimacy is seen as important key in securing public feelings of obligation and responsibility toward the law; (2) legitimacy is perceived as granted by the public (and by the political system) to specific spheres of police action and power; and (3) legitimacy inside the police organization has an important influence on officer behavior and police culture.

According to Hinsch's (2008) normative concept of legitimacy, the individual's decision to accept the power of police authority and to accept the justification of that power cannot be ignored. Moral alignment between people and the criminal justice system is in the forefront of the discussion. In addition, Jackson and Bradford (2010) follow Beetham's (1991b) and Tankebe's (2008) definition of police legitimacy and stress three criteria that are common to the notion that the police are "appropriate, proper and just." The authors define and measure police legitimacy as a multidimensional concept with three elements: (1) *the obligation to obey*, where the perceived legitimacy of the police is measured by peoples standpoints on obligation to the law and police authority; (2) *moral alignment or normative justifiability*, where the perceived legitimacy of the police is measured by people's standpoints on moral credibility and values; and (3) *legality*, where the perceived legitimacy of the police is measured by peoples standpoints on police authority and trust.

Jackson and Bradford (2010: 4) stress that the above described elements of police legitimacy are interconnected and all three have to coexist when establishing the legitimacy of the relationship between the police and the public. Thus Jackson, Bradford, Hough, Myhill et al. (2012: 1055) see a difference between an obligation to obey the police and moral alignment with the police, and between obligation to obey the police and obligation to obey the law.

Hough et al. (2010) ascertained that legal cynicism, together with perceived police legitimacy and personal morality, affects the willingness of the people to cooperate with the police. The police are aware that such cooperation is very important for them, because without it "policing in developed democracies would become essentially unworkable" (Hough et al., 2010: 209–210). The authors emphasize that according to procedural justice theory, ignorance and violation of the rights and entitlements of the public by justice system or authorities can lead to growing deficit in legitimacy, which is evident in reduced compliance with the law and growing legal cynicism. Sampson and Bartusch (1998) compare perceived low legal legitimacy with cynicism about the law and emphasize that is reflected as a belief that an individual does not need to comply with the law simply because it is the law. Moreover, in an extreme way, legal cynicism is reflected as active antagonism and a personal validation of deviant behavior (Jackson, Bradford, Hough, & Murray, 2012). Finally, Jackson, Bradford, Hough, and Murray (2012: 29–30) define police legitimacy as an "obligation to obey and moral alignment" and link it with legal legitimacy/cynicism and compliance with the law. Nevertheless, deriving from the fact that young people are generally more cynical towards the authorities, the question of the present paper, discussed in the section below, is how law students understand police legitimacy and how binding for them are (criminal) justice rules and regulations.

5 Young People's Attitudes Towards the Police and Criminal Justice

> Adolescence is a key period of attitude formation on policing and the law. A substantial literature on the socialization process from childhood to adulthood records an often conflictual relationship with police during adolescence, as young people challenge the authority of police, other legal agencies and social institutions. (Hinds, 2009: 11)

In contemporary society, the transition to adulthood and the extension of family life of an young adult is prolonged due to structural causes (difficulty in entering the labor market, higher level of study, difficulty in finding houses), and cultural aspects (greater freedom and less intergenerational conflicts) (Scabini, 1996). This phenomenon is known as "prolonged adolescence." Scabini (1996) describes it as a time of life that constitutes a bridge between two conditions (young and adult), thereby "young adult phase." Furthermore, Galland (2001) notes that comparisons internationally revealed that the cultural tendencies and institutional setup are factors that have an impact on this phase of life.

Attitudes of youth towards legal institutions (e.g., police, courts) are similar to their attitudes towards other social institutions (e.g., schools, social centers) suggesting an "anti-authority syndrome" orientation during adolescence (Clark & Wenninger, 1964: 488). Easton and Dennis (1969) emphasized that behavior, formed in the adolescence period, can have a lasting influence on adults' judgments of the police. In addition, young people usually form their beliefs according to direct experiences (Nelsen, Eisenberg, & Carroll, 1982). From the perspective of the relationship between youth and police, this means that young people normally respond to the treatment they receive from the police in direct contact with the police officers and do not follow the generally socially accepted attitude about the police and policing (Hinds, 2009). Cunneen and White (1995), Loader (1996) and Hinds (2009) stress that contacts between young people and the police are anything but rare, because as noted by White (1994), police officers are often the only agents of the criminal justice system in daily contact with young people. Moreover, young people are extensive users of public space and thereby are often the subjects of involuntary and generally negatively experienced contacts with the police (Cunneen & White, 1995; Hinds, 2009; Loader, 1996). As Leiber, Nalla, and Farnworth (1998) emphasized that juveniles present a relatively large percent of the population that is subjected to police contacts and arrests, Walker (1992) focused on police perspective of juveniles and deviance and discovered that juveniles are by police officers seen as "special set of problems," forcing them to become incorporated into school system and cooperate with other social service agencies.

Wu and Sun (2010) studied global and specific perceptions of the police by college students in China during the summer and fall, 2008. In addition to attitudes toward the police, the study included demographic characteristics, crime and criminal justice experiences, perceptions of quality of life, and locality. Three groups of factors shape public perceptions of the police: (1) individual demographics (e.g., race, gender, age, class); (2) experiential factors (e.g., crime and criminal justice experiences, media influence); and (3) attitudinal factors (e.g., quality of life). Results show that respondents' satisfaction with the police and their evaluation of police fairness, effectiveness, and integrity are significantly correlated with their crime and criminal justice experiences, perceived quality of life, and their origin (differences between rural and urban areas). On the contrary, background characteristics have a weak impact on their attitudes toward the police (Wu & Sun, 2010: 106–107).

Reisig et al. (2012) identified a strong correlation between procedural justice and police legitimacy among a group of young Slovene adults. Thus, results revealed that police legitimacy has an impact on cooperation with the police. Reisig et al. (2012: 162) emphasize the importance of educational programs and training that teach and promote fair and just police practices, based on their finding that police can rely more on residents if people in local community perceived police as legitimate, exercising their authority in a fair and just way.

In 2012, Ilie, Eman, Bogush, and Meško (2013) conducted a survey whereby they tested the importance of perceptions of legal cynicism among law students in Slovenia, Romania, and Russia. The results revealed that legal cynicism is quite high in all three countries, but it is the highest in Romania, followed by Russia and Slovenia. Legitimacy, moral credibility and deterrence are perceived in a negative way, but the students are willing to report crimes and other offences to the police and serve as witnesses in criminal investigations. In addition, legal compliance is found to be quite high. The authors concluded that such findings imply a challenge for the police and the criminal justice system, because law students are not representative of the population, but a certain percentage of them will work in the fields of law enforcement and criminal justice in the future (Ilie et al., 2013: 449–450).

Meško, Fields, Šifrer, and Eman (in press) analyzed law students' perceptions of police authority and trust in policing in eight countries of Central and Eastern Europe. The results show that law students in general question their willingness to comply with laws and cooperate with the police. Regression analysis indicated that police authority and procedural justice are related to trust in the police in all the studied countries and police effectiveness in Slovenia, Russia, Romania, Poland, Bosnia and Herzegovina, and Croatia. The authors suggested that if the police wish to improve trust and legitimacy of policing, the police should strive primarily to improve their effectiveness, authority and procedural justice (Meško et al., in press). The question that remains and is discussed below, is why young people in South-Eastern Europe view police authority as legitimate and do they defer to them?

6 The Present Study

This paper presents the overall findings from a cross-national survey on legitimacy of policing conducted in Slovenia, Croatia, Bosnia and Herzegovina, Serbia, Romania, Poland, and Russia in the spring of 2013. The survey examined law students' perception of police legitimacy and related variables, such as police authority, police effectiveness, procedural justice, distributive justice, cooperation, moral credibility, deterrence, obligation to obey, legal cynicism, and legal compliance. All of the countries are characterized by a transition from communist to democratic political regimes and from a planned to a market economy. The collapse of the communist regime started after the fall of the Berlin Wall as well as a separation of the republics of the former Yugoslavia. Significant changes have occurred throughout Eastern Europe, impacted by the development of democratic changes of the political systems and later with joining the European Union (e.g., Poland, Slovenia, Romania, and Croatia), interventions of international institutions in post-conflict areas (e.g., Bosnia and Herzegovina, Croatia, and Serbia), international conflicts (Bosnia and Herzegovina), and efforts to modernize the criminal justice system in all the countries of Central and Easter Europe. There have been significant changes in the democratization of policing and criminal justice in the last two decades. Nevertheless, the criminal justice system and the police still are still challenged to pursue the development of democratic law enforcement (Meško, Fields, Lobnikar, & Sotlar, 2013a).

Studies on legitimacy in the region (Reisig et al., 2012) show a potential to study legitimacy and related constructs also in Eastern European countries. Project Euro-Justis (Hough & Sato, 2011) showed that levels of legitimacy and trust are quite similar in all post-communist countries. Therefore, we are interested in how potential future criminal justice professionals (law students) perceive legitimacy of policing and related variables.

6.1 Method

6.1.1 Data Collection

The results of the law student legitimacy survey conducted in seven Central and Eastern European countries[7] (Slovenia, Croatia, Bosnia and Herzegovina, Serbia, Romania, Poland and Russia)[8] are presented in the following section. The survey previously used by Reisig et al. (2012) was translated from English into the native languages of the participating countries. Research partners from faculties of law presented the survey to their students and discussed every item in the survey regarding their meaning and possible differences in the connotative meaning of the survey statements. After preliminary tests, the survey was published on the Web (https://www.1ka.si/) and the students who were enrolled in criminal law and criminology courses were given a certain period of time to complete the online survey. The Web survey was administered in the native languages of the respondents in spring 2013, and we assured internet access for all students in the faculties of law in the respective countries. The survey was accessible only to the law students who received a Web address and a specific code provided by their criminal law and criminology lecturers.

Law students were selected primarily due to the nature of their studies (i.e., legal orientation) and the assumption that they are planning to be future professionals in law enforcement or criminal justice agencies. A convenience sample of

[7] Central and Eastern Europe generally presents a political and geographical entity, thus for the understanding of the area in the present chapter, Central and Eastern Europe includes countries within the borders of Germany to the West, Russia to the East, the Baltic states to the North and Former Yugoslav Republic of Macedonia to the South (Meško, Fields, Lobnikar, & Sotlar, 2013b).

[8] We would like to thank our colleagues Elmedin Muratbegović from Bosnia and Herzegovina, Irma Kovčo Vukadin from Croatia, Janina Czapska and Daria Wójcik from Poland, Andra-Roxana Ilie from Romania, Gleb Bogush from Russia, and Đorđe Ignjatović from Serbia who helped us to collect data in their countries. We agreed with them that the national data could be used for this comparative paper.

undergraduate law students ($N = 1,368$) from Slovenia (Faculty of Law at the University of Ljubljana and Faculty of Law at the University of Maribor; $n = 143$), Croatia (Faculty of Law at the University of Zagreb; $n = 82$), Bosnia and Herzegovina (Faculty of Law at the University of Sarajevo; $n = 139$), Serbia (Faculty of Law in Belgrade; $n = 149$), Romania (Faculty of Law at the Bucharest University; $n = 245$), Poland (Faculty of Law at the Jagiellonian University, Faculty of Law and Administration of the University of Warsaw, Faculty of Law and Administration of the University of Gdańsk, Faculty of Law and Administration of the Nicolaus Copernicus University in Toruń, Faculty of Law and Administration of the Adam Mickiewicz University in Poznań, Faculty of Law and Administration of the University of Silesia in Katowice, and Faculty of Law, Administration and International Relations of the Andrzej Frycz Modrzewski Krakow University; $n = 488$), and Russia (Faculty of Law at the Moscow State University; $n = 147$) was used. The response rate varied between 1.5 and 5 % of the entire law student population in the universities included in the study, while the response from groups of students who were taking a criminology/criminal law course at the time of data collection is more than 50 %. The sample consisted of 981 female and 410 male respondents, with a modal age of 21 years ($n = 293$), and the majority of students are enrolled in the second year of the law programs ($n = 336$). Six hundred and eighty four students have already had some experience with the police and criminal justice system, either as someone who reported a crime ($n = 215$), an eye witness ($n = 264$), as a hearsay witness ($n = 238$), as someone who committed a minor offence ($n = 363$), as a crime suspect ($n = 33$) or as a crime victim ($n = 334$). Some respondents appeared in several different roles (e.g., someone who reported a crime, a victim, and a hearsay witness). Students were victimized by theft (241), fraud (51), burglary (69), assault (90), street robbery (26), sexual assault (21), and other minor crimes (73). Some students reported more than one criminal victimization; of 470 students who reported criminal victimization, 124 of them indicated that this victimization did not have any effect on them, 117 students reported that they handled their victimization well, 152 of them felt that their victimization was bad but they are not suffering any more, and 77 victimized students were still suffering the consequences of their victimization. Perception of police and criminal justice professionalism of those who have already had experience with the police and the criminal justice system is divided into three groups; those who perceived police and criminal justice professionals as "professional" ($n = 474$), "unprofessional" ($n = 191$), and "extremely unprofessional/abusive" ($n = 19$).

6.1.2 Variables

Factor analysis (maximum likelihood) was used to test all constructs (scales). KMO tests of sampling adequacy and reliability by Cronbach's alpha were calculated for each factor, new variables (factors) were computed after factor analysis, and descriptive statistics for each factor (means and standard deviations; and median) and percentage of agreement/disagreement with each variable are also presented in

Table 1 Factor analysis

Factors ranked by *α*	KMO and Cronbach Alphas	*N*	*M*	SD	Me	Agree/disagree (%)
Procedural justice[a**]	(KMO = 0.95; *α* = 0.93)	1,368	2.26	0.54	2.44	34.5/65.5
Trust in police[a*]	(KMO = 0.92; *α* = 0.91)	1,368	2.33	0.60	2.29	41.4/58.6
Moral Alignment[*]	(KMO = 0.74; *α* = 0.83)	1,368	2.05	0.56	2.42	25.8/74.2
Police effectiveness[a**]	(KMO = 0.82; *α* = 0.82)	1,368	2.37	0.52	3.23	42.0/58.0
Distributive justice[a*]	(KMO = 0.78; *α* = 0.77)	1,368	2.22	0.53	2.00	26.3/73.7
Police legitimacy[a**]	(KMO = 0.72; *α* = 0.73)	1,368	2.39	0.54	2.36	44.4/55.6
Police cooperation [b**]	(KMO = 0.71; *α* = 0.72)	1,368	3.13	0.66	2.29	81.5/18.5
Obligation to obey[a*]	(KMO = 0.61; *α* = 0.68)	1,368	2.37	0.63	2.16	42.1/57.9
Deterrence[c*]	(KMO = 0.73; *α* = 0.67)	1,368	2.58	0.57	1.67	59.0/41.0
Moral credibility[a**]	(KMO = 0.64; *α* = 0.60)	1,368	2.15	0.58	2.00	26.5/73.5
Legal cynicism[a*]	(KMO = 0.62; *α* = 0.54)	1,368	1.83	0.58	2.60	12.4/87.6
Legal compliance[d*]	(KMO = 0.62; *α* = 0.50)	1,368	2.35	0.30	2.51	94.2/5.8

[a]1—Strongly disagree, 2—Disagree, 3—Agree, 4—Strongly agree
[b]1—Never, 2—Rarely, 3—Occasionally, 4—Frequently
[c]1—Very unlikely, 2—Unlikely, 3—Likely, 4—Very likely
[d]1—Not wrong, 2—Somewhat wrong, 3—Very wrong
Levene statistics for One-way ANOVA—*excluded from further analysis; **included in further analysis

the Table 1. The factors legal cynicism and legal compliance were excluded from further analyses due to low values of reliability coefficients (lower than 0.60).

We analyzed data using one-way analysis of variance and *t*-test. The primary outcome measure, *legal compliance*, is a six-item additive index. Specifically, survey respondents were asked to report their opinion as to how wrong is it for someone to commit a variety of legal infractions, such as relatively minor violations ("illegally disposed of trash and litter"), traffic infractions ("broke traffic laws"), drug use ("used marijuana or some other drug"), and more serious violations ("bought something you thought might be stolen"). Previous research has employed similar compliance scales (see, e.g., Jackson, Bradford, Hough, & Murray, 2012; Reisig et al., 2007; Tyler, 1990). Each item featured a close-ended response set ranging from 1 (not wrong) to 3 (very wrong). The level of internal consistency exhibited by the scale is acceptable (KMO = 0.62, Cronbach's $\alpha = 0.50$, var. = 30.2 %). This variable is coded so that higher scores reflect higher levels of compliance with the law. a variable similar to legal compliance is *deterrence*. It is also a six-item additive index where respondents are asked to report how often are they caught and punished if they commit a variety of six above described legal infractions. Each item featured a close-ended response set ranging from 1 (very unlikely) to 4 (very likely). The level of internal consistency exhibited by the scale is acceptable (KMO = 0.73, Cronbach's $\alpha = 0.67$, var. = 43.8 %).

Two process-based measures are included in the current study. *Police legitimacy* is a summated scale comprised of two components: *obligation to obey the police* ("You should do what the police tell you to do even if you disagree" and "You should accept police decisions even if you think they are wrong") and *trust in police* ("The police in my community are trustworthy" and "I am proud of the police in this community"). The second process-based measure, *procedural justice*, is a ten-item additive scale that also consists of two components: *quality of interpersonal treatment* ("The police are courteous to citizens they come into contact with" and "The police treat everyone with dignity") and *quality of decision-making* ("The police make decisions based on facts" and "The police explain their decisions to the people they deal with"). The operationalization of these two process-based scales is consistent with that used in prior research (see, e.g., Sunshine & Tyler, 2003). The process based items featured a closed-ended response set ranging from "strongly disagree" (coded 1) to "strongly agree" (coded 4). The level of internal consistency for police legitimacy (KMO = 0.72, Cronbach's $\alpha = 0.73$, var. = 55.9 %) and procedural justice (KMO = 0.95, Cronbach's $\alpha = 0.93$, var. = 60.2 %) is acceptable. Scales are coded so that higher scores reflect more positive procedural justice judgments and higher levels of perceived police legitimacy.

An instrumental variable was created to address concerns with endogeniety bias. It is always preferred that the number of instruments (i.e., exogenous variables that are correlated with the endogenous regressor) exceed the number of potentially problematic variables (e.g., police legitimacy). Accordingly, two instruments are used in this study. Research shows that perceptions of how well the police handle crime are linked to legitimacy perceptions (Sunshine & Tyler, 2003; Tankebe, 2008). *Police effectiveness* is a seven-item additive scale ("The police are doing well in controlling violent crime" and "The police do a good job maintaining order in my neighborhood"). The level of internal consistency exhibited by the scale is acceptable (KMO = 0.82, Cronbach's $\alpha = 0.80$, var. = 48.1 %). The next variable created, *police cooperation*, is a four-item additive scale ("If the police were looking for witnesses in a case where someone's wallet was stolen, how likely would you be to volunteer information if you witnessed the theft?" and "Imagine that you were out and saw someone steal a wallet. How likely would you be to call the police?"). The level of internal consistency exhibited by the scale is acceptable (KMO = 0.71, Cronbach's $\alpha = 0.72$, var. = 55.6 %). Another variable with a four-item additive scale ("The police always obey the law" and "The police act in ways that are consistent with my own moral values") is *moral alignment*. The level of internal consistency exhibited by the scale is acceptable (KMO = 0.74, Cronbach's $\alpha = 0.83$, var. = 66.9 %).

Moral credibility ("Most people in my community believe that the law punishes criminals the amount they deserve") and *legal cynicism* ("To make money, there are no right or wrong ways anymore, only easy ways and hard ways") are variables with a five-item additive scale, and *distributive justice* ("The police provide the same quality of service to all citizens" and "The police make sure citizens receive the outcomes they deserve under the law") is variable with a five-item additive scale. The closed-ended response sets that accompanied the survey items used to create the instrumental variable ranged from 1 (strongly disagree) to 4 (strongly agree). The level of internal consistency for moral credibility (KMO = 0.64, Cronbach's $\alpha = 0.60$, var. = 56.0 %), legal cynicism (KMO = 0.62, Cronbach's $\alpha = 0.54$, var. = 53.0 %), and distributive justice (KMO = 0.78, Cronbach's $\alpha = 0.77$, var. = 53.1 %) is acceptable. These variables are coded so that higher scores reflect more positive evaluations of police effectiveness and more favorable moral credibility judgments.

7 Results

A comparison between countries indicates (Table 2) statistically significant differences among all countries for police legitimacy, police effectiveness, and willingness to cooperate with the police, procedural justice, and moral credibility. These results are similar to the findings of Taylor, Turner, Esbensen, and Winfree (2001), which support the idea of social context influencing citizens' attitudes towards the police, especially young people's attitudes. Legitimacy of the police is perceived in the most positive way by Polish law students, followed by Slovenians, while Russian and Serbian students perceive it the lowest. The results for police legitimacy are also presented graphically (Fig. 2). Police effectiveness is most positively perceived in Slovenia, followed by Romanian students, while Bosnian and Russian students perceived it in the most negative way. Willingness to cooperate with the police is the highest in Croatia followed by Slovenia. The most negative results for police cooperation are typical for Russian and Polish students. Procedural justice is

Table 2 One-way ANOVA—comparison between the countries

	Legitimacy	Effectiveness	Cooperation	Procedural justice	Moral credibility
M/SD	*M*/SD	*M*/SD	*M*/SD	*M*/SD	
Slovenia	2.49/0.54	2.55/0.56	3.27/0.60	2.41/0.50	2.09/0.59
Croatia	2.24/0.54	2.36/0.50	3.40/0.58	2.16/0.55	2.07/0.55
B&H	2.25/0.51	2.19/0.50	3.19/0.67	2.16/0.54	2.19/0.61
Serbia	2.24/0.54	2.27/0.52	3.23/0.61	2.61/0.56	2.20/0.55
Romania	2.39/0.51	2.44/0.48	3.12/0.68	2.23/0.49	2.22/0.61
Poland	2.51/0.55	2.42/0.51	3.05/0.66	2.40/0.54	2.20/0.57
Russia	2.24/0.47	2.19/0.47	2.96/0.68	1.99/0.48	1.88/0.50
F	12.14	11.53	7.28	15.67	7.37
p	0.00	0.00	0.00	0.00	0.00

ANOVA computed for variables where the assumptions of homogeneity of variances have not been violated (Levene's test is non-significant; $p > 0.05$)

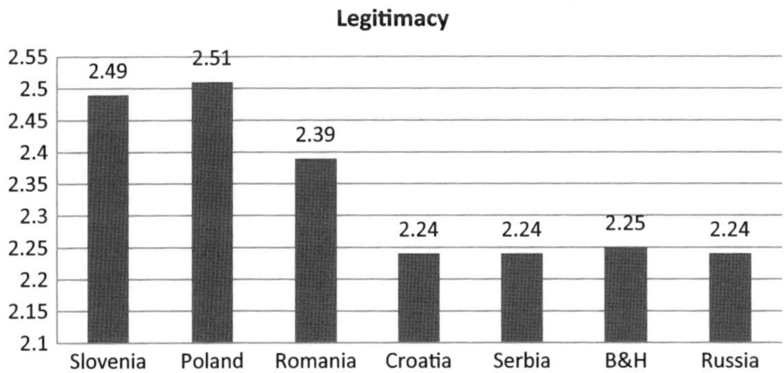

Fig. 1 Perceived police legitimacy

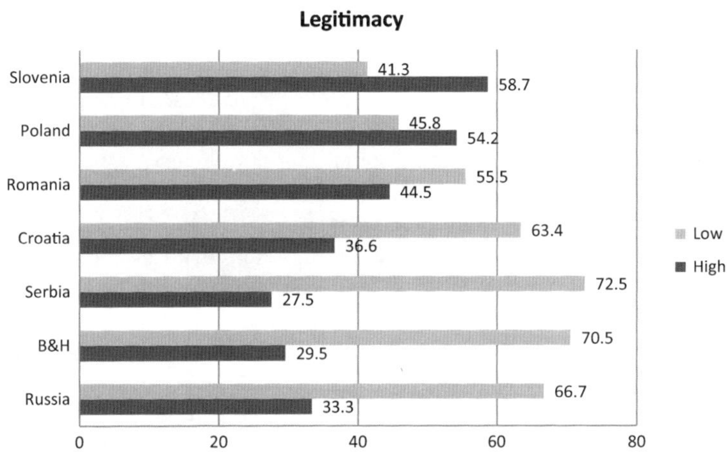

Fig. 2 Percentage of students' agreement/disagreement for factor police legitimacy within country

the most positively perceived in Serbia and Slovenia and the most negative in Russia, followed by Bosnian and Croatian students. Beliefs about moral credibility of the legal system are the highest in Serbia and Poland, and the lowest in Russia and Croatia. Detailed results are presented in Table 2. In addition, we took only one variable—police legitimacy—to show the differences among countries. These results are presented in Figs. 1 and 2.

In addition to legitimacy, other indicators, such as a democracy index, a corruption perception index and the GINI index of social inequality show similar differences between countries as compared in Figs. 1 and 2. These indicators were not included in the analysis in the present chapter, but we suggest taking them into consideration in the future studies. Moreover, differences in legitimacy and other variables can be also taken into account using a criterion of the European Union membership (see Table 2).

We also used the *t*-test to compare male and female respondents' attitudes, and found that only differences in moral credibility and deterrence were found statistically significant. Female respondents believe more than males that deterrence works and have a more positive attitude about the moral credibility of criminal justice. This finding is consistent with prior studies on young people's attitudes towards the police. Taylor et al. (2001: 296–298) reviewed studies over a 40-year period on attitudes towards the police and criminal justice, and determined that: gender is important variable, because female usually rate police more positive compared to males irrespective of the age group. Other possible reasons for difference in attitudes towards the police between boys and girls are: different socialization process, prejudicial social control and parental supervision, and different role expectations and limitations for males and females. On the other hand, girls have far fewer contacts with the police than boys therefore possible positive attitudes toward the police by females compared to males.

Nevertheless, police officers act differently towards young female and male suspects during police procedures—police officers exercise discretionary powers more often with girls than boys. The comparison between students who have had experiences with the police and criminal justice system shows that those who have had experiences with the police in the past have more negative opinions about police authority, obligation to obey the police, distributive justice, police effectiveness and their legitimacy. Furthermore, comparison of those who have had experiences with the police and criminal justice assessed their experience through their perception of police professionalism. The results imply that those who had a more positive experience with the police (i.e., perceived police as professional) assessed their experience in a more positive manner regarding all the measured variables (police authority, obligation to obey the police, trust in police, procedural and distributive justice, police effectiveness, moral credibility, deterrence and police legitimacy) than those who believed that the police were unprofessional. Similar to findings of the project Euro Justice (Hough & Sato, 2011) and the European Social Survey (Jackson et al., 2011), our research results revealed that personal contact with police officers is a key predictor of people's trust judgments.

Hough et al. (2010) established that there is good support between different European countries based on the connection between trust in the police and people's perceptions of the police legitimacy. Their survey showed that trust in police and belief in their fairness, are very important factors of police legitimacy in the European space. On the contrary, a comparison between all seven countries showed that significant differences existed between the variables compared (police legitimacy, police effectiveness, police cooperation, procedural justice, and moral credibility). The results imply that countries went through different developments of democratization of their criminal justice system, and those countries which have been members of the European Union for some time, have higher values regarding legitimacy and effectiveness than in other countries. Police reforms have taken place in Bosnia and Herzegovina, Serbia, and Croatia (post-conflict countries) but results of the reform are still vague (Kešetović, 2013; Kovčo Vukadin, Borovec, & Ljubin Golub, 2013; Šikman & Lalić, 2013). The results of the comparison imply perception of different traditions of policing and criminal justice—"former-Yugoslav" (Slovenia, Croatia, Bosnia and Herzegovina, and Serbia), Romanian, Polish and Russian (for more see Ponsaers, 2013). Changes in policing and criminal justice have also been noticed in Russia with police and criminal justice reforms. The impact of reforms is yet unknown (Sergevnin & Kovalyov, 2013). The majority of the countries referred to their police forces as militia prior to the fall of the Berlin Wall. All police militias were renamed to police forces in the early 1990s, except the Russian militia which did so more recently (Sergevnin & Kovalyov, 2013: 193). We need to comment on the results for Slovenia as they were the most positive regarding legitimacy. The democratization of policing and criminal justice started in the 1990s, and police and criminal justice reforms have been taking place for more than two decades. In addition, the Slovenian government had to meet the requirements in the areas of law enforcement and justice to join the European Union. The unification and harmonization of legislation and crime control practices contributed to the development of the democratization of the police and criminal justice. About the same developments have occurred in other countries (e.g., Poland) as well, and new European Union member countries (e.g., Romania and Croatia), while some countries are still at the beginning of this process.

Our results resemble the findings of Hinds and Murphy (2007) in that people who believe that the police use procedural justice more likely view them as legitimate and are more satisfied with their services. The results are also very interesting because the majority of students express a willingness to cooperate with the police (81.5 %), low legal cynicism (87.6 %), and high legal compliance (94.2 %). We believe these are good starting points for the police to work with the youth more effectively and convince them that they do serve the public and maintain public order and do crime control on behalf of citizens. Our findings on police authority (moral alignment) and policing are similar to Tyler's (2011), emphasizing that new approaches to policing have to focus on police legitimacy and include public compliance with the law, acceptance of police authority and cooperation with the police in responding to crime. On the other hand, student' perceptions calls for more professional policing, more police authority, and more procedural and distributive justice. Trust and legitimacy could also be improved in order to perform a more democratic policing and law enforcement.

A comparison of respondents who have had experiences with the police and criminal justice show that an experience per se did not have a significant impact on an individual and did increase negative attitudes towards the police. This finding is related to the results from the study of Hinds and Murphy (2007) showing that a person's evaluation of police legitimacy are based on their personal views about the way police treat them and independent of their individual views about how well police perform their. In a group of students who perceived the police as unprofessional or professional, statistical differences are found in all the important measured dimensions. Additional regression analyses for trust in the police and legitimacy (not shown) give the same results as found in the overall sample of students. In addition, surveys about citizens' attitude towards the police and willingness to cooperate showed that attitudes towards police vary with age

(Campbell & Schuman, 1972; Jesilow et al., 1995; Sullivan et al., 1987); and the contact, cooperation, and satisfaction with the police depending on the prior interaction and experience in police procedures (Hagan et al., 2005; Rusinko et al., 1978). We can conclude that young people believe that the same factors are important for the improvement of trust in the police and legitimacy of policing. Let us explain this a little more in detail. Procedural justice, police effectiveness, and police authority were found to be significant in both models (trust and legitimacy), so therefore we believe that they are crucial in the improvement of police professionalism in the studied region. Procedural justice, also referred to as procedural fairness, is important in law enforcement, as their clients perceive police officers in different ways. Even students who have not had any experiences with the police, believe that procedural justice is crucial in addition to legality of police procedures. Respondents require the police to perform their tasks effectively, to clear up criminal offences, and deal professionally and effectively with criminal and other suspects, to effectively collect evidence and contribute to the quality of criminal and other proceedings. Police authority can be maintained by exercising a high level of integrity and professional practice of law enforcement as well as community policing and other police–citizen relations (e.g., counselling victims, establishing of social control networks to improve police effectiveness).

In addition, the police have to bear in mind that they are not tools of the government but a public institution, serving the citizens and protecting their constitutional rights. As emphasized by Tyler (2012), police forces have to bear in mind that people fulfil the need to create shared principles of justice and then use them as a tool for cooperation and solve conflicts. In case of police legitimacy, this means that when the police make decisions and try to achieve justice, it is really important how they "make their decisions legitimate to all the parties in a conflict" (Tyler, 2012: 367), to be accepted. As all mean values were quite low, we assume that police forces in the region have a huge challenge to work with the youth to convince them that they serve citizens and not only the government, performing their duties not in the best possible manner. There is a lot of optimism because the majority of students are willing to support and cooperate with the police.

References

Beetham, D. (1991a). Max Weber and the legitimacy of the modern state. *Analyse & Kritik, 13*(1), 34–45.

Beetham, D. (1991b). *The legitimation of power*. Houndmills: Macmillan.

Beetham, D. (1993). In defence of legitimacy. *Political Studies, 41*(3), 488–491.

Bradford, B., Huq, A., Jackson, J., & Roberts, B. (2013). What price fairness when security is at stake? Legitimacy in South Africa. *Regulation and Governance*. doi:10.1111/rego.12012.

Bradford, B., Jackson, J., & Hough, M. (2013). Police futures and legitimacy: Redefining 'good policing'. In J. Brown (Ed.), *Future of policing* (pp. 79–99). Oxon: Routledge.

Campbell, A., & Schuman, H. (1972). A comparison of black and white attitudes and experiences in the city. In C. M. Haar (Ed.), *The end of innocence: A suburban reader* (pp. 97–110). Glenview: Scott Foresman.

Carr, P. J., Napolitano, L., & Keating, J. (2007). We never call the cops and here is why: A qualitative examination of legal cynicism in three Philadelphia neighbourhoods. *Criminology, 45*(2), 445–480.

Carter, D. L. (1985). Hispanic perception of police performance: An empirical assessment. *Journal of Criminal Justice, 13*(6), 487–500.

Clark, J. P., & Wenninger, E. P. (1964). The attitude of juveniles toward the legal institution. *Journal of Criminal Law, Criminology, and Police Science, 55*(4), 482–489.

Corkin, J. (2008). Science, legitimacy and the law: Regulating risk regulation judiciously in the European community. *European Law Review, 33*(4), 360.

Cunneen, C., & White, R. (1995). *Juvenile justice: An Australian perspective*. Melbourne: Oxford University Press.

Dvoršek, A., Maver, D., & Meško, G. (2006). Policijsko delo z oškodovanci premoženjske kriminalitete—Med prijaznostjo in učinkovitostjo [Police work with victims of property crime—Between kindness and efficiency]. *Revija za kriminalistiko in kriminologijo, 57*(1), 57–68.

Easton, D., & Dennis, J. (1969). *Children in the political system: Origins of political legitimacy*. New York, NY: McGraw-Hill.

Feldman, Y., & Lobel, O. (2008). Decentralized enforcement in organizations: An experimental approach. *Regulation and Governance, 2*(2), 165–192.

Galland, O. (2001). Adolescence, post adolescence, youth: A re-appraisal on a number of interpretations. *Revue Francaise De Sociologie, 42*(4), 611–640.

Gallup, G. (1999). *The Gallup poll: Public opinion 1999*. Wilmington: Scholarly Resources.

Goodman-Delahunty, J. (2010). Four ingredients: New recipes for procedural justice in Australian policing. *Policing, 4*(4), 403–410.

Hagan, J., Shedd, C., & Payne, M. (2005). Race, ethnicity and youth perceptions of criminal injustice. *American Sociological Review, 70*(3), 381–407.

Harris, L. (1999). *The Harris poll: March*. New York, NY: Louis Harris and Associates.

Herbert, S. (2006). Tangled up in blue: Conflicting paths to police legitimacy. *Theoretical Criminology, 10*(4), 481–504.

Hinds, K. (2009). Youth, police legitimacy and informal contact. *Journal of Police and Criminal Psychology, 24*(1), 10–21.

Hinds, L., & Murphy, K. (2007). Public satisfaction with police: Using procedural justice to improve police legitimacy. *The Australian and New Zealand Journal of Criminology, 40*(1), 27–42.

Hinsch, W. (2008). Legitimacy and justice. In J. Kuhnelt (Ed.), *Political legitimation without morality?* (pp. 39–52). London: Springer.

Hough, M., Jackson, J., Bradford, B., Myhill, A., & Quinton, P. (2010). Procedural justice, trust, and institutional legitimacy. *Policing, 4*(3), 203–210.

Hough, M., Jackson, J., & Bradford, B. (2013a). Legitimacy, trust, and compliance: An empirical test of procedural justice theory using the European Social Survey. In J. Tankebe & A. Liebling (Eds.), *Legitimacy and criminal justice: An international exploration* (pp. 326–352). Oxford: Oxford University Press.

Hough, M., Jackson, J., & Bradford, B. (2013b). Trust in justice and the legitimacy of legal authorities: Topline findings from European comparative study. In S. Body-Gendrot, M. Hough, K. Kerezsi, R. Lévy, & S. Snacken (Eds.), *The Routledge handbook of European criminology* (pp. 243–265). Oxon: Routledge.

Hough, M., & Sato, M. (Eds.). (2011). *Trust in justice: Why it is important for criminal policy, and how it can be measured: Final report of the Euro-Justis Project*. Helsinki: Institute for Criminal Policy Research. Retrieved from http://www.eurojustis.eu/fotoweb/HEUNI_Report_70_revised_09112011.pdf.

Igličar, A. (2013). *The outline of sociology of law*. Saarbrücken: Lap Lambert Academic Publishing.
Ilie, A.-R., Eman, K., Bogush, G., & Meško, G. (2013). Legal cynicism in Romania, Slovenia and Russia: A comparative approach of crime and criminal justice related variables. In E.-M. Fodor (Ed.), *Efficiency of legal norms* (pp. 441–451). Bucureşti: Hamangiu.
Jackson, J. (2010). *Trust in justice and the legitimacy of legal authorities: Pilot data from a comparative European analysis*. Retrieved from http://www.tasa.org.au/uploads/2008/12/Jackson-Jonathan.pdf.
Jackson, J., & Bradford, B. (2010). *Police legitimacy: A conceptual review*. Social Science Research Network. Retrieved from http://papers.ssrn.com/sol3/papers.cfm?abstract_id=1684507
Jackson, J., Bradford, B., Hough, M., Myhill, A., Quinton, P., & Tyler, T. R. (2012). Why do people comply with the law? Legitimacy and the influence of legal institutions. *British Journal of Criminology, 52*(6), 1051–1071.
Jackson, J., Bradford, B., Hough, M., & Murray, K. H. (2012). Compliance with the law and policing by consent. In A. Crawford & A. Hucklesby (Eds.), *Legitimacy and compliance in criminal justice* (pp. 29–49). New York: Routledge.
Jackson, J., Bradford, B., Stanko, B., & Hohl, K. (2013). *Just authority? Trust in the police in England and Wales*. Abingdon: Routledge.
Jackson, J., Hough, M., Bradford, B., Pooler, T., Hohl, K., & Kuha, J. (2011). *Trust in justice: Topline results from round 5 of the European Social Survey*. European Social Survey. Retrieved from http://www.icpr.org.uk/media/32166/Topline%20Results%20from%20Round%205%20of%20the%20ESS.pdf.
Jacob, H. (1971). Black and white perceptions of justice in the city. *Law and Society Review, 6*(1), 69–89.
Jesilow, P., Meyer, J., & Namazzi, N. (1995). Public attitudes toward the police. *American Journal of Police, 14*(2), 67–89.
Jonathan-Zamir, T., & Weisburd, D. (2013). The effects of security threats on antecedents of police legitimacy: Findings from a quasi-experiment in Israel. *Journal of Research in Crime and Delinquency, 50*(1), 3–32.
Kešetović, Ž. M. (2013). Serbian police: Troubled transition from police force. In G. Meško, C. B. Fields, B. Lobnikar, & A. Sotlar (Eds.), *Handbook on policing in Central and Eastern Europe* (pp. 217–238). New York, NY: Springer.
Kovčo Vukadin, I., Borovec, K., & Ljubin Golub, T. (2013). Policing in Croatia: The main challenges on the path to democratic policing. In G. Meško, C. B. Fields, B. Lobnikar, & A. Sotlar (Eds.), *Handbook on policing in Central and Eastern Europe* (pp. 31–56). New York, NY: Springer.
Lasley, J. R. (1994). The impact of the Rodney King incident on citizen attitudes towards police. *Policing and Society, 3*(4), 245–255.
Leiber, M. J., Nalla, M. K., & Farnworth, M. (1998). Explaining juveniles' attitudes toward the police. *Justice Quarterly, 15*(1), 151–173.
Lind, E. A., & Tyler, T. R. (1988). *The social psychology of procedural justice*. New York, NY: Plenum Press.
Loader, I. (1996). *Youth, policing and democracy*. Basingstoke: Macmillan Press.
Meares, T. L. (2000). Norms, legitimacy and law enforcement. *Oregon Law Review, 79*(2), 391–416.
Meško, G., Fields, C. B., Lobnikar, B., & Sotlar, A. (Eds.). (2013a). *Handbook on policing in Central and Eastern Europe*. New York, NY: Springer.
Meško, G., Fields, C. B., Lobnikar, B., & Sotlar, A. (2013b). Introduction to handbook of policing in Central and Eastern Europe. In G. Meško, C. B. Fields, B. Lobnikar, & A. Sotlar (Eds.), *Handbook on policing in Central and Eastern Europe* (pp. 1–4). New York, NY: Springer.
Meško, G., Fields, C. B., Šifrer, J., & Eman, K. (in press). Understanding trust in police and legitimacy in Central Eastern Europe: The law student survey. *CEPOL Research and Science Bulletin*, 15 p.

Meško, G., & Umek, P. (2002). Čustveni odzivi oškodovancev kaznivih dejanj [Emotional reactions of crime victims]. In A. Dvoršek, V. Gorenak, B. Lobnikar, D. Maver, G. Meško, M. Pagon, & P. Umek (Eds.), *Stališča oškodovancev premoženjskih kaznivih dejanj do postopkov policistov: Končno poročilo [Standpoints of property crime victims on police procedures: Final report]* (pp. 39–40). Ljubljana: Visoka policijsko-varnostna šola.
Murphy, K. (2005). Regulating more effectively: The relationship between procedural justice, legitimacy, and tax non-compliance. *Journal of Law and Society, 32*(4), 562–589.
Murphy, K., Tyler, T. R., & Curtis, A. (2009). Nurturing regulatory compliance: Is procedural justice effective when people question the legitimacy of the law? *Regulation and Governance, 3*(1), 1–26.
Nelsen, E. A., Eisenberg, N., & Carroll, J. L. (1982). The structure of adolescents' attitudes towards law and crime. *Journal of Genetic Psychology, 140*(1), 47–58.
Piquero, A. R., Paternoster, R., Pogarsky, G., & Loughran, T. (2011). Elaborating the individual difference component in deterrence theory. *Annual Review of Law and Social Science, 7*, 335–360.
Ponsaers, P. (2013). Policing in Central and Eastern Europeans an epiphenomenon of geopolitical events. In G. Meško, C. B. Fields, B. Lobnikar, & A. Sotlar (Eds.), *Handbook on policing in Central and Eastern Europe* (pp. 5–14). New York: Springer.
Reisig, M. D., Bratton, J., & Gertz, M. G. (2007). The construct validity and refinement of process-based policing measures. *Criminal Justice and Behaviour, 34*(8), 1005–1028.
Reisig, M. D., & Lloyd, C. (2009). Procedural justice, police legitimacy, and helping the police fight crime: Results from a survey of Jamaican adolescents. *Police Quarterly, 12*(1), 42–62.
Reisig, M. D., & Meško, G. (2009). Procedural justice, legitimacy, and prisoner misconduct. *Psychology Crime and Law, 15*(1), 37–54.
Reisig, M. D., Tankebe, J., & Meško, G. (2012). Procedural justice, police legitimacy, and public cooperation with the police among young Slovene adults. *Varstvoslovje, 14*(2), 147–164.
Reiss, A. J. (1971). *The police and the public*. New Haven, CT: Yale University Press.
Rusinko, W. T., Johnson, K. W., & Hornung, C. A. (1978). The importance of police contact in the formulation of youths' attitudes toward police. *Journal of Criminal Justice, 6*(1), 53–67.
Sampson, R. J., & Bartusch, D. J. (1998). Legal cynicism and (subcultural?) tolerance of deviance: The neighborhood context of racial differences. *Law and Society Review, 32*(4), 777–804.
Scabini, R. C. (1996). The perception of support and communication in families with late adolescents. *International Journal of Psychology, 31*(3–4), 2377.
Sergevnin, V., & Kovalyov, O. (2013). Policing in Russia. In G. Meško, C. B. Fields, B. Lobnikar, & A. Sotlar (Eds.), *Handbook on policing in Central and Eastern Europe* (pp. 191–216). New York, NY: Springer.
Šifrer, J., Meško, G., & Bren, M. (2013). Zakaj mladi spoštujejo zakone—Empirična izhodišča Tylerjeve teorije [Why young people obey the law—Empirical backgrounds of the Tyler's theory]. *Varstvoslovje, 15*(1), 45–63.
Šikman, M., & Lalić, V. (2013). A new concept of the police and policing in Republika Srpska (Bosnia and Herzegovina). In G. Meško, C. B. Fields, B. Lobnikar, & A. Sotlar (Eds.), *Handbook on policing in Central and Eastern Europe* (pp. 287–303). New York, NY: Springer.
Skitka, L. J., & Houston, D. A. (2001). When due process is of no consequence: Moral mandates and presumed defendant guilt or innocence. *Social Justice Research, 14*(3), 305–326.
Škrinjar, K. (2010, May 20). Demonstracije ušle izpod nadzora [The demonstrations got out of control]. *Delo.si*. Retrieved from http://www.delo.si/novice/slovenija/demonstracije-usle-izpod-nadzora.html.
Sullivan, P. S., Dunham, R. G., & Alpert, G. P. (1987). Attitude structures of different ethnic and age groups concerning police. *Journal of Criminal Law and Criminology, 78*(1), 177–196.
Sunshine, J., & Tyler, T. R. (2003). The role of procedural justice and legitimacy in shaping public support for policing. *Law and Society Review, 37*(3), 513–547.
Tankebe, J. (2008). Policing, procedural fairness and public behaviour: A review and critique. *International Journal of Police Science & Management, 11*(1), 8–19.

Tankebe, J. (2013). Viewing things differently: The dimensions of public perceptions of police legitimacy. *Criminology, 51*(1), 103–135.

Taylor, T. J., Turner, K. B., Esbensen, F.-A., & Winfree, L. T., Jr. (2001). Coppin' an attitude: Attitudinal differences among juveniles toward police. *Journal of Criminal Justice, 29*, 295–305.

Thibaut, J., & Walker, L. (1975). *Procedural justice: A psychological analysis.* Hillsdale, MI: John Wiley.

Tyler, T. R. (1990). *Why people obey the law.* New Haven, CT: Yale University Press.

Tyler, T. R. (1997). The psychology of legitimacy: A relational perspective on voluntary deference to authorities. *Personality and Social Psychology Review, 1*(4), 323–345.

Tyler, T. R. (2003). Procedural justice, legitimacy, and the effective rule of law. In M. Tonry (Ed.), *Crime and justice: A review of research* (pp. 283–357). Chicago, IL: University of Chicago Press.

Tyler, T. R. (2004). Enhancing police legitimacy. *Annals of the American Academy of Political and Social Science, 593*, 84–99.

Tyler, T. R. (2006a). *Why people obey the law.* Princeton, NJ: Princeton University Press.

Tyler, T. R. (2006b). Legitimacy and legitimating. *Annual Review of Psychology, 57*, 375–400.

Tyler, T. R. (2011). Trust and legitimacy: Policing in the USA and Europe. *European Journal of Criminology, 8*(4), 254–266.

Tyler, T. R. (2012). Justice and effective cooperation. *Social Justice Research, 25*(4), 355–375.

Tyler, T., & Blader, S. (2000). *Cooperation in groups: Procedural justice, social identity, and behavioural engagement.* Philadelphia, PA: Psychology Press.

Tyler, T. R., & Darley, J. M. (2000). Building a law-abiding society: Taking public views about morality and the legitimacy of legal authorities into account when formulating substantive law. *Hofstra Law Review, 28*(3), 707–739.

Tyler, T. R., & Fagan, J. (2008). Legitimacy and cooperation: Why do people help the police fight crime in their communities. *Ohio State Journal of Criminal Law, 6*(1), 231–275.

Tyler, T., & Huo, Y. (2002). *Trust in the law: Encouraging public cooperation with the police and courts.* New York, NY: Russell Sage.

Tyler, T. R., & Lind, E. A. (1992). A relational model of authority in groups. In M. Zanna (Ed.), *Advances in experimental social psychology* (pp. 115–191). New York, NY: Academic.

Tyler, T. R., & Wakslak, C. J. (2004). Profiling and police legitimacy: Procedural justice, attributions of motive, and acceptance of police authority. *Criminology, 42*(2), 253–281.

Walker, S. (1992). *Taming the system: The control of discretion in criminal justice, 1950–1990.* Oxford: Oxford University Press.

White, R. (1994). Street life: Police practices and youth behaviour. In R. White & C. Alder (Eds.), *The police and young people in Australia* (pp. 16–29). Cambridge: Cambridge University Press.

Winter, S. C., & May, P. J. (2001). Motivation for compliance with environmental regulations. *Journal of Policy Analysis and Management, 20*(4), 675–698.

Wu, Y., & Sun, I. Y. (2010). Perceptions of police: An empirical study of Chinese college students. *Policing, 33*(1), 93–113.

Police Self-Legitimacy, Use of Force, and Pro-organizational Behavior in Slovenia

Justice Tankebe and Gorazd Meško

1 Introduction

In many ways, these are the best times for legitimacy in criminology. Unlike sociology and political science, legitimacy had long been peripheral in criminological research. This inattention to legitimacy was due to a general historical tendency for criminologists to avoid normative issues (Bottoms, 2002). The situation today is different; legitimacy is now an established topic in criminological studies, with an explosion in empirical research about its antecedents and consequences. The impetus for the remarkable change of fortune for legitimacy is undoubtedly traceable to the pioneering work of Tom Tyler, beginning with his *Why People Obey the Law* (Tyler, 1990). Tyler's procedural justice arguments have been studied in different contexts, focusing principally on everyday interactions between criminal justice agents—such as prisons and police officers—and citizens. The results from these studies consistently show that public perceptions of police legitimacy shape general compliance with the law (Papachristos, Meares, & Fagan, 2012; Piquero, Fagan, Mulvey, Steinberg, & Odgers, 2005; Sunshine & Tyler, 2003) and cooperation with legal authorities (Jackson, Bradford, Stanko, & Hohl, 2012; Murphy & Cherney, 2012; Reisig, Tankebe, & Meško, 2012; Tankebe, 2013).

Notwithstanding this important advancement in our understanding of legitimacy, some areas of legitimacy theorization and research remain underdeveloped.

J. Tankebe (✉)
Institute of Criminology, University of Cambridge, Sidgwick Avenue, Cambridge CB3 9DA, UK
e-mail: jt340@cam.ac.uk

G. Meško
Faculty of Criminal Justice and Security, Slovenia, University of Maribor, Kotnikova 8, 1000 Ljubljana, Slovenia
e-mail: gorazd.mesko@fvv.uni-mb.si

G. Meško, J. Tankebe (eds.), *Trust and Legitimacy in Criminal Justice*,
DOI 10.1007/978-3-319-09813-5_12

One of these is the police's views of their own legitimacy. To date, the dominant approach to legitimacy is from the standpoint of citizens; thus, various empirical analyses attempt to assess the conditions associated with citizens' views of the legitimacy or otherwise of the police (Tyler, 1990; Sunshine & Tyler, 2003; Jackson, Bradford, Stanko & Hohl, 2012). Yet one must equally be attentive to the belief and the confidence that officers have in their own legitimacy, because such a belief can have important implications for how carry out their work and for the cultivation of legitimacy among citizens. Max Weber, to whom we owe much for the stature of legitimacy in contemporary social science, emphasized the duality of legitimacy (see further below).

This dimension of legitimacy from the standpoint of power-holders is what has been described as *power-holder legitimacy* or *self-legitimacy* (Bottoms & Tankebe, 2012). Self-legitimacy refers to a belief on that part of power-holders, such as the police, that the positions they occupy and their attendant roles are morally acceptable and justified to themselves. It is, in other words, about the self-recognition of entitlement to power. Unlike organization legitimacy, which focuses on power-holders' views of the organization, self-legitimacy is concerned with power-holders' views of their own individual legitimacy. What relationship exists, if any, between self-legitimacy and organizational legitimacy is yet to be empirically examined.

The essay presents a brief theoretical analysis of self-legitimacy, hypothesizing a number of factors that might shape officers' self-legitimacy. It also discusses the consequences of police self-legitimacy.

2 Understanding Police Self-Legitimacy

There are various definitions of legitimacy. For example, Tyler (2011: 256) defines "the legitimacy as the belief that police authority ought to be accepted and people should voluntarily defer to police decisions and directives." This definition is problematic. Among other things, it appears to reduce legitimacy to decision acceptance. However, while legitimacy and decision acceptance may be related, they are different concepts that should not be conflated (Bottoms & Tankebe, 2012; Kaina, 2008). Moreover, discussions of police legitimacy had (until recently) focused exclusively on the views of the *audiences* of power. That is to say, the rightness of power as perceived by those over whom power is exercised (Bottoms & Tankebe, 2012, 2013; Tankebe, in press). In doing so, legitimacy scholars had overlooked what Bottoms and Tankebe (2012) call *power-holder legitimacy*. This dimension of legitimacy describes the confidence or self-belief that those in positions of power (e.g., police officers) have in the rightness of their power.

The idea of a dual conception of legitimacy is not new to social scientists. For example, writing in the *Encyclopaedia of the Social Sciences*, Sternberger (1968: 244) defined legitimacy as "the foundation of such governmental power as is exercised both with a consciousness on the government's part that it has a right to govern and with some recognition by the governed of that right." However, this conception of legitimacy can be traced to the work of Max Weber. Weber argued that power-holders have a need to cultivate legitimacy of their power and positions not only for the purposes of securing the cooperation of their power-subjects, but for their own personal consumption. As he put it, the powerful have a need to "persuade *themselves* that their fates are deserved and therefore rightful" (Weber in Kronman, 1983: 41). In Weber's conception, self-legitimacy is a necessary pre-condition for claiming legitimacy among citizens. "To the extent that he anticipates and understands the criticism of those who are less fortunate, the man of good fortune must already be a critic himself." (Weber in Kronman, 1983: 41).

Weber did not develop his analysis of this dimension of legitimacy as fully as he did the audience dimension. Nonetheless, Bottoms and Tankebe (2012) argue that because of the central place that Weber assigned to formal legality in his treatise on audience legitimacy, it might be reasonable to suspect that it would have been the grounds on which power-holders would seek to justify the rightness of their power to themselves. In other words, police officers will believe in their own legitimacy if and only if they ensure that the positions they occupy, the powers they wield, and the manner in which such powers are exercised on a day-to-day basis are formally and legally correct. Yet legality is not sufficient to establish legitimacy; in addition to legality, those in power must also be able to convince themselves that their claims to legitimacy is justified in terms of a society's shared values and beliefs (Botttoms & Tankebe, 2012). Wrong (1995: 51) has emphasized this need for reference to the shared beliefs held both by rulers and by those who are governed, when he notes that power holders have "a need to believe that the power they possess is morally justified, that they are servants of a larger collective goal or system of values surpassing mere determination to perpetuate themselves in power, [and] that their exercise of power is not inescapably at odds with hallowed standards of morality."

As Bottoms and Tankebe (2012) have noted, however, analysis of self-legitimacy in the political science literature had focused entirely on rulers. In this way, the role of "junior power-holders," including frontline officers, who are in direct contact with citizens and often exercise a significant degree of local power on a daily basis, is overlooked (Bottoms and Tankebe, 2012, 2013). Yet, such junior power-holders are a special group; they are "the state made flesh. [...] they are the most direct representatives of the state for citizens given their visible, uniformed, 24-hour presence on the streets and their crucial involvement in social intervention and law enforcement" (Punch, 2000: 322). The nature and outcome of everyday police–public interactions may lead to outcomes that necessitate a recalibration of the modes of audience legitimacy and a transformation of police practices and procedures. Given this, it would seem that the problem of ordinary police officers' cultivation of belief in moral rightness of their power and role should be taken seriously. Indeed, Tankebe (2014) speculates that the further one climbs downwards on the rungs of organizational structure, the greater the energy, time, and intensity of legitimation for the confirmation of claims to authority.

As noted previously, police researchers have not yet paid sufficient attention to self-legitimacy in their empirical analyses of legitimacy. It is nonetheless important to note that the main thrust of this dimension of legitimacy is at least implicit in Muir's (1977) in-depth study on good policing, as well as an empirical description of ways in which police deviate from it. A core element of Muir's argument is that police officers are moral animals and that they wrestle with justifying their actions in moral terms. That is, they need to construct moral arguments about "the rightness of their cause." This is a central idea in the analysis of police self-legitimacy. As it is well known, Muir identified four "types" of officers—*Professionals, Enforcers, Reciprocators,* and *Avoiders*—each with different orientations to their work but all seeking some way to cultivate legitimacy for their roles. Officers with a greater sense of self-legitimacy approximate Muir's (1977: 144–145) professional officers: "The professional response never involved an indefensible violation of the law. Any apparent illegality, if there was one, was always put in an understandable and acceptable light, openly and publicly justified. Nor did the professional response amount to the naked assertion of the law. The law was invoked after careful preparation of a foundation of knowledge, or fearfulness, or both."

3 What Factors Might Promote Self-Legitimacy?

Practically and theoretically, the task of understanding the conditions that help to create and sustain police confidence in self-legitimacy is of immense importance. However, empirically, not much is known about those conditions. Part of the reason is that this dimension of legitimacy has been undeveloped. However, it is possible to hypothesize a number of such factors that might relate to officer self-legitimacy. Barbalet (2001: 87) has argued that "feelings of confidence arise from acceptance and recognition in social relationships." For police officers, there are at least three main social relationship involved: relationships with *supervisors, colleagues,* and *citizens* (Tankebe, in press), such that the feeling of acceptance in each of these relationship could shape the level of confidence officers have in their own legitimacy.

Relationships with supervisors bring to the fore the issues of procedural justice. Procedural justice is now an established area of criminological research. It refers to the perceived fairness of the procedures used to determine specific outcomes. In more developed work, procedural justice has itself been shown to comprise two separate elements: namely, *quality of decision-making* (e.g., did the citizen have a fair opportunity to state his/her point of view?), and *quality of treatment* (i.e., how far was the citizen treated as a person with human dignity and respect?).

There is a growing body of empirical studies that show procedural justice is the predominant determinant of citizens' perceptions of police legitimacy. Among power-holders, a study by Tyler, Callahan, and Frost (2007: 476) found that perceptions of legitimacy made by law enforcement agents and soldiers were significantly influenced by the views about procedural justice from their supervisors. Tyler and his colleagues were concerned with evaluations of organizational legitimacy, rather than the individual officers' self-confidence in their own legitimacy. Yet it is reasonable to hypothesize that procedural justice can be important in promoting self-legitimacy among police officers. This is because procedural justice communicates one's status in a group; it signals to subordinates in a power relationship to extent to which they are considered full members of the social group to which they belong. It is in this sense that we should expect it to predict confidence in self-legitimacy. In his study with frontline police officers in Ghana, Tankebe (in press) found that procedural justice from supervisors was the main driver of self-legitimacy. However, in Durham, Bradford and Quinton (2014) reported that procedural justice from supervisors was associated with a decrease, not an increase, in self-legitimacy.

As indicated above, a second party in the relationship triad of officers is their colleague officers within the same rank or unit. According to Coleman (1988: 101), "a group within which there is extensive trustworthiness and extensive trust is able to accomplish much more than a comparable group without that trustworthiness and trust." It is a group characterized by the so-called "relational social capital," and is considered "an aid in accounting for different outcomes at the level of individual actors" (Coleman, 1988: 101). The general notion of social capital is not new to criminology; there is a strong body of evidence demonstrating the role of conventional social capital suppresses offending and protects against victimizations (McCarthy, Hagan, & Martin, 2002), while criminal social capital facilitates it (Hagan & McCarthy, 1997). Among police officers, the police subculture literature suggests the presence of relational social capital among officers can be an important resource for getting police work done as much as it can facilitate misconduct among officers.

However, the quality of interpersonal relations among officers may also have other functions beyond facilitating misconduct. Indeed, it is our hypothesis that such relationships can help to predict the levels of self-legitimacy officers have. This is consistent with expectations from Barbalet's (2001) arguments about the social foundations of self-confidence. In his ethnographic work in the USA, Muir (1977) found that an officer's attachment to and views about relations with peers was key understanding such an officer's belief in the moral rightness of her power. In Tankebe's (in press) study in Ghana, relations with colleagues explained self-legitimacy, albeit indirectly. The effects were mediated by the influence of supervisors.

Finally, we consider relations with citizens. Police officers engaged in daily routine patrol are lowly actors in the hierarchy of their organization. Yet to the citizen they are in possession of enormous power, including the power to arrest and detain; and, as power-holders, they regularly engage in legitimacy dialogues as their authority is challenged by citizens in one way or another (Bottoms & Tankebe, 2013). For Tyler (2011), everyday police–citizen encounters are a "teachable moment" in which people learn about the legitimacy or otherwise of their police. What is not known is whether, and to what extent, the reactions of citizens' shape police officers' sense of legitimacy. Extrapolating from Barker's (2001) analysis of power-holder legitimacy, Tankebe (in press) hypothesized that citizens' response will have the least influence on police confidence in their self-legitimacy. This hypothesis was informed by Barker's (2001: 125) argument that "rulers do not need subjects, or citizens, to enable them to legitimate themselves or to cultivate their governing identities. Their first mirror is themselves, and subjects are at the edge of the outer circle."

Two previous studies have sought to examine the influence of relations with citizens on officer self-legitimacy. In Tankebe's (in press) study in Ghana, officers who felt accepted by citizens expressed greater confidence in their own legitimacy; however, this influence was indirect, being mediated by the quality of relationships with supervisors. In Durham, Bradford and Quinton (2014) reported that perceptions of public support increased feelings of self-legitimacy. Extrapolating from these two studies, we expect police audience legitimacy (as perceived by the police themselves) to predict self-legitimacy.

4 Self-Legitimacy and Police Behavior

Why should police researchers and police managers take police self-legitimacy seriously? Is it merely an interesting theoretical concern, or it has practical implications for everyday police work? There is evidence to show that self-legitimacy predicts police organizational commitment (Tankebe, 2010). What is not known is whether self-legitimacy can help to explain police decision choices. Yet it is possible to speculate on a few potentially important consequences, which might be the subject of future empirical analysis. In this chapter, we focus on the effects of self-legitimacy on two behavioral outcomes: police decision to use force and police pro-organizational behavior. According to Croft (in Lersch, Bazley, Mieczkowski, & Childs, 2008: 285),

> "police use of force is of theoretical importance because it represents a delegated governmental power over the citizenry; as agents of the state, police can legitimately use force in meeting their law enforcement and order maintenance responsibilities. The questions how and why police use force, therefore, are central not only to an examination of police activities but also to the broader political issue of the proper role and function of government in a modern democratic society."

Unsurprisingly, police use of force (of varying degrees of seriousness) has attracted criminological interest. Drawing on data from official records, field observations, and surveys, various prior studies have examined when (situation), against whom (suspect characteristics) officers use force, and the factors that account for these decision choices (e.g., Bittner, 1970; Johnson & Kuhns, 2009; Terrill & Reisig, 2003; Weisburd, Greenspan, Hamilton, Williams, & Bryant, 2000). Explanations for the decision to use force have been sought in terms of personal characteristics of officers (e.g., McElvain & Kposowa, 2008; Rydberg & Terrill, 2010; Worden, 1989), personal characteristics and reactions of suspects (Alpert & Dunham, 2004; Lersch et al., 2008; Terrill & Reisig, 2003), police sub-culture (Skolnick, 1994), and organizational policies and expectations (Fyfe, 1988). We aim to contribute to this quest to account for police decision choices by considering the possible role of police self-legitimacy.

The British sociologist, Archer (2003: 139), argues that people with different identities will "evaluate the same situations quite differently and their responses will vary accordingly." As Bottoms and Tankebe (2012) have noted, the implications of Archer's observation is that it leads us to expect individual differences in officers' beliefs about their self-legitimacy to influence how they "perceive, evaluate, and respond to situations." In Muir's (1977: 145) work, he found that unlike the "professional" officer, the "enforcer" was "more aggressive ... more impatient and unenlightening, unresponsive to the possible changes going on inside the citizen's head and heart." Similarly, different levels of self-legitimacy may help to explain differences among officers in their use of power, in the quality of interactions with citizens, and decision choices, including the decision to use (deadly) force (Bottoms & Tankebe, 2013). The argument is that officers who lack confidence in their own legitimacy are likely to be less reflective and more impulsive in their reactions to situations, and consequently more likely to resort to force (Tankebe, 2009). Using survey data from a sample of frontline officers in Ghana, Tankebe (2013) examined the link between self-legitimacy and attitudes to the use of force. The results did not support the relationship. In Tankebe's (2013) study, officers were invited to express their agreement or disagreement to a series of statements about use of force (e.g., "It is sometimes necessary to use more force than what is legally allowed to make an arrest."). Our study moves beyond this approach by asking officers to consider a decision-making scenario.

Beyond the decision to use force, we also hypothesize a link between police self-legitimacy and police *pro-organizational behavior*. Pro-organizational behavior describes largely discretionary behaviors, not often formally rewarded but that help to promote the effectiveness of an organization (Organ, 1988). It is a matter of personal choice the omission of which is not ordinarily punishable (Kohan & Mazmanian, 2003). This type of behavior is usually contrasted with *mandatory behavior*, which refers to "behavior that is dictated or required by group rules or norms. Some rule or policy of the group prescribes the terms and guidelines of the behavior" (Tyler & Blader, 2000: 4). There is evidence to show that employee pro-organizational behavior is shaped by fair treatment from supervisors (Moorman, Niehoff, & Organ, 1993; Tyler & Blader, 2000). Using survey data from the USA, Kohan and Mazmanian (2003) found a correlation between perceptions of organizational procedures and pro-organizational behavior. More recently, Bradford and his colleagues reported that procedural justice treatment from supervisors predicted self-reported pro-organizational behavior, or what they called "extra-role activity," among police officers in a police force in England (Bradford, Quinton, Myhill, & Porter, in press).

Part of our aim in this chapter is to explore the role of self-legitimacy in promoting pro-organizational behavior. Bottoms and Tankebe (2013) have argued that "human groups always need to find ways not only to allow the healthy self-development of individuals and to encourage social cooperation, but also to discourage acts of harmful selfishness." The fundamental claim of police organizations is that they seek to serve the collective good of society by preventing social disorder. Indeed, as Loader and Walker (2001) argue, policing is a "public good" in the sense that it is "inexorably connected with the quality of our association with others." In this way, we should expect officers who believe in the legitimacy of their own power to contribute more than the minimum required of them in order to ensure the effective production of social order. It is therefore the hypothesis of this study that the more confident an officer in her own legitimacy, the greater the likelihood of pro-organizational behavior.

5 Methods and Data

The data for the study came from a survey of random sample of 529 officers in eight regional police directorates (from three police stations per each directorate) in Slovenia. The survey was translated from English to Slovene by the second author who conducted preliminary testing of the survey understanding on a sample of 30 police officers studying as part-time undergraduate students at the Faculty of Criminal Justice and Security, University of Maribor, Slovenia. Trained assistants from the Faculty of Criminal Justice and Security, University of Maribor conducted the data collection. Visits at the police stations took place during daily briefings, mainly between two shifts (morning/afternoon) between 13.00 and 15.00 in June 2013.

There was no dropout from the participation after the introductory explanation was made. A total of 529 police officers completed a paper & pencil survey that took them about 30 min. Gender was 20 % female, 22.6 % were between the ages of 20 and 29, 50.7 % were between 30 and 39 years, and 26.8 % were 40 years or older. The breakdown of length of service was 18.6 % had 1–5 years, 21.7 % had 6–10 years, 25.1 % had 11–15 years, and 34.5 % had served for 16 years or more. Regarding education, about two-thirds of the officers (73.1 %) had high school education, 12.6 % had vocational education, and only 14.2 % had university education.

5.1 Measurement of Variables

Self-legitimacy. Ten items were used to measure officers' sense of their own legitimacy: (1) I feel that I represent the values of the public in my local community. (2) I believe it is right for me as an officer to have special powers over my fellow citizens (e.g., powers to stop, search, or make arrests. (3) I sometimes worry that I am not really up to the job. (4) When on duty, I feel that I have a special kind of authority. (5) The powers I have as a police officer are morally right. (6) I am sure I can give a good reason to members of the public as to why my powers as an officer are morally proper. (7) I believe I occupy a special position in society. (8) I believe my role as an officer is necessary to prevent crime. (9) I often find it hard to convince myself that my role as an officer is necessary. (10) I believe my local community would be better off without the police. Each question had the following Likert-type response set: 1—strongly disagree to 5—strongly agree. These responses then were combined to create a self-legitimacy index ($\alpha = 0.73$; mean = 3.74; standard deviation [SD] = 0.54).

Relations with Colleagues. This was measured with six items: (1) I have a good working relationship with colleagues in my police station. (2) I feel that my colleagues trust me. (3) I feel supported by my colleagues. (4) My colleagues treat me with respect. (5) I find it hard to trust my colleagues. (6) My views about what is wrong and right in police work are very similar to the views of my colleagues. Each question had the following Likert-type response set: 1—strongly disagree to 5—strongly agree. These responses then were combined to create a "Relations with colleagues" index ($\alpha = 0.82$; mean = 3.92; standard deviation [SD] = 0.67).

Supervisor Procedural Justice. This was measured with seven items: (1) I feel that my supervisor treats me with respect and dignity. (2) My supervisor usually gives me an explanation for the decisions s/he makes that affect me. (3) My supervisor takes account of my needs when making decisions that affect me. (4) I am treated fairly in my police force. (5) The decisions of my supervisor are equally fair to every officer. (6) Decisions by my supervisor are always based on facts, not personal biases. (7) My supervisor can be rough with officers when trying to get them to do what he/she wants. Each question had the following Likert-type response set: 1—strongly disagree to 5—strongly agree. These responses then were combined to create a Supervisor Procedural Justice index ($\alpha = 0.90$; mean = 3.24; standard deviation [SD] = 0.91).

Audience legitimacy. This was measured with the following items: (1) The police are doing a good job in tackling drug dealing and drug use. (2) The police treat them fairly. (3) Police officers always obey the law. (4) Police officers take time to explain the reasons for their decisions. (5) Officers are biased against them. (6) Police officers doing well in tackling gun crime. (7) Police officers take bribes. Each question had the following Likert-type response set: 1—strongly disagree to 5—strongly agree. These responses then were combined to create a Audience Legitimacy index ($\alpha = 0.83$; mean = 3.15; standard deviation [SD] = 0.65).

Pro-organizational behavior. Officers were asked to indicate how often they had: (1) Volunteered to do things that not required in order to help my police department. (2) Helped your supervisor even when not asked to do so. (3) Put extra effort into doing your job well, beyond what is normally expected. Each question had a response category ranging from 1—Never to 4—Three times or more. These responses then were combined to create a Pro-organizational Behavior index ($\alpha = 0.71$; mean = 2.86; standard deviation [SD] = 0.97).

Use of force. To measure officer decision choices regarding the use of force, we asked respondents to consider a hypothetical traffic encounter. The scenario was as follows: "Late in the night you pull over/stop a driver who seems to be drunk.

You ask him to step out of the car and then he starts blaming you that you are foolish/stupid." The respondents were asked how far they would go in dealing with the scenario. The response categories were and the proportion of officers in the respective categories was: 1 = Verbal warning to stop (32.5 %); 2 = Warning to use physical force (65.8 %); 3 = Use physical force (0.4 %); 4 = Warning to use a gun (0.6 %); and Withdraw and call for backup (0.8). Our analysis focused on the first two categories. These were recoded as 0 = Verbal warning, and 1 = Warning to use physical force.

6 Results

We begin by examining the predictors of self-legitimacy, the results of which are displayed in Table 1. The first key question was to establish the factors that explained the belief officers had in their own individual legitimacy. Model 1 considers the influence of individual-level variables. These variables accounted for only 4 % of the variation in self-legitimacy (F-test = 5.22, $p < 0.05$). As can be seen from the results, only length of service was associated with self-legitimacy, but even here the relationship was weak ($p < 0.10$). Specifically, and in comparison

Table 1 OLS regression predicting supervisor PJ, relations with colleagues, and audience legitimacy, on self-legitimacy

	Model 1		Model 2	
	(s.e.)	β	(s.e.)	β
Gender	0.06	−0.03	0.05	−0.03
Age (20–29)				
30–39	0.07	0.00	0.06	−0.04
40 or older	0.09	−0.02	0.08	−0.10
Length of service (1–5 years)				
6–10 years	0.08	−0.11†	0.07	−0.09†
11–15 years	0.08	0.07	0.07	0.04
16 years or more	0.09	0.11	0.08	0.08
Education (high school)				
Vocational	0.07	0.02	0.06	0.01
University	0.07	0.05	0.06	0.01
Relations with colleagues			0.03	0.26***
Supervisor procedural justice			0.03	0.21***
Audience legitimacy			0.03	0.19***
F statistic		2.55*		16.88***
R^2		4 %		25 %

Note: Standard errors in parentheses
†$p < 0.10$
*$p < 0.05$
***$p < 0.001$

with officers who were new on the job, officers with 6–10 years of service felt less legitimate.

Model 2 introduced our consideration of the influence of procedural justice, interpersonal relations with colleagues, and perceptions of audience legitimacy. The effects reported for length of service persisted, with the overall model accounting for 25 % of the variation in self-legitimacy. Further, the three variables incorporated in Model 2 predicted self-legitimacy ($p < 0.001$). Specifically, being treated procedurally justly by one's supervisor and having good interpersonal relations with colleagues were both associated with increased belief in self-legitimacy. Additionally, officers who believed the public perceived them to be legitimate were the officers more likely to see their own power as legitimate. As the sizes of the standardized regression coefficients appear to show, the effects of interpersonal relations with colleagues was the strongest among the three.

Next we turned to the influence of self-legitimacy on the decision choices of officers by considering their responses to a traffic scenario. Table 2 reports the logistic regression results for three models. Considering demographic predictors and self-legitimacy first (Model 1), the results show that none of those

Table 2 Logistic regressions: what predicts the decision choices of officers?

	Model 1			Model 2			Model 3		
	B	(s.e.)	Exp (*B*)	*B*	(s.e.)	Exp (*B*)	*B*	(s.e.)	Exp (*B*)
Gender	0.21	0.28	1.24	0.30	0.29	1.35	0.28	0.29	1.32
Age									
30–39	0.15	0.33	1.16	0.21	0.34	1.23	0.19	0.34	1.20
40 or older	0.65	0.42	1.92	0.69	0.43	2.00	0.64	0.43	1.89
Length of service									
6–10 years	−0.12	0.36	0.89	−0.18	0.36	0.84	−0.21	0.36	0.81
11–15 years	−0.69	0.39	0.50	$-0.74^{\dagger}$	0.39	0.48	−0.72	0.39	0.49
16 years or more	−0.95	0.43	0.39	−0.98*	0.42	0.38	−0.94*	0.43	0.39
Education									
Vocation	−0.26	0.30	0.77	−0.24	0.30	0.78	−0.23	0.30	0.79
University	−0.37	0.28	0.69	−0.31	0.29	0.73	−0.30	0.29	0.74
Self-legitimacy	−0.54**	0.20	0.58				$-0.40^{\dagger}$	0.23	0.67
Procedural justice				−0.27*	0.13	0.76	$-0.22^{\dagger}$	0.13	0.80
Relations with colleagues				$-0.31^{\dagger}$	0.17	0.74	−0.22	0.18	0.80
Audience legitimacy				0.15	0.17	1.16	0.21	0.17	1.24
Log likelihood	586.94			584.12			580.91		
Pseudo-*R*	0.05			0.06			0.07		

Note: S.E. = standard errors
$*p < 0.05$
$^{\dagger}p < 0.10$

characteristics (age, gender, level of service, and education) predicted whether an officer would respond with verbal warning or threat of physical force. The only statistically significant predictor is self-legitimacy, which yields a negative coefficient ($b = -0.54$). That is to say, officers who with a greater sense of self-legitimacy tended to opt for verbal warning rather than threat of physical force.

Model 2 examined the effects of procedural justice, perceived audience legitimacy, and relationship with colleagues on the decision choices of officers. The results show that officers who are treated more justly tended to opt for verbal warning. Similar effects were found for interpersonal relations with colleagues, but the effects were weaker ($p < 0.10$). How officers believed the public viewed them (audience legitimacy) did not predict the nature of their responses. Unlike Model 1, the length of service predicted officers' choices. Officers with at least 16 years of services were more likely than new officers to choose verbal warning over physical force ($p < 0.05$). There is also a difference between new officers and officers who have 10–15 years of service, but the difference was significant at $p < 0.10$)

Model 3 incorporates all demographic variables, self-legitimacy, procedural justice, quality of interpersonal relations with colleagues, and the perceived audience legitimacy. As in Model 2, length of services predicted the decision choices of officers, such that officers with at least 16 years of services were more likely to respond with verbal warning than with a threat to use physical force ($b = -0.94$, $p < 0.05$) The finding about education is particularly noteworthy given prior results from the USA showing that education was negatively associated with the use of force (Rydberg & Terrill, 2010). The weak effects of relations with colleagues disappeared in Model 3, while the relative strong effects of self-legitimacy (Model 1) and procedural justice (Model 2) weakened ($p < 0.10$). Overall, though, these results appear to suggest that officers who experience procedural justice from their supervisors and those who belief in their own legitimacy were less inclined to threaten the use of physical force.

Next, we investigate the correlates of self-reported pro-organizational behavior of officers. The results are presented in Table 3. Model 1 examined the influence of self-legitimacy, while controlling for age, length of service, and gender. We found that self-legitimacy was positively associated with pro-organizational behavior ($\beta = 0.16$, $p < 0.001$). That is to say, the more officers expressed belief in their own legitimacy, the more likely they were to engage in pro-organizational behavior. The results also show that middle age and older officers were both more likely than younger officers to engage in pro-organizational behavior. Further officers with vocational and university level education were more likely than those with high school education to report pro-organizational behavior. As can be seen, however, the model explained only 14 % of the variance in pro-organizational behavior.

Model 2 showed the effects of procedural justice, interpersonal relations with colleagues, and perceived audience legitimacy. Here, we found that officers who had positive interpersonal relations with colleagues ($\beta = 0.17$, $p < 0.001$) were more likely to report engaging in pro-organizational behavior. Procedural justice

Table 3 OLS regressions of pro-organizational behavior on self-legitimacy, procedural justice, relations with colleagues, and perceived audience legitimacy

	Model 1		Model 2		Model 3	
	(s.e)	β	(s.e)	β	(s.e)	β
Gender	0.11	0.00	0.11	−0.01	0.11	−0.01
Age						
30–39	0.12	0.13*	0.12	0.12	0.12	0.12
40 or older	0.16	0.15*	0.16	0.24†	0.16	0.15*
Length of service						
6–10 years	0.13	0.10†	0.13	0.10†	0.13	0.11†
11–15 years	0.15	0.12†	0.15	0.12†	0.15	0.13†
16 years or more	0.16	0.13†	0.15	0.13†	0.15	0.12
Education						
Vocational	0.13	0.16***	0.13	0.16***	0.13	0.16***
University	0.12	0.19***	0.12	0.18***	0.12	0.17***
Self-legitimacy	0.08	0.16***			0.09	0.08
Procedural justice			0.05	0.09†	0.05	0.08
Relations with colleagues			0.07	0.17***	0.07	0.15**
Audience legitimacy			0.07	−0.02	0.07	−0.03
F statistic		9.22***		8.87***		8.38***
R^2		14.4 %		16.6 %		17 %

Note: S.E. = standard errors
*$p < 0.05$
**$p < 0.01$
***$p < 0.001$
†$p < 0.10$

by supervisors was only weakly associated with pro-organizational behavior ($p < 0.0$), but perceived audience legitimacy had no effects. While the age differences reported in Model 1 diminished, that of education persisted. Model 2 explained approximately 17 % of the variance in pro-organizational behavior.

Finally, in Model 3, the influence of self-legitimacy, procedural justice, interpersonal relations with colleagues, and perceived audience legitimacy were assessed simultaneously. With the exception of interpersonal relations with colleagues ($\beta = 0.15$, $p < 0.01$), none of these factors predicted pro-organizational behavior among the officers. In other words, self-legitimacy appeared not to have any independent influence on the likelihood that officers will engage in pro-organizational behavior. Officers' levels of educational attainment continued to predict pro-organizational behavior. Unlike the results reported in Model 2, the difference between younger and older officers was stronger in Model 3

Conclusion

Legitimacy is now an established concept in criminological analysis, with an explosion in empirical studies on the correlates and consequences of police legitimacy. However, the extant literature had tended to focus almost exclusively on public perceptions; far less is known about police officers' belief in the legitimacy of their own individual power and positions. The aim of this chapter was twofold. First, we sought to understand the factors that explain police self-legitimacy. Second, we investigated the role of self-legitimacy in predicting decision choices of officers, in particular, the decision to use force and to engage in pro-organizational behavior. The data for the study came from a survey of police officers in Slovenia.

Three main findings emerged from the data. First, we found that self-legitimacy was shaped by the quality of social interactions officers had with their supervisors and colleagues, and their sense of the how the public perceived them. Considering the sizes of the regression coefficients, it emerged that relationships with colleagues had the strongest effects on self-legitimacy, followed by procedural justice from supervisors, and perceived audience legitimacy. This appears to contradict Tankebe's (in press) findings in Ghana. In his study, only the reactions of supervisors had a direct impact on self-legitimacy; relations with colleagues and treatment by supervisors did not. In Slovenia, all three factors had a direct impact on self-legitimacy. Our findings appear to support Barker's (2001) theoretical arguments. To recall, Barker (2001) argues that self-legitimacy is best conceptualized as occurring; as one moves further away from the center of that circle, the energy and resources vested in cultivating self-legitimacy decreases. Thus, argues Barker (2001), the views of those within the immediate circles of power are far more critical to the affirmation of a power-holder's sense of rightful entitlement to power than those of citizens who are far removed from the centers of power. Although our findings appear to support these theoretical arguments, it is important to note that our model explain only small proportion of the variation in self-legitimacy. In other words, there appeared to be other drivers of police self-legitimacy that our model did not capture.

Second, our analysis showed that procedural justice from supervisors and self-legitimacy predicted how officers responded to situations. Specifically, we found that officers who believed in their own legitimacy and who were treated fairly by their supervisors were more likely to use verbal warning, rather than threat of physical force, to take control of situations. To our knowledge, no prior studies exist on the correlation between procedural justice and police decision choices. Tyler et al. (2007) study was based on survey data requiring officers to respond to general statements about rule adherence. Our study was based on officers' responses to scenarios as close to actual police–citizens encounter as possible. Although the effects in both

(continued)

cases were weak, the findings point to potentially promising new avenue for further research aimed at understanding police decision choices.

Third, it emerged that although self-legitimacy predicted the self-reported pro-organizational orientation by officers, the influence was not independent of other factors. Specifically, the influence of self-legitimacy on pro-organizational behavior was mediated by the quality of interpersonal relations officers had with their colleagues. These findings support the findings from a study conducted by Phibbs (2011) who found out that the quality of internal communication and interpersonal relations help to bond personnel to the organization and acts as a link between efficient operation and employees' willingness to perform.

References

Alpert, G., & Dunham, R. (2004). *Understanding police use of force: Officers, suspects, and reciprocity*. New York, NY: Cambridge University Press.

Archer, M. S. (2003). *Structure, agency and internal conversation*. Cambridge: Cambridge University Press.

Barbalet, J. (2001). *Emotions, social theory and social structure: A macrosociological approach*. Cambridge: Cambridge University Press.

Barker, R. (2001). *Legitimating identities: The self-presentation of rulers and subjects*. Cambridge: Cambridge University Press.

Bittner, E. (1970). *The functions of the police in modern society*. Cambridge: Oelgeschlager, Gunn, & Hain.

Bottoms, A. E. (2002). Morality, crime, compliance and public policy. In A. E. Bottoms & M. Tonry (Eds.), *Ideology, crime and criminal justice: A symposium in honour of Sir Leon Radzinowicz* (pp. 15–60). Cullompton, Devon: Willan.

Bottoms, E. A., & Tankebe, J. (2012). Beyond procedural justice: A dialogic approach to legitimacy in criminal justice. *Journal of Criminal Law and Criminology, 102*(1), 119–170.

Bottoms, A., & Tankebe, J. (2013). Voice within: Powerholders' perspectives on authority and legitimacy. In J. Tankebe & A. Liebling (Eds.), *Legitimacy and criminal justice: An international exploration* (pp. 60–82). Oxford: Oxford University Press.

Bradford, B., & Quinton, P. (2014). *Self-legitimacy, police culture and support for democratic policing in an English constabulary*. Oxford Legal Studies Research Paper, No. 14/2014. Retrieved from http://papers.ssrn.com/sol3/papers.cfm?abstract_id=2406350

Bradford, B., Quinton, P., Myhill, A., & Porter, G. (in press). Why do 'the law' comply? Procedural justice, group identification and officer motivation in police organizations. *European Journal of Criminology*. doi:10.1177/1477370813491898

Coleman, J. (1988). Social capital in the creation of human capital. *American Journal of Sociology, 94*, S95–S120.

Frow, J. (2000). Economies of value. In J. L. Machor & P. Goldstein (Eds.), *Reception study: From literary theory to cultural studies* (pp. 294–318). London: Routledge.

Fyfe, J. J. (1988). Police use of deadly force: Research and reform. *Justice Quarterly, 5*(2), 165–205.

Hagan, J., & McCarthy, B. (1997). *Mean streets: Youth crime and homelessness*. New York, NY: Cambridge University Press.

Jackson, J., Bradford, B., Stanko, E. A., & Hohl, K. (2012). *Just authority? Trust in the police in England and Wales*. Oxford: Routledge.

Johnson, D., & Kuhns, J. B. (2009). Striking out: Race and support for police use of force. *Justice Quarterly, 26*(3), 592–623.
Kaina, V. (2008). Legitimacy, trust and procedural fairness: Remarks on Marcia Grimes' study. *European Journal of Political Research, 47*(4), 510–521.
Kohan, A., & Mazmanian, D. (2003). Police work, burnout, and pro-organizational behavior: A consideration of daily work experiences. *Criminal Justice and Behavior, 30*(5), 559–583.
Kronman, A. (1983). *Max Weber*. London: Edward Arnold.
Lersch, K. M., Bazley, T., Mieczkowski, T., & Childs, K. (2008). Police use of force and neighbourhood characteristics: An examination of structural disadvantage, crime, and resistance. *Policing Society, 18*(3), 282–300.
Loader, I., & Walker, N. (2001). Policing as a public good: Reconstituting the connections between policing and the state. *Theoretical Criminology, 5*(1), 9–35.
McCarthy, B., Hagan, J., & Martin, M. J. (2002). In and out of harm's way: Violent victimization and the social capital of fictive street families. *Criminology, 40*(4), 831–866.
McElvain, J. P., & Kposowa, A. J. (2008). Police officer characteristics and the likelihood of using deadly force. *Criminal Justice and Behavior, 35*(4), 505–521.
Moorman, R. H., Niehoff, B. P., & Organ, D. W. (1993). Treating employees fairly and organizational citizenship behavior: Sorting the effects of job satisfaction, organizational commitment, and procedural justice. *Employee Responsibilities and Rights Journal, 6*(3), 209–225.
Muir, W. K. (1977). *Police: Streetcorner politicians*. Chicago, IL: University of Chicago Press.
Murphy, K., & Cherney, A. (2012). Understanding cooperation with police in a diverse society. *British Journal of Criminology, 52*(1), 181–201.
Organ, D. W. (1988). *Organizational citizenship behavior: The good soldier syndrome*. Lexington, KY: Lexington Books.
Papachristos, A. V., Meares, T. L., & Fagan, J. (2012). Why do criminals obey the law? The influence of legitimacy and social networks on active gun offenders. *Journal of Criminal Law and Criminology, 102*(2), 397–440.
Phibbs, M. W. (2011). Analyzing organizational performance from the bottom up. *FBI Law Enforcement Bulletin*. Retrieved from http://www.fbi.gov/stats-services/publications/law-enforcement-bulletin/december-2011/analyzing-organizational-performance.
Piquero, A., Fagan, J., Mulvey, E., Steinberg, L., & Odgers, C. (2005). Developmental trajectories of legal socialization among serious adolescent offenders. *Journal of Criminal Law & Criminology, 96*(1), 267–298.
Punch, M. (2000). Police corruption and its prevention. *European Journal of Criminal Policy and Research, 8*(3), 301–324.
Reisig, M. D., Tankebe, J., & Meško, G. (2012). Procedural justice, police legitimacy, and public cooperation with the police among young Slovene adults. *Varstvoslovje, 14*(2), 147–164.
Rydberg, J., & Terrill, W. (2010). The effect of higher education on police behavior. *Police Quarterly, 13*(1), 92–120.
Skolnick, J. H. (1994). *Justice without trial: Law enforcement in democratic society* (3rd ed.). New York, NY: Wiley.
Sternberger, D. (1968). Legitimacy. In D. L. Sills (Ed.), *The international encyclopaedia of the social sciences* (pp. 244–248). New York, NY: Free Press.
Sunshine, J., & Tyler, T. (2003). The role of procedural justice and legitimacy in shaping public support for policing. *Law & Society Review, 37*(3), 513–348.
Tankebe, J. (2009). Self-help, policing and procedural justice: Vigilantism and the rule of law in Ghana. *Law & Society Review, 43*(2), 245–269.
Tankebe, J. (2010). Legitimation and resistance: Police reform in the (un)making. In L. K. Cheliotis (Ed.), *Roots, rites and sites of resistance: The banality of good* (pp. 197–219). London: Palgrave.
Tankebe, J. (2013). Viewing things differently: The dimensions of public perceptions of police legitimacy. *Criminology, 51*(1), 103–135.

Tankebe, J. (2014). Police self-legitimacy. In G. Bruinsma & D. Weisburd (Eds.), *Encyclopaedia of criminology and criminal justice* (pp. 3735–3742). New York, NY: Springer.

Tankebe, J. (in press). Rightful authority: Exploring the structure of police self-legitimacy. In A. Liebling, J. Shapland, & J. Tankebe (Eds.), *Crime, justice and social order: Essays in honour of A. E. Bottoms*. Oxford: Oxford University Press.

Terrill, W., & Reisig, M. D. (2003). Neighborhood context influence on the level of force used in citizen-police encounters. *Journal of Research in Crime and Delinquency, 40*(3), 291–321.

Tyler, T. (1990). *Why people obey the law*. Yale: Yale University Press.

Tyler, T. (2011). Trust and legitimacy: Policing in the USA and Europe. *European Journal of Criminology, 8*(4), 254–266.

Tyler, T., & Blader, S. (2000). *Cooperation in groups: Procedural justice, social identity, and behavioral engagement*. Philadelphia, PA: Psychology Press.

Tyler, T., Callahan, P., & Frost, J. (2007). Armed, and dangerous (?): Motivating rule adherence among agents of social control. *Law & Society Review, 41*(2), 457–492.

Weisburd, D., Greenspan, R., Hamilton, E. E., Williams, H., & Bryant, K. A. (2000). *Police attitudes toward abuse of authority: Findings from a national study*. Washington: National Institute of Justice.

Worden, R. (1989). Situational and attitudinal explanations of police behavior: A theoretical reappraisal and empirical assessment. *Law & Society Review, 23*(4), 667–711.

Wrong, D. (1995). *Power: Its forms, bases and uses*. London: Transaction.

Index

G. Meško, J. Tankebe (eds.), *Trust and Legitimacy in Criminal Justice*,
DOI 10.1007/978-3-319-09813-5

Printed by Printforce, the Netherlands